G. Lloyd Jones

The discovery of Hebrew
in Tudor England:
a third language

Manchester University Press

492.4
J77d

Published by Manchester University Press
Oxford Road, Manchester M13 9PL
and
51 Washington Street, Dover,
New Hampshire 03820, U.S.A.

British Library cataloguing in publication data

Jones, G. Lloyd
   The discovery of Hebrew in Tudor England.
   1. Hebrew language 2. Hebrew literature
   I. Title
   933   PJ5001

   ISBN 0–7190–0875–1

Library of Congress cataloging in publication data

Jones, G. Lloyd
   The discovery of Hebrew in Tudor England.
   Bibliography: p.
   Includes index.
   1. Hebrew language—Study and teaching—Great
Britain. 2. Great Britain—Intellectual life—16th
century. 3. Judaism—Relations—Christianity.
4. Christianity and other religions—Judaism. I. Title.
PJ4538.G7J66 1982   492.4′07′041   82-20875
ISBN 0-7190-0875-1

86-2644

Photoset in Plantin by
Northern Phototypesetting Co., Bolton
Printed in Great Britain by
Butler & Tanner Ltd,
Frome and London

Contents

Preface

In contrast to its Classical counterpart, the study of Hebrew learning
in Tudor England remains a rather neglected area of intellectual
history. Apart from a few articles in learned journals dealing with
different aspects of the subject, there is, to my knowledge, no published
work which considers the question as a whole. While David Daiches'
book on the Authorised Version of the Bible (*The King James Version
... An Account of the Development and Sources of the English Bible
of 1611 with special reference to the Hebrew Tradition*, Chicago 1941)
provides a brief but useful survey of Hebrew studies in England during
this period, that is not the author's primary intention. G. S. Paine in
The Learned Men (New York 1959) gives a popular and selective
account of the translators of the Authorised Version among whom
were prominent sixteenth-century Hebraists, but he does not attempt
to assess their achievements as Hebrew scholars. There are, however,
two seminal articles which ought to be mentioned. In the *Bulletin of
the John Rylands Library*, Vol. XXIV, No. 1, 1940, E. I. J. Rosenthal
assessed the influence of Rashi on the English Bible and suggested that
Hebrew scholarship in Elizabethan England warranted deeper study.
In 1956 Israel Barroway took the matter further and outlined some
profitable lines of approach in 'Towards understanding
Tudor–Jacobean Hebrew studies' (*Jewish Social Studies*, Vol. 18). To
both of these scholars I am greatly indebted. The only full account of
the subject is to be found in an unpublished doctoral thesis submitted
to London University in 1944 by A. Schper entitled 'Christian
Hebraists in sixteenth century England'. Though stimulating and
informative, Schper's work tends to be inconclusive. It offers little,
even in its final chapter, by way of appraisal of the achievements of
English Hebraists. Furthermore, its treatment of the continental
influence seems to me to be inadequate.

In this book I marshal afresh the existing evidence for the status of
Hebrew and the Hebraic tradition in English educational circles
during the period in question. I attempt to give two interdependent
studies. The one is concerned with the knowledge of and interest in the

Hebrew language shown by sixteenth-century English scholars; the other is the attitude towards the Jews and Jewish thought which this development encouraged. I am adopting a thematic not a chronological approach, for I do not intend the study to be all-inclusive. Rather than catalogue many, I concentrate on key individuals and institutions. The *terminus ad quem* is set at 1603 in order to exclude the Authorised Version of the Bible produced in 1611, for the Hebrew scholarship which lies behind this translation is a subject in itself. Only those A.V. translators whose major works appeared before the accession of James I will come within the scope of this enquiry.

Although I am aware of the tendency of 'backgrounds' to get out of hand, I feel that an introductory chapter is justified. It has a twofold aim. First, to provide a brief description of the work of leading mediaeval Jewish exegetes and grammarians, so that later references to them will not require explanation. Second, by considering the extent to which Hebrew was studied by Christians, it seeks to justify the claim that the study of Hebrew was not entirely unknown in England before the Reformation. There is even a case, however slender, for referring to the 'rediscovery' of Hebrew in Tudor England.

The main part of the book is divided into three sections. The first considers the influences brought to bear on English scholars by their continental counterparts. Just as the history of the Reformation in England is to a large extent the history of continental influence on English minds, so the development of Hebraic studies must be traced to continental centres of learning. Mention is therefore made of some of those to whom English Hebraists turned for help and inspiration as they struggled with a third language in addition to Latin and Greek. The second section examines the reasons for the sudden flourishing of Hebrew studies in England during this period. The desire to reform the Church from within, the decision to have the Bible in the vernacular, the prominence of theological controversy and an interest in Kabbalah and apocalyptic all played their part in promoting the study of Hebrew and Jewish literature. Finally, in the third section attention is focussed on the opportunities afforded for the development of the study and on the achievements of individual scholars. The extent of instruction at school and university is considered, together with the availability of suitable books.

Acknowledgements

The debts which I have incurred in the preparation of this work will be obvious from the notes appended to each chapter. I wish, however, to acknowledge the generous assistance given to me during the past few years by individual scholars. I am grateful to Dr E. I. J. Rosenthal, who first suggested that this subject warranted further study, for his continued and enthusiastic support; to Professors R. Loewe and P. R. Ackroyd for valuable advice during the early stages of the study; to the Revd Dr B. Hall and Professor J. K. McConica for many useful suggestions with regard to the work as a whole; to the late Professor Ch. Wirszubski for expounding Pico's view of the Kabbalah; to Mr R. J. Roberts for his help in deciphering the manuscript of John Dee's library catalogue; to Dr E. S. Leedham-Green for providing much of the material from which Appendix III was compiled and for constructive comments on the contents of the final chapter; to Mr A. H. May for bibliographical assistance; to three Bangor colleagues, Miss H. Miller, Dr M. E. Thrall and Principal R. Tudur Jones for reading the manuscript and making many improvements; and finally to another colleague, Dr E. W. Davies, for meticulously checking the proofs.

Publication was made possible by grants from the following sources: The Bethune-Baker Fund, The Twenty-Seven Foundation, The Pusey and Ellerton Fund, The Cecil Roth Trust, The Harold Hyam Wingate Foundation and The Max Richter Foundation. I am deeply grateful to the trustees for their generous help.

I wish to thank Mrs G. Birkett, Mrs B. Llewellyn and Mrs J. Jones for typing the manuscript, and I appreciate the care and skill with which the publishers have guided the book through the press.

Bangor,   G. Lloyd Jones
Gwynedd, Wales

Abbreviations

ASTI	*Annual of the Swedish Theological Institute* (Jerusalem)
BJRL	*Bulletin of the John Rylands Library*
CBQ	*Catholic Biblical Quarterly*
CHB	*Cambridge History of the Bible*
CWE	*Complete Works of Erasmus*
DNB	*Dictionary of National Biography*
EHR	*English Historical Review*
EJ	*Encyclopaedia Judaica*
HTR	*Harvard Theological Review*
HUCA	*Hebrew Union College Annual*
JBL	*Journal of Biblical Literature*
JE	*Jewish Encyclopaedia*
JHI	*Journal of the History of Ideas*
JR	*Jewish Review*
JTS	*Journal of Theological Studies*
JQR	*Jewish Quarterly Review*
JWCI	*Journal of the Warburg and Courtauld Institutes*
L and P	*Calendar of Letters and Papers, Henry VIII*
MGWJ	*Monatsschrift für Geschichte und Wissenschaft des Judentums*
RTAM	*Recherches de Théologie Ancienne et Médiévale*
STC	*Short Title Catalogue*
TCBS	*Transactions of the Cambridge Bibliographical Society*
TJHSE	*Transactions of the Jewish Historical Society of England*
VCH	*Victoria County History*

Place and date of publication and the full title are given in the footnotes only when a book is cited for the first time. In all quotations from sixteenth- and seventeenth-century writings the spelling and punctuation have been modernised.

Introduction

The Golden Age of Jewish literature (A.D. 900–1500)

The Gaonic era in Jewish history is noted for the rapid progress that was made in the related fields of grammar, lexicography and biblical exegesis. Although the intensive study of Hebrew, as developed among the Jews of Babylon at the beginning of the tenth century A.D., was primarily regarded as a means of understanding the Scriptures, the leaders of traditional Judaism during this period had a twofold task. On the one hand they were called upon to respond to a challenge from within Jewry itself, and on the other to defend their ancestral faith against attack. They attempted both to affirm the traditional beliefs of Rabbinic Judaism in the face of Karaite opposition, and to maintain their Jewish identity in spite of Christian polemics and missionary activity.

The Karaites, or *Bene Mikra'* (The Scripturalists) as they called themselves, gave strict allegiance to the literal meaning of the Bible, and were convinced that they could find in it all that they required to lead their lives as Jews. Whereas the rabbis claimed that Scripture alone was insufficient, and that it had to be supplemented by another law given to Moses on Sinai and preserved by oral transmission from generation to generation, the Karaites were anxious to appreciate the Bible afresh, independently of the tradition which had surrounded it for the past four centuries. Under the leadership of Anan ben David (*c.* 750) they made clear their refusal to accept the rabbinic interpretation of biblical passages. They objected to the anthropomorphic haggadah of the Midrash and Talmud and denied the authority of the Mishna. They clung to the Written Law and found the concept of Oral Law, with its tendency to widen and modify the written word, totally unacceptable. They rejected talmudic methods in favour of a direct approach to the Scriptures, for in their view the Talmud was 'a web of lies'. Their slogan, 'Search the Bible thoroughly for all is in it', was taken with the utmost seriousness and led them to place great emphasis on grammar and lexicography in an effort to lay bare the literal meaning of the text.[1]

Although its impact was felt somewhat later, the claim of the Christian Church to be the 'true Israel' gave the Jew of the west an added impetus to pursue linguistic and exegetical studies with vigour. Christian preachers and teachers, regurgitating patristic arguments, searched the Old Testament for its mystical sense at the expense of the literal sense. If the rabbis were to protect the faith of their fathers from what they considered to be an unwarranted interpretation of their own writings, they had to insist on a literal exegesis based on sound philological studies. It was towards the end of the first millennium A.D. that Rabbinic Jewry began taking this twofold threat seriously. The period was primarily one of *peshat*. Biblical exegetes endeavoured to understand the plain meaning of the words and to present the sense of the contents as lucidly as possible. Studies and investigations in Hebrew grammar and lexicography prepared the way for this kind of exegesis and made it possible. One of the first to enter the battle against the foes of Jewish tradition was Saadia Gaon (872–942), a philosopher, theologian and linguist, who, through his literary achievements had a lasting influence on subsequent generations of scholars. While remaining faithful to the rabbinic conception of Judaism, Saadia saw the need for a fresh and authoritative interpretation of the Bible, and he spared no effort in trying to establish the plain meaning of the text. He fought the Karaites with their own weapons.

Saadia's willingness to champion the cause of Rabbinic Judaism against the Karaite heresy led to his being recognised as the founder of Hebrew philology among the Jews.[2] He produced a Hebrew dictionary and a Hebrew grammar, for he regarded philological studies as a prerequisite for anyone who wished to discover the true meaning of Scripture. As well as emphasising philology, Saadia realised the importance of having a vernacular version of the Bible. If the traditionally Rabbinic Jews of the Arab world were to hold their own against the Karaites, they must have an Arabic translation of the Hebrew Bible which would also serve as an interpretation. He undertook this great work single handed, and in addition wrote commentaries on almost all the books of the Bible. An important and interesting feature of his exegesis is the introduction with which each biblical book is prefaced, where he comments on the principal ideas of the book, outlines its structure and notes any difficulties. By establishing this scientific study of the Scriptures and of the Hebrew language Saadia gave Rabbinic Judaism superiority in the special province of Karaism, and clearly influenced all the major Jewish exegetes who followed him. His life and labour ushered in a new era.

During the latter part of the tenth century A.D. the centre of gravity of Hebrew studies moved from Babylon to Europe. Moslem Spain quickly acquired a prominent position as a seat of Jewish learning by producing a host of grammarians and commentators who influenced the course of biblical scholarship among both Jews and Christians for centuries. Before mentioning Abraham ibn Ezra, one of Spanish Jewry's most notable sons, we must turn for chronological reasons to the French rabbinic schools. The leading light in biblical studies among the Jews of northern France was Rashi (1040–1105), a commentator who wrote primarily for the school and family, and whose writings soon came to be admired and loved by Jews throughout Europe. His literal exegesis is combined with midrashic elements which appealed to the hearts of the devout. This combination of *peshat* and *derash* was adopted by his contemporaries and later became one of the distinguishing marks of the French school of exegetes. But although there was little that was original in Rashi's comments, he was not uncritical of traditional exegesis. 'Rashi's commentary', says Bacher, 'has in many respects the character of a compilation of Midrash collections; but he takes from the traditional literature chiefly those explanations that he can best harmonise with the wording and the connection of the Biblical text; and he expressly rejects those that he can not bring into such agreement'.[3] It is possible that he was stimulated to produce his short running commentary on the whole Bible by the availability to Christians of the *Glossa ordinaria*, and that his succinctness and success are the result of his improving on his model.[4] His simple exegetical method appealed to Jew and Christian alike, and after the first expulsion of the Jews from France in 1181 Rashi's influence spread widely through Germany, Poland, Spain and Italy.[5]

During a lifetime of ceaseless wandering Abraham ibn Ezra (1092–1167) mediated the achievements of Spanish exegetes to the Jews of Italy and northern France.[6] His biblical commentaries, though mainly composed far from Spain, were based on the results of the grammatical and exegetical work of earlier scholars associated with Spanish Jewry. But Abraham ibn Ezra was more than the mediator of the work of others; he propounded some theories of his own. He hinted, for example, that parts of the Pentateuch were later than the

time of Moses, and that chapters 40–55 of Isaiah were written during
the Babylonian Exile. His insistence on the importance of *peshat* led
him to emphasise the literal as opposed to the spiritual meaning of the
sacred text, but his literalism was held in check whenever halachic
considerations (i.e. the biblical source for constitutional Judaism)
involved a construction of the text which strict grammatical or
syntactical analysis would in fact not allow. His comments are very
compressed, almost into note form at times, and he is in the habit of
circumspectly hinting at difficulties of a doctrinal nature by saying
'there is a mystery here'. Although his writings appealed more readily
to intellectuals than to the man in the street, his commentary on the
Pentateuch was second in popularity only to that of Rashi.

The twelfth century saw the rise of another centre of Jewish
learning in Provence. Joseph Kimchi and his two sons Moses and
David followed in the steps of Saadia, Rashi and Ibn Ezra as exegetes
and philologists. Moses wrote a grammatical treatise which was
studied widely in Jewish academies and even translated into Latin to
be used by Christian Hebraists of a later century. Among the
important contributions made by David (1160–1235) were two related
works, the *Michlol* and *Sefer Ha-Shorashim*, the former a grammar
and the latter a dictionary or 'book of roots'. His intention in the
Michlol was to systematise and simplify existing grammatical studies.
He makes no claim to originality but seeks to offer the student a short
cut which will enable him to grasp the rudiments of Hebrew more
quickly and more easily. He writes thus in his introduction:

The Lord has stirred my spirit and strengthened my heart to write a book
concisely. I come thus like the gleaner after the reaper, following in the
footsteps of my predecessors, but abridging their material. I called this book
Mikhlol, for I intend to include therein succinctly both the grammar and the
lexicography of the Hebrew language and to make it easily and readily
available for the student.[7]

David excelled also in the field of exegesis. He shared Ibn Ezra's
insistence on *peshat*, and like Rashi made great use of the Targumim.
His grammatical knowledge is often reflected in his commentary, and
his style is clear and brief. Following in the footsteps of his
predecessors, he sought to strengthen the faith of his fellow Jews and to
enable them to withstand the polemics associated with Christian
missionary activity. His comments on the Psalms are especially
illustrative of his frequent emphasis on the literal interpretation of
certain passages and his opposition to exegesis which was specifically

Christian.[8]

Don Isaac Abravanel was 'the last representative of the golden period in the life of the Jews in Spain'.[9] Born in Lisbon in 1437, he spent almost thirty years of his life in exile from his native Portugal and died in Venice in 1508. Although he had the obvious advantage of being able to build on the foundations laid by his eminent predecessors, he is not uncritical of their efforts. He places an unambiguous emphasis on *peshat*, taking Ibn Ezra to task on account of his predilection for speaking in riddles, and Rashi for too great a dependence on Midrash.[10] Unlike his forerunners in the field of exegesis he comments on a chapter in sections rather than verse by verse. Another feature of his work is the introduction with which he prefaces each biblical book, where he comments at some length on authorship, date, composition, the purpose of the writer, and any difficulties which may arise out of the text. His achievements have led him to be regarded as the 'pioneer of the modern science of Bible propaedeutics'.[11] In addition to scriptural commentaries, he wrote philological treatises and books dealing with the messianic age.

For illumination of difficult passages Abravanel turns not only to Jewish scholars but also to Christian writers such as Jerome, Albertus Magnus and Nicholas of Lyra. At times he even dismisses the exegesis offered by those of his own race, claiming that he has found a rational explanation among the writings of Christian commentators. S. Gaon has drawn attention to the influence which Alphonsus Tostado, a fifteenth-century bishop of Avila, exercised over Abravanel. This is particularly apparent in the latter's commentary on the Pentateuch, where he divides the five books into sections and introduces each section with six questions related to difficulties and inconsistencies in the text – a method borrowed directly from Tostado. His introduction to the Book of Numbers is apparently a 'precis of Tostado's Introduction', and there are occasions when he totally disregards the rabbis to follow the bishop.[12] It was presumably this openness to Christian exegetical methodology that made Abravanel acceptable to such scholars as Richard Simon, the seventeenth-century French orientalist, who felt that he could 'reap more advantages in the translating of the Scripture from Don Isaac Abravanel, than from any other Jew'.[13]

Our brief survey of exegetical and philological studies among mediaeval Jewry would not be complete without mentioning Elijah Bachur (1469–1549) or Elias Levita, as he was known to Christians.

Of German–Jewish stock, Levita led a wandering life much of which was spent in Italy. He was an accomplished poet, grammarian and lexicographer whose chief contribution was to mediate the works of mediaeval Jewish philologists to Christian Hebraists of the sixteenth century. He cannot be regarded as an original scholar comparable to those who laid the foundations of Hebrew philology in earlier centuries. But he was an excellent populariser, and because of his congenial personal qualities was well-liked in Christian humanist circles.[14] In his own time, however, Levita's willingness to help Christians who wished to learn Hebrew was not wholly appreciated by fellow Jews. In the preface to his principal work, *Masoreth Ha-Masoreth*, he shows how Italian rabbis resented the fact that he revealed Hebrew wisdom to Christians. His co-religionists felt that the desire for such knowledge stemmed from a polemical motive rather than from a genuine interest in or friendship towards the Jews. Christians, it is true, were eager to read Jewish works in the hope of finding support for Christian beliefs in the writings of the Jews themselves. Thus, any Jew who taught Hebrew to a gentile was regarded as a traitor. 'I swear by my Creator', writes Levita, 'that a certain Christian encouraged me and brought me thus far. For fully ten years without interruption he was my pupil. I meanwhile lived in his house and instructed him. On this account there was a great outcry against me, for it was not considered proper. Some rabbis did not approve of what I had done, and pronounced woe on me, because I taught the Law to a Christian'. The Christian by whom he was befriended and to whom he taught Hebrew was Cardinal Egidio of Viterbo, General of the Augustinians, and an enthusiastic patron of Hebrew studies during the early decades of the sixteenth century.[15]

The six hundred years which separated Saadia Gaon from Elias Levita was a period of great literary activity among the Jews. Spurred on by their desire to defend Rabbinic Judaism from the assaults of Christians and Jewish sectaries, exegetes and grammarians pooled their resources and bequeathed to their successors, within Jewry and without, a legacy which has been greatly valued. The names of Saadia, Rashi, Ibn Ezra, Kimchi, Abravanel and Levita recur with increasing prominence in the writings of English biblical scholars of the sixteenth century. But before we come to that aspect of our study, account must be taken of some of the earliest Christian Hebraists in an attempt to discover the extent to which Hebrew was studied by non-Jews up to the Renaissance.

Early Christian Hebraists (A.D. 200–1350)

In recent years scholars have laid considerable emphasis on the Jewish background to the New Testament. C. G. Montefiore, H. J. Schoeps and W. D. Davies, to mention but a few, have demonstrated the importance of recognising the close contact which existed between Christianity and Judaism at the beginning of the current era. Although the Church and the Synagogue eventually went their separate ways, Christian exegetes did not entirely forsake their Jewish heritage. Whatever their motives may have been, a few did make the effort to learn Hebrew and enlisted the assistance of Jews in overcoming difficulties encountered in the biblical text.[16]

One of the first Fathers of the Church to acknowledge Jewish help in elucidating difficult words and perplexing passages in the Old Testament is Origen (*c.* 186–255). In spite of the fact that the Early Church on the whole regarded Judaism in an unfavourable light, Origen's voluminous works offer evidence of his indebtedness to contemporary Jewish commentators and of his appreciation of rabbinic exegetical works. His knowledge of Jewish customs, and his frequent references to 'a Hebrew', suggest that he had Jewish friends and teachers. Origen's proficiency in Hebrew has been much discussed. Eusebius and Jerome claim that his excellent grasp of the language was common knowledge. A detailed study, however, of Origen's writings leads N. de Lange to a less enthusiastic conclusion. He suggests that 'we shall not be far from the truth if we conclude that Origen could not speak or read Hebrew, but that he was fortunate in having acquaintances who did, and who gave him such help as he demanded'.[17]

Pride of place among the Christian Hebraists of the Early Church must go to St Jerome (348–420). Following his insistence that the Old Testament should be translated into Latin from what he called the *hebraica veritas*, it is not surprising that he persevered in linguistic studies. In his writings he gives us a detailed account of his efforts to learn Hebrew while he was in the desert near Antioch. The enterprise involved him in much toil, but to his great joy he could finally say 'I give thanks to the Lord that from that bitter seed of study I now pluck the sweet fruits'.[18] This personal testimony to his own ability to translate directly from the Hebrew is substantiated by B. Kedar-Kopfstein in an unpublished thesis on the text of the Vulgate. 'There can be no doubt', he writes, 'that Jerome's ardent desire to trace the

Scripture's text back to its source caused him to devote the most important years of his life to the Hebrew Bible. ... That which is impressive is the profound seriousness and consistency of Jerome's efforts to gain mastery of the Hebrew language'.[19] In his discussion of the text from which Jerome worked Kedar-Kopfstein asks, 'was Jerome's *Vorlage* a Greek or Latin version, while the Hebrew original served as a mere corrective, or else did Jerome read and translate the Hebrew Bible, availing himself of every possible source of information for a better understanding of it?'[20] The writer's conclusion is that Jerome was in fact working independently from a Hebrew original, and the overall picture which emerges from this study of the text of the Vulgate is that of a man who prepared himself for the work of Bible translation persistently and successfully. In contrast to the negative evaluation of some critics,[21] Jerome's growing proficiency in Hebrew must be stressed. Much of his Hebrew learning was incorporated into the Vulgate, with the result that his version is much nearer to the original than was once supposed.[22] It is clear that he, like Origen, had close contacts with Jews and that he sought their assistance in procuring Hebrew manuscripts and in perfecting his knowledge of the language. His commentaries contain much exegetic material which he received from his Jewish teachers.

In spite of the example set by Jerome, his immediate successors in the scholarly circles of the Christian Church were not such enthusiastic Hebraists, so that with him an entire era in the study of Hebrew by Christians came to an end. Indeed, the study of the language lapsed to the extent that Charles Singer could say with justification, 'For centuries during the Dark Ages the Hebrew alphabet and language stood for something odd, strange, and difficult'.[23] The Venerable Bede (673–735) has been acclaimed as the most learned man of his age in Western Europe, yet his knowledge of Hebrew was very rudimentary. That he was familiar with it must be conceded, otherwise he would not have drawn attention in his commentaries to the equal sound of *sin* and *samech*, or to the similarity in shape between *daleth* and *resh*.[24] But allowing for the conclusion that he may have grasped the essentials of the language, E. F. Sutcliffe points to the difficulty of deciding how he did so. There were no books available; instruction would therefore have to be oral. There is, however, no evidence to suggest that Jews resided in England before the Norman conquest, and as far as one can tell Bede never left the country. This leads Sutcliffe to conclude that he had 'no knowledge of

Hebrew beyond the few scraps of information he was able to glean from the writings of Jerome. His appreciation of the importance of the language for a correct understanding of the Bible is apparent from the intelligent use he makes of the little knowledge he could gather at second hand'.[25] Alcuin (735–804), a native of Yorkshire, pioneered important educational work in France and played a significant part in the transmission of the text of the Vulgate, but there is no clear evidence that he knew much Hebrew. Hailperin draws attention to Rabanus Maurus (776–856), Archbishop of Mainz, and makes the exaggerated claim that his writings are 'saturated with Hebrew and Rabbinic learning even more than Jerome's commentaries'.[26]

Although the revival of learning which is associated with the reign of Charles the Great (742–814) did have its Old Testament and Jewish aspect, the most probable explanation of what some would regard as examples of Hebrew scholarship in the writings of Bede, Alcuin and even Rabanus, is to be found in the twenty-volume work of Isidore of Seville (*c.* 560–636) entitled *The Etymologies*. Isidore was no Hebraist either, but he was an encyclopaedist whose works became a 'storehouse of knowledge freely utilized by innumerable mediaeval authors'.[27] Through his *Etymologies*, which was a compendium of the knowledge of the times, Isidore mediated the Hebrew scholarship of Jerome to the mediaeval Church, and the scant knowledge of the language evinced by Bede and Alcuin is almost certainly derived from this source.

The twelfth century witnessed the pursuit of Hebrew learning among European Christians on a somewhat greater scale. Stephen Harding, the English abbot of Cîteaux, recognised the importance of the language for establishing a correct text of the Old Testament. A manuscript edition of the Bible written under the personal supervision of the abbot was preserved at Cîteaux up to the time of the French Revolution. Not content with consulting only Latin manuscripts, Harding sought the assistance of the rabbis whenever he was faced with a difficult reading.[28] Nevertheless, it is improbable that his Hebrew amounted to very much, and it seems safer to regard it as little more than the invocation of Jewish assistance to purge the Vulgate text of pre-Carolingian patristic accretions. Beryl Smalley has published a study of an early twelfth-century commentary on the literal sense of Leviticus, in which the unknown exegete made use of Jewish sources to help him unravel the meaning of the legalia in the text and obviously struggled with the Hebrew language.[29] The school of the Victorines in Paris put Hebrew studies on an even firmer footing. Hugh of St Victor (*c.* 1096–1141), in his exegesis of the Old Testament, went beyond the customary sources, and his English pupil Andrew of St Victor (*c.* 1104–1175) claims to have received instruction from Jews on the literal sense of the Pentateuch.[30] By paying serious attention to the study of Hebrew and Jewish tradition Hugh was breaking new ground and blazing the trail for Andrew whose works must be regarded as a major contribution to Hebraic scholarship during the Middle Ages.

To return to England. Herbert of Bosham (*c.* 1120–1190) was the companion and secretary of St Thomas à Becket. An investigation of his writings has shown that he also merits a place of some importance in the history of mediaeval Hebrew scholarship. The conclusion of R. Loewe, based on a detailed study of Herbert's commentary of Jerome's *Hebrew Psalter*, is that 'in Herbert we have the most competent Hebraist whom the Western Church produced between Jerome himself and Pico de Mirandola and Reuchlin in the late fifteenth century, with the possible exception of Raymond Martini in the thirteenth. Excluding, that is, Jewish converts to Christianity; since Herbert's father was a priest, there seems no reason to believe that he had any recent Jewish ancestry'. There is little doubt, in Loewe's opinion, 'that Herbert's main Jewish source throughout his book is the biblical commentary of Rashi'.[31] Two younger contemporaries of Herbert were Ralph Niger (*c.* 1150–1200) and Alexander Neckam (1157–1217), both of whom had at least a smattering of Hebrew. Niger was an English biblical scholar and chronicler who lived in exile in France. Although there is apparently little in his Old Testament commentaries to testify to his knowledge of Hebrew, his work on the interpretation of Hebrew proper names indicates that he was familiar with the rudiments of the language and that he had access, through a Jewish convert, to the dictionary of the tenth-century lexicographer Menachem ben Saruq.[32] Alexander Neckam, abbot of Cirencester, had taught at both Paris and Oxford. An examination of his treatise *De naturis rerum* leads Loewe to conclude that while his Hebrew scholarship is not comparable to that of Herbert, he does evince an elementary knowledge of the grammar and a 'considerable familiarity with Jewish exegesis'.[33] The sixteenth-century antiquary John Leland, in his account of English writers, mentions monks of Ramsey Abbey who had some knowledge of Hebrew. He relates how, at the dissolution of the monasteries, Robert Wakefield, the first Hebrew lecturer at Cambridge, had purloined a Hebrew dictionary compiled by Laurence Holbeach (d. *c.* 1410), a monk of the abbey. In the monastery library

Holbeach had discovered books which a former prior, Gregory of Huntingdon (d. *c.* 1290), had bought from Jews on their expulsion from England, among them a dictionary which Gregory himself had started. Holbeach had completed the work early in the fifteenth century.[34]

The study of Hebrew was regarded by the missionary religious orders of the thirteenth century as an essential duty; it became a favoured child of the church militant. The Dominicans began to see that violence and abuse were not conducive to the making of converts from Judaism. If its adherents were to be won for Christ, the Jewish faith had to be studied and understood, and to this end Hebrew must be learned. Furthermore, if Jewish interpretations of certain Old Testament passages were to be successfully refuted, a knowledge of the work of the rabbis and of the Talmud was indispensable. The moving spirit in this sphere of Christian endeavour was Raymund de Penaforte, a Spanish priest who became Master General of the Dominicans in 1238. He established centres within the order for the study of Arabic and Hebrew and encouraged Paulus Christiani (a convert from Judaism) and Raymund Martini, two prominent fellow members of the Order of Preachers, in their study of Jewish writings. Both became ardent advocates of the study of Oriental languages among the Dominicans for the purposes of conversion to Christianity. The Franciscans were similarly motivated. Their first great teacher in England, though not a member of the order, was Robert Grosseteste (1175–1253) who later became Bishop of Lincoln. The extent of Grosseteste's knowledge of Hebrew is disputed. L. I. Newman classes him among the 'distinguished English Hebraists' of the thirteenth century, whereas S. H. Thomson feels that the tradition that Grosseteste knew Hebrew to any appreciable extent is late and apocryphal. D. A. Callus, quoting Nicholas Trivet's observations on this point, is a little less sceptical; but even so, it is his opinion also that Grosseteste's Hebrew did not amount to very much.[35]

Despite his doubtful proficiency in the language, Grosseteste was certainly enthusiastic in urging his contemporaries to learn it. One of his most promising pupils at Oxford was Roger Bacon (*c.* 1210–1290), who displays great veneration for Hebrew, regarding it as the medium through which God revealed his philosophy to his saints.[36] In an illuminating passage S. A. Hirsch comments thus on Bacon's reasons for learning Hebrew:

But all such ancillary motives, as the improvement of Church management, the interests of theology and science, the spread of Christianity, the annihilation of incurable infidels, the understanding of the spiritual meaning of the Scriptures, were not the only levers that moved Bacon's mind towards the study of languages. He was, besides, powerfully affected by another fundamental incentive, of which, however, he was perhaps less conscious than of any of the other, purely subservient, motives. Bacon possessed the true philological instinct; he had a keen perception of the connexion subsisting between the various dialects belonging to groups of languages.[37]

This interest in philology led Bacon to emphasise the importance of learning grammar, and even to write a Hebrew grammar himself.[38] He was, however, distrustful of the work of all translators and copyists — especially that of the latter, because of their ignorance of the original languages. While it is not entirely clear how extensive his knowledge of Hebrew actually was, it probably exceeded the little that appears in his grammar, and there can be no doubt that he passionately believed in the necessity for all Christian scholars to learn the language. Moreover, he advocated the study of it for other than missionary purposes.[39] He claimed that he could teach any diligent person to understand Hebrew perfectly in three days! If he followed the recommended method, the student would soon be able to appreciate the comments of the Fathers on the Bible and even to correct the Hebrew text if necessary.[40] It may well have been a disciple of Bacon who was responsible for the literal translation of the Hebrew Scriptures into Latin which was begun in England sometime during the thirteenth century.[41]

Nicholas of Lyra (*c.* 1270–1340), another Franciscan, was one of the most famous biblical commentators of the late Middle Ages. Though not the first to apply rabbinic exegesis to Christian interpretation of the Scriptures, Nicholas' thorough knowledge of Hebrew and the writings of Jewish exegetes, especially Rashi, is indisputable. His *Postillae* give clear evidence that he had recourse not only to the Hebrew text of the Bible but also to the mediaeval commentators.[42] Rashi's emphasis on the literal sense of Scripture obviously appealed to him, but also like Rashi, he made good use of *derash* when occasion demanded. Indeed, Nicholas reflects Rashi to such an extent that a later commentator, Johann Reuchlin, could say that not much would be left of the *Postillae* if the references to 'Rabbi Solomon' were omitted. By harsher critics of his work Nicholas was called 'the ape of Rashi'. Whatever view one takes of Nicholas, his

importance lies in the fact that he introduced Jewish interpretations of
the Old Testament to Christian theologians on a far greater scale than
had been done before, and secured a place for traditional Jewish
exegesis in the thought of the Protestant Reformers.

Grosseteste and Bacon were respected representatives of thirteenth-
century learning at Oxford. The following two centuries witnessed the
impact made on biblical studies by the friars at Cambridge. In the
words of J. R. H. Moorman, 'In Cambridge in the fifteenth century
there were, no doubt, in the Franciscan convent friars of conservative
instincts who viewed with dismay the growth of a critical attitude
towards the sacred text, but there were certainly some who turned
eagerly to the study of Hebrew and Greek in order that they might
understand more clearly the literal meaning of the Bible'.[43] One of
these was Henry de Costesy who was appointed lector at the university
in *c.* 1326. An able scholar, he proved to be a competent and original
biblical commentator. His interest in the literal meaning of Scripture
and his reputed knowledge of Hebrew may be traced to Nicholas of
Lyra under whom he probably studied at Paris. He owned a Hebrew
Psalter which had belonged to a convert from Judaism and a copy of
the *superscriptio lincolnensis* (a Hebrew text of the Psalms with an
interlinear Latin translation) which had once been the property of
Grosseteste. Another erudite Franciscan was Richard Brinkley who
resided at Cambridge during the early decades of the Tudor period (*c.*
1480–1518). The manuscripts in his possession suggest that he too was
a student of Greek and Hebrew.[44] He borrowed a copy of the Psalms in
Hebrew from the Abbey of Bury St Edmunds in 1502.[45]

The link between Christian exegetes and their Jewish counterparts can
be traced, though sometimes only with difficulty, from Origen to
Nicholas of Lyra. Whatever their motives may have been, a few
Christian scholars, Englishmen among them, did make the effort to
learn Hebrew. Some were more enthusiastic than others and had
greater success. Bede, Harding and Grosseteste knew very little, if any,
Hebrew, but they must be credited with realising the importance of
studying the language and commending it to their pupils. The
contribution of the Victorines, Herbert of Bosham, Roger Bacon,
Alexander Neckam and Nicholas of Lyra, was more substantial. The
last two in particular evince a familiarity, not only with the Hebrew
language, but also with the explanations and comments of the rabbis.
As a result of this interest the quest for the literal sense of the sacred

text received fresh impetus. Although the legacy which they bequeathed to others in the field of Christian Hebrew studies was not great, scholars of a later generation did profit from their labours.

Notes

1 See L. Simon, 'Jewish Sectaries II: the Karaites', *JR*, vol. 3, 1912–13, pp. 68f. Also N. Wieder, *The Judean Scrolls and Karaism*, London 1962, pp. 57f for the difference between Karaite and rabbinic exegesis.

2 E. Rosenthal, 'Saadia Gaon: an appreciation of his biblical Exegesis', *BJRL*, vol. 27, No. 1, 1943, p. 168 (reprinted in *Studia Semitica*, Cambridge 1971, vol. I, pp. 86ff).

3 *JE*, Vol. III, p. 168.

4 This is suggested by R. Loewe in 'Christian hebraists (1100–1890)', *EJ*, vol. 8, col. 11.

5 See M. Liber, *Rashi*, Philadelphia, Pa. 1936, chs. 11 and 12.

6 E. Rosenthal, 'The study of the Bible in mediaeval Judaism', *CHB*, vol. 2, pp. 266f.

7 *David Kimḥi's Hebrew Grammar*, ed. W. Chomsky, New York 1952, p. 9.

8 On Kimchi as an exegete see F. E. Talmage, *David Kimḥi: the Man and the Commentaries*, Cambridge, Mass. 1975, ch. III.

9 M. Gaster, 'Abravanel's literary work', *Isaac Abravanel*, ed. Trend and Loewe, Cambridge 1937, p. 41. For the details of his life see B. Netanyahu, *Don Isaac Abravanel: Statesman and Philosopher*, 2nd ed., Philadelphia, Pa. 1968, Part One.

10 E. Rosenthal, 'Don Isaac Abravanel: financier, statesman and scholar', *BJRL*, vol. 21, No. 2, 1937, p. 456 (reprinted in *Studia Semitica*, vol. 1, pp. 21ff).

11 L. Ginsberg, art. 'Abravanel', *JE*, vol. I, p. 127.

12 S. Gaon, 'The influence of Alphonsus Tostado on Isaac Abravanel', unpublished Ph.D. thesis, London 1943, p. 170.

13 *Histoire Critique du Vieux Testament*, Rotterdam 1678, Eng. trans. by A Person of Quality, London 1682, Book III, ch. 6, p. 34.

14 See I. Zinberg, *A History of Jewish Literature*, Eng. trans. by B. Martin, New York 1974, vol. IV, pp. 48ff. Also G. E. Weil, *Elie Lévita: Humaniste et Massorète (1469–1549)*, Leiden 1963.

15 Elijah Levita, *Masoreth Ha-Masoreth*, ed. C. D. Ginsburg, London 1867, Intro., p. 96. J. W. O'Malley, *Giles of Viterbo on Church and Reform*, Leiden 1968, ch. 3.

16 See *EJ*, vol. 5, cols. 550ff for a survey of the relationship between the Church Fathers and the Jews.

17 *Origen and the Jews*, Cambridge 1976, p. 22. See also R. P. C. Hanson, *Allegory and Event*, London 1959, pp. 167ff.

18 Quoted by J. Barr, 'St. Jerome's appreciation of Hebrew', *BJRL*, vol. 49,

No. 2, 1967, p. 289. For Jerome's Hebrew scholarship see also E. F. Sutcliffe, 'Jerome', *CHB*, vol. 2, pp. 80ff.

19   'The Vulgate as a translation', Hebrew University, Jerusalem 1968, p. 50.

20   *Ibid.*, p. 53.

21   See e.g. F. C. Burkitt, 'The debt of Christianity to Judaism', *The Legacy of Israel*, Oxford 1927, p. 91.

22   The notion of 'the Vulgate' is, of course, an oversimplification. Each book, or group of books, has its own inner text history, and in some cases, notably the *Psalterium juxta Hebraeos*, which was excluded from the Vulgate, the heritage of Jerome is much more marked than in others. For a detailed study of the textual history of the Vulgate see R. Loewe, 'The mediaeval history of the Latin Vulgate', *CHB*, vol. 2, pp. 102ff. For the influence of Jewish exegesis on parts of the Vulgate see C. H. Gordon, 'Rabbinic exegesis in the Vulgate of Proverbs', *JBL*, vol. 49, 1930, pp. 384ff.

23   'Hebrew scholarship in the Middle Ages among Latin Christians', *The Legacy of Israel*, p. 287.

24   See S. A. Hirsch, 'Early English hebraists: Roger Bacon and his predecessors', *JQR*, O.S. vol. 12, 1900, p. 38 (reprinted in *A Book of Essays*, London 1905, pp. 1ff).

25   'The Venerable Bede's knowledge of Hebrew', *Biblica*, vol. 16, 1953, pp. 305ff.

26   *Rashi and the Christian Scholars*, Pittsburgh, Pa. 1963, p. 10.

27   *Oxford Dictionary of the Christian Church*, 2nd ed. F. L. Cross and E. A. Livingstone, London 1974, p. 717. Cf. R. Loewe, 'The mediaeval Christian Hebraists of England', *TJHSE*, vol. 17, 1951–52, p. 227, 'In an age of intellectual stagnation, it is not surprising that Jerome and Isidore were mercilessly plagiarised by numerous lesser writers'.

28   J. H. Newman, *The Cistercian Saints of England*, London 1844, p. 129. See also R. Loewe, *op. cit.*, *CHB*, vol. 2, pp. 143f for the Cistercian contribution to Hebraic studies.

29   'An early twelfth-century commentator on the literal sense of Leviticus', *RTAM*, Tome 36, 1969, pp. 78–99.

30   B. Smalley, *The Study of the Bible in the Middle Ages*, 2nd ed. Oxford 1952, p. 126.

31   'Herbert of Bosham's commentary on Jerome's Hebrew Psalter: a preliminary investigation into its sources', *Biblica*, vol. 34, 1953, pp. 54ff. It would be more accurate to say that in Herbert we have *one* of the most competent Hebraists between Jerome and Pico.

32   See G. B. Flahiff, 'Ralph Niger: an introduction to his life and works', *Mediaeval Studies*, vol. II, 1940, p. 121 for Ralph's 'smattering of Hebrew'.

33   'Alexander Neckam's knowledge of Hebrew', *Mediaeval and Renaissance Studies*, vol. IV, 1958, p. 22.

34   *Commentarii de Scriptoribus Britannicis*, ed. A. Hall, Oxford 1709, p. 452.

35   See Newman, *Jewish Influence on Christian Reform Movements*, New

York 1925, p. 81; Thomson, *The Writings of Robert Grosseteste*, Cambridge 1940, p. 38; Callus, *Robert Grosseteste: Scholar and Bishop*, Oxford 1955, pp. 35ff.

36 'Revelavit igitur Deus primo philosophiam sanctis suis, quibus et legem dedit; nam philosophia utilis est legi Dei, ad intellectum, ad promulgationem, ad probationem, ad defensionem, et multis aliis modis, ut patet per opera qua scribo. Et ideo primo tradita est principaliter et complete in lingua Hebraica', *Fr. Rogeri Bacon Opera Quaedam Hactenus Inedita*, ed. J. S. Brewer, Rolls Series, London 1859, vol. 1, Opus Tertium, p. 32.

37 'Early English Hebraists ...', *JQR*, O.S. vol. 12, 1900, p. 65. See further S. A. Hirsch, 'Roger Bacon and philology', in *Roger Bacon: Commemoration Essays*, ed. A. G. Little, Oxford 1914, pp. 101ff.

38 For his *Hebrew Grammar* see *The Greek Grammar of Roger Bacon and a Fragment of his Hebrew Grammar*, ed. E. Nolan and S. A. Hirsch, Cambridge 1902.

39 For his insistence on the importance to the Church of linguistic studies see his remarks in 'Linguarum Cognitio', *The 'Opus Maius' of Roger Bacon*, ed. J. H. Bridges, London 1900, vol. 1, pp. 92ff.

40 *Fr. Rogeri Bacon Opera Quaedam Hactenus Inedita*, ed. Brewer, vol. 1, p. 65.

41 S. Berger, *Quam Notitiam linguae Hebraicae habuerunt Christiani medii aevi temporibus in Gallia*, Nancy 1893, pp. 49ff.

42 Hailperin, *Rashi and the Christian Scholars*, Part IV.

43 *The Grey Friars in Cambridge 1225–1538*, Cambridge 1952, p. 121.

44 A. G. Little, *Franciscan Papers, Lists and Documents*, Manchester 1943, pp. 140ff.

45 Now in the Bodleian Library, MS. Bodl. Laud. Orient. 174.

Part one

Influences

I
Two Christian Kabbalists

After the death of Nicholas of Lyra in *c.* 1350 what little interest had been shown by Christians in Hebrew studies waned. For over a century no one seems to have taken up the quest for the literal sense of the Old Testament and to have made a specific study of the language in which it was originally written. What contributed to this lack of enthusiasm during the century immediately preceding the Reformation? What hindered the learning of Hebrew and the study of rabbinic exegesis by non-Jews? The first, and perhaps foremost reason was directly connected with Nicholas himself. So thorough was his work that he effectively killed Christian Hebrew studies for over a century. His *Postillae*, which were replete with references to rabbinic works, seemed to the ecclesiastical public to have done the job for them; there was nothing more left to do. A good example of this attitude may be seen in the writings of Geronimo de Santa Fe (*fl. c.* 1414). In the second chapter of his treatise *Ad convincendum perfidiam Judaeorum* he shows that according to Jewish tradition the Messiah was expected to come shortly before the destruction of the Second Temple, and in support of this view he refers the reader to Nicholas of Lyra in whose works he would find the matter 'stated plainly and sufficiently and in accordance with the true Faith'.[1] Since Nicholas had combed the commentaries of Rashi on most major exegetical issues his successors were quite prepared to take his *Gloss* as their final authority on Jewish matters, and thus absolve themselves from any serious study of Hebrew.

There were, however, other reasons. A marked mistrust of the Jews had developed among Christian scholars. It was claimed that they had wilfully falsified the text of Scripture and given erroneous explanations, especially in those parts which were capable of a Christological interpretation. The text of the Vulgate might well stand in need of correction, but there was no guarantee that the Hebrew text was any less corrupt. There was a solid phalanx of Christian teachers and exegetes who rejected the Jewish tradition and could see no value whatsoever in it.[2] But even if a Christian had wanted to learn Hebrew, he would not have found it easy to obtain a teacher. During the High Middle Ages Jews had been expelled from several European countries, and in those places where they remained they were not always willing to teach Hebrew. Furthermore, Hebrew books were scarce. Since the beginner could not use a grammar written in Hebrew, he had to rely on the grammars of Bacon and Richard of Bury (*fl. c.* 1330), and on the six-page introduction of the Dominican Peter Nigri to his volume *Stella Messiae* (1477). But these were scarcely satisfactory from the point of view of a serious student since they contained only the basic rudiments of the language. Finally, the cause of Hebrew scholarship was certainly weakened by being left to individuals and not placed on an official footing. An attempt had been made at the General Council of the Church held in Vienne in 1311 to establish chairs of Hebrew, Arabic, Syriac and Greek in the four 'studia generalia' of Christendom, Oxford, Paris, Bologna and Salamanca. Each university was to have two teachers for each language who were to be responsible for giving instruction and for producing Latin translations of important works. The decree was prompted by missionary ideals and by the desire to advance the cause of biblical exegesis. Yet, in spite of the fact that the Church was now putting its stamp of approval on what the Franciscans and the Dominicans had already been doing, the injunction was a dead letter. It failed because of lack of financial support and because the attitude of the hierarchy was, to say the least, lukewarm. Although the decree was reissued by the Council of Basle in 1434, nothing more was heard of it in England until the sixteenth century.[3]

The father of Christian Kabbalah

When Giovanni Pico (1463–1494), a Count of Mirandola and a prominent figure in Renaissance Italy, began taking a scholarly and cultural interest in Hebrew, he was thus entering a field of study not at all well known in Christian Europe. There was a marked lack of competent Christian teachers and no substantial grammar or dictionary to help the aspiring student. Admittedly, there was no dearth of educated Jews in fifteenth-century Italy, for by 1492, after their expulsion from Spain and Sicily, Italy was the only country in Christian Europe open to them.[4] In spite of the Church's nervousness at the geographic expansion of Italian Jewry from the middle of the fourteenth century onwards, which resulted in an outbreak of antisemitism, there was no general persecution of the Jews in Italy. Whenever the friars demanded a reimposition of the old ecclesiastical disciplines and preached frenzied sermons against unbelievers, the Vatican held them in check. But the desire of Christians to learn Hebrew from their Jewish compatriots was not universally welcomed by Italian Jews. Elias Levita, as we have already noted, refers to the animated debate among his fellow Jews on the appropriateness of imparting the mysteries of the Torah in its original language to gentiles.

Despite the difficulties encountered in finding suitable instructors, scholars and ecclesiastical dignitaries did make considerable progress in linguistic studies, with the result that two Renaissance popes, Nicholas V and Sixtus IV, were inspired to make valuable collections of Hebrew manuscripts and to commission Latin translations of Jewish works. But although Christians, ordained and lay, began to employ Jews as teachers in their homes, there can be little doubt that this interest in Hebrew lore was motivated by polemical rather than academic considerations. The attitude of the Florentine statesman and scholar Giannozzo Manetti (d. 1459) towards Judaica is typical of his age. He reiterates the principle laid down by the missionary orders when he emphasises that Christians must know Hebrew and be familiar with Jewish literature, if they are to be successful in conducting polemics against the Jews. The controversial writings of Manetti himself offer ample evidence of competence in Hebrew and of a determination to come to grips with the works of Jewish authors for apologetic purposes. Like many of his contemporaries he kept a converted Jew in his household with whom, it is claimed, he spoke only in Hebrew.

Gradually, however, the emphasis shifted from polemics to scholarship. Humanist scholars, especially those associated with the Platonic Academy in Florence, were anxious to acknowledge Hebrew as one of the three historic languages of the west and to learn it in the same way as they had learned Latin and Greek. Knowledge of the language would give them direct access to the Old Testament in its original form and to post-biblical Jewish literature, the usefulness of which for the Christian exegete they were eager to discover. Hence we find Marsilio Ficino, leader of the Academy, making use of rabbinic writings in his *De Christiana religione* (1474).[5] Though his quotations from Saadia, Rashi and Gersonides may have been obtained through translations or secondary sources, such as Nicholas of Lyra's *Postillae*, thus necessitating hardly any knowledge of Hebrew, it is clear that Ficino utilised the Hebraic tradition and wished to promote the study of it among his colleagues.

Pico, a Christian layman, stood in the forefront of this movement. He wanted to be able to read rabbinic literature, and to this end he applied himself to the study of Hebrew and Aramaic. His teachers were Jews and Jewish converts to Christianity.[6] Leone Ebreo, the son of Isaac Abravanel, was a close friend and a member of the Florentine circle. Johanan Allemanno, a Jewish religious philosopher and biblical exegete whose erudition was held in high regard, helped Pico to furnish his library with Jewish works. Elijah del Medigo, the noted Jewish Averroist, taught him at Padua and agreed to translate into Latin various works extant only in Hebrew. Flavius Mithridates, a Sicilian Jew who, after his conversion, lectured at the Sapienza in Rome and produced Latin translations of several rabbinic works, was responsible for instructing him in Oriental languages. But despite the help of Jewish teachers the precise extent of Pico's knowledge of Hebrew is still an open question. In the autumn of 1486 he wrote to Ficino stating that he had spent a whole month studying the language day and night, and that although he was not yet very proficient he had made enough progress to write a tolerable letter in Hebrew.[7] Chaim Wirszubski is of the opinion that Pico's correction of the first ten chapters of the Vulgate of the Book of Job, made sometime before March 1489, betrays the hand of 'a competent collaborator', namely Mithridates, and that Pico's knowledge of Hebrew at the time did not amount to very much.[8] It was presumably Mithridates who mediated to Pico the comments of Gersonides on Job which were incorporated into the annotations found in the margin.

His Jewish teachers introduced Pico to the Kabbalah, the secret meaning of the Written Law revealed by God to the elect in the distant past and preserved by a privileged minority. Kabbalistic teachings fall into three main categories. First, they contain doctrines about the relation between God and creation based on Neoplatonic and Gnostic schemes of emanation. In this way they try to explain the immanent activity of a transcendent God. Second, they contain messianic and apocalyptic doctrines of a more specifically Jewish character. Finally, they offer techniques of scriptural exegesis which are intended to enable the reader to discover profound spiritual significance and hidden meanings in the most trivial passages of Scripture. All these aspects, especially the first and the third, proved to be of absorbing interest to Renaissance Kabbalists, and Pico was no exception. To assist him in his difficult enterprise he had at his elbow Mithridates' Latin translation of a book entitled *Sefer Ha-Shorashim*. This was 'a glossary of kabbalistic symbols, words and expressions meant to be an introduction to the study of the Kabbalah and a kabbalistic companion to the interpretation of Scripture and the sayings of the Rabbis'.[9]

Pico was not the first Christian to take an interest in the writings of Jewish mystics. In a previous century the Spanish Franciscan missionary Raymund Lull had made use of kabbalistic works in his attempts to proselytise among the Jews. A contemporary of Pico, the converted Jew Paulus de Heredia, tried to demonstrate in his *Epistola de secretis* and *Ensis Pauli* that fundamental Christian truths were to be found in the Kabbalah.[10] But he wrote with an avowed missionary purpose, and for that reason won few readers among Christian humanists. Like Paulus and other converts from Judaism, Pico maintained that the main doctrines of Christianity were to be found in the writings of the Kabbalists. Using II Esdras 14:5–6 as an authoritative scriptural reference to the Kabbalah he writes thus in his *Oratio de dignitate hominis*:

Among the Hebrews of the present day these books are cherished with such devotion that it is permitted no man to touch them unless he be forty years of age. When I had purchased these books at no small cost to myself, when I had read them through with great diligence and with unwearying toil, I saw in them ... not so much the Mosaic as the Christian religion. There is the mystery of the Trinity, there the Incarnation of the Word, there the divinity of the Messiah; there I have read about original sin, its expiation through Christ, the heavenly Jerusalem, the fall of the devils, the orders of the angels, purgatory and the punishments of hell, the same things we read daily in Paul and Dionysius, in Jerome and Augustine. ... Taken altogether, there is absolutely no controversy between ourselves and the Hebrews on any matter, with regard to which they cannot be refuted and gainsaid out of the cabalistic books, so that there will not be even a corner left in which they may hide themselves.[11]

Clearly Pico's speculation about the Kabbalah led him to conclusions similar to those of other Christians. Although he does not sound so blatantly polemical as some of his predecessors, he too believed in the value of kabbalistic works for controverting Jewish teachings. But his interest did not spring primarily from missionary motives. He sought rather to present the Kabbalah as a new way of confirming Christian truth. This he could do because he believed that in it he had found an original divine revelation to man which had been lost. He regarded it as authoritative because he accepted the claim of the Jewish mystics that their writings were based on a secret tradition that went back in oral form to biblical times. The Kabbalah was the way of wisdom. Since it came from God it could provide new insights into the meaning of the biblical texts. This in turn would strengthen, not undermine, the Christian faith. Under the auspices of sacred tradition the Kabbalah introduced conceptions borrowed from Hellenistic thought which were attractive but previously suspect.[12]

Pico published his theological views in nine hundred theses, seventy-two of which are derived from kabbalistic sources and twenty-six are described as 'Conclusiones magicae'.[13] In 1486 he offered to discuss his theses publicly in Rome and wrote his *Oratio de dignitate hominis* as an introductory speech for the disputation. The debate, though promised by the Church, never took place. Instead the Pope appointed a commission to examine the theses, with the result that Pico was charged with heresy. Thirteen of the nine hundred theses were singled out for special attack. Among them was that which strikes the keynote of his contribution to Hebrew scholarship during the Renaissance by creating a Christian interpretation of the Kabbalah: 'There is no knowledge which makes us more certain of the divinity of Christ than magic and Kabbalah'.[14] In defence of this thesis Pico explains that 'knowledge' (scientia) refers to non-revealed knowledge, 'magic' to nature's mysterious revelation of God, and 'Kabbalah' to God's mysterious revelation of himself. Eventually, under pressure from the ecclesiastical authorities he modified his original statement to read, 'Magic and Kabbalah make us more certain of the divinity of Christ than any other non-revealed knowledge'.

The trilingual miracle

'Whatever had been done before his time', writes J. L. Blau, 'it was Pico who first attracted his fellow humanists in any considerable number to the Cabala', and for this reason he can be legitimately regarded as the 'father' of Christian Kabbalah.[15] His most important disciple was the German savant Johann Reuchlin (1455–1522) whom he met in Florence in 1490 and to whom he communicated his passion for Jewish mystical writings. In Israel Abrahams' view this was the most influential episode of Pico's life, for it was from this interview that Reuchlin's interest in post-biblical literature sprang.[16] But there is evidence to suggest that he had started to learn Hebrew several years previously. As far back as November 1483 Rudolph Agricola, 'the prince of German humanism', wrote to him mentioning their mutual interest in the language.[17] If Melanchthon is correct, he was instructed in the rudiments of Hebrew by John Wessel of Gansfort while he was a student at the University of Paris in 1473.[18] Reuchlin himself, however, names Jacob Loans, private physician to the Emperor Frederick III, as his first teacher. It is evident that he held Loans in high regard for he refers to him as 'humanissimus praeceptor meus . . . doctor excellens'.[19] Although he never forgot his debt to the learned physician, Reuchlin also employed the services of Obadiah ben Jacob Sforno in the furtherance of linguistic studies. Sforno was renowned for his exegetical and philosophical writings, and towards the end of his life founded a talmudic school at Bologna. He taught Reuchlin while the latter was in Rome on diplomatic service for the German Emperor from 1498 to 1500. Thanks to his teachers Reuchlin's passion for Hebrew and the Hebraic tradition was never quenched, for in October 1508 he wrote to a certain Abbot Leonard stressing the importance of the knowledge of Hebrew for a proper understanding of the Bible: 'I assure you that not one of the Latins can explain the Old Testament unless he first becomes proficient in the language in which it was written. For the mediator between God and man was language, as we read in the Pentateuch; but not any language, only Hebrew, through which God wished his secrets to be made known to men'.[20]

After his meeting with Pico in Florence Reuchlin went home determined to perfect his knowledge of Hebrew and to study the Kabbalah. Four years later he produced his first kabbalistic work, the *De verbo mirifico*, a dialogue in three parts between an Epicurean, a Jew and a Christian.[21] In it he tries to make the morphology of Jewish mystical writings intelligible and to give the Kabbalah a prominent place in the current debate about magic and the occult. The 'wonder-working word' of the title is the Tetragrammaton (YHWH) and the Pentagrammaton (YHSWH: the letters of the Hebrew form of the name 'Jesus') whose power and properties are discussed in the second and third parts of the book respectively. By showing that the practice of Jewish mysticism led ultimately to Jesus Christ, and that the essential doctrines of Christianity were to be found in the Kabbalah, Reuchlin was attempting to vindicate Pico's Conclusions and to defend him against his many opponents. But the *De verbo mirifico* was the work of a beginner. By 1517, the year in which he produced his *De arte cabalistica*, he had become a very proficient Hebraist, a 'trilingue miraculum' as he was called by his friends, and was clearly the leading Christian authority on post-biblical Jewish writings. In this second volume Reuchlin examines further the magical properties of the divine names but also lays considerable stress on the 'art' or the practical application of the Kabbalah. Through the invocation of angels and by observing correct ritual procedures man could protect himself from evil and reach the divinity.[22] Like Pico, Reuchlin depended on Jewish help to unravel the mysteries of the Kabbalah, and a study of his library has shown that his chief sources in this connection were the works of Joseph ben Abraham Gikatilla,[23] a thirteenth-century Spanish Kabbalist who, in his *Ginnat Egoz* (*A Garden of Nuts*) and *Sha'arei Orah* (*Gates of Light*), made an original attempt to give a detailed yet lucid and systematic exposition of kabbalistic teaching.[24]

Reuchlin's main concern was with the Christian interpretation of the Kabbalah. But since the study of Hebrew was essential for a true appreciation of it, he also devoted his energies to providing students with the necessary apparatus for learning the language. In 1506 he published his *De rudimentis hebraicis*, a Hebrew grammar and dictionary of which he was very proud, for on the last page he quotes Horace, 'I have erected a monument more lasting than bronze'. In this book he demonstrates a close affinity with David Kimchi's *Book of Roots*, and quotes at first hand from Rashi. In 1512 he edited a text of the penitential psalms to which he appended a translation and commentary specifically for the use of students; it was the first Hebrew text to be printed in Germany. *De accentibus et orthographia linguae hebraicae*, a work dealing with pronunciation, accents and synagogue music, was issued in 1518.

In spite of Reuchlin's admiration for his teachers and his enthusiasm for Judaica, the fact remained that early in the sixteenth century it was unwise for a Christian to display too great an interest in Hebrew. For one thing the teaching contained in Jewish books was regarded by the ecclesiastical authorities as being blasphemous. If studied by a Christian, it could have a most corrupting influence. The Kabbalah and the commentaries of the rabbis might be read by qualified persons for apologetic and missionary purposes, but they were of no use whatsoever in elucidating biblical passages. Even if they did possess a limited value, the works of Christian commentators had surely rendered them obsolete. Had not Nicholas of Lyra and some of his illustrious predecessors provided the Christian exegete with all the help that he required? Furthermore, there was no need to learn Hebrew in order to arrive at the true meaning of Scripture, for Jerome's Vulgate was the Bible of Christendom and it was upon the renderings of this version that the Church of Rome based its doctrinal teaching. Christian scholars who ventured to swim against the tide to seek the help of Jewish tradition in elucidating Old Testament passages were promptly branded as Judaisers. Ignorant and illiterate monks, alarmed by the progress of the new learning, thundered from the pulpit that a new language had been discovered called Greek, of which people should beware, since it was that which produced all the heresies. A book called the New Testament written in this language was now in everyone's hands, and was 'full of thorns and briers'. There was also another language called Hebrew, which should be avoided at all costs since those who learned it became Jews.[25] Reuchlin was well aware of the trouble that lay ahead if he persisted in advocating the study of Hebrew. In his *De rudimentis* he wrote:

Enemies will rise against my dictionary in which the translations of many are frequently censured. 'Oh! what a crime', they will exclaim. 'Nothing is more unworthy of the memory of the Fathers, no crime more cruel, since that most audacious man strives to overthrow so many and such saintly men who were inspired by the divine spirit. As Pope Gelasius attests, the Bible of the most blessed Jerome was accepted in the Church. The venerable father Nicholaus of Lyra, the common expositor of the Bible, is approved as an irreproachable man by all faithful to Christ. Now a certain puff of smoke, a little Reuchlin, has appeared, who indicates that these have ignorantly translated in a great many places'. I answer these threatening shouts with these few words: to allow me what was allowed to these very famous luminaries.[26]

Just as Jerome had criticised earlier translations and Nicholas of Lyra had criticised Jerome, so Reuchlin felt that he had a right to make a judgement on the work of his predecessors, and so promote the study of Hebrew and Jewish literature.

The battle of the books

In view of the prevailing attitude of the Church towards Judaism, it is not surprising that early in 1510 a converted Jewish butcher, named Johann Pfefferkorn, came to Reuchlin with a strange request. The Jews of Cologne and Frankfurt had appealed against an order made by the Emperor Maximilian at the instigation of the Dominicans, that all

Hebrew books considered inimical to the Christian faith should be burned. Reuchlin was asked by Pfefferkorn, who was acting as the spokesman of the ecclesiastical authorities, to assist in the case, and from his vast knowledge of Jewish writings to decide which books should be condemned. Predictably, Reuchlin sprang to the defence of the Jews and their literature. Although he regarded them as mistaken in their religious convictions, and traced their endless misery to blind unbelief rather than to the uncharitable attitude of the Church throughout the centuries, he insisted that the Jews should be accepted by Christians as fellow human beings. As a graduate in law from the University of Orléans, he was aware that whatever deprivations they had suffered during the Middle Ages, they had always been treated with fairness and equality in legal matters. He knew of the charters granted by popes and emperors which guaranteed their religious liberty and permitted them to keep their prayer-books and doctrinal works.[27] Neither the Dominicans nor anyone else had the right to confiscate their property. Pfefferkorn's campaign offended Reuchlin's sense of justice and made him all the more eager to protect the Jews on humanitarian grounds.

With regard to Jewish books, Reuchlin brought religious and humanistic arguments to bear on Pfefferkorn and his colleagues. In a short memorandum he divided Jewish literature into several classes, only one of which ought to be destroyed.[28] The Old Testament, naturally, must be kept. The Talmud might well contain anti-Christian remarks, but how many Christians in Germany could read it, much less be offended by what it said; he admitted that he had not read it himself. If, as its opponents maintained, it deserved to be condemned and destroyed, surely Christians in previous centuries would have long since dealt with it. As for the Kabbalah, even popes had recognised its usefulness to Christians and had gone so far as to commission Latin translations of kabbalistic works. Furthermore, had not the learned Pico della Mirandola shown convincingly that it contained the principal doctrines of Christianity? Exegetical works, such as the commentaries of Rashi, Kimchi, Ibn Ezra and other notable rabbis, should be regarded by every serious student as an indispensable aid to the understanding of the Old Testament. Little would remain of Nicholas of Lyra's *Postillae* if they were shorn of their rabbinic quotations. Liturgical works, which gave instruction in matters of worship and ceremonial, could in no way be regarded as a threat to Christianity. Only writings which contained insults to Christ,

such as *Toledoth Yeshu* (the Jewish *Life of Jesus*) and *Ha-Nissachon*
(*The Victory*), were to be burned. To add weight to his
recommendation Reuchlin pointed out that what is forbidden usually
attracts men; confiscation would only lead to greater interest. He
urged Christians to direct their efforts to the conversion of the Jews,
not to persecution and the wilful destruction of their literary heritage.
Those who rejected Christ must be brought to see the error of their
ways by discussion and debate. But if Christians were to enter into a
meaningful dialogue with Jews, they must first have a thorough
knowledge of the writings of Jewish exegetes and philosophers. In
order to achieve this purpose he proposed the foundation of two chairs
of Hebrew in every German university with provision for the teaching
of biblical and rabbinic Hebrew. The Jews should be asked to supply
the students with books.

This, however, was not what Pfefferkorn wanted, and the result of
their disagreement was a bitter controversy which quickly went
beyond the original quarrel and lasted for almost a decade. Behind
Pfefferkorn were the Dominicans of Cologne; behind Reuchlin were
many learned Germans. Reuchlin's opponents were the mendicant
Orders and the universities which they controlled (e.g. Louvain, Paris,
Erfurt); his friends were the leaders of the literary movements in
Europe who realised that his cause was their own.[29] The true
significance of the controversy is a matter of debate. Many historians
of the Renaissance and the Reformation have regarded it as a conflict
between humanism and scholasticism, between scholarship and
ignorance, between the new and the old, between light and darkness.
According to this view the Dominicans were not merely criticising
Reuchlin for supporting the Jews, but attacking the humanist
movement as a whole. In H. Holborn's opinion, 'the humanists were
endangered. Basically the question was not simply as to the retention
of the Jewish books, but as to something much more fundamental.
Should the humanists have a voice in the affairs of faith and the
Church?'[30] Unlike their Italian counterparts, the German humanists
were being drawn into theological disputation. While the friars
condemned Reuchlin for bringing his philological studies to bear on
his interpretation of the Bible, the humanists gave him their
wholehearted support. A clash was inevitable.

Those, like Holborn, who see the Reuchlin affair as a battle between
two intellectual traditions have been influenced by the views of Ulrich
von Hutten, an outspoken critic of all who opposed the development of

Renaissance ideals. Hutten, a younger contemporary of Reuchlin, was violently anti-clerical. He regarded the Pope not only as an enemy of the Emperor, but as an enemy of Christ himself. The corruption with which he considered the Church to be rife, he blamed on illiterate and immoral priests. Since these same clerics opposed Reuchlin they could be attacked with renewed vigour in the name of the new learning. Hutten, and others of a similar persuasion formed a closely-knit group under the leadership of Konrad Muth, a canon of Gotha. According to L. W. Spitz, Muth was 'the key figure in the humanist movement of central Germany', and as such, a vigorous opponent of scholasticism.[31] In advocating the study of the Scriptures and the works of the early Fathers, he made plain his admiration for Pico and quoted him as an excellent example of this type of study.[32] Yet he did not support Reuchlin without reservation. He was never convinced that the mysteries of the Kabbalah should have been popularised and made freely available to all. However, though not an activist himself, Muth certainly stirred others to action. His scholarship was profound, his personality attractive. So great was the respect in which he was held that the group of friends and scholars which surrounded him at Gotha and the neighbouring University of Erfurt called themselves the Mutianic Circle. Crotus Rubeanus, one of the more influential members of the circle, wrote to Reuchlin, 'You do not lack supporters: you have on your side the illustrious Mutianic order which is comprised of philosophers, poets, orators, and theologians, all ready to fight for you if you so desire'.[33] Such enthusiastic backing was not confined to Germany. Lefèvre d'Etaples, the leading French Catholic Erasmian, wrote to Reuchlin from Paris in 1514, 'If you conquer, we conquer with you'.[34]

Further encouragement from the humanist camp came barely a year later. During the final weeks of 1515, when the controversy between Reuchlin and the Dominicans was at its height, there appeared in Germany a slim volume of less than forty pages entitled *Epistolae obscurorum virorum*. Though the name of the author was not given, it was widely recognised that the letters originated from the Mutianic Circle, and in particular from the pen of Hutten and Rubeanus. The title suggested satire, for in the previous year Reuchlin had published *Clarorum virorum epistolae*, a collection of the letters sent to him by prominent humanists in support of the new learning. The 'obscure men', however, wrote letters complaining of the current state of affairs to Ortwin Gratius, professor at the University of

Cologne, who, though an enthusiastic humanist, shared Pfefferkorn's antisemitic views. A monk reports how he castigated two Jews who dared revile Pfefferkorn for converting to Christianity. 'I was wroth and answered them, you speak thus out of hatred to Herr Pfefferkorn. He is as good and zealous a Christian as any in Cologne, . . . he gladly hears Mass, and when the priest elevates the host he looks at it devoutly, and does not (as his revilers claim) look down, except to spit, and he does this because he is troubled by phlegm and takes cough medicine in the morning'.[35] The letters, fictitious creations of Reuchlin's admirers, are all written in a similar vein and are designed to exhibit the foolishness and pedantry of the opposing party. They bear eloquent testimony to 'the slaying power of satire'.

Jewish historians, however, have taken a different view of the controversy. They have regarded it primarily as a battle, not between humanists and obscurantists but between antisemites and those Christians who were anxious to uphold the right of the Jews to practise their religion and preserve their devotional writings. The attempt by the Dominicans to destroy Jewish books was not new. Three centuries previously, during the pontificates of Gregory IX and Innocent IV, they had instigated the burning of the Talmud in Paris.[36] This time they were thwarted in their purpose by one of the most respected scholars in Europe, who not only disapproved of the condemnation of Jewish literature, but also demanded that the persecution of the Jews should stop. Heinrich Graetz depicts the Dominicans as vicious antisemites rather than as the opponents of humanistic learning, whereas Reuchlin was friendly towards the Jews and persistently advocated toleration and respect. 'Unquestionably', writes Graetz,

since the Jews had been ill-used and persecuted by the Christians, they had never found so friendly an advocate as Reuchlin, who declared himself in their favour in an official document, to be placed before the Chancellor of the Empire, and even before the Emperor himself. Two points on which Reuchlin had laid stress were especially important to the Jews. The first was, that the Jews were citizens of the holy Roman Empire, and were entitled to its full privileges and protection. This was in a sense the first stammering utterance of that liberating word of perfect equality, which required more than three centuries to be absolutely enunciated and acknowledged. . . . The second point which Reuchlin emphasized was of equal importance: that the Jews must not be considered or treated as heretics. Since they stood without the Church, and were not bound to hold the Christian faith, the ideas of heresy and unbelief – those terrifying and lethal anathemas of the Middle Ages – did not apply to them.[37]

In Graetz's view the conflict was between antisemites and those who were prepared to follow Reuchlin in declaring that the Jews had rights. S. W. Baron also emphasises the role played by Reuchlin in defending Jewish rights, and quotes his statement to the effect that as 'fellow citizens of the same Roman Empire' both Jews and Germans 'lived on the basis of the same law of citizenship and internal peace'.[38] In a recent re-examination of the case J. H. Overfield comes to a conclusion similar to that of these two leading Jewish historians. After scrutinising the contributions of the various participants in the debate he concludes that Reuchlin's opponents 'were motivated by anti-Semitism rather than antihumanism. Their books and pamphlets give no evidence that they viewed the controversy as a showdown between humanism and scholasticism. What they sought from the onset was a justification for the confiscation of the Jews' books'.[39]

In view of the support given by many prominent humanists, whatever their motives may have been, to all that Reuchlin stood for, the equivocal attitude of Erasmus to the study of the Hebraic tradition occasions surprise and disappointment. Surprise, because of his passionate concern for the new learning and his recognition of the importance of Greek for New Testament studies; disappointment because of the great respect in which he was universally held as a scholar and because of the influence he had over his English friends. One might agree or disagree with him, but one could not ignore him. By means of his vast correspondence, he propagated his ideas and made his opinions known to the whole scholarly world of his day. That he learned some Hebrew is certain. In December 1504 he wrote to John Colet, who later became Dean of St Paul's, stating his intention of embarking upon a thorough study of the Bible:

Hereafter I intend to address myself to the Scriptures and to spend all the rest of my life upon them. Three years ago, indeed, I ventured to do something on Paul's Epistle to the Romans, and at one rush, as it were, finished four volumes; and would have gone on, but for certain distractions, of which the most important was that I needed the Greek at every point. Therefore for nearly the past three years I have been wholly absorbed by Greek; and I do not think my efforts have been altogether wasted. I began to take up Hebrew as well, but stopped because I was put off by the strangeness of the language, and at the same time the shortness of life and the limitations of human nature will not allow a man to master too many things at once.[40]

Although he soon became proficient in Greek, his attempt at mastering Hebrew seems to have been abandoned very quickly. While he may well have been inhibited by 'the strangeness of the language', and perhaps hampered in his efforts by the difficulty of finding a good teacher, the true reason for his reluctance probably lay elsewhere. Like most of his contemporaries he was anti-Jewish at heart, and just as he feared that the revival of Greek literature would lead to a resurgence of paganism, so he feared that the study of Hebrew would lead men to Judaism, a religion which he found totally meaningless. In February 1517 he wrote to Wolfgang Capito whom he greets as 'a true expert in the three tongues', expressing his fear that the rebirth of Hebrew studies might 'give Judaism its cue to plan a revival, the most pernicious plague and bitterest enemy that one can find to the teaching of Christ'.[41] While he may have valued the humanist ideal of *hebraica veritas*, his interest in it was overshadowed by a fear of the erroneous creed of the Jews.[42] His attitude to the Kabbalah and the Talmud was entirely negative. In another letter to Capito he writes, 'Talmud, Cabala, Tetragrammaton, Gates of Light, these are but empty names. I would rather see Christ infected by Scotus than by that rubbish. Italy has very many Jews; Spain has hardly any Christians'.[43] He persistently refused to accept that the writings of mediaeval Jewish mystics could have any value whatsoever for a Christian.

But in spite of a fundamental difference of opinion over the importance of Hebrew and Judaica for the Christian, Erasmus supported Reuchlin and admired his erudition. It seems, from at least one of his letters, that he sympathised with him in his battle against the friars because he realised that this was no isolated case, and that humanist scholarship in general was being attacked by the obscurantists. From London in 1515 he wrote on Reuchlin's behalf to Raphael Riario, Cardinal of San Giorgio and one of the most powerful men in Rome. He ends his letter thus:

One thing I had almost forgotten. I beg and beseech you earnestly, in the name of those humane studies of which your eminence has been an outstanding patron, that that excellent man Doctor Johann Reuchlin should find you fair-minded and friendly in his business. At one stroke you will render a great service to literature and to all literary men, for the greater their learning the greater their enthusiasm for him. He has all Germany in his debt, where he was the first to awake the study of Greek and Hebrew. He is a man with an exceptional knowledge of the languages, accomplished in many subjects, eminent and well-known throughout Christendom for his published works. . . . The time had come when for his part he deserved to enjoy at his time of life a pleasant harvest from his honourable exertions, and we on our part looked to see him bring out the results of so many years' work for the common good. And so it seems outrageous to all men of good feeling, not Germans only but English and French as well, to whom he is well-known through his letters, that a man of such distinction and such outstanding gifts should be persecuted with such unpleasant litigation. . . . Believe me, whoever restores Johann Reuchlin to the arts and letters will win countless men's grateful devotion.[44]

Although this paragraph admittedly comes at the end of a letter which discusses other matters, and seems to have been added as an afterthought, it does testify to Erasmus' concern for the ageing Reuchlin and to the high regard in which he held him as a scholar. He makes another spirited defence of Reuchlin in one of his colloquies published shortly after the Hebraist's death in 1522. Entitled 'The Apotheosis of that Incomparable Worthy, Johann Reuchlin', he depicts Reuchlin being escorted to heaven by Jerome, the great exemplar of Christian scholars. The dialogue ends with the following collect to be used to honour the scholar's memory:

O God thou lover of mankind, who through thy chosen servant Johann Reuchlin has renewed to the world the gift of tongues, by which thou didst once from heaven, through thy Holy Spirit, instruct the apostles for the preaching of the gospel, grant that all men everywhere may preach in every tongue the glory of thy son Jesus. Confound the tongues of false apostles who band themselves to build an impious tower to Babel, attempting to obscure thy glory whilst minded to exalt their own; since to thee alone, with Jesus thy Son our Lord, and the Holy Spirit, belongs all glory, for ever and ever, Amen.[45]

It is also worth noting in this context Erasmus' willingness to co-operate with Jerome Busleiden in establishing a college at Louvain specifically for the study of the three languages, Latin, Greek and Hebrew.

Yet, while Erasmus defended Reuchlin sincerely and eloquently on occasion, he took care not to associate himself too closely with his cause, especially during Reuchlin's own lifetime. His attitude has been explained in various ways. It is certain that he wanted peace at all costs. He maintained that the revival of letters would flourish only if men were at peace with one another and for this reason he disapproved of the *Letters of Obscure Men* and saw no point in crossing swords with Pfefferkorn, who though 'a fool with a forehead of brass', was a dangerous man. In a letter addressed to Albert, Archbishop of Mainz, he expressed his views on the controversies caused by both Luther and Reuchlin. Although Albert was an educated man and favourable to the

new learning, Erasmus felt it necessary to deny any close alliance with
the two chief controversial figures of the day. 'I must make it plain', he
writes, 'that I never had anything to do either with the Reuchlin affair
or with the case of Luther. Cabbala and Talmud, whatever they are,
never appealed to me. Those bitter clashes between Reuchlin and the
supporters of Jacob Hochstrat have greatly displeased me'.[46] Further,
Erasmus was anxious to steer clear of conflict, not so much on account
of personal timidity, or a desire to be acceptable to his royal and
ecclesiastical patrons, but out of prudence. His letter to Albert was
written from Louvain where he had become an object of suspicion and
attack by the Carmelites because of the growing alarm in the Church
at large over Luther. Under such circumstances, Erasmus felt that
party labels were of no advantage. He did not want to be associated
with Luther or Reuchlin, and he forestalled the accusation of
Judaising by denying any knowledge of or interest in post-biblical
Jewish writings. Yet another reason, recently put forward by Charles
Zika, for Erasmus' reluctance to give Reuchlin his unqualified
support, was his opposition to the excessive emphasis on ceremonial
and ritual which found expression in the latter's kabbalistic works.
Such ceremonies as were advocated in the *De arte cabalistica*, though
they conformed to orthodox Christian practice, would not in Erasmus'
view help to bring about the reform of the Church he so passionately
desired. Salvation would come, not by adopting the esoteric practices
advocated by Jewish mystics, but by leading an ethical and moral
life.[47] Not only did the study of the Kabbalah open the door to the
pernicious influence of Judaism, it also encouraged a form of piety
which was the complete antithesis of all that Erasmus stood for.

   In the light of recent research it must be recognised that support for
Reuchlin was not as widespread as was once supposed. Though leading
German humanists did espouse his cause, not many did so
unambiguously, and of those who did, few shared his concern for
protecting Jewish interests. His work was condemned even by Pope
Leo X, an action which appears all the more surprising in view of Leo's
patronage of learning. In acting as he did the Pope was presumably
bowing to the demands of the friars, for the Dominicans became
threatening, and Leo X realised that if they were his servants they
were also the mainstay of his power, and therefore his masters.[48]
Ironically for Reuchlin's enemies theirs was a barren triumph, for
indirectly the activity of Pfefferkorn and his associates stimulated
German scholars to a serious study of Hebrew and Jewish literature,

which was precisely what Reuchlin wanted.

Apart from his work on the Kabbalah, Reuchlin's importance in the field of scholarship is that he established philology as a recognised and independent discipline entitled to discuss the meaning of biblical words. He claimed that where a theologian may err in his interpretation, the philologist may arrive at the truth. It was in his search for the truth that he discovered for his fellow Christians a Jewish literature which was eventually to become an important branch of study at almost every seat of higher learning.[49] Behind Reuchlin stood Pico. Without the active encouragement of this brilliant Florentine Orientalist it is doubtful whether the German would have pursued the study of Hebrew and Judaica with such passion. Behind both of them were Jews and converts from Judaism who were prepared to teach Hebrew to gentiles.

My objectives in this chapter have been strictly limited. I have tried to show that Pico and Reuchlin are chiefly remembered for the attempt which they made to form a synthesis between Christian theology and kabbalistic motifs. For them, however, the Kabbalah was important in a practical as well as a speculative sense. Through the power with which it was invested it could be employed to tap the supercelestial spirits of the universe. For this reason it was to be recommended to the Renaissance magician and used alongside the Hermetic tradition of natural magic propagated by Ficino in Florence. Both Pico and Reuchlin saw a parallelism between the writings of Hermes, the ancient Egyptian lawgiver, and the secret Jewish tradition which claimed to go back to Moses. They urged that the holy magic of the Kabbalah be used to strengthen the natural magic of Hermes.[50]

The scholarly endeavours of these two Christian Kabbalists are of great significance. Their advocacy of a specifically Christian interpretation of the Kabbalah marks a turning point in the attitude of the Church towards the learning of Hebrew and the study of Jewish literature. Admittedly Pico may have failed, because of his attempt to employ Jewish mystical writings, to give an acceptable presentation of the creed of Christendom. Likewise Reuchlin, on account of his missionary interests, may have done but little to lessen the age old antagonism between Christianity and Judaism. Both of them, because of their preoccupation with the occult and with ceremonial, may not have succeeded in persuading their contemporaries of the abiding value of the Kabbalah. Nevertheless, they were men of considerable influence, whose achievements eventually brought several prominent Christian scholars to a deeper understanding and a greater appreciation of rabbinic literature. It is to those men who perpetuated some of their ideals in Tudor England that we shall turn later when we look for the motives for the acceptance of Hebrew by Christians as a necessary branch of the study of divinity, and as a third language alongside Latin and Greek.

Recognition of the influence of continental scholars is crucial to our understanding of the position adopted in England towards the Hebraic tradition. As the century progressed this influence became more pervasive. Even the practical Kabbalah found some adherents. In the next two chapters, therefore, we shall examine further the part played by European men of letters in disseminating Jewish learning. Translators and exegetes also were responsible for awakening an interest in the study of Hebrew among sixteenth-century Englishmen, and for transmitting the legacy of the rabbis to all who were anxious to receive it.

Notes

1   See A. Lukyn Williams, *Adversus Judaeos*, Cambridge 1935, p. 263.
2   See W. Schwarz, *Principles and Problems of Biblical Translation*, Cambridge 1955, pp. 63ff.
3   See R. Weiss, 'England and the decree of the Council of Vienne on the teaching of Greek, Arabic, Hebrew and Syriac', *Bibliothèque d'Humanisme et Renaissance*, tome XIV, 1952, pp. 1–9. Weiss concludes that a converted Jew taught Hebrew briefly at Oxford from 1320.
4   See C. Roth, *The History of the Jews of Italy*, Philadelphia, Pa. 1946, pp. 153ff; M. Shulvass, *The Jews of the World of the Renaissance*, Leiden 1973, pp. 148ff.
5   *Marsilio Ficino: Opera Omnia*, ed. P. O. Kristeller, Turin 1962, vol. I, pp. 31–105. See especially the section on 'Testimonia Prophetarum de Christo', pp. 60–76.
6   For Pico's contacts with Italian Jews see U. Cassuto, *Gli Ebrei a Firenze*, Firenze 1918, pp. 282–316.
7   Quoted by Chaim Wirszubski, 'Giovanni Pico's Book of Job', *JWCI*, vol. XXXII, 1969, p. 173.
8   *Ibid.*
9   Chaim Wirszubski, 'Giovanni Pico's companion to kabbalistic symbolism', *Studies in Mysticism and Religion Presented to G. Scholem*, Jerusalem 1967, p. 353.
10 See F. Secret, 'L'Ensis Pauli de Paulus de Heredia', *Sefarad*, vol. 26,

1966, pp. 79–102, 253–71.

11   *The Renaissance Philosophy of Man*, ed. E. Cassirer, P. O. Kristeller, J. H. Randall Jr., Chicago, Ill. 1948, p. 252.

12   See P. O. Kristeller, 'Giovanni Pico Della Mirandola and his sources', in *L'Opera e il Pensiero di Giovanni Pico della Mirandola*, Florence 1965, vol. I, pp. 35ff.

13   *Johannes Picus Mirandulanus: Opera Omnia*, ed. E. Garin, Turin 1971, pp. 104–13.

14   *Ibid.*, p. 105.

15   *The Christian Interpretation of the Cabala in the Renaissance*, New York 1944, p. 19.

16   'Pico della Mirandola', *HUCA*, Jubilee Volume, 1925, p. 325.

17   *Johann Reuchlins Briefwechsel*, ed. L. Geiger, Stuttgart 1875, Letter 5, p. 7.

18   *Corpus Reformatorum*, vol. XI, Halle 1843, 'Oratio continens historiam Ioannis Capnionis', col. 1002. See also M. Brod, *Johannes Reuchlin und sein Kampf*, Stuttgart 1965, p. 80 for a reference to an otherwise unknown Jew named Calman who taught Reuchlin Hebrew in 1486.

19   See L. Geiger, *Johann Reuchlin: sein Leben und seine Werke*, Leipzig 1871 (reprinted 1964), p. 106, n. 3, quoting Reuchlin's *De rudimentis*, p. 619.

20   *Reuchlins Brief.*, Letter 102, p. 105.

21   For a detailed account of the *De verbo mirifico* see C. Zika, 'Reuchlin's *De Verbo Mirifico* and the magic debate of the late fifteenth century', *JWCI*, vol. XXXIX, 1976, pp. 104ff.

22   A French translation of this work with introduction and notes has been prepared by F. Secret, *La Kabbale (De Arte Cabalistica)*, Paris 1973. An English translation with facsimile text and introduction has been made by M. D. and S. J. Goodman, *De Arte Cabalistica*, Abaris Books, New York 1982.

23   K. Christ, *Die Bibliothek Reuchlins in Pforzheim*, Leipzig 1924.

24   G. Scholem, *EJ*, vol. 7, col. 566.

25   J. I. Mombert, *English Versions of the Bible: a Handbook*, New York 1883, p. 77, quoting Hody, *De textibus bibliorum*, p. 456.

26   Quoted in trans. by W. Schwarz, *Principles and Problems*, p. 88.

27   G. Kisch, *Zasius und Reuchlin*, Constance 1961, pp. 23–36, argues that legal training rather than literary interests inspired Reuchlin to defend the Jews. For papal protection of the Jews see S. Grayzel, *The Church and the Jews in the XIIIth Century*, Philadelphia, Pa. 1933, pp. 76ff. For favourable legal treatment of the Jews by the state up to *c.* 1350 see G. Kisch, 'The Jews in Mediaeval Law', *Essays on Antisemitism*, ed. K. S. Pinson, 2nd ed. rev., New York 1946, pp. 103ff. For a concise account of the controversy see S. A. Hirsch, 'Johann Pfefferkorn and the battle of the books', *A Book of Essays*, pp. 73ff.

28   See L. Geiger, *Johann Reuchlin*, pp. 227ff.

29   See *Ulrichi Hutteni Opera*, ed. E. Boking, Leipzig 1859 (reprinted 1963), vol. I, pp. 130f for a list of some of Reuchlin's supporters, 'Capnionis Defensores Acerrimi, viri Germaniae totius literatissimi

splendidissimique'.

30 *Ulrich von Hutten and the German Reformation*, Eng. trans. by R. H. Bainton, New Haven, Conn. 1937, p. 54.

31 *The Religious Renaissance of the German Humanists*, Cambridge, Mass. 1963, p. 130.

32 C. Krause, *Der Briefwechsel des Mutianus Rufus*, Kassel 1885, Letter 137, p. 174.

33 *Ulrich Hutteni Opera*, vol. 1, Letter 14, p. 29.

34 Lefèvre's letter to Reuchlin, 30 August 1514, Herminjard, *Correspondance des Réformateurs*, Paris 1866, vol. 1, p. 17.

35 *Epistolae Obscurorum Virorum*, edited with Eng. trans. by F. G. Stokes, London 1909, p. 94.

36 See E. A. Synan, *The Popes and the Jews in the Middle Ages*, New York 1965, pp. 107–111.

37 *History of the Jews*, London 1892, vol. IV, pp. 473f.

38 *A Social and Religious History of the Jews*, vol. XIII, New York 1969, p. 188 quoting Reuchlin in *Der Augenspiegel*, Tübingen 1511.

39 'A new look at the Reuchlin affair', *Studies in Mediaeval and Renaissance History*, vol. VIII, ed. H. L. Adelson, Lincoln, Neb. 1971, p. 191.

40 *CWE*, vol. 2, Letter 181, p. 87.

41 *CWE*, vol. 4, Letter 541, p. 267.

42 W. L. Gundersheimer, 'Erasmus, humanism and the Christian Cabala', *JWCI*, vol. XXVI, 1963, p. 43.

43 *Opus Epistolarum Des. Erasmi Roterodami*, ed. P. S. Allen, Oxford 1910, vol. III, Letter 798, p. 253.

44 *CWE*, vol. 3, Letter 333, pp. 90f. For Erasmus' negative attitude see also M. Krebs, 'Reuchlins Beziehungen zu Erasmus von Rotterdam', *Johannes Reuchlin 1455–1522*, ed. M. Krebs, Pforzheim 1955, pp. 139ff.

45 *The Colloquies of Erasmus*, Eng. trans. by C. R. Thompson, Chicago, Ill. 1965, p. 86.

46 *Opus Epistolarum*, vol. IV, Letter 1033, p. 100.

47 'Reuchlin and Erasmus: humanism and occult philosophy', *Journal of Religious History*, vol. 9, 1977, p. 232.

48 W. Popper, *The Censorship of Hebrew Books*, New York 1899, p. 25.

49 'Johann Reuchlin: the father of the study of Hebrew among Christians', *JQR*, O.S. vol. 8, 1896, p. 451 (reprinted in *A Book of Essays*, pp. 116ff).

50 See further Frances A. Yates, *Giordano Bruno and the Hermetic Tradition*, London 1964, pp. 20ff.

II
The bridge builders

The authoritative version of the Bible in the Western Church during the Middle Ages was Jerome's Vulgate. Although it was given official sanction only at the Council of Trent in 1546, it had been used everywhere and by everyone. The existence of a well-established tradition coupled with the complete ignorance of Hebrew among the great majority of biblical exegetes made its position secure, so that whenever a translation into the vernacular was made the Vulgate was used as the original. But with the Renaissance the tide turned, and early in the sixteenth century both Catholics and Protestants took up the battle cry of the humanists enshrined in the motto *ad fontes* and applied it to the Scriptures.

This adoption by biblical scholars of the humanist attitude towards the primary sources had two important consequences. In the first place it drew attention to the original texts, thus stressing the importance of Hebrew and Greek. Secondly, by emphasising the necessity of discovering the *hebraica veritas*, it appeared to impugn the authority and, some would claim, lower the prestige of the Vulgate.[1] By insisting that due recognition be given to the languages in which the Bible was written, the Christian humanists gave biblical translation a new impetus. They no longer felt bound by a traditional reverence for the Vulgate. The version provided by Jerome was less readily accepted, in some circles, as the final authority in textual matters, and the attempt was made to bypass it by making new Latin translations of the Old and New Testaments from the original languages. 'This last age', wrote the French exegete Richard Simon in 1678, 'has abounded in translations of the holy Scriptures in the western Church. Some learned men who had learned Hebrew, fancied they could make from the Hebrew text a better translation of the Bible, than the ancient vulgar one attributed to St Jerome. Thus in a little time we saw a great many translations very different one from the other, although all affirmed they translated the Bible from the same original Hebrew'.[2] In spite of Simon's disapproval of this drive for fresh translations, the fact remains that these new and independent Latin versions of the Old Testament quickly assumed an important role in the field of biblical scholarship, and some of them were destined to play a crucial part in the transmission of rabbinic exegesis to those concerned with Hebrew studies. In this chapter we shall consider briefly the contribution of four translators towards the establishment of the Hebraic tradition in Tudor England, noting their dependence on mediaeval Jewish commentators for the elucidation of difficult words and phrases in the Hebrew text.

Sanctes Pagninus (1470–1536)

The Italian scholar Sanctes Pagninus was born in Lucca, and at the age of sixteen entered the Order of Preachers. After studying for the priesthood at Fiesole, where he came under the influence of Savonarola who doubtless taught him how to preach and impressed upon him the importance of the Scriptures, the young Dominican went to Florence and soon demonstrated his penchant for Oriental languages. By 1513 he was teaching Semitics in Rome and for a while acted as prefect of the Vatican library. The year 1524 found him lecturing at Lyons where he did his most important academic work, remaining there until his death. He has been described as one of the most learned Hebraists of his day, a man deeply versed in rabbinic literature, and one of the glories of his order.[3]

Early in the sixteenth century Pagninus decided to make his own translation of the Bible from Hebrew and Greek, and in the preface he explains to Pope Clement VII why he undertook such a task. As a result of careful investigation he had come to the conclusion that the ancient versions of the Bible were unreliable. He pointed out that even Jerome in his commentaries offered proof of textual variations and admitted that he was perplexed over the meaning of many words. The venture was approved and financed by Pope Leo X and after twenty-five years of painstaking labour, at a time when aids to the study of Hebrew were few, Pagninus published his *Veteris et Novi Testamenti nova translatio* in 1528. The approbation of the Church for such a project was further emphasised in the prefatory letters of Pope Adrian VI and Pope Clement VII which were appended to the finished work licensing the printing of it. But his contribution to biblical scholarship did not come to an end with his new translation. To help students in their efforts to read the Old Testament in the original he also published a grammar and a dictionary, both of which were based on the works of Kimchi. His *Institutiones hebraicae* was modelled on the *Michlol* and his *Thesaurus linguae sanctae seu lexicon hebraicum* was derived mainly from the *Book of Roots*. In the year of his death he completed a six-volume anthology of the works of Jewish and Christian commentators on the Five Books of Moses entitled *Catena argentea in pentateuchum*.

Our main concern here is with Pagninus' translation of the Old Testament, for in it he employed to advantage the comments of mediaeval rabbis whenever he came to a problematic word or phrase in the Hebrew text. It would not be difficult to give a host of instances where he depends entirely on rabbinic exegesis to elucidate textual problems. Three examples, taken from his translation of the Book of Ezekiel, must suffice.

The ancient versions all differ in their understanding of the word *hedh*, used in the final phrase of Ezekiel 7:7 to describe the day of doom with which the land is threatened. The Septuagint, presumably in an effort to make sense of a corrupt text, claims that the day will come 'neither with tumult nor with pangs', while the Vulgate ('gloria') obviously reads *hodh*. The Targumic 'and there is no salvation in the strongholds of the mountains' likewise seems to be of little help. David Kimchi, however, both in his commentary *ad loc.* and in the *Book of Roots* suggests that the word means 'an echo', and in explanation of this text says that the approaching day of doom will be a day of tumult and not like a mountain echo; it will be real, not imaginary. In his translation Pagninus accepts this exposition directly with no explanatory note and renders the phrase 'et non echo montium'. But in his *Thesaurus* he acknowledges his debt to Kimchi and ends his comment by expressing his satisfaction at this particular rendering with the words, 'Et haec magis placet'.[4] In Ezekiel 7:11 neither the Septuagint nor the Targum offers any help in the elucidation of *noah*, a *hapax legomenon*. The Vulgate presupposes *noach* which it renders 'requies'; when the day of doom comes there will be no rest for the wicked. Rashi and Kimchi, however, take the word to mean 'lamentation' or 'mourning' from the root *nahah*. So great will be the tragedy that the survivors will not even lament for the dead. Pagninus' 'nec erit lamentum in eis' follows this rendering exactly and once more refers to Kimchi as the source.[5] Although the literal translation 'they shall not gird themselves in sweat' is grammatically possible for the last phrase in Ezekiel 44:18, what this injunction actually meant for the Levitical priests is not immediately obvious. The Septuagint clearly found difficulty with *ba-yaza* ('in sweat'), another *hapax legomenon*, and translated it as *bia*, 'with force' or 'tightly'. The Targum's paraphrase offers little help, while the Vulgate gives the word its literal translation, 'in sudore'. But Rashi and Kimchi cite the explanation that the priests are commanded not to gird themselves 'in any place where they sweat' i.e. not as high as the armpits nor as low as the loins. This reflects the instruction given to priests in *Tal. Zeb.* 18b where this verse is quoted and explained. Again Pagninus follows the lead given by traditional Jewish exegesis by translating the phrase as 'non accingent se in locis sudoris'.[6] In each of these three cases Pagninus' suggestion is reproduced in either the text or the margin of the Authorised Version of 1611.

Within a short time of its publication Pagninus' translation was extolled by both Jews and Christians as the best Latin version ever made from the Hebrew. Sixtus of Siena in his *Bibliotheca sancta* (1626) informs us that the learned Dominican 'collated many of the best Hebrew MSS. available and in his Latin version he restored the Hebrew proper names to their original form, unlike the Latin dress in which previous translators had presented them. So carefully was his work done that the most learned of the Hebrew rabbis prefer his version to all others'.[7] But to some critics the literalness of his translation seemed harsh and unnatural, and his reliance on rabbinic sources did not find universal favour. Génébrard, who taught Hebrew in Paris from 1566 to 1591, heartily disapproved of the version, claiming that it was 'too ambitious, too odd, too grammatical, too close to the hair-splitting methods of the rabbis'.[8] Richard Simon likewise accuses Pagninus of 'neglecting the ancient interpreters of Scripture, to rely upon the opinion of the Rabbis'.[9] The eighteenth-century Roman Catholic scholar Alexander Geddes, although he records the enthusiasm of Jews and Christians for the version, finds it to be 'a barbarous composition, despicable in almost every point of view, but that of grammatical glossary: as such it may be of considerable use in giving an idea of Hebrew idiom, and a superficial knowledge of the language to grown up Biblical students who are too idle to turn over the leaves of a lexicon or con their Buxtorf'.[10] It was, however, this extreme literalness which made Pagninus' translation of invaluable assistance to those who, without the knowledge of Greek and Hebrew, wished to understand the simple meaning of the original text and to appreciate the explanations of lexical and exegetical difficulties offered by Jewish commentators.

The Latin version of Sanctes Pagninus was revised and reprinted by his admirers several times during the sixteenth century, but the most far-reaching and significant tribute to it was its inclusion in the Royal Polyglot Bible printed by Christopher Plantin at Antwerp in 1572 under the auspices of the King of Spain.[11] It seems that Plantin was anxious to undertake a truly monumental project which would bring him fame and fortune, and had considered reissuing the Complutensian Polyglot edition which was already scarce since many copies of it had been lost in a shipwreck off the Italian coast. But he decided to produce a new polyglot and sent specimen sheets to Philip II of Spain in an attempt to persuade him to give financial support. The king responded enthusiastically and dispatched Benito Arias Montano (1527–1598) to Antwerp to correct the proofs and supervise the work. Montano, a Spanish priest, had learned Hebrew at the University of Alcalá and had been initiated into the spirit of humanist scholarship and philological exegesis in Seville, 'a town where Erasmianism flourished freely'.[12] It is clear from the articles on grammar and lexicography appended to the polyglot that Montano was an accomplished Hebraist, and that he favoured the work done by Protestants and those on the fringes of Roman Catholicism to further the cause of Semitic scholarship. In the final volume he included the Syriac grammar and dictionary of Andreas Masius (whose commentary on the Book of Judges was eventually put on the *Index*) and a list of variant readings in the Talmud compiled by Franciscus Raphaelengius, who later became a Calvinist. He was clearly impressed by the fine team of scholars which Plantin had assembled in Antwerp, for in a letter to Sayas, secretary to the King of Spain, he writes enthusiastically of his colleagues: 'God has brought together in this city five men who are assisting me in this work, and who are knowledgeable about the corrections. . . . Without hesitation I dare to assert that in no land and at no time have been brought together men with greater linguistic erudition. . . . I shall make their names known in the Prologue'.[13]

Montano's enthusiasm for Hebrew studies was strong, and in spite of violent opposition he remained undaunted in his task of promoting the best possible Latin translation of the Scriptures. Although he published it in the polyglot, in accordance with the decision of the censors of Louvain to place the authorised Catholic version alongside the Hebrew text, in his heart Montanus regarded the Vulgate as 'a philological absurdity'.[14] His sympathies lay with Pagninus, and in his determination to produce a Bible which incorporated the fruits of contemporary scholarship he included the Dominican scholar's version in the penultimate volume of the Royal Polyglot. An explanation of the editor's purpose and of the method adopted for presenting the work appears on the title-page. Pagninus' translation is interlineated with the Hebrew text and refined by Montano and his associates whenever they feel that it does not do justice to the original. These emendations appear in italics while Pagninus' own renderings are printed in the margin together with etymological notes.

Despite the powerful support of Philip II the new polyglot was by no means universally accepted. Pope Pius V refused to give his approval because the Holy Office had not had time to scrutinise it for heresy. Montano himself was bitterly attacked by Leon de Castro, Dean of the Faculty of Theology and Professor of Greek at Salamanca, who believed that any scholar who went behind the Vulgate by consulting the Hebrew original and consorting with rabbis should be condemned as a Judaising heretic.[15] After much debate on the legitimacy of the enterprise a committee of Spanish theologians led by the Jesuit Juan de Mariana was allowed by Pope Gregory XIII to have the last word on the matter. The progressive party triumphed, and Mariana, though not without qualification, agreed with Montano, thereby saving the work from being condemned. This decision, finally taken in 1579, to permit the new Bible to circulate freely secured for Pagninus' translation a new lease of life and an even more prominent place in the scholastic equipment of those studying the Old Testament in the original Hebrew in Tudor and Jacobean England. Due to Montano's efforts it was given a place in an edition of the Bible which was of great significance in the field of sixteenth-century scholarship. For the Royal Polyglot represented the climax of Erasmianism in Spain. It was an example of what was best in Tridentine Catholicism inasmuch as it was the Catholic answer in biblical studies to a biblically based Protestantism. It has been described as 'the Counter-Reformation in folio'.[16]

Sebastian Münster (1489–1552)

One of Pagninus' most celebrated contemporaries was the German scholar Sebastian Münster, professor of Hebrew at Basle from 1528 until his death. As a Christian Hebraist he was equal, if not superior, to Reuchlin. A former Franciscan, he became a Protestant in *c.* 1526 and soon proved to be a prolific author and translator. Between 1527 and 1552 he published seventy-five works, over half of which were concerned with the study of Semitic languages. For the benefit of non-Jews he translated the works of Jewish authors from Hebrew into Latin.[17] Although he appreciated the value of the Hebraic tradition for elucidating the Old Testament, Münster was also motivated by polemic and conversionist considerations. He composed three missionary works intended specifically for the Jews. The first, which took the form of a dialogue between a Christian and a Jew, appeared in 1529. Written in Hebrew, so that Jews could read it, it was remarkably eirenic in character. Throughout, the discussion was conducted amicably, the Christian making little effort to propagate the faith or to counter Jewish arguments. As such, it is quite untypical of sixteenth-century missionary tracts. The only suggestion of conflict appears when the Christian upbraids the Jew for his obstinacy in refusing to believe that Jesus of Nazareth was the Messiah:

Your rabbis do always seduce you, saying, behold, at this time the Messiah shall come, and when that is past, again they say, at that time he shall come. How will you believe these lying words? Consider, you have no hope and salvation is deferred from you, and God is departed from you and you have no consolation, not a prophet nor vision: therefore be converted, and acknowledge your Saviour and our Saviour, our Lord Christ.[18]

His second attempt at converting the Jews followed the Reformation principle of giving the people a copy of the Bible in their own language. In 1537 he made a Hebrew translation of the Gospel of Matthew. By now his attitude towards the Jews had hardened. The lengthy introduction contained more than a hint of ill-feeling. It is doubtful whether any Jew reading it would have persevered as far as the biblical text. The third tract, *The Christian and Jewish Messiah*, was a revision of the first. It was published in 1539 and translated into English in the seventeenth century. Whereas the dialogue remains unchanged, in the introduction we catch a glimpse of a much more virulent anti-Jewish polemic. After attacking contemporary Jewish apologists, he adds:

Today the Jews, although they live freely among Christians, abuse their venerable language and spout blasphemous words. . . . These perfidious people should have been banned from all Christian lands, had not the

Redeemer himself wished that that infidel race survive until the end of the age as an example to his faithful and in order that all things predicted in the Scriptures by dictation of the Holy Spirit should be fulfilled.[19]

Happily such outbursts are few and far between, even in tracts written with an avowedly missionary or polemic purpose, with the result that the author is chiefly remembered as one of the leading transmitters of Jewish exegesis to Christian scholars.

Münster acquired his early knowledge of Hebrew from Konrad Pellican of Zurich who was himself a pupil of Reuchlin. Through Pellican (1478–1556) he would have become acquainted with Reuchlin's Hebrew grammar and David Kimchi's *Michlol*. Of more direct and lasting influence, however, was his Jewish teacher Elias Levita. It is doubtful whether he would have been able to understand, let alone make use of rabbinic literature without the help afforded by Kimchi's works and by Levita's instruction.[20] Between them his teachers provided Münster with a sound grammatical knowledge. Through them he came to regard Jewish writers as important authorities in the field of biblical exegesis and to realise that their explanations of difficult passages could be of great value for the Christian in his understanding of Scripture. This appreciation of the Hebraic tradition is to be seen nowhere more clearly than in his Latin version of the Old Testament, which was printed alongside the Hebrew text and published in Basle in 1535. The work, dedicated to the 'invincible' King Henry VIII of England, is prefaced by a lengthy introduction in which the translator mentions the sources from which his comments and marginal notes have been taken. He claims to have used the Targum, Rashi, David Kimchi, Ibn Ezra and several others, and to have followed in the more obscure places whatever exposition appeared to him to be the most suitable. In his translation Münster gave Christian readers a fully annotated version of the Old Testament which was heavily dependent on the rabbis. As the following examples from the Book of Daniel will demonstrate, Jewish exegesis was worked into the translation itself and was also given a prominent place in the copious marginal notes.

The reason why Nebuchadnezzar, in Daniel 4:24 (Aramaic, English 4:27), is encouraged to break with his past is variously interpreted. The ancient versions suggest that if the king 'breaks off his sins by practising righteousness' God will forgive him. But the Jewish commentators offer two other interpretations. Rashi sees a reference to a long and peaceful reign as a reward for doing right and translates 'perhaps there will be a lengthening of thy peace'. Ibn Ezra, followed by Gersonides,[21] takes the phrase to refer to the king's reformed life and translates it as 'perhaps there will be a healing of thine error'. Münster adopts this latter explanation in his text, 'id enim erit sanitas pro errore tuo', but in the margin he notes the former and renders it 'prolongatio pro pace tua'. Both these interpretations find a place in the A.V., one in the text itself and the other in the margin. In Daniel 6:18 we read that King Darius was so distraught after locking Daniel in the lions' den that he lay down fasting and allowed no *dachwan* to be brought before him. Theodotion and Jerome both take the word to signify 'food', but this precise translation is not adopted by any of the later versions. Rashi enlists the support of the Mishna and Dunash ibn Labrat in taking it to mean 'table' and so, presumably, 'food'. Ibn Ezra comments briefly, 'music and song', an explanation which clearly influenced Gersonides who says that the word means 'musical instruments'. Disregarding the other interpretations, Münster, without any acknowledgement, follows this one and renders the word by 'melodia instrumentorum' which is adopted verbatim by the A.V. The promise is made in Daniel 9:25 that Jerusalem will be rebuilt and given new streets and fortifications. The English translations follow the Vulgate and Theodotion in rendering *charutz* as 'wall', which in this sense is a *hapax legomenon* in the Hebrew Bible. The mediaeval rabbis, however, are unanimous in suggesting that the word means 'ditch'. (Cf. the Aramaic *charitza*, 'channel'.) Although Pagninus prefers to reproduce the traditional understanding ('murus'), Münster tacitly adopts the Jewish explanation and translates the word by 'fossa', which is preserved by the A.V. in the margin.

Münster, like Pagninus, has not been without his critics. His penchant for consulting rabbinic authorities on difficult points, at the expense of the Septuagint and Vulgate, has been regarded by some as a weakness. In the opinion of Richard Simon his translation

would have been more exact had he joined the ancient Greek and Latin translations with the rabbis' books, because he would then more thoroughly have understood the Hebrew tongue. . . . He declares he follows the modern Jews, . . . he would have done better to have followed the method of Conrad Pellican, his Hebrew master, who was in the right in thinking we ought only to borrow the grammar from the rabbis; and that as for the sense, we ought to consult as well the ancient as modern interpreters of the Bible.[22]

In a similar vein B. Hall claims that Münster's version 'would have been better if he had heeded the opinion of other reformers, for example Luther, that one should take grammar from the Jews but not their interpretation of the sense of the Hebrew text'.[23] But it was precisely on account of his firm grasp of Hebrew and his constant use of the rabbinic commentaries that his translation was hailed by many as the *hebraica veritas*. Although, after 1546, his version gradually lost ground before those of other scholars such as Pagninus, it was Münster above all others who introduced the Targum and the works of the rabbis to the biblical scholars of Tudor England. As we shall see, Archbishop Parker's instructions to those responsible for the Bishops' Bible bear witness to the esteem in which his work was held in Britain. It is also noteworthy that his marginalia were incorporated, together with those of other famous exegetes, in the *Critici sacri* of 1660.

Leo Jud (1482–1542)

Ulrich Zwingli, the pioneer and chief promoter of Hebrew studies among the Swiss Reformers, was surrounded by a group of learned men who shared his enthusiasm. Leo Jud, a close friend and associate of the Zurich leader, is of particular interest.[24] A native of Alsace, Leo was the son of a Catholic priest whose family name would suggest Jewish lineage. But despite his surname, Leo's Jewish background is by no means certain. According to L. I. Newman his parents were 'indisputably Christian, and no Jewish strain in the family is known to have existed'.[25] C. Pestalozzi on the other hand considers it highly probable that he was of Jewish extraction and quotes Leo's son as saying that his father almost certainly came from one of the many Jewish families in Alsace which had converted to Christianity.[26] Whatever his origins, Leo became a sound Hebrew scholar. After exchanging medicine for theology he came to Basle in 1505 to study under Thomas Wyttenbach, and it was here that his lifelong friendship with Zwingli commenced. Before following the Reformer to Zurich in 1519, and later becoming the first Evangelical pastor of St Peter's church (a post which he held for the rest of his life), he ministered at Basle and Einsiedeln and in his spare time studied the works of Reuchlin and Luther. It was here too that he embarked on a German translation of Erasmus' paraphrase of the New Testament.

Although, as Zwingli's adviser, Leo made an important contribution to the Zurich Bible of 1529, his fame rests on his independent Latin translation of the Old Testament published at

Zurich in 1543, a year after his death. He was assisted in his task by Bibliander, Zwingli's successor as professor of divinity at Zurich, and by Konrad Pellican. Bibliander in fact completed the work after Leo's death, and according to Richard Simon was responsible for translating the last eight chapters of Ezekiel, Daniel, Job, Ecclesiastes, the Song of Songs and psalms one hundred and three to the end.[27] Another close associate was Michael Adam, a baptised Jew and citizen of Zurich who may well have acquainted him with the points of rabbinic exegesis which found their way into the margin of the new translation.

A good example of Jud's reliance on the Hebraic tradition when faced with a perplexing word or phrase in the Massoretic Text is to be found in Daniel 2:5. In describing what will happen to the magicians and sorcerers if they fail to give King Nebuchadnezzar a satisfactory interpretation of his dream, the Hebrew original uses the word *nebali*. Theodotion and Jerome take it to refer to the destruction or confiscation of property, hence the Vulgate's 'et domus vestrae publicabuntur'. Rashi, however, followed by Gersonides, comments tersely *'ashpa*, 'dunghill'. While Ibn Ezra's personal opinion is that 'ruin' is indicated, he does quote Rabbi Joshua ben Judah, an eleventh-century Karaite, who explains it by *domen*, a word which is synonymous with *'ashpa*. Pseudo-Saadia offers *biza*, meaning 'plunder', as his own interpretation of the difficulty, but quotes two other possible explanations, the former agreeing with that of Rashi and Rabbi Joshua and the latter with that of Ibn Ezra.[28] Pagninus and Münster clearly follow one of the rabbinic explanations and translate the word as 'latrinas' and 'sterquilinium' respectively, though neither of them offers any explanation of how they arrived at a translation so far removed from that found in the Vulgate. Leo Jud, however, despite rendering *nebali* in his version by a general term signifying shame or abomination, 'detestabiles', in a marginal note draws the reader's attention to the various Jewish interpretations: 'Certain Jews explain *nebali*, which Jerome interprets as referring to the public confiscation of property, as "something contemptible"; others as "ruin"; and others as "dunghill" or "latrine" '.

Persian terms which appear in the Massoretic Text in Hebrew characters caused difficulties for Jewish and Christian commentators alike. In Daniel 3:2, which contains a list of the officials whom Nebuchadnezzar assembled for the dedication of the image of gold, Jerome seems to follow Theodotion in translating the word *adhargazerayya* by 'duces', thus taking it as a general term referring to the leaders of the people. Ibn Ezra in his comment on this verse admits that he does not know what this or the following words mean, but he does quote 'a savant of Spain' who explains it as 'magisterial decision makers'. Gersonides translates it simply as 'judges'. Whereas Münster comes close to this meaning with 'magistratus', Leo Jud renders it by 'nomophylaces' which he supports with a marginal note to the effect that it signifies 'principal judges' or 'custodians of the law', a clear reflection of the interpretation offered by Jewish commentators.

Such references to rabbinic explanations are a marked feature of Leo Jud's translation thus making it an important link in the chain of transmission from the mediaeval rabbis to sixteenth-century English scholars.

Immanuel Tremellius (1510–1580)

Born at Ferrara to Jewish parents, Immanuel Tremellius was converted to Roman Catholicism under the influence of Cardinal Pole and soon found himself teaching students who were preparing for ordination. At the age of thirty-one he became an instructor in Hebrew at a seminary in Lucca, a city which at the time had more converts to Protestantism than any other in Italy.[29] One of its leading lights was Peter Martyr Vermigli, an Augustinian friar who was rector of the seminary and pastor of a church in the town which showed a marked leaning towards the reformed faith. It was in order to combat this drift towards heresy that Pope Paul III issued the Bull *Licet ab initio* in July 1542, thus establishing the Roman Inquisition which resulted in the persecution of Italian Protestants beginning with those at Lucca.[30] Since Tremellius had by now become actively interested in Protestant teachings he had no option but to flee, in the company of Peter Martyr, to Strasbourg where he stayed for some time earning a meagre living as a teacher of Hebrew. Having finally embraced the doctrines of the Reformers, he came to England in 1547 on Archbishop Cranmer's invitation, and two years later replaced another immigrant, Paul Fagius, as a teacher of Hebrew at Cambridge. Such was his love for his subject that he was prepared to give lessons free of charge, and would presumably have continued to do so had he not found it necessary to return to the Continent on Queen Mary's accession. It was during this brief period at Cambridge that Tremellius became friendly with Matthew Parker, Master of Corpus Christi College, and in 1551 we find him acting as godfather to Parker's third son. Despite the Hebraist's return to the Continent the two men remained firm friends, and on a further visit to England in 1567 Tremellius stayed with Parker, by now Archbishop of Canterbury, for six months.

It was while he held the chair of Old Testament Studies at Heidelberg that Tremellius at last had the leisure to write and publish several important academic works. A Latin translation of Targum Jonathan on the Twelve Minor Prophets appeared in 1567. Two years later he produced an Aramaic and Syriac grammar and an edition of the Syriac New Testament with a Latin translation which was dedicated to Queen Elizabeth I. His *magnum opus*, however, carried out in co-operation with his son-in-law Franciscus Junius, was a Latin translation of the Old Testament in which each biblical book was prefaced by an introduction and almost every verse was carefully annotated in the margin. A comparison of this version, published at Frankfurt in 1579, with the Vulgate shows how far removed Tremellius' translation was from that which had by now been authorised by the Church of Rome.

Like those of his three illustrious predecessors, Tremellius' Latin version frequently reproduces the rabbinic explanation of difficult words and phrases. Three instances will be given. In Daniel 1:11 Daniel is reported to have spoken to *ha-meltsar* and requested a special diet for himself and his companions. This word, found only in the Book of Daniel, was taken by the ancient versions and by the majority of the sixteenth-century translators, including Pagninus, Münster and Leo Jud, as a proper name, following Jerome's 'et dixit Daniel ad melasar'. The mediaeval Jewish commentators, however, recognised it as a foreign word descriptive of an office, and not as a name. According to Rashi, in his comment on this verse, the *meltsar* was the official responsible for 'setting out the portions and bowls' in the royal household, and he attempts to clarify the meaning of the word by using a French gloss.[31] Ibn Ezra and Gersonides explain the word similarly. Among Christian translators the Spanish scholar Arias Montano is the first to hint at this meaning when he explains *meltsar* by 'archimagirus' (chief cook) in the margin of the Antwerp Polyglot Bible. But Tremellius is even more specific when he translates the word with 'promo' (butler), which appears in the margin of the A.V. as 'steward'.[32] In their translation of Daniel 3:14 Pagninus, Münster and Leo Jud all choose to follow the Septuagint and Vulgate in rendering Nebuchadnezzar's question with, 'Is it true, O Shadrach, Meshach and Abednego, that you do not serve my gods or worship the golden image which I have set up?' While this is a perfectly plausible translation, Tremellius points out that the word *hatsda'*, 'Is it true?', can have a quite different meaning. Noting in the margin Rashi's explanation of the verb *tsadhah* in Exodus 21:13 as signifying 'to lie in wait with evil intent for someone', he suggests that the question should begin with the words 'An certo concilio, Schadrach . . .?' According to this interpretation, the king wishes to know, not if it is true that Daniel's three companions have disobeyed him, but if they did so deliberately, an understanding which is perpetuated by the A.V. in a note on this verse. In his version of the last phrase in Daniel 5:5 Jerome follows Theodotion in taking *pas* to refer to the 'joints' of the hand responsible for the writing on the wall at Belshazzar's feast. Gersonides explains it by *kaph*, meaning 'palm'; a suggestion which, although rather difficult to appreciate since the king actually saw the *pas* of the hand as it wrote, is adopted by both Pagninus and Münster. Tremellius, however, follows Ibn Ezra by translating it as 'the part of the hand that wrote', a rendering which is found verbatim in the A.V.

Although Tremellius' version was not universally acclaimed, there is no question that the scholarship of its translators was greatly respected. Tremellius himself was in close and constant touch with some of the most distinguished men of the age. He was a prolific writer, and his translation of the Bible was received by Protestants with much approbation. Above all else, Tremellius communicated the scholarship of the mediaeval rabbis to the group of eminent linguists responsible for the Authorised Version of 1611.[33]

These are four of the many independent Latin translations of the Old Testament made during the sixteenth century.[34] Since Latin was the language of the school and the university, Protestants realised that versions of the Bible in Latin were essential for the spread of new doctrines among the educated classes of Europe, and so Münster, Leo Jud and Tremellius quickly followed the lead given by Pagninus. The major characteristic which they all share is close adherence to the Hebrew text and the acceptance of the guidance of the rabbis in difficult places. They are of considerable importance in a study of the revival of the Hebraic tradition in England inasmuch as they formed the link between rabbinic scholarship and those engaged in translating the Bible into English.[35] They succeeded in demonstrating the value of Jewish commentaries for a better understanding of the Old Testament, and thus prepared the way for the significant contributions to Hebrew studies made by future generations. Used in schools and seminaries, by teachers, priests and ministers, they became an essential part of the equipment of every exegete and translator.

Inevitably these new translations were given a mixed reception. Because of the stress which they laid on the value of the Scriptures, and because of the threat which they posed to the Vulgate, Protestants rather than Catholics were their chief supporters. It is, however, important to note that in spite of the declaration of the Council of Trent in favour of the Vulgate as the 'authentic' version of the Bible, the Church of Rome neither condemned these independent translations out of hand nor tried to prevent its adherents from consulting them.

It was expressly added', writes E. F. Sutcliffe with reference to the Council's decision, 'that other translations would not thereby be rejected in so far as they helped to the understanding of the one version declared authoritative. ... The Vulgate was not declared intrinsically superior to other Latin versions nor were these others in any way condemned. As far as they are concerned the decree is purely negative. They are left in exactly the condition in which they were. Only to no other was given the juridical recognition of authority which was accorded to the Vulgate.[36]

This, in theory, was the standpoint of the Roman Catholic Church during the second half of the sixteenth century, but in fact the violent opposition of Leon de Castro to the Antwerp Polyglot would suggest that such broadmindedness towards versions other than the Vulgate was by no means general.

Notes

1   V. Baroni, *La Contre-Réforme devant la Bible*, Lausanne 1943, p. 41.
2   *Histoire Critique du Vieux Testament*, Eng. trans. Bk. II, p. 140.
3   For the details of his life see J. D. Gauthier, 'Sanctes Pagninus O.P.', *CBQ*, vol. 7, No. 2, 1945, pp. 175ff.
4   *Thesaurus*, col. 507.
5   *Ibid.*, col. 1529.
6   *Ibid.*, cols. 931f.
7   See H. Pope, *English Versions of the Bible*, rev. ed. S. Bullough, St Louis, Miss. 1952, p. 109, quoting Sixtus in translation.
8   Quoted by Richard Simon, *op. cit.*, Eng. trans. Bk. II, p. 144.
9   *Ibid.*, p. 142.
10 *A Prospectus of a New Translation of the Holy Bible*, Glasgow 1786, p. 75.

11   See further L. Voet, *The Golden Compasses: a History and Evaluation of the Printing and Publishing Activities of the Officina Plantiniana at Antwerp*, Amsterdam 1969, pp. 62ff; C. Clair, *Christopher Plantin*, London 1960, pp. 88ff.

12   B. Rekers, *Benito Arias Montano 1527–98*, Studies of the Warburg Institute vol. 33, London 1972, p. 1. On the importance of Seville for Erasmianism in Spain see also M. Bataillon, *Erasme et l'Espagne*, Paris 1937, pp. 562ff.

13   Rekers, *op. cit.*, p. 48, quoting a letter from Montano to Zayas written on 23 March 1569. There were about twenty translators in all, but Montano's chief assistants were Postel, Raphelengius, Masius, and Guy and Nicholas Boderianus.

14   Rekers, *op. cit.*, p. 49.

15   A. F. G. Bell, *Benito Arias Montano*, Hispanic Society of America 1922, p. 24.

16   B. Hall, *The Great Polyglot Bibles*, Book Club of California, San Francisco, Cal. 1966, n.p.

17   For a list of his works see K. H. Burmeister, *Sebastian Münster: Eine Bibliographie mit 22 Abbildungen*, Wiesbaden 1964. For his life see same author, *Sebastian Münster: Versuch eines biographischen Gesamtbildes*, Basel und Stuttgart 1963.

18   Eng. trans. by Paul Isaiah, London 1655, p. 209.

19   The Introduction was not translated by Paul Isaiah. On Münster's missionary motives see further A. K. E. Holmio, *The Lutheran Reformation and the Jews*, Hancock, Mich. 1949; J. Friedman, 'Sebastian Münster, the Jewish mission, and Protestant antisemitism', *Archiv für Reformationsgeschichte*, vol. 70, 1979, pp. 238ff. This article has an illuminating discussion of Münster's motives in writing his tracts.

20   'Sebastian Muenster's knowledge and use of Jewish exegesis', in *Essays Presented to J. H. Hertz, Chief Rabbi*, ed. Epstein, Levine, Roth, London 1942, p. 361 (reprinted in *Studia Semitica*, vol. I, pp. 127ff).

21   Levi ben Gerson (d. 1344), a native of Provence, who besides being a biblical commentator was an accomplished physician, philosopher and astronomer.

22   *Histoire Critique du Vieux Testament*, Eng. trans., Bk. II, pp. 149f.

23   *CHB*, vol. 3, p. 71.

24   For Jud's association with Zwingli see O. Farner, 'Leo Jud, Zwinglis treuster Helfer', *Zwingliana*, vol. 10, No. 4, 1955, pp. 201ff.

25   *Jewish Influence on Christian Reform Movements*, p. 507.

26   Art. in *Leben und ausgewählte Schriften der Väter und Begründer der reformierten Kirche*, vol. IX, ed. K. R. Hagenbach, Leipzig 1861, p. 2.

27   *Histoire Critique du Vieux Testament*, Eng. trans., Bk. II, p. 152.

28   The 'Saadia' commentary printed in the Rabbinic Bible (Warsaw ed. 1864, anastatic reprint Jerusalem 1957) is recognised as being later than the time of Saadia Gaon and therefore cited as Pseudo-Saadia.

29   See G. K. Brown, *Italy and the Reformation to 1550*, Oxford 1933, pp. 160ff.

30 See B. J. Kidd, *Documents Illustrative of the Continental Reformation*, Oxford 1911, pp. 247ff.

31 In his commentary he writes *senesk'al* which is an unmistakable reference to 'seneschal', the Old French for 'sénéchal' meaning 'steward' or 'major domo' whose duties included quartermastering and dining arrangements. See A. Darmesteter, *Les Gloses françaises de Raschi dans la Bible*, Paris 1909, p. 132.

32 The edition of the King James Version or the Authorised Version of the Bible referred to throughout this study is an exact reprint of that published in 1611 with an introduction by A. W. Pollard, London 1911.

33 See L. Wolf, *Papers read at the Anglo-Jewish Historical Exhibition*, London 1887, p. 59.

34 Another Roman Catholic who produced his own Latin version was Isidore Clarius. For a comprehensive list of independent Latin translations of the Bible by Protestants printed before 1570 see J. M. Lenhart, 'Protestant Latin Bibles of the Reformation from 1520–1570: a bibliographical account', *CBQ*, vol. 8, No. 4, 1946, pp. 430f.

35 For the importance of these independent Latin versions as mediators of rabbinic exegesis to the translators of the English Bible see further E. I. J. Rosenthal, 'Rashi and the English Bible', *BJRL*, vol. XXIV, No. I, 1940, pp. 138ff (reprinted in *Studia Semitica*, vol. I, pp. 56ff); G. Lloyd Jones, 'Jewish exegesis and the English Bible', *ASTI*, vol. VII, 1968–69, pp. 53ff.

36 'The Council of Trent on the "Authentica" of the Vulgate', *JTS*, vol. 49, 1948, p. 36. Cf. R. Loewe, *EJ*, vol. 8, col. 17: 'When the Council of Trent asserted the "authenticity" of the Latin Vulgate, this was on grounds of its embodying of a linkage with "officially" endorsed patristic exegesis (analagous to the position of Targum Onkelos within Judaism), and not by way of depreciation of the greater accuracy of the new translations'.

III

The continental Reformers

The Renaissance had attempted to highlight the importance of Hebrew for the biblical exegete; the Reformation emphasised it still further. It was the Reformation which gave the study of the language among Christians its true significance by providing it with a definite goal: namely, a serious and impartial understanding of the Holy Scriptures freed from the mediaeval hermeneutic. Since the dissemination of vernacular versions of the Bible based on the original texts was high on their list of priorities, Hebrew scholarship came to play an increasingly important part in the educational pattern of the leading Protestants.[1] If the principle of 'Sola Scriptura' was to have any real meaning, scholars had to be trained to cope with the Bible in the languages in which it was first written. Commentaries on biblical books had to be provided which were not bound to the mediaeval method of 'the four senses' but based primarily on the literal sense of the text. In this field the chief continental Reformers, Luther, Zwingli and Calvin, together with their associates, acted as pioneers. It is their knowledge of Hebrew and their attitude to the Hebraic tradition which forms the subject of the present chapter, as we consider further the influences to which those concerned with the rediscovery of Hebrew in Tudor England were subjected.

Wittenberg

Although Martin Luther devoted most of his scholastic career to the study and elucidation of the Old Testament, he was at least thirty years old before he could claim to have gained more than a rudimentary knowledge of Hebrew. As a student he spent two periods at the University of Erfurt, a fourteenth-century foundation which ranked among the most prestigious centres of learning in Germany. During the first period, which lasted from 1501 to 1505, he followed a course in liberal arts, and soon became known among his friends as 'the erudite philosopher'. There is no suggestion that either he or the university, old and renowned though it was, showed any interest whatever in linguistic study. But when, after a two-year novitiate with the Augustinian Hermits, he returned to the same university to resume his studies, the influence of the new learning, if only in controversial debates, was beginning to be felt. By 1507 the open antagonism between humanism and scholasticism had found its way into the university, and could hardly fail to affect the young friar.[2] Yet there is no strong evidence to connect him directly with the Mutianic Circle, despite the fact that as a student he shared a room for a time with Crotus Rubeanus. The only hint we have of his intention to pursue linguistic studies this early in his career comes from a letter written many years later to Johann Lang, a one-time fellow Augustinian, in which he recalls that during his early days at Erfurt he had purchased a copy of Reuchlin's *De rudimentis* (1506). This sudden burst of enthusiasm should not, however, be taken to imply that he soon mastered Hebrew, for even the most dedicated student would find the new grammar difficult without the aid of a competent teacher, and this facility was something the university could not as yet provide, for humanism, though introduced, was not gaining ground at Erfurt. If anything, the opposite was true. When asked to pass judgement on Reuchlin's *Augenspiegel* the theological faculty had declared it heretical, a decision which infuriated Muth and prompted him to write to a friend in 1514 expressing his disgust at the obscurantist views which still seemed to predominate at Erfurt. He complained bitterly that 'the apes of theology occupy the whole university, teaching their students the figures of Donatus, a most unintelligible thing; the figures of Parvulus, pure nonsense; exercises in complexities, the silliest stuff. With such chatter they burden their students'.[3] Whatever else he may have learned from his *alma mater*, the Reformer is not likely to have been introduced to Hebrew.

Even if we regard Luther's purchase of Reuchlin's grammar in *c.* 1507 as an indication of his interest in languages, it was an interest which soon waned. Schwiebert's claim[4] that he knew but little Greek or Hebrew by 1511 is borne out by an examination of his first course of lectures on the Psalms, the *Dictata super Psalterium*, delivered at Wittenberg between 1513 and 1515. In his preparations for these lectures he based his studies chiefly on the text of the Vulgate as given in Lefèvre's *Psalterium quincuplex* of 1509 and was clearly unaware, at this stage, of the importance of the original Hebrew for a correct interpretation.[5] This must not however be taken to suggest that he knew hardly any Hebrew. It is clear from his comments on individual psalms that he had made some progress in his study of the language between 1511 and 1513. But it is equally clear from his frequent references to Jerome's *Psalterium juxta Hebraeos* and to the commentaries of Nicholas of Lyra and Paul of Burgos that he relied heavily on previous recognised interpreters to help him with the Hebrew text. One can also be certain that Reuchlin's grammar and his Latin translation of the seven penitential psalms with a Hebrew glossary (1512) were never far away.

It was not until 1519, the year in which he published his second set of lectures on the Psalms, the *Operationes in Psalmos*, that Luther's mastery of Hebrew began to be apparent.[6] By this time he had grown sceptical of the accuracy of the Vulgate. He was now ready to base his observations on the Hebrew and to accept it as the determinative text.[7] In a three-volume work dealing with the Reformer's use of the Massoretic Text, S. Raeder shows the great progress he had made as an exegete and linguist between 1515 and 1519, and demonstrates in some detail the way in which his knowledge of Hebrew helped him in his exposition of the Psalter.[8] In the light of the evidence presented by Raeder it is impossible to claim, as older biographies did, that Luther never knew much Hebrew,[9] though admittedly there is a *Table Talk* which suggests that he did not pursue the study of the language to a very great extent:

If I were younger [he is reported to have said in 1530], I would want to learn this tongue [Hebrew] because without it one can never rightly understand the Sacred Scriptures. The New Testament, though written in Greek, is full of Hebraisms and Hebraic expressions. Therefore they have said correctly, "The Hebrews drink from the spring, the Greeks out of the small stream which flows from the spring, the Latins, however, drink out of the puddles." I am no Hebraist as regards grammar and rules for I do not allow myself to be bound, but pass freely through. . . . If I were to study Hebrew I would take as guides the purest and best grammars such as those of David Kimchi and Moses Kimchi who are excellent grammarians.[10]

Despite this modest disclaimer, in which he seems to be saying that his knowledge of the finer points of grammar was not what it might be, by 1530 Luther's command of Hebrew was good, but perhaps not good enough to enable him to read at first hand the rabbinic commentaries which Lyra quoted so often. Throughout his career he depended on others for advice on philological questions. In his *Rules for translating the Bible* (1532) he admits, 'If the meaning is ambiguous I ask those who have a better knowledge of the language than I have whether the Hebrew words can bear this or that sense which seems to me to be especially fitting'.[11] It is clear from his *Lectures on the Book of Genesis* that Nicholas of Lyra, with whose works he had become familiar during his student days at Erfurt, had introduced him to the writings of Rashi. Pagninus, whom he describes as a 'learned philologist',[12] and Münster, for whose scholarship he had great respect,[13] likewise mediated to him Jewish explanations of *cruces interpretum* in the Hebrew text. During the twelve year period spent in preparing his German version of the Bible (1522–1534), he was heavily dependent on a group of advisers which included Bernard Ziegler, a renowned Hebraist from Leipzig, and Matthew Aurogallus (*c.* 1490–1543), who succeeded Adrianus as professor of Hebrew at Wittenberg in 1521 and later became Rector of the university. A distinguished linguist, Aurogallus was the author of one of the several works on Hebrew grammar and lexicography produced during the first quarter of the sixteenth century.[14] Andreas Osiander, who taught at Nuremberg and was probably the best Hebriast among the German Reformers, was also available to offer advice, as was Caspar Cruciger the elder, professor of Hebrew at Wittenberg from 1528 to 1548.[15]

But the scholars of Wittenberg, though proficient in Hebrew, were by no means anxious to propagate the explanations of Jewish rabbis among Christians. Johann Förster (1495–1556), another member of the 'Sanhedrin' (as Luther called his circle of Old Testament pundits), produced a Hebrew dictionary in 1543 which contained on its title-page an explicit denial of any dependence on Jewish works.[16] Although he was one of Reuchlin's favourite students, Förster did not share his teacher's regard for Jewish exegetes. In the introduction to his dictionary he complains that 'among Christians the rabbinic commentaries are controlling the work of translation and explanation' and expresses his astonishment at the feeblemindedness of his Christian colleagues who have embraced without discernment the commentaries of the Jews, in which there is no light, no knowledge of God, no spirit, and not even a proper understanding of Hebrew. Jewish dictionaries and commentaries have, in the author's opinion, brought into Christ's church more obscurity and error than light and truth.

Luther's opinion of the rabbis is no different from that of some of his colleagues; if anything he is even more antagonistic. In spite of his regard for the Hebrew language and his determination to learn it, even with the aid of Kimchi, he rejects, ridicules and condemns rabbinic

exegesis. His *Lectures on the Book of Genesis*, written during the last
decade of his life when, on his own admission, he was weary and one-
eyed, contain numerous examples of his opposition to those who
deliberately rejected a christological interpretation of the Old
Testament. While ostensibly offering an exposition of the text, he
seems to go out of his way to refute the traditional Jewish explanations
and castigates the rabbis for their mishandling of God's Word. In the
introduction to his *Treatise on the Last Words of David* (1543) he is
more direct and urges his readers to pay no attention whatever to what
the rabbis say or think for

> after all they are not in agreement among themselves, and they expound
> scripture arbitrarily and quote out of context. . . . If we were to heed them, we
> could never acquire a uniform Bible, since every rabbi claims to be superior to
> the other. Furthermore, they all have to admit that the words in many a
> passage are incomprehensible to them. They are far from having one,
> harmonious, perfect and flawless Hebrew Bible, even from the point of view
> of grammar, to say nothing of theology, where they are so very incompetent.
> . . . Their opinion would not impel me to learn a single letter of the Hebrew
> language. The reason for that is this: We Christians have the meaning and
> import of the Bible because we have the New Testament, that is Jesus
> Christ.[17]

Given the choice between Augustine's interpretation of Scripture and
that of the rabbis he writes without hesitation, 'I would let the Jews
with their interpretation and their letters go to the devil, and I would
ascend into heaven with St Augustine's interpretation without their
letters'. The Old Testament must be interpreted 'whenever that is
feasible, in the direction of the New Testament, in opposition to the
interpretation of the rabbis'.[18]

Like Förster, Luther utterly failed to understand how his fellow
Christians could possibly accept the opinions of these 'pernicious
perverters of Holy Writ'. Referring to the rabbinic exposition of
Genesis 5:29, he registers his amazement that this particular point of
view pleases Lyra and that he even adopts it. 'He should have been
familiar with that usual habit of perverting the Scriptures to which the
Jews everywhere adhere'.[19] Excellent though Lyra is in every respect,
'when he follows his Rabbi Solomon [Rashi], how meaningless and
unimpressive it sounds; it has neither hands nor feet, despite his good
command of words and letters'.[20] Sebastian Münster comes in for
similar criticism. 'Münster's Bible pleases me', he is quoted as saying
in a *Table Talk*, 'but I wish he had been here and had conferred with

us here. He still makes too many concessions to the rabbis, although he is also hostile to the Jews, but he doesn't take it so much to heart as I do'.[21] If only Münster had consulted the 'Sanhedrin' at Wittenberg while he was engaged on his translation he would have been far less dependent on the Hebraic tradition, and as a result would have produced a much better version of the Old Testament.

The reasons for such harsh treatment of Jewish biblical commentators have been examined by Arnold Ages who pinpoints three main areas of criticism.[22] In the first place the rabbis, in Luther's opinion, erred miserably in their exposition of the Old Testament because of their preoccupation with grammatical minutiae at the expense of the inner meaning of the text. Indeed it is doubtful whether they could find the inner meaning even if they tried. Scripture deals with spiritual matters such as life, death and resurrection, of which the Jews, who are spiritually bankrupt, understand nothing. They are certainly 'familiar with the language but have no knowledge of the subject matter; that is, they are not theologians. Therefore they are compelled to twaddle and to crucify both themselves and Scripture'.[23] Secondly, in their eagerness to oppose Christianity, the rabbis are guilty of purposely distorting the text of the Bible. Because of such fabrications those who read them are advised to do so 'with careful judgement', for although the Jews 'had in their possession certain facts through tradition from the patriarchs, they nevertheless corrupted these facts in various ways. Consequently, they often deceived Jerome too. The poets have not filled the world with their fabrications to the extent to which the ungodly Jews have filled Scripture with their silly opinions. Hence it causes us much work to keep our text free from their misleading comments'.[24] For this reason they should be shunned and despised by every Christian. 'The rabbis very much deserve to be detested, for whatever Scripture has that is very excellent they pervert most execrably'.[25] Finally, the Jewish exegetes are guilty of inconsequential bantering. Instead of engaging in serious discussion they inevitably become frivolous whenever they are faced with a real problem. Thus it is hardly surprising that they never achieve anything worthwhile for 'in their commentaries men twice thirty and even older prattle most childishly about these extremely important matters'.[26] Adverse criticism of this kind inevitably leads one to conclude that Luther's hatred of the great Jewish teachers appears to have had no limit. He cannot find one good word to say for them. They distort, pervert, swear and contaminate. They are ignorant, absurd, pernicious, unscholarly, and superficial. They are nothing more than deceptive husks, empty bubbles and dung.

When we go beyond works which deal specifically with the interpretation of Scripture we find that Luther's antagonism is directed not only towards the official representatives of rabbinic scholarship but towards any and every Jew. Admittedly, such undisguised prejudice is not characteristic of the younger Luther. Early in his career as a Reformer he fully expected that he would be able to persuade the Jews of the error of their ways and witness a mass conversion to Christianity. Accordingly, whatever his true feelings towards the Jewish people, he adopted a friendly attitude. In *That Jesus Christ was born a Jew* (1523) he argues that since the Jews were of the lineage of Christ they were within their rights in resisting conversion. In any case, who would want to become a Christian once he had discovered the ignorance and corruption prevalent within the Church? 'If I had been a Jew', he writes, 'and had seen such dolts and blockheads govern and teach the Christian faith, I would sooner have become a hog than a Christian'.[27] He deplores the methods currently adopted by the Catholics for making converts from Judaism. He appeals to Christians to deal more kindly with Jews and in this way draw them to Christ. Slandering them, treating them like dogs, forbidding them to work and denying them any business with Christians will do no good at all.

If we really want to help them we must be guided in our dealings with them not by papal law but by the law of Christian love. We must receive them cordially, and permit them to trade and work with us, that they may have occasion and opportunity to associate with us, hear our Christian teaching and witness our Christian life. If some of them should prove stiffnecked, what of it? After all, we ourselves are not all good Christians either.[28]

Thus wrote Luther in a tract which, because of its eirenic nature, was immediately hailed by Christians as an important missionary document.

But such cordiality was short lived. Despite Luther's blandishments the Jews of Germany continued to resist conversion to Christianity. Angered by such stubbornness, and also annoyed that a radical Anabaptist sect in Moravia was adopting Jewish laws, thus to all appearances relapsing into Judaism, he produced a trilogy of tracts which evince a quite different attitude from that found in his earlier writings. *On the Jews and their Lies, Of the Shem Hamphoras and the Race of Christ* and *The Last Words of David* followed one another in quick succession and appeared in 1543. In the first of these, which fortunately became a worst seller, Luther repeats the ancient lies about Jews drinking the blood of Christians, ritual murder and the poisoning of wells. He warns his fellow Christians of the dangers inherent in even associating with Jews, and, because of the blasphemies of which they were guilty, makes several practical proposals how they should be treated. He recommends that, among other things, synagogues should be burned, Jewish homes destroyed and their occupants made to wander from place to place like gypsies, rabbis forbidden on pain of death to teach the faith, and that safe conduct on the highways should no longer be provided for Jewish travellers.[29] In the other two pamphlets, which are no more than an exegetical appendix to the first, he fiercely attacks the Jews for rejecting the christological interpretation of the Old Testament.[30]

The tirade of abuse which greets the reader in these three tracts suggests that the author was familiar with the contents of polemical writings against the Jews which were popular during the first half of the sixteenth century. The Spanish Dominican Raymund Martini had written his *Pugio fidei* in 1278, and although it was not printed until 1651 it was plagiarised and used extensively by late mediaeval writers who wished to incite Christians to a hatred of the Jews.[31] Alfonso de Spina, a General of the Franciscans, wrote *Fortalitium fidei* in 1495, 'a venomous book' the primary object of which was to protect Christians from the abominations of the Jews.[32] The influence of the Carthusian Salvatus Portchetus' *Victoria adversus impios Hebraeos*, written in the fourteenth century but published in 1520, is clearly discernible throughout the first half of the *Shem Hamphoras*. Even Nicholas of Lyra and Paul of Burgos, Luther's tutors in rabbinics, had penned anti-Jewish writings. But above all it was the work of the Jewish convert Antonius Margaritha which had the greatest effect on the Reformer. In 1530 Margaritha published in German what purported to be a full description of contemporary Judaism entitled *The Whole Jewish Faith* in which he paid particular attention to any anti-Christian prayers and practices found in the Jewish liturgy. It was the third edition of this book which Luther read to his friends at table, claiming that it had come as a revelation to him, confirming his fears that the Jews were blasphemers.[33] Such manifestations of Christian antisemitism were a common inheritance which, despite his early protestations against Rome's harsh treatment of the Jews, Luther was never quite able to shake off. Catholic authors, unacceptable though they may have been in many other respects, could be read with profit when it came to anti-Jewish propaganda.

In view of such bitter animosity on Luther's part it is not surprising that Rabbi Josel of Rosheim, the famous sixteenth-century apologist and campaigner for Jewish freedom, utterly failed to understand how 'a man who had bowed in fear and humility before the infinite majesty of God' could have been capable of producing such crude, inhuman and abusive writings, and genuinely thought that Luther was suffering from a spell of madness. 'Never', he wrote, 'has it been contended by any scholar that we Jews ought to be treated with violence and much tyranny; that none was bound to honour any obligation towards us or keep the peace of the land where we were concerned, because we decline to believe what Luther believes'.[34] Although it may justifiably be claimed with E. G. Rupp that the anti-Jewish writings to which Josel refers were written with an apologetic rather than a polemic purpose, and that Luther's attitude towards the Jews never really changed over the years, only the expression of it, there can be little doubt that his three most defamatory pamphlets did cause much hardship for Jews in Germany and beyond. Whatever the intention, the effect was catastrophic. Jacob Marcus goes so far as to say that Luther was responsible for the bitterest anti-Jewish statements 'in all Christian literature'.[35] They were brought about more by an irrational fear that Christianity was being contaminated by Judaism than by frustration and anger at the Jews' continued rejection of Christ.

Given this negative approach to the value of the Hebraic tradition for the Christian theologian, Luther's German Bible cannot be regarded as a primary channel of Jewish exegesis in the way that the versions of his three contemporaries, Pagninus, Münster and Leo Jud, were. Although, as a vernacular Bible, it ranks above these Latin translations, those using it would not often find rabbinic explanations of difficult words being preferred to the renderings of the Septuagint and Vulgate. Furthermore, his biblical commentaries, as we have seen, were not calculated to encourage his fellow Christians to look for the elucidation of problematic passages in the works of the rabbis or to turn to members of the local Jewish community for help with the text of the Old Testament. Yet throughout his career his attitude towards the Hebrew language was very positive. He was obviously convinced that a thorough knowledge of it was an essential part of the training of every serious student of the Old Testament. Addressing the Bohemian Brethren in 1523 on the subject of the adoration of the sacrament he ends his treatise by criticising their method of theological education and appeals to them to include Greek and Hebrew in their syllabus:

If I could bring it to pass among you I should like to ask that you do not neglect the languages but, since it would not be difficult for you, that you have your preachers and some of your gifted boys learn Latin, Greek and Hebrew well. I know for a fact that one who has to preach and expound the Scriptures and has no help from the Latin, Greek and Hebrew languages, but must do it entirely on the basis of his mother tongue will make many a pretty mistake. For it has been my experience that the languages are extraordinarily helpful for a clear understanding of the divine Scriptures.[36]

This piece of advice demonstrates that as an educator Luther held views similar to those of the humanists, but with one important difference. While the German humanists regarded linguistic study as an integral part of a liberal education, Luther was strongly motivated by theological and religious considerations. For him knowledge of the languages was a means to an end, the end being the exposition of Scripture. It was essential that pastors should be properly trained to expound the biblical message. If such training was to be effective the foundations had to be laid in the schools, and it was with this realisation that Luther wrote in 1524 to the civic authorities throughout Germany urging them to revitalise the educational system. He was not sorry to see the larger schools freed from the control of the religious orders, for they had, in his opinion, become 'unchristian' and 'devoted only to men's bellies'. But with the decay of the schools came another threat: the belief of ordinary people that it was no longer necessary to study the ancient languages. Since the Bible could be read in the vernacular, what need was there to learn the languages in which it was originally written? Such an apathetic attitude to formal education alarmed Luther, with the result that in the recommendations for reform which he made to the state authorities he insisted that a prominent place be given to the study of Greek and Hebrew. It is only when the languages have been properly grasped that the faith can be adequately defended:

When our faith . . . is held up to ridicule, where does the fault lie? It lies in our ignorance of the languages; and there is no other way out than to learn the languages. Was not St Jerome compelled to translate the Psalter anew from the Hebrew because, when we quoted our [Latin] Psalter in disputes with the Jews, they sneered at us, pointing out that our texts did not read that way in the original Hebrew? Now the expositions of all the early fathers who dealt with Scripture apart from a knowledge of the languages (even when their teaching is not in error) are such that they often employ uncertain, indefensible, and inappropriate expressions. They grope their way like a blind man along the wall, frequently missing the sense of the text and twisting it to suit their fancy. . . . Even St Augustine himself is obliged to confess, as he does in his *Christian Instruction*, that a Christian teacher who is to expound the Scriptures must know Greek and Hebrew in addition to Latin. Otherwise it is impossible to avoid constant stumbling; indeed there are plenty of problems to work out even when one is well versed in the languages.[37]

This eloquent plea for the promotion of the languages demonstrates not only that Luther had an enlightened interest in education, but also that he was uncompromising in his insistence on the importance of Hebrew for biblical study.

The positive attitude towards Hebrew studies evinced in these two letters is attributable in part to the Reformer's close friend and collaborator Philip Melanchthon (1497–1560). Educated under the supervision of his uncle Johann Reuchlin, Melanchthon had been steeped in humanist learning from an early age. On his appointment as professor of Greek at Wittenberg in 1518 this promising young educator had delivered an inaugural address entitled *The Improvement of Studies* in which he challenged the obscurantists and called for the promotion of Latin, Greek and Hebrew within the university. He made a strong plea that students of theology and the liberal arts should be given the opportunity of 'returning to the sources' by acquiring a thorough grounding in the ancient languages.[38] Luther had been impressed, and in a letter to Spalatin claimed that he would want no other Greek teacher at Wittenberg as long as they had Melanchthon.[39] But although he was appointed to the chair of Greek the new professor proved to be a proficient Hebraist who, throughout his life, remained faithful to the principles laid down by Reuchlin. He may not have seen eye to eye with his illustrious uncle on the value of rabbinic exegesis for an understanding of the Old Testament, yet in 1546 and 1549 he was able to deliver two enthusiastic orations in favour of the study of Hebrew among Christians. The world of psalmist and prophet would become intelligible only to those who had mastered the language of the sacred writers.[40] Luther was greatly influenced by this 'quiet Reformer', and with his co-operation he had made Wittenberg one of the leading trilingual universities of Europe by the mid 1530s.

Zurich

A cursory glance at Ulrich Zwingli's biblical commentaries is enough to leave the reader in no doubt that the Swiss Reformer knew Hebrew. Time and again he refers to the Massoretic Text and even discusses the meanings of different forms of the Hebrew verb. But despite such obvious manifestations of linguistic ability, like many of his contemporaries Zwingli began his study of the language comparatively late in life. Four years (1502–1506) at the University of Basle had brought him into contact with the new learning and it is possible that Thomas Wyttenbach had persuaded him to start learning Greek, but there is no indication that he received instruction in Hebrew. However, the seeds of humanist scholarship had been sown in good ground for on his appointment to the parish of Glarus, after leaving the university, the young priest made clear his intention of continuing his education. The ten year period which he spent in this small rural pastorate was crucial to Zwingli's intellectual development, for it proved to be a time of sustained and enthusiastic study. In addition to the Latin Classics he began to apply himself in earnest to the Bible and to the works of the Fathers. He became a devoted disciple of Erasmus, and according to Bullinger had 'read almost all the works of John Pico della Mirandola, particularly the *Resolutions on the Propositions* which were advanced for discussion in Rome'.[41] For entertainment he read the *Letters of Obscure Men*. The considerable library which he accumulated during this period is evidence of his humanist and biblical interests.

In 1516 Zwingli moved to the neighbouring village of Einsiedeln to act as chaplain to the pilgrims who visited the shrine of the Black Virgin at the famous Benedictine abbey. It was here, according to E. Christen,[42] that he began his Hebrew studies, though hardly with any help from the monks since at this particular time the fortunes of the monastery were at a very low ebb. If his heavily annotated copy of Reuchlin's *De rudimentis*, now in the Zwingli Library in Zurich, belongs to this period then it suggests that he had tried to teach himself. After moving to Zurich early in 1519 he secured the services of the gifted teacher Andreas Böschenstein, but he cannot have persevered, for on 24 July 1520 he wrote to a friend that he was about to resume his study of the language.[43] This time he seems to have been inspired by the visit to Zurich of Jacob Ceporinus, one of Reuchlin's more promising pupils. But again progress was slow, for two years later in a letter to Beatus Rhenanus he claims that he has once more 'started to learn Hebrew. But good heavens! how distasteful and heartbreaking a study it is. Nevertheless, I shall persist until I derive some benefit from it'.[44] Even in 1526 he claims that his knowledge of the language is inconsiderable.[45]

Although Hebrew did not come easily to Zwingli, he felt that it had a grace and beauty all of its own. Gradually he came to like it.

After I had begun not only to comprehend Hebrew, but also to cherish it, I found the holy language cultivated, graceful and dignified beyond all belief. Despite the paucity of its vocabulary, this lack is hardly felt because of the use one is able to make of it in a varied fashion. . . . No other language expresses so much with so few words, . . . none so greatly delights and quickens the human heart.[46]

But in spite of its many attractive qualities, Zwingli was led to study the language from theological rather than humanist motives. During his student days at Basle he had shown an interest in the Bible, and at Glarus and Einsiedeln he consistently preached biblically-based sermons. His belief in the centrality and self-sufficiency of the Scriptures, coupled with the influence of Erasmus, led inevitably *ad fontes*. Though he loved and used the Vulgate, he was not slow in pointing out passages where Jerome had been mistaken and had 'twisted the Gospel'. In order to appreciate the true meaning of God's Word every preacher, teacher and scholar must have recourse to the original texts. The biblical languages could be used even in sermons, and Zwingli often made a point of doing so, much to Luther's annoyance. 'Oh, how I hate people', said the latter in a *Table Talk*, 'who use so many languages as did Zwingli: at Marburg he spoke Greek and Hebrew from the pulpit'.[47] On matters of doctrine the ability to go to the original versions was even more important. At the many disputations in which the Swiss Reformers were involved, the Hebrew and Greek Bibles were given a place equal to that of the Vulgate. 'If I have erred', said Zwingli at the First Zurich Disputation in January 1523, 'and err now, I may be better instructed, since there are here present Bibles in the Hebrew, Greek and Latin languages'.[48] But if the knowledge of Hebrew was useful in preaching and of the greatest significance in the search for truth, for a proper understanding of the Bible it was axiomatic. In the introduction to his translation of the prophecy of Isaiah Zwingli writes:

Ignorance of Hebrew forms of expression is responsible for many erroneous interpretations of scriptural passages not only by ignorant and reckless men, who, the more ignorant they are the more arrogantly express broad opinions on all ancient matters, but also by genuinely pious and learned persons. Certain figures of speech are so native and peculiar to Hebrew that they cannot be rendered into any other language.[49]

The result of such ignorance of the nuance of Hebrew words leads only to obscurity and violent invective.

Zwingli's determination to persist with his Hebrew studies bore fruit. Between 1526 and his death in 1531 he produced commentaries on several Old Testament books, all of which testify to his linguistic ability. In his exegesis of Genesis he applies grammatical and philological rules to the text and even discusses the exact meaning of the *Hithpa'el*.[50] His comments on Exodus show an acquaintance with the Targum and rabbinic works; in one instance he mentions Kimchi by name.[51] References to Jewish authorities are more frequent in his exposition of the prophecies of Isaiah and Jeremiah. Though he often borrows from them without admitting it, he cites the rabbis several times to settle questions of grammar and lexicography. He is reluctant to admit to any indebtedness to them on theological matters, yet he delights to enlist their support for his point of view.[52] L. I. Newman's careful analysis of these commentaries leads him to conclude that Zwingli deserves to be regarded as one of the leading continental Hebraists of the sixteenth century.[53] If ever this knowledge failed him he could rely on the advice of several competent linguists. Leo Jud, Jacob Ceporinus, Andreas Böschenstein, Konrad Pellican, Johannes Oecolampadius were all on hand to assist him in his efforts to come to grips with the Hebrew Bible and with its mediaeval Jewish exponents. On the Jewish question itself he was far less outspoken than Luther. His attitude towards the Jews of antiquity and those of his own day is consistent. Their major sin is their rejection of Christ, but though they stubbornly refuse to convert they should not be hounded without mercy.[54]

Like his illustrious contemporary at Wittenberg, Zwingli was anxious to promote the study of biblical languages by every possible means. In an essay entitled *Of the Upbringing and Education of Youth in Good Manners and Christian Discipline* (1523) he discusses what he considers to be the essential ingredients of a Christian education. The work belongs to the period when he was actively reforming the life of the Church in Zurich and it sets out the principles which governed his proposed reforms of the system. After its reorganisation the Minster school consisted of two parts, the one a grammar school and the other a theological seminary. Yet Zwingli's essay contains very little about education in its widest sense. His primary concern is for the training of ministers of religion. For such people a knowledge of the three biblical languages is the primary objective. Greek and Hebrew must follow hard on the heels of Latin:

I put Hebrew last because Latin is in general use and Greek follows most conveniently. Otherwise I would willingly have given Hebrew the precedence, for in many places even amongst the Greeks those who are ignorant of Hebrew forms of speech have great difficulty in attempting to draw out the true sense of Scripture. . . . If a man would penetrate to the heavenly wisdom, with which no earthly wisdom ought rightly to be considered, let alone compared, it is with such arms that he must be equipped.[55]

Mastering the skill necessary to be able to 'penetrate to the heavenly wisdom' was the province of the Minster's trilingual school, but the practising of it became an integral part of 'prophesyings', daily gatherings for the express purpose of expounding the Scriptures. Bullinger gives us this description of such a meeting:

All the clergy, preachers, canons, chaplains and senior scholars gathered in the choir of the Great Minster occupying the stalls. . . . Mr. Ulrich Zwingli opened with a prayer. . . . Then one of the students read out so much of the lesson from the Bible as was to be expounded. This he read in Latin since the Bible was then translated into Latin. So they began to read the Bible from the beginning and proceeded steadily every day throughout the year with the exception of Sundays and Fridays. When all the books of the Old Testament were completed they started the Bible again from the beginning. In this reading nothing was produced except the Old Testament. After the student had read out the Latin, Jakob Ceporinus stood up and read the same passage again, this time in Hebrew, for the Old Testament was originally written in Hebrew, and he expounded the Hebrew in Latin. Then Zwingli read the same passage in Greek from the Septuagint and likewise expounded it in Latin showing the proper meaning and intent of any uncertain passages. Finally a preacher set out in German what had been said in the other languages, adding a prayer.[56]

All those who participated in such gatherings were considered in some way superior to ordinary ministers. Their linguistic achievements led others to look to them for advice and instruction.

The Minster school and seminary were Zurich's substitute for a university. Zwingli's concept of education was narrow. He seems to have thought that 'high-quality Sunday schools and a kind of extended theological college with special facilities for the study of Latin, Greek and Hebrew, were all that was needed'.[57] Nevertheless, by the time of his death in 1531 he had laid a firm foundation for trilingual studies on which his associates could build.

Geneva

Much time and energy would have been saved if John Calvin had stated in a preface to one of his many biblical commentaries when and where he learned Hebrew. Unfortunately he tells us nothing. Lefranc, who is followed by A. M. Hunter, suggests that he was introduced to the language by his lifelong friend Melchior Wolmar during his early student days at the University of Orléans.[58] But there is no evidence that Wolmar knew any Hebrew, though he was proficient in Greek, as Calvin himself attests in a dedicatory letter attached to his commentary on II Corinthians.[59] It is more likely that Calvin embarked on Hebrew when he went to Paris to improve his Greek soon after his conversion in *c.* 1530. There he could have availed himself of the instruction offered at Le Collège de France, a royal foundation recently opened for the promotion of humane letters and where there were no less than three teachers of Hebrew.

First and foremost there was François Vatable (d. 1547), a man of great erudition which he knew how to communicate to his students. Even Jews were to be found among the large audiences which attended his lectures.[60] A pupil of Girolamo Aleander, the renowned Italian humanist and opponent of Luther who taught Semitics at Orléans and Paris, Vatable was a recognised Hebrew scholar who was anxious to introduce his students to mediaeval Jewish exegesis, as his commentary on the Book of Zechariah entitled *Zecharias cum commentariis R. David Kimchi* (1540) suggests. One of Vatable's colleagues from 1530 to 1540 was Agathias Guidacerius (1477–1540) who had been appointed to teach Hebrew together with Pagninus at the University of Rome in 1513. When the city was sacked in 1527 he lost his valuable library and was forced to flee the country and seek sanctuary with Cardinal Sadoleto in Avignon. A loyal Catholic, with little sympathy for the Reformation, he had applied for a Hebrew lectureship at the trilingual college in Louvain. But he was unsuccessful and the year 1530 found him at Le Collège de France. Evidently, his stay in Paris was productive, for in a bibliographical appendix to an article on his academic achievements H. Galliner lists fifteen items, many of which were published during the 1530s.[61] He was the author of biblical commentaries, works on Hebrew grammar and an edition of Kimchi's *Michlol*. Lefranc does not put his exegetical writings in the same class as those of Vatable; nevertheless, he regards him as a meticulous and conscientious teacher.[62] The third Hebrew reader in Calvin's day was Paul Paradis, a converted Jew of Viennese origin, who was at the college from 1531 to 1549. Testimony to his expert knowledge of Talmud and Kabbalah comes from the sixteenth-century French scholar Jean Chéradame, who was himself a noted Hebraist.[63]

A. J. Baumgartner finds it difficult to believe that Calvin did not commence his study of Hebrew under these eminent lecturers in Paris. In a review of Baumgartner's book, however, H. Vuilleumier disputes this claim and maintains that at this point in his career (i.e. on his second visit to Paris in 1531) Calvin was still studying law and had as yet shown no great interest in the Bible. He refers to Nicholas Colladon's biography of the Reformer published in 1556 where it is stated that it was at Basle that Calvin began to study Hebrew.[64] The same point is made by Theodore Beza in his *Life of Calvin*. Neither biographer connects him with Vatable and his colleagues in Paris.[65] But Baumgartner regards the testimony of Colladon as insufficient evidence since it is not related to any available documents.

Whatever the extent of Calvin's knowledge of Hebrew when he fled from France in 1533, it was without doubt considerably increased during the time he spent at Basle. More than any other city Basle was the spiritual home of many northern humanists, and as such it was one of the most important European centres of the new learning. Academically speaking, it was a free city.[66] When Calvin arrived there Sebastian Münster was just seeing his *Biblia hebraica* through the press, and the opportunity of sitting at the feet of this renowned scholar must have presented itself to the young Frenchman. It would be surprising if he had missed it. There was also at Basle another renowned linguist, Simon Grynaeus who, as his epitaph in the cathedral close says 'is worthy of praise and an eternal memorial for his knowledge of Latin, Greek and Hebrew'.[67] As a mark of respect Calvin dedicated his commentary on the Letter to the Romans to his learned teacher.

During his exile from Geneva between 1538 and 1541 Calvin spent most of his time in Strasbourg, a city noted for its friendliness towards persecuted Protestants and for its pioneering work in education.[68] Its tolerance towards every shade of religious opinion had made it the venue of those who sympathised with humanistic studies. Two of its most illustrious teachers were Wolfgang Capito and Martin Bucer (1491–1551), both of whom had been invited there by the Stettmeister in 1523 to expound 'the authentic sense of the Scriptures'. Their presence, together with that of the Hebraist Gregor Caselius, suggests that Hebrew and biblical studies were taken seriously. Capito (1478–1541) held qualifications in law and medicine as well as theology, and had learned Hebrew from Matthew Adrianus. He had previously been professor of Old Testament and cathedral preacher at Basle and was a friend and defender of Erasmus. The latter considered him to be one of Europe's most accomplished Hebraists; in a letter to John Fisher he describes him as 'a much better Hebrew scholar than Reuchlin'.[69] Like Erasmus, Capito was convinced that the only proper way of studying any subject, especially theology, was by means of the ancient languages. In the introduction to his Hebrew grammar of 1518 he wrote: 'I commend to you the three languages, which are the foremost and greatest supports to the whole world of learning'.[70] But apart from his interest in the Hebraic tradition from the scholarly standpoint, Capito was also friendly with Jews. This protector of the persecuted and the most broadminded of all the German Reformers felt that Christians should deal more kindly with their Jewish neighbours, hence his close relationship with Rabbi Josel of Rosheim who attended his sermons regularly 'because of his great learning'.[71]

Bucer's commentary on the Psalms (1529) offers ample evidence of the author's knowledge of classical Hebrew and of his positive attitude to rabbinic exegesis. In the preface he singles out David Kimchi and Abraham Ibn Ezra as particularly helpful guides on philological matters, but in the body of the work he refers frequently to the Targum and to Rashi as well. As Gerald Hobbs has shown, he makes extensive use of rabbinic sources so that he can establish the historical and literal interpretation of the text.[72] Only psalms 50 and 85 out of the whole Psalter were interpreted christologically. This famous commentary, which appeared in English in 1530, eventually ran into five editions and was hailed by Calvin as one of the magisterial works of the age. In view of Bucer's success Calvin considered his own exposition of the Psalter superfluous and undertook it only to please his friends. Addressing Grynaeus in the preface of his *Commentary on Romans* he makes plain the admiration he has for Bucer as a biblical scholar: 'For that man (as you know) besides the hidden learning and abundant knowledge of many things, . . . is chiefly to be commended in this, that none in our time hath used more exact diligence in expounding the Scriptures than he'.

Yet, in spite of his debt to the rabbis and his obvious appreciation of the Hebraic tradition, Bucer's attitude towards the Jews of his own day was far from friendly. It was put to the test quite by chance while Calvin was at Strasbourg. In 1538 Philip the Landgrave of Hesse sought from his advisers a definite ruling on the legal position of Jews living within his domain. A seven-point proposal was drawn up and sent to six leading theologians for their approval. After due consideration they condemned it for being too tolerant and suggested that Bucer's *Counsel concerning the Jews (Judenratschlag)* be adopted instead.[73] Surprisingly, the Cassel Advice, as this plan was called, was marked by a strong aversion to the Jewish people: Jews were opposed to the true religion, dishonest in their dealings with Christians and clearly condemned by God for idolatry in Deuteronomy 13. Hence, if they wanted to live in a Christian country certain conditions had to be met. They must agree not to denigrate Christianity, not to build new synagogues, and not to use the Talmud as their authority in any disputation. Attendance at church sermons ought to be made obligatory for them. They should be made to pay higher taxes and prevented from working in industry and commerce. All economic activity between Jews and Christians should be stopped. But since they were unlikely to adhere to such conditions, the final recommendation was that all Jews should be expelled from Hesse. Fortunately Philip listened to his counsellors not to his theologians, and the Jews were allowed to stay. In all this Bucer's standpoint does not differ materially from that of Luther in *The Jews and their Lies*. Both reiterate the mediaeval anti-Jewish arguments. In spite of such harsh stipulations, Hastings Eells is at pains to exonerate Bucer from hatred of the Jews. According to Eells, his purpose in drawing up his plan was to protect the Christian faith from what he believed to be a very real threat. He did not embark on a deliberate policy of intolerance, and in later writings never once did he seek an opportunity to attack the Jews. He was asked for his opinion and after giving it he let the matter drop.[74] Admittedly, the cruel measures advocated in the Advice are quite out of character for Bucer, but it is hard to believe that he was not motivated by something other than the desire to defend Christianity. One may be grateful that he did not pursue the matter further.

Though the architects of reform at Strasbourg were men like Capito and Bucer, the educational programme for which the city became famous was the work of John Sturm (1507–1589). A graduate of the trilingual college at Louvain, Sturm first visited Strasbourg in 1528 and attended with interest Bucer's lectures on the Psalms. By the time of Calvin's arrival he had finally settled there and was busily introducing new pedagogical methods. In his curriculum the emphasis was on Latin and Greek with Hebrew offered as an optional subject, for Sturm did not share the enthusiasm with which many of his contemporaries greeted the revival of Hebrew associated with Pico and Reuchlin. He felt that while future pastors should be given every opportunity to study the language, there was no obligation for the ordinary Christian to learn it. Such reservation stems from two causes. In the first place, he is afraid that students would spoil the purity of their classical prose style by using Semitic idioms. Secondly, he believes that too great a stress on the biblical languages may lead to a Protestant scholastic, as inimical to the humanities as the mediaeval scholastic.[75] But despite Sturm's moderation in the study of Hebrew, it appears that many students chose it as an option. Peter Martyr, who replaced Capito as Old Testament lecturer, wrote to his friends at Lucca in December 1543 saying that he was at the time going through the prophecy of Amos, 'and because the most part in this school have knowledge in Hebrew, I expound the Hebrew text in Latin'.[76]

Paris, Basle and Strasbourg offered Calvin the chance of learning Hebrew from internationally acclaimed scholars. In the absence of any definite information, we must assume that he took it. It is also possible that he had been persuaded to apply himself to the language by his cousin Robert Olivetan, who was himself a Hebraist and appreciative of the Hebraic tradition. But pressure from his cousin apart, Calvin is likely to have studied Hebrew simply because it was fashionable to do so. The humanist scholars, by whom he had been influenced since he was a teenager, had developed an enthusiasm for the antique. Like their English counterparts, they admired the simple clarity of the Fathers compared with the complicated arguments of the Schoolmen. French humanists saw in the biblical piety which they attributed to the Fathers a justification for their own aversion to the scholastic method and for their insistence on a return to the sources in the original languages. For them, as it had been for the early Fathers, the scriptural page was central. The Bible must be studied and understood. The critical examination of the Vulgate went hand in hand with the study of Greek and Hebrew. Calvin would have sympathised with these principles, for he was a lawyer before he became a theologian, and his method of studying the Scriptures is typical of the humanist lawyers among whom he had been trained. The law school of Bourges had taught him to go beyond the gloss to the earliest sources. This he did when commenting on the Bible. He strove always to present to his listeners and readers the plain meaning of the original text unencumbered with idle speculation.[77] Calvin and his contemporaries were part of the Erasmian literary revival with its stress on philology and linguistic study. Furthermore, Hebrew was disesteemed at the Sorbonne, a fact which made the learning of it even more attractive in humanistic circles.

But, given his interest in the language, to what extent can Calvin be regarded as a competent Hebraist? During his time as a teacher and writer in Geneva what was his attitude towards the Hebraic tradition? On the question of his competence Richard Simon was of the opinion that, despite these golden opportunities to learn Hebrew, he got no further than the alphabet.[78] Such scepticism, however, has not gone unchallenged, for A. M. Hunter claims that he 'was more than adequately equipped to deal authoritatively with the originals of both Old Testament and New Testament'.[79] This latter estimation of Calvin's linguistic ability is now universally accepted. And not without good reason, for there is ample evidence in his Old Testament commentaries of his proficiency in Hebrew. His commentary on the Psalms contains very many allusions to the original text, and in his lectures on the twelve chapters of Daniel he comments on over a hundred Hebrew and Aramaic words. The printer's preface to the Daniel commentary states that it was his custom, when lecturing, first to read each verse in the original Hebrew or Aramaic and then to translate it into Latin.

His attitude to the rabbis is ambivalent. In a discussion of the Hebrew text of Genesis 3:1 he sides with the Targum and with David Kimchi, whom he regards as 'the most correct expositor among the rabbis'.[80] But such compliments are rare. Jewish exegetes are frequently condemned for seeking 'new and subtle interpretations' and for being 'actuated by pure malice' when expounding certain passages.[81] They wilfully misrepresent crucial parts of the Old Testament by denying their Christian interpretation. He considers Isaac Abravanel to be an ingenious commentator, yet he is quick to hurl abuse at him whenever his exposition of a text differs from that hallowed by Christian tradition. In his exegesis of the Book of Daniel, Abravanel proves to be nothing more than a 'twister' and a 'trifler' who is 'impure' and 'obstinate' to boot. He is a 'brawler', brazenly babbling 'about matters utterly beyond his knowledge'.[82] This familiarity with rabbinic sources comes through intermediaries such as Lyra, Pagninus and Vatable. A colleague, the renowned Hebraist Anthony Chevallier (1523–1572), had drawn his attention to Abravanel's commentary on Daniel. Unlike Luther, he had little contact with contemporary Jewry, for between 1490 and 1780 all Jews were banished from Geneva.[83] Although he published a pamphlet entitled *An Answer to a Certain Jew's Questions and Objections*, in which he went over the age old theological differences between Jew and Christian, Calvin wrote nothing which could be compared with Luther's *The Jews and their Lies*.[84] In general, he displays a more tolerant attitude towards the Jews, possibly as a result of his association with Capito and other Strasbourg Reformers.

Although sermons and lectures were a prominent feature of life in Geneva during the 1550s, the provision for the formal instruction of the young was inadequate. The Collège de Rive, founded by William Farel in 1535, was still functioning, but a precarious financial situation was making its future uncertain. The city lacked an efficient educational institution, and it was a source of great sorrow for Calvin that he was unable to provide one until only five years before his death. Despite numerous difficulties a school and an academy were opened on 5 June 1559. The school offered preparatory courses for the academy; the academy trained future ministers. Since the exposition of the Bible was central to the sermon, Calvin ensured that the biblical languages were given primary place in the curriculum and spared no effort in trying to attract competent teachers. The first principal was Theodore Beza, who though chiefly remembered as a Greek scholar, was an enthusiastic promoter of Hebrew. In his *Icones*, pen portraits of famous scholars which he dedicated to James VI of Scotland, he included at least six Christian Hebraists.[85] The details of the scholarly pursuits of Reuchlin, Förster, Münster, Fagius, Tremellius and Vatable were meant both to inspire the young monarch and to promote the new learning. Initially Calvin's attempt to fill the chair of Hebrew met with little success. Both Jean Mercier of the trilingual college in Paris and Immanuel Tremellius, who was at the time lecturing in Heidelberg, politely refused his invitation. But with his third choice he was lucky. Anthony Chevallier, recently expelled from the Bernese Academy in Lausanne together with several other scholars, gladly accepted the post. According to the regulations he was to give eight hours of Hebrew instruction per week, five of which were to be devoted to grammar and three to the exposition of 'some books of the Old Testament with the rabbinic commentaries'.[86] Chevallier served with distinction as the academy's Hebrew lecturer until 1566. Since he came to England a few years later we shall have occasion to consider his contribution to Hebraic studies in greater detail in another context.

Chevallier was the first in a long line of eminent Hebraists who taught at the Geneva Academy. His successor was Corneille Bertram, a Frenchman schooled at the feet of Jean Mercier in Paris. Like other Hebrew scholars of his own day, Bertram could appreciate the contributions of Jewish authors to grammatical and exegetical studies. In the preface to a comparative grammar of Hebrew and Aramaic published in 1574, he acknowledges his debt to Kimchi, Elias Levita and Tremellius. Another of his published works was a new edition of Pagninus' lexicon, the *Thesaurus linguae sanctae*, which he had revised and enriched by means of the scriptural commentaries of Chevallier and Mercier. In 1587 Bertram was followed by a native of Geneva, Pierre Chevallier. Though no relation of his famous namesake and predecessor, he was one of his students. Inspired by Anthony, he had continued his study of Semitics at Basle and Heidelberg before coming to Geneva. During the final years of the century the professorship was held by Jean Diodati (1576–1649), the son of Italian Protestants who had fled to Geneva from Lucca. Beza was so impressed with his grasp of Oriental languages that he recommended him for the chair when he was only twenty-one. Diodati established his reputation as a scholar with his translation of the Bible into Italian in 1607.

The Geneva Academy was undoubtedly Calvin's most important institutional legacy to his adopted city.[87] His plans for it were influenced by what he had experienced in Basle and Strasbourg. The example of humanistic learning which he had observed elsewhere, coupled with his own enthusiasm for biblical studies, secured a prominent place for Hebrew in the curriculum. As one would expect, this interest in Hebrew is reflected also in the library holdings. The 1572 catalogue lists over fifteen items which were related to the study of Hebrew and Aramaic, including three copies of Bomberg's Rabbinic Bible.[88] It is noteworthy that there were far more books on the Old Testament than on the New; a sure indication that from Calvin's time onwards the Jewish Bible was given pride of place in Geneva. The study of it was rooted in the original language, and on questions of grammar and lexicography it was illuminated by the comments of the rabbis.

The recognition by Europe's leading Reformers of the relevance of Hebrew for understanding the Scriptures had a considerable impact on the world of learning. The Old Testament commentaries produced on the Continent, with their discussion of individual words and their allusions to the rabbis, stimulated an interest on this side of the Channel in the Hebrew Bible and its Jewish exegesis. By 1529 Luther's writings were so popular in England that they were put on an index of prohibited books, what E. G. Rupp has called a 'forbidden-Book-of-the-Month Club'. But the existence of the index did not have the desired effect. English scholars were not prevented by it from paying close attention to his ideas; in fact they did much more. They engendered in the universities an awareness of and an interest in the biblical interpretation propounded by Luther and other emerging continental Reformers. In 1535 Melanchthon's works replaced those of Duns Scotus as part of the syllabus for divinity students at Oxford and Cambridge. But as the century progressed, foreign influence came less from Wittenberg and more from Zurich, Basle, Strasbourg and Geneva. At Zurich the English exiles formed a 'community of scholars' under the guidance of Bullinger, Zwingli's successor. Oecolampadius attracted students to Basle. The pre-eminence of Sturm and Bucer ensured that Strasbourg became an important educational centre. The Geneva Academy succeeded in drawing students from many different countries, with the result that Calvinist scholars became some of the leading Christian Hebraists of the seventeenth century.

In the following chapters it will become increasingly obvious how significant these European centres of learning were for the development of Hebrew studies in England.

Notes

1 A. J. Baumgartner, *De l'Enseignement de l'hébreu chez les Protestants à partir de l'époque de la Réformation*, Lausanne 1889, p. 8.
2 R. W. Scribner, 'Reformation, society and humanism in Erfurt, *c.* 1450–1530', unpublished Ph.D. thesis, London 1972, p. 121.
3 Quoted by R. H. Fife, *The Revolt of Martin Luther*, New York 1957, p. 56.
4 E. G. Schwiebert, *Luther and his Times*, St Louis, Miss. 1950, p. 281.

5 W. Schwarz, 'Studies in Luther's attitude towards humanism', *JTS*, N.S. vol. VI, Pt. 1, 1955, p. 66.

6 *Luthers Werke*, Weimar ed., vol. V.

7 H. Boehmer, *Road to Reformation*, Philadelphia, Pa. 1946, p. 56.

8 *Das Hebräische bei Luther untersucht bis zum Ende der ersten Psalmenvorlesung*, Tübingen 1961; *Die Benützung des masoretischen Texts bei Luther in der Zeit zwischen der ersten und zweiten Psalmenvorlesung (1515–1518)*, Tübingen 1967; *Grammatica Theologica: Studien zu Luthers Operationes in Psalmos*, Tübingen 1977. Cf. the statement of J. M. Reu to the effect that by 1518 Luther 'had gained a thorough mastery of the Hebrew language', in *Luther's German Bible*, Columbus, Ohio 1934, p. 118.

9 T. M. Lindsay, *Cambridge Modern History*, Cambridge 1903, vol. II, p. 119. Cf. H. E. Jacobs, *Martin Luther*, New York 1898, pp. 105, 208, 225, for a similar viewpoint.

10 *Tischreden*, Weimar ed., vol. I, No. 1040, pp. 524f.

11 *Luther's Works*, American ed., vol. 54, p. 43.

12 *Ibid.*, vol. 1, p. 297.

13 *Tischreden*, Weimar ed., vol. IV, No. 5003, p. 608, 'Ego hodie huius laborem laudo'.

14 *Compendium Hebraeae Grammatices*, Wittenberg 1523. See further O. Eissfeldt, 'Mathaeus Aurogallus' Hebräische Grammatick 1523', *Wissenschaftliche Zeitschrift der Universität Halle–Wittenberg, gesellschaftswissenschaftlichsprachwissen-schaftliche*, Reihe VII, 1957–8, pp. 885ff. For a complete list of Aurogallus' works see G. Bauch, 'Die Einführung des Hebräischen in Wittenberg', *MGWJ*, Band 48, N.F. 12, 1904, pp. 479f.

15 See *Neue Deutsche Biographie*, vol. 3, pp. 427ff.

16 *Dictionarium Hebraicum Novum, non ex Rabbinorum commentis, nec nostratium doctorum stulta imitatione descriptum.*

17 *Luther's Works*, vol. 15, p. 267.

18 *Ibid.*, p. 270.

19 *Ibid.*, vol. 1, p. 353.

20 *Ibid.*, vol. 15, p. 270.

21 *Ibid.*, vol. 54, p. 445.

22 'Luther and the Rabbis', *JQR*, N.S. vol. LVIII, 1967–8, pp. 63ff.

23 *Luther's Works*, vol. 1, p. 296.

24 *Ibid.*

25 *Ibid.*, p. 349.

26 *Ibid.*, p. 3.

27 *Ibid.*, vol. 45, p. 200.

28 *Ibid.*, p. 229.

29 *Ibid.*, vol. 47, pp. 267ff.

30 See e.g. *ibid.*, vol. 15, pp. 279, 290.

31 A. Lukyn Williams, *Adversus Judaeos*, Cambridge 1935, pp. 248f. For the influence of the *Pugio fidei* on other writers see also G. F. Moore, 'Christian writers on Judaism', *HTR*, vol. XIV, No. 3, 1921, pp. 203ff.

32 A. Lukyn Williams, *op. cit.*, p. 277.

33   *Luther's Works*, vol. 54, p. 436.
34   Quoted by S. Stern, *Josel of Rosheim: Commander of Jewry in the Holy Roman Empire of the German Nation*, Eng. trans. by G. Hirschler, Philadelphia, Pa. 1965, p. 192.
35   *The Jew in the Mediaeval World*, New York 1960, p. 165. On Luther's attitude to the Jews see R. Lewin, *Luthers Stellung zu den Juden*, Berlin 1911; A. K. E. Holmio, *The Lutheran Reformation and the Jews*, Hancock, Mich. 1949; A. Siirala, 'Luther and the Jews', *Lutheran World*, vol. 11, No. 3, 1964, pp. 337ff.; W. Maurer, *Kirche und Synagoge*, eds. C. H. Rengstorf and S. von Kortzfleisch, Stuttgart 1968, vol. I, ch. 5; C. Cohen, 'Martin Luther and his Jewish contemporaries', *Jewish Social Studies*, vol. 25, No. 3, 1963, pp. 195ff.; E. G. Rupp, *Martin Luther and the Jews*, Robert Waley Cohen Memorial Lecture, Council of Christians and Jews, London 1972; J. Brosseder, *Luthers Stellung zu den Juden im Spiegel seiner Interpreten*, Munich 1972; C. B. Sucher, *Luthers Stellung zu den Juden: eine Interpretation aus germanistischer Sicht*, Nieuwkoop 1977.
36   *Luther's Works*, vol. 36, p. 304. See also W. Koenig, 'Luther as a student of Hebrew', *Concordia Theological Monthly*, vol. 24, 1953, p. 849.
37   *Ibid.*, vol. 45, pp. 362f.
38   *Corpus Reformatorum*, vol. XI, cols. 15ff.
39   *Luther's Works*, vol. 48, p. 78.
40   *Corpus Reformatorum*, vol. XI, cols. 718ff, 867ff.
41   G. R. Potter, *Huldrych Zwingli* (Documents of Modern History), London 1978, p. 5 quoting from Bullinger, *Reformationgeschichte nach dem Autographon*.
42   *Zwingli avant la Réforme de Zurich: Histoire de son développement intellectuel et religieux*, Geneva 1899, p. 84.
43   Schüler and Schulthess, eds., *Zwingli Opera*, Zurich 1829–42, vol. VII, p. 145.
44   *Ibid.*, p. 194.
45   *Ibid.*, p. 534.
46   *Ibid.*, vol. V, p. 547.
47   P. Smith, *The Life and Letters of Martin Luther*, London 1911, p. 244.
48   S. M. Jackson, ed., *Selected Works of Zwingli*, New York 1901, p. 63.
49   Schüler and Schulthess, eds., *Zwingli Opera*, vol. V, pp. 550f.
50   *Ibid.*, p. 26.
51   *Ibid.*, p. 226.
52   *Ibid.*, p. 774, 'Nobiscum sentiunt Rabbini'.
53   *Jewish Influence on Christian Reform Movements*, p. 486; cf. the views of E. Egli, 'Zwingli als Hebräer', *Zwingliana*, 1900, Nr. 2, pp. 153ff.
54   For Zwingli's attitude to contemporary Jewry see E. Künzli, 'Zwinglis Stellung zu den Juden', *Festgabe Leonhard von Muralt*, Zurich 1970, pp. 309ff.
55   G. W. Bromiley, ed., *Zwingli and Bullinger* (The Library of Christian Classics vol. XXIV), London 1953, p. 109.
56   G. R. Potter, ed., *Huldrych Zwingli*, p. 64.
57   G. R. Potter, *Zwingli*, Cambridge 1976, p. 224.

58   J. Lefranc, *La Jeunesse de Calvin*, Paris 1888, p. 81; A. M. Hunter, 'The education of Calvin', *Evangelical Qtly*, vol. 9, 1937, p. 24.

59   *Commentary on II Corinthians*, Calvin Trans. Soc. 1849, p. 101, 'Under your direction and tuition, I conjoined with the study of Law, Greek literature, of which you were at that time a most celebrated Professor'.

60   A. J. Baumgartner, *Calvin hebraïsant et interprète de l'Ancien Testament*, Geneva 1889, p. 15. See also J. Lefranc, *Histoire du Collège de France*, Paris 1893, pp. 175ff. For a list of the professors of Hebrew at the college see *Le Collège de France: Livre Jubilaire*, Paris 1932, p. 19.

61   'Agathias Guidacerius 1477(?)–1540: an early Hebrew grammarian in Rome and Paris', *Historia Judaica*, vol. 2, No. 1, April 1940, pp. 100f.

62   *Histoire du Collège de France*, p. 181.

63   See F. Secret, *Les Kabbalistes Chrétiens de la Renaissance*, Paris 1964, p. 171, n. 61.

64   *Revue de Théologie et de Philosophie*, March 1889, pp. 213f.

65   *Tracts and Treatises on the Reformation of the Church*, Eng. trans. by H. Beveridge (reprinted London 1958), vol. I, p. lxv.

66   B. Hall, 'The Reformation city', *BJRL*, vol. 54, No. 1, 1971, p. 108. M. Doumergue, *Les Hommes et les choses du temps de Calvin*, Lausanne 1889–1927, vol. I, p. 504.

67   W. Vischer, 'Calvin, exégète de l'Ancien Testament', *La Revue Réformée*, vol. 18, 1967, p. 8.

68   See M. V. Chrisman, *Strasbourg and the Reform*, New Haven, Conn. 1967.

69   *CWE*, vol. 3, Letter 413, p. 294. See also J. M. Kittelson, *Wolfgang Capito: from Humanist to Reformer*, Leiden 1975, p. 22: Capito 'soon became known as one of Europe's most accomplished Hebrew scholars'.

70   *Institutionum Hebraicorum: libri duo*, Basle, 1518.

71   S. Stern, *Josel of Rosheim*, Eng. trans., p. 178.

72   'Martin Bucer on Psalm 22: a study in the application of rabbinic exegesis by a Christian Hebraist', *Histoire de l'exégèse au XVIe siècle*, eds. O. Fatio and P. Fraenkel, Geneva 1978.

73   See further W. Nijenhuis, *Ecclesia Reformata: Studies on the Reformation* (Kerkhistorische Bijdragen III), Leiden 1972, pp. 38ff.

74   'Bucer's plan for the Jews', *Church History*, vol. VI, 1937, p. 135.

75   See P. Mesnard, 'The pedagogy of Johann Sturm (1507–1589) and its evangelical inspiration', *Studies in the Renaissance*, vol. 13, 1966, pp. 213ff.

76   G. D. Gorham, *Gleanings of a Few Scattered Ears during the Period of the Reformation in England*, London 1857, p. 22. For Hebrew teaching at Strasbourg see A. Schindling, *Humanistische Hochschule und freie Reichstadt: Gymnasium und Akademie in Strassburg 1538–1621*, Wiesbaden 1977, pp. 262f.

77   B. Hall, *John Calvin: Humanist and Theologian*, London 1956, p. 34. On Calvin's exegetical method see also J. H. Leith, 'John Calvin – theologian of the Bible', *Interpretation*, vol. 25, No. 3, 1971, p. 336; Q. Breen, *John Calvin: a study in French Humanism*, 2nd ed., Archon Books, Grand Rapids 1968, ch. 3.

78 *Histoire Critique du Vieux Testament*, Eng. trans., vol. III, p. 98.
79 'The erudition of John Calvin', *Evangelical Qtly*, vol. 18, 1946, p. 203.
80 *Commentary on the Psalms*, Calvin Trans. Soc. 1845, vol. IV, p. 326.
81 *Ibid.*, vol. II, p. 10; vol. IV, p. 278.
82 *Commentary on Daniel*, Calvin Trans. Soc. 1852, vol. II, p. 207.
83 A. Nordman, 'Histoire des Juifs à Genève de 1281 à 1780', *Revue des Etudes Juives*, vol. 80, 1925, p. 40.
84 On Calvin's attitude to the Jews see J. Courvoisier, 'Calvin et les Juifs', *Judaica*, vol. II, No. 3, 1946, pp. 203ff; S. W. Baron, 'John Calvin and the Jews', *Harry Austryn Wolfson Jubilee Volume*, Jerusalem 1965, pp. 141ff; G. W. Locher, 'Calvin spricht zu den Juden', *Theologische Zeitschrift*, vol. 23, No. 2, 1967, pp. 180ff.
85 *Icones 1580*, Selected and ed. by J. Horden, London 1971, *passim*.
86 See 'Leges Academiae Genevensis' in C. Borgeaud, *Histoire de l'Université de Genève: l'Académie de Calvin 1559–1798*, Genève 1900, p. 631.
87 E. W. Monter, *Calvin's Geneva*, New York 1966, p. 113.
88 A. Ganoczy, *La Bibliothèque de l'Académie de Calvin: le catalogue de 1572 et ses enseignements*, Genève 1969, pp. 159ff.

Part two

Motives

IV

A church Catholic but reformed

In A.D. 1500 Western Christendom was still one and the learned of the age were cosmopolitan. During the fifteenth century it was not uncommon for European scholars to visit England and for their English counterparts to spend several years studying on the Continent. Exchanges between England and Italy were particularly popular. Although the Renaissance in England came almost a century later than the Renaissance in Italy, there had been a continuous interchange of scholars between the two countries for several decades. Italian humanists crossed the Channel in pursuit of knowledge, and an English College was founded at Padua, one of the foremost mediaeval universities, as early as 1446. English men of letters regarded Italy as the fount of all learning, and were especially attracted by the opportunities offered in the Italian universities to study Greek. G. B. Parks lists the permanent entry of Greek into England as one of the four main achievements of those English students who went to Italy during the second half of the fifteenth century, for by the late 1490s instruction in Greek had become firmly established at Oxford.[1]

But although the Italian city states were unsurpassed during this period as centres of culture, Italian humanists were not the only ones to influence the development of the new learning in England. Instead of a movement which relied on imported Italians, we find in early sixteenth-century England a group of English humanists with interests of its own, interests which are largely centred on 'the Erasmian blend of classical culture and religious reform'.[2] It was in England that Erasmus found some of his most enthusiastic patrons. His insistence that true Christianity could be revived only by studying the sources in their original form, 'unwarped by ecclesiastical tradition' and with the help of philology, was recognised and accepted by many prominent scholars and statesmen. The scores of letters which passed between him and his English friends suggest that there was strong support for his ideas among the leading figures in the spiritual and intellectual life of England. Likewise, the message of Johann Reuchlin did not go unheeded. Though the German Hebraist himself never once set foot on English soil, he was present in spirit, and his insistence on the importance of the philological principle in biblical exegesis found ready acceptance among a small but powerful group of scholars, divines and statesmen, who exercised considerable influence on educational developments at Oxford and Cambridge. 'The spread of humanism', writes F. G. Stokes, 'within our own shores is illustrated by the fact that among the "army of Reuchlinists" were numbered many Englishmen of light and leading. Sir Thomas More; Fisher, Bishop of Rochester; Linacre, scholar and physician; Grocyn, first teacher of Greek at Oxford; Colet, Dean of St. Pauls; Hugh Latimer; and Tunstall, afterwards Bishop of London, were all instinctively drawn into the confederation'.[3] It is to some of these men, and others of a like mind, the representatives of Christian humanism in England, that we must turn first in seeking the motives for the study of Hebrew. Some of them were prominent in educational circles, others at the royal court.

At Oxford and Cambridge

Reuchlin's English supporters during the first two decades of the sixteenth century could not be described as Hebraists themselves, yet they were, to a man, imbued with the spirit of the new age and were ready in principle to promote Hebraic studies among their compatriots. In a letter written from Antwerp in 1516 Erasmus reminds Reuchlin of the esteem in which he is held by the whole scholarly world, and especially by two prominent Englishmen:

You have been the acquaintance and friend of so many of our greatest men; you are even now so dearly beloved by all our noblest men and our best scholars that, were you their father, you could not be more intimately beloved by all of them. The bishop of Rochester has an almost religious veneration for you. To John Colet your name is sacred. Had not his servant lost your letter, he would keep it, he told me, among his holy relics.[4]

Most of these English Reuchlinists had attended the Italian academies and gained first hand experience of the flowering of Renaissance culture south of the Alps. Furthermore, many of them had been educated at Oxford, which, as Roberto Weiss shows, had been responsive to Italian ideas since 1470, and where there was a growing appreciation of the works of humanistic authors.[5]

The most senior member of the group was William Grocyn, who, even in his own day, was referred to as 'the patriarch of English learning'. On his return from Italy in 1491 he inaugurated Greek lectures at Oxford, and although he was presented with the living of St Lawrence Jewry in 1496, there is evidence to suggest that he did not actually leave Oxford before the turn of the century. But whether in Oxford or London, Grocyn continued to be at the centre of the movement for the revival of learning. Thomas Linacre, founder of the Royal College of Physicians, took a degree in medicine at Padua, but on his return to England he taught Greek at Magdalen College, Oxford; Thomas More was numbered among his pupils. Though not mentioned by Stokes, William Latimer was a close friend of Grocyn and Linacre with whom he had studied in Italy, and despite no extant evidence that he published anything, his proficiency in Greek is demonstrated by the fact that Erasmus asked him to read through the text of his New Testament.

The dominant figure in this Oxford company of Reuchlinists was John Colet. Although, in common with many of his fellow humanists, he published little, he exercised considerable influence over his colleagues and students, and was held in high regard as a scholar. Erasmus, on his first visit to Oxford in the autumn of 1499, attended Colet's lectures, and in December of the same year wrote to a former pupil, Robert Fisher, who was then in Italy. It is obvious from his letter that Erasmus was very happy at Oxford. He had never found a place he liked so much, and the scholarship was of such a high quality that he had little desire left to go to Italy, except to be able to say that he had visited it. Above all, he was particularly impressed by John Colet. 'When I am listening to Colet', he writes, 'it seems to me that I am listening to Plato himself'. J. Huizinga sums up the opinion of Erasmus' many biographers when he states that Colet's influence 'definitely decided the bent of Erasmus' many-sided mind'.[6] Where Colet received his initial degree is uncertain. The consensus of his biographers is that he went to Oxford, graduating B.A. in 1487 and M.A. in 1490. W. R. Godfrey, however, has challenged this assumption and made out a possible case for regarding him as a Cambridge man who later moved to Oxford.[7] Whatever his academic pedigree, after obtaining his master's degree Colet went abroad. He decided to fulfil the requirements for the B.D., four years of reading and listening to lectures, at various Italian universities. Although his travels must have been of crucial importance for his intellectual development, very little is known about his itinerary or of any contact he may have made with humanist scholars. Seebohm contends that 'he can hardly have visited Italy without visiting Florence, as Grocyn and Linacre had done before him', but there is no direct evidence that he ever went there.[8] A letter written to Marsilio Ficino after he had returned to England suggests that he did not go to Florence, for in it he expresses the hope that one day he will meet Ficino in person.[9]

Even if this period in his life must remain something of a mystery, it is clear that Colet left Italy imbued with the reforming zeal of men like Pico and Savonarola. On his return to Oxford in 1496, finding biblical study at a very low ebb, he replaced the customary lectures on the *Sentences* of Peter Lombard, a twelfth-century bishop of Paris, with lectures on the Bible. He took Paul's Letter to the Romans as his starting point, treating it as a whole and not as an arsenal of unrelated texts. These lectures, the object of Erasmus' admiration in his letter to Robert Fisher, proved to be 'a milestone in the history of Christian scholarship', for compared to the usual provision made for students of theology they were fresh and original, with the result that they attracted large audiences. Although he deliberately rejected the scholastic method of interpretation then in vogue, Colet did not attack the schoolmen, he simply ignored them. He set aside the mediaeval commentaries and three out of four of their customary interpretations (moral, allegorical and anagogical), affirming that Scripture had but one meaning, the obvious, literal sense. His concern was with what the biblical authors actually meant, and he was always anxious to communicate to his students the basic sense of a biblical passage, rather than give the long list of authorities common to lectures and devotional sermons during the Middle Ages. To achieve this end he followed the example of the Early Church Fathers and the continental humanists of his own day, thus inaugurating a new method of textual examination.[10] In Colet 'we can begin to see the silhouette of a new kind of Christian scholar, convinced of the importance of the original sources, endowed with a fresh sense of historical perspective, disillusioned with scholastic philosophy, yet at the same time warmly committed to preaching Christ and to reforming ecclesiastical abuses'.[11]

But in spite of his interest in the original sources and in the literal sense of the Bible, Colet's text was the Vulgate. He knew no Hebrew, and although he had encouraged Erasmus to learn Greek many years previously, it was 1516 before he was inspired by the latter's *Novum instrumentum* to study it himself. Unlike his contemporaries he had not used his time in Italy to learn Greek, and in a letter to Erasmus he laments his ignorance of the language:

Personally I like your work and welcome your new edition, but in a way that rouses mixed feelings. At one time I am sorry that I never learned Greek, without some skill in which we can get nowhere; and then again I rejoice in the light which is shed by your genius like the sun. . . . I will join you, if you permit me, and will attach myself to your side, making myself your pupil even for the learning of Greek, although I am now getting on in years and am almost an old man. I have not forgotten that Cato learned Greek at a great age, and I know that you, who are level with me in years, are now studying Hebrew.[12]

Though he was well into middle age when he wrote this letter, it is obvious that Colet realised the importance of mastering the language in which the New Testament was originally written. A similar attitude to the study of Hebrew emerges clearly from the advice he gives to Radulphus in 1497. His correspondent, whose identity is not known, had been attempting to expound 'the dark places of Scripture' beginning with the words of Lamech in Genesis 4:23, 24. Colet's reply to the questions raised by Radulphus is based in part on Pico's treatment of the biblical account of Creation found in his *Heptaplus*. He emphasises that this is not the first instance of a 'dark place' in the Bible by drawing his friend's attention to Genesis 1, and in several letters, four of which have been preserved, discusses some of the difficulties in the Creation story. He demonstrates that the narrative is shrouded in obscurity which cannot be satisfactorily penetrated without the knowledge of Hebrew, a fact which Origen and Jerome had appreciated.

All things in it are so hidden [he writes of Genesis 1], as to furnish matter for opinions and words without end, and there is hardly anyone but may say what he will thereupon, so long as what he says is consistent with itself. But his result of self-consistency will be more easily attained, than that of harmony with the words of Moses; unless the one who is discussing the beginning of Genesis is versed in the Hebrew tongue, and has the means of consulting Hebrew commentaries. For without the help of this, I suppose that the Mosaic records can be understood by no one. It is a resource with which Origen, and Jerome, and all the most careful investigators of Holy Writ, were well acquainted.[13]

This indicates the stand Colet was prepared to take. During the final decade of the fifteenth century, long before the *Letters of Obscure Men* had ridiculed the views of the obscurantists, he was urging all serious students of the Old Testament, not only to learn Hebrew, but also to avail themselves of the help afforded by the rabbinic commentators in the elucidation of difficult passages.

It is tempting to suppose that Colet's appreciation of the importance of Hebrew and of the significance of Jewish writings for the Christian exegete was increased by the visit of Cornelius Agrippa von Nettesheim to London in 1510. Agrippa, a native of Cologne, made his first public appearance as a scholar by expounding Reuchlin's *De verbo mirifico* at the University of Dôle in Burgundy during the course of the previous year. Though his knowledge of Hebrew was slight, he had been profoundly influenced by Pico and Reuchlin and had become acquainted with the teachings of the Kabbalists early in his career.[14] He went to great lengths to defend the orthodoxy of the Kabbalah. The study of the long neglected writings of the Jewish mystics would, he claimed, in true Reuchlin fashion, provide new insights into the meaning of biblical texts, and as a result, the Christian faith would be strengthened, not undermined. But since the 'Battle of the Books' was to begin barely a year later, it is hardly surprising that the young scholar's defence of the renowned German humanist brought down the wrath of Rome. In a Lenten sermon, Jean Catilinet, provincial superior of the Franciscans in Burgundy, accused him of being a judaising heretic who had introduced into Christian schools the criminal, condemned and prohibited art of Kabbalah. Despising the Fathers and Catholic doctors he had made it clear that he preferred the Jewish rabbis, and had bent sacred letters to heretical arts and to the Talmud. Although Agrippa freely admitted that he did not disparage the Hebraic tradition and that he had frequent recourse to rabbinic works, he strenuously denied the charge of heresy; it was the ignorance of the Kabbalah among his opponents that led to such a monstrous accusation.[15] His defence, which was written in London at St Paul's Deanery where he was lodging as Colet's guest, contains several quotations from the Pauline Letters, quotations which undoubtedly betray the dean's influence, and elsewhere in his writings Agrippa tells us that with the learned and virtuous John Colet as his teacher he learned many things.[16]

But in spite of his guest's passion for the Kabbalah, Colet was not finally convinced of its usefulness for the Christian. Scholars might profit from consulting rabbinic commentaries when attempting to expound particular passages in the Old Testament, but they had nothing to gain from trying to unravel the enigmatic writings of the Jewish mystics. In a letter written to Erasmus in 1517 he comments on

Reuchlin's newly published *De arte cabalistica* and says:

It is a book about which I dare not pronounce an opinion. I am aware how
ignorant I am and how dimsighted in matters so transcendental, and in the
works of so great a man. And yet, as I read, it seemed to me at times that the
wonders were more verbal than real; for according to this system, Hebrew
words have something mysterious in their very characters and combinations.
Erasmus! Of books and knowledge there is no end. But for this short life there
is nothing better than that we should live in purity and holiness, and daily
endeavour to be purified and enlightened and fulfil what is promised in those
Pythagorean and Cabbalistic treatises of Reuchlin. This result, in my
judgement we shall attain by no other way, than by an ardent love and
imitation of Jesus Christ. Wherefore, leaving detours, let us take a short road
to attain it quickly.[17]

With the humility that is characteristic of him Colet bows to
Reuchlin's erudition, but feels nevertheless that he must draw the line
at the Kabbalah. The pursuit of Hebrew studies for a better
understanding of Scripture was one thing, but to seek Christ in the
works of the Kabbalists was another.

This negative attitude on Colet's part appears in marked contrast to
the opinion he had expressed some twenty years previously in his
Treatises on the Hierarchies of Dionysius. There, he regards the
Kabbalah as the true interpretation of the Law given by God to Moses
on Sinai, for kabbalistic writings 'openly contain all the secret things
and mysteries which are veiled in the literal Law. These secret things,
as Origen perceives, are called by St. Paul "the oracles of God", giving
life to the Law; without which life-giving spirit the Law is dead'.
Moreover, the Kabbalah is of significance to the Christian since 'in
these books all our doctrines plainly appear'.[18] These words
presumably reflect Colet's initial reaction to Pico's Kabbalistic
Conclusions and Reuchlin's first kabbalistic work, the *De verbo
mirifico*. By the time Reuchlin's second and much more detailed study
of the Jewish mystical tradition had appeared, with its system of angel
invocation and its stress on the practice or the 'art' of Kabbalah, he
was far less enthusiastic. Furthermore it is of possible significance that
Cornelius Agrippa's most notable work, the *De occulta philosophia*,
originally written in 1510, outlined a highly ritualistic religion in
'which the concern for the objects and forms which constitute religious
ritual and ceremony – sacrifice, oblation, blessing, purification,
solitude, holy water, incense, oil, bells and so so – is given even more
emphasis than with Reuchlin'.[19] Since the study of the Kabbalah could
also lead men to emphasise what he would have regarded as

inessentials, Colet may well have felt it prudent to side with Erasmus and give Jewish mysticism a wide berth. But whatever his reservations about certain aspects of the Hebraic tradition, John Colet must be regarded as one of the pioneers of linguistic study in sixteenth-century England, not because he was an accomplished linguist himself, but because he saw the relevance of the ancient languages for the interpretation of Scripture.

Despite the fact that Colet and his friends had pressed for a reformation of educational methods and for a revision of the curriculum at Oxford before the end of the fifteenth century, it was only in 1516 that a school of humanist studies was actually established within the university. This was done at the instigation of Richard Fox, Bishop of Winchester, who had long been prominent in educational circles. He had served for three years as Chancellor of the University of Cambridge, and from 1507 to 1519 had been Master of Pembroke College in the same university. Before her death in 1509 the Countess of Richmond had appointed him to be one of the executors of her will. As such he had played a leading part in the foundation of St John's College, and thus in promoting the new learning at Cambridge. Oxford also benefited from the bishop's zeal for educational reform when he was invited to write new statutes for Balliol College in 1507. Although the changes in the statutes were not as sweeping as one might have expected and left much to be desired from the standpoint of the ideal Renaissance foundation, the new code did bear the stamp of Fox's individuality. In contrast with the vagueness of the earlier statutes there was a coherent pattern running through it.[20] As an educator the Bishop of Winchester clearly had earned the right to be listened to with respect.

Like many of his contemporaries in England and on the Continent, Fox firmly believed that the Church ought to be totally committed to the revival of letters. In order to make some contribution towards the provision of competent clergy he proposed to set up a house of study in Oxford for the benefit of the monks of St Swithin's monastery at Winchester. His decision to abandon this project in favour of something more directly linked with ideals of the Renaissance was due to the intervention of Hugh Oldham, Bishop of Exeter and a lifelong friend of Fox, who persuaded him 'that monkery had done its work', and that the new opportunities for learning which now presented themselves should be grasped.[21] Oldham, perhaps best remembered as the founder of Manchester Grammar School, was yet another member of the English bench of bishops who must be regarded as one of the pioneers of humanistic studies during this period. In the opinion of his biographer his educational work at Oxford has not received sufficient notice, and has always been regarded as ancillary to that of Richard Fox and William Smyth. Further research, however, suggests that 'he was a creative thinker and a leader rather than a follower'.[22] As a result of his friend's intervention, instead of a seminary Fox founded Corpus Christi College for which he provided the statutes in June 1517. Oldham himself contributed no less than four thousand pounds towards the venture.

The regulations laid down by Fox for the new college bear the unmistakable imprint of the Renaissance, especially those concerning the subjects which were to be included in the curriculum. In the statute entitled 'Of the Public Lecturers' it was decreed that the college should appoint three readers, one in Latin, one in Greek and one in divinity. In this explicit provision for the teaching of Greek we witness the first official recognition of the importance of the language in the university, a recognition strengthened by an appeal to the authority of the Council of Vienne. A Greek reader was to be appointed 'because the Holy Canons have established and commanded, most suitably for good letters, and Christian literature especially, that such a one should never be wanting in this University of Oxford, in like manner as in some other most famous places of learning'.[23] The reader in divinity was expected to base all his lectures on both the Old and the New Testaments and to rely for his exegesis on the Greek and Latin Fathers, rather than on Nicholas of Lyra, Hugh of Vienne and other mediaeval commentators 'who as in time, so in learning are far below them'.[24] This emphasis on the Scriptures and the early Fathers at the expense of the *Sentences* and the works of mediaeval exegetes was, as we have seen, typical of the humanist scholarship of the Renaissance.

Under the presidency of John Claymond, another exponent of the new learning and a competent Classical scholar, the college quickly drew the attention of some of the leading humanists of the day. Erasmus, writing to Claymond in 1519, refers to the interest shown by Wolsey, Henry VIII and Cardinal Campeggio in the new foundation. He predicts that it will soon be recognised throughout the world as one of the glories of Britain and that its 'trilingual library' will attract more scholars to Oxford than were formerly attracted to Rome.[25] What prompted this description of the library as 'trilingual' is not clear, since among the hundred and fifty books and manuscripts presented to the college by Fox the only Hebrew book was Reuchlin's *De rudimentis hebraicis* (Pforzheim 1506). Apart from this single volume the college possessed no Hebrew books until 1537 when Claymond made a bequest of seven Hebrew manuscripts.[26] But deserved or not, the reputation of Corpus Christi for trilingual instruction grew rapidly so that John Fisher could speak of it in 1527 as a college which was 'well endowed with teachers in Hebrew, Greek and Latin, and in whatever ministers to the true study of Theology'.[27] Again, there seems to be no basis for the claim that Hebrew was taught at the college, except in so far as the study of the language was implicit in the study of divinity. Nevertheless, it must be recognised that Fox's foundation offers evidence of a new and positive attitude towards linguistic studies on the part of some Oxford scholars.

We now turn to Cambridge. 'Cambridge humanism was still in its infancy when the Tudors came to the throne':[28] thus Roberto Weiss commenting on the lack of enthusiasm for the new learning on the part of Cambridge scholars during the latter half of the fifteenth century. The long chancellorship of John Fisher (1504–1535), however, ushered in a new era, for the influence of Fisher on the revival of letters in Cambridge was deep and lasting, first as a scholar and educational reformer himself, and second as a patron of other scholars. He matriculated in 1483, but learned neither Hebrew nor Greek until the second decade of the following century. In a letter dated 29 September 1516 Erasmus informed Reuchlin that Colet had at last, in spite of his age, started to learn Greek, and that the Bishop of Rochester was now making good progress in the language.[29] Already both More and Erasmus had tried to persuade William Latimer to teach Fisher, claiming that such an able scholar would need no more than a month's tuition to perfect his Greek. But Latimer was unwilling to accede to their request. The reasons he gives for his refusal are interesting.

Greek [he writes in his reply to Erasmus in 1517] is a complex and many-sided business, as you know, and more than a little involved; and though it is toilsome rather than difficult yet it needs time, at least until it can be got by heart. Do not think I judge other people's mental powers by my own slow pace. I am sure, and have been told so by many people, that the bishop is unusually able and capable of greater undertakings than that you now propose. You write of his willingness, and how greatly he longs to learn Greek, and from this I see clearly that he will also work very hard; and all this shows me that I can hope for as much progress as anyone could hope for from a man of considerable powers, great industry and an incredible desire to learn. But how great that progress can be in so short a space of time, I find it hard to say. You seem to hope for much; and I too think it will be much in relation to the time available, but small in absolute terms. . . . So, if you want the bishop to make progress and arrive at some results in the language, make him send to Italy for someone well versed in all this, who is also willing to stay with him long enough for him to feel himself strong and secure, so that he can not only creep along but raise himself and stand up and even go forward. In this way, it seems to me, you will do more for his future skill in the language than if, while he is lisping still and can barely utter childish cries, you abandon him like a baby in its cradle.[30]

Despite Latimer's reluctance to become Fisher's tutor, there is evidence that the bishop had made sufficient headway by his own efforts to be able to read the New Testament in Greek by the 1520s. In his *Defence of the Sacred Priesthood*, published in 1525 as a rejoinder to Luther but originally written at least two years earlier, he makes several references to the meaning of Greek words and appears to be quite familiar with the text of the New Testament in the original.[31]

When he turned his attention to Hebrew, Fisher was fortunate in finding a competent teacher in Robert Wakefield, a noted Hebraist whose contribution to the study of the language will be examined in another chapter. Although it is not known how much Wakefield actually taught him, it is clear from Fisher's own writings that he was capable of commenting on the meaning of particular Hebrew words and phrases, and that he was acquainted, to some extent, with rabbinic writings. In his *Defence of the Sacred Priesthood* he discusses at length the nature of Melchizedek's sacrifice in Genesis 14:8 and quotes several rabbinic authorities in support of his explanation. He refers to Moses Ha-Darshan, an early eleventh-century French exegete and haggadist, to Pinchas ben Jair and Simeon ben Johai, two second-century rabbis, to Rashi, Kimchi and the Targums as affirming that the sacrifice of the Messiah will be of the same substance as that of Melchizedek, namely bread and wine or a wheaten loaf.[32] But direct quotations from the rabbis are rare. The very fact that in this instance he gives a long list of authorities, some of which it would have been difficult for an inexperienced Hebraist to read, leads one to suspect that he was relying on intermediaries for his knowledge of Jewish opinion. He did, however, have his personal copy of Bomberg's Hebrew Bible and Pagninus' lexicon, both of which he bequeathed to Christ's College.

Whatever the measure of his own competence in the biblical languages, John Fisher was a firm supporter of the revival of learning. His admiration for Reuchlin and his eagerness to meet him emerge from Erasmus' correspondence, for in a letter to Reuchlin dated 27 August 1516 Erasmus writes:

No words of mine can possibly express the enthusiasm and the deep respect felt for you by that great champion of good letters and religion, the bishop of Rochester, so much so that, though he had a very high opinion of Erasmus, he now comes near to thinking nothing of him in his admiration for Reuchlin. ... He never sends me a letter (and he writes quite often) without making most honourable mention of you.... Have no hesitation in addressing a letter to him often, and Colet as well. Both of them have a very high opinion of you.[33]

During the previous year Fisher himself had written to Erasmus with reference to Reuchlin, 'If he has published any book which is not yet in our hands, pray see that it is brought to us. For I am very pleased with his erudition: I do not think there is another man alive that comes near to Giovanni Pico. ... Commend me warmly to Reuchlin, whom I should certainly visit myself, were it not for these my sacred garments'.[34] In Fisher's opinion Reuchlin surpassed all living authors in his knowledge of theology and philosophy.

Although he became Bishop of Rochester in 1505, Fisher's life was spent among books. An assiduous student himself, he was also a keen promoter of learning and an active agent for the intensified study of Latin, Greek and Hebrew. It was through Fisher's persuasion that Erasmus became the first teacher (though not professor) of Greek at Cambridge in 1511, a post in which he was succeeded by Richard Croke, another protégé of the bishop. When he was elected Vice-Chancellor of the university in 1501 Cambridge was impoverished through lack of wealthy patrons, but Fisher did much to remedy the situation by persuading the Lady Margaret Beaufort, Countess of Richmond, to become a benefactor. On his advice she founded the professorship of divinity in 1503, made large bequests to the university and played a prominent part in founding Christ's College. Although she intended to give the rest of her charities to the monastery at Westminster, on the presumption that she had done enough for educational institutions, she was dissuaded from doing so by Fisher who pointed out to her that the abbey was wealthy enough but that places of learning were still in need of financial support. She changed her mind and provided for the foundation of St John's College, Cambridge, on 9 April 1511.

The statutes of St John's, which were first drawn up by Fisher himself in 1516 and revised in 1524 and 1530, give a prominent place to the study of Hebrew in the curriculum. Under the first statutes, in a chapter entitled 'De sociorum exercitamento scholastico', he recommended that some students should study both Greek and Hebrew.[35] Eight years later, in a revision of the statutes based on those provided by Bishop Fox for Corpus Christi College, Fisher again emphasised the importance of the study of the three languages, and even decreed that fellows and scholars were to converse in Latin, Greek or Hebrew except when they were in their own rooms or celebrating a major feast.[36] But despite his stringency, trilingual studies at St John's do not seem to have flourished, for in 1530 he complained of the past neglect of Hebrew and Greek and instituted two lectureships at the college, one in Greek for the benefit of the younger students, and the other in Hebrew for the seniors. A salary of £3 and £5 per annum was decreed respectively to the two lecturers in the hope of better results.[37]

The founding of St John's College was without doubt Fisher's chief contribution to the study of the biblical languages during the early decades of the sixteenth century. As a theologian he could see the absolute necessity of Hebrew and Greek for a proper study of the Bible and the Fathers. In this he was both a Renaissance figure and a Christian humanist. But Fisher not only realised the importance of Hebrew for a proper understanding of the biblical message, he also took positive steps to place the language on an academic footing and to offer English students the opportunity to learn it.

The pattern of trilingual studies which began to emerge in England under the guidance of men like Fisher and Fox had been foreshadowed on the continent of Europe. The first attempt at establishing a college where the three languages could be studied on an equal footing was made in March 1498 when Francisco Ximénez de Cisneros, Cardinal Archbishop of Toledo and Provincial of the Franciscans in Castile, laid the foundation stone of the College of San Ildefonso at Alcalá de Henares a few miles north-east of Madrid. Ximénez, who was passionately concerned with the reformation of the Church, intended the new university to play a prominent part in ecclesiastical renewal, both as a centre of biblical scholarship and as a seminary for the Spanish clergy.[38] Like his English contemporaries he believed that the study of the Bible and the early Fathers was the *sine qua non* of any course in theology, but he also realised the difficulties which faced any serious student of the Scriptures on account of the poor state of the Vulgate. To change or correct the text itself would have been an insult to the memory of Jerome, so Ximénez decided to reproduce the ancient versions side by side in what eventually became known as the Complutensian Polyglot edition of the Bible. But if he was to achieve his aim he needed scholars who were able to read the Bible in the original Hebrew and Greek. It was his intention that Alcalá should supply such scholars, and four years after the university was officially opened in 1508 Alfonso de Zamora was appointed the first professor of Hebrew. A convert from Judaism, Alfonso received his education at Zamora, a noted centre of Jewish learning in northern Spain where his father had been a rabbi. Steeped as he was in the Hebrew language and in traditional Jewish exegesis, Alfonso was able not only to read the Old Testament in the original but also to utilise the works of the mediaeval rabbis and bring their comments and explanations to bear on Christian biblical study in his native Spain. A master of the grammatical and lexicographical learning of the Kimchis, he was instrumental in adapting it to Catholic exegesis. In order to promote his cause he translated several Hebrew works into Latin, and during the years he spent at Alcalá he made the university a recognised centre of Hebraic studies.[39]

The drive to establish Hebrew as a respectable and recognised subject among Christian scholars was given further impetus by Jerome Busleiden who endowed the University of Louvain, the educational centre of the Netherlands, with the most famous of its institutions, the Collegium Trilingue.[40] Although Busleiden himself died long before the actual inauguration of the college in October 1520, his intentions were faithfully carried out by Erasmus, who in a letter to John Lascar in 1518 set out his plans for the kind of teaching which he envisaged for the students enrolled at the new foundation. 'Free and public instruction is to be given in the three tongues, Hebrew, Greek and Latin, in return for a substantial salary of about seventy ducats, which can, however, be increased according to the person appointed. The Hebrew teacher is already in residence, and so is the Latin. For the Greek chair there are a number of candidates'.[41] The professor of Hebrew mentioned here was Matthew Adrianus, another convert from Judaism who had already taught in Italy and Germany, and was, according to Erasmus in a letter to Capito, 'an accomplished Hebraist and successful in all that he has done'.[42] Adrianus was one of the first Christian scholars to draw up a systematic course of instruction in Hebrew, and Louvain must be credited with providing all other universities with an example of what could be done to promote Hebraic studies. The college was Erasmus' attempt to put his theories into practice and to make the three languages an integral part of a course in theology. It was through his constant encouragement that the venture succeeded.

At the royal court

Not everyone shared the enthusiasm of these English educational reformers for the new learning, and in some circles the emphasis on biblical and linguistic study was causing alarm. As we have already noted in the case of Reuchlin, the Church as a whole was not prepared for the great changes that were to take place as a result of the Renaissance. Her apologetics were out of date and incapable of countering the attacks of the biblical critics. Indeed, the aversion to learning Greek was so strong in some quarters that 'Beware of the Greeks lest you become a heretic' had become a popular tag among obscurantists. In 1530 Tyndale could ask More whether or not he remembered 'how within this thirty years and far less, and even unto this day, the old barking curs, Dun's disciples, and like draff called Scotists, the children of darkness, raged in every pulpit against Greek, Latin and Hebrew'.[43] Even as late as 1555, John Cheke the first Regius Professor of Greek at Cambridge commented in a letter to Stephen Gardiner, Bishop of Winchester, that Hebrew still had its detractors; to study it would almost certainly undermine one's scholarly reputation.[44] These opponents of the new learning were not confined to the ranks of itinerant friars and popular preachers; they were to be found also in academic circles. Resistance came not only from unlettered clergy but also from men who might have been expected to welcome the revival of letters. The contention of some of those engaged in teaching and scholarly pursuits was that the new learning was detrimental to religion and should on no account be permitted in the universities. It was not for nothing that Bishop Fox appealed to one of the canons of a Council of the Church in order to sanction his introduction of Greek into the university curriculum. He did so because he realised that he would face the virulent opposition of those who regarded the promoters of the new learning as agitators. Reference to a two hundred year old decree promulgated by the authorities was calculated to silence, if not convince, the most intransigent antagonists, and made the official introduction of Greek at Oxford appear to be an act of ecclesiastical obedience.

But, granted that there was opposition, effective and extensive resistance to the educational ideals of the humanists was prevented, not only by the persistence of men like Fisher and Fox, but also by the positive attitude to the revival of letters adopted by the royal court. Even if there is some basis for the claim that Henry VIII 'inherited none of his grandmother's interest in higher education' and as a result 'gave no more than conventional patronage to any scholar',[45] there can be no denying that he was a learned man or that his court numbered among its members those who were anxious to promote the educational aims of John Colet and his circle. Perhaps it is of some significance with regard to the recognition of Hebrew that in 1545, on the tenth anniversary of his becoming supreme head of the Church, he struck a commemorative medal inscribed in Latin, Greek and Hebrew. Two years later Edward VI followed his father's example by producing two coronation medals bearing Hebrew inscriptions.[46] The goodwill of the sovereign and of those who moved in courtly circles was crucial, for if the study of the biblical languages was to flourish in England it had to find greater support among influential statesmen and ecclesiastics than it had found hitherto. Such support was forthcoming in the persons of Tunstall, More, Pace, Warham and Wolsey.

Cuthbert Tunstall, bishop successively of London (1522) and Durham (1530), spent most of his life in diplomatic circles. Educated at both Oxford and Cambridge during the final decade of the fifteenth century, he continued his studies in Italy, spending six years at the English College in Padua where he became a friend of Jerome Busleiden and made the acquaintance of Lefèvre d'Etaples. On his return to England he became closely associated with More and Erasmus, both of whom had a high opinion of his scholarship. Thomas Stapleton in his *Life* of More (1588) states that 'More's most intimate friendship was with Tunstall. Him More could never extol highly enough: of his company he was never tired: in his letters, his wit, his judgement, his virtues, his piety, he took inexpressible delight. In the epitaph which More composed for himself he speaks thus of Tunstall: "In the whole world could scarcely be found one more learned, more wise, more virtuous than he" '.[47] Erasmus, in reply to Latimer's suggestion that a capable Italian ought to be employed to teach Fisher Greek, claimed that if a man could have Linacre and Tunstall as teachers of the Classical languages he would have no need of anyone from Italy.[48] According to Godwin, Tunstall was little short of a polymath, 'A very good Grecian, well seen in the Hebrew tongue, a very eloquent rhetorician, a passing skilful mathematician, . . . a great lawyer, . . . and a profound divine, a man whose equal in learning, wisdom, and virtue is seldom seen in the world today'.[49] Exaggerated praise perhaps, but it is of interest inasmuch as it comments on his knowledge of Hebrew which he presumably gained in Italy.

But the bishop was not only a competent scholar in his own right, he was also a generous benefactor and patron to whom those actively engaged in any branch of Renaissance learning could turn for help. Polydore Vergil, the author of a critical history of England, owed much to Tunstall, whom he described as 'the best of bishops' who contributed 'so much and so constantly to the advancement of learning'.[50] Although he seems at times to have been excessively cautious for the age in which he lived, Tunstall sided with other Catholic reformers in his desire to educate the clergy and in his distrust of zeal without knowledge.[51] Despite the fact that he consigned Tyndale's English New Testament to the fire, he was one of the chief patrons of Erasmus' *Novum instrumentum*, and it is recorded that he presented a copy of the Complutensian Polyglot Bible to Cambridge University Library in 1528. Conservative by instinct, he could nevertheless see the significance and value of the revival of learning and, inasmuch as it did not threaten the unity of Christendom, he gave it his sympathetic support.

Although Thomas More, unlike most of his contemporaries, never visited Italy he studied under those who had been there, and as a result became familiar with the teachings of the Italian humanists. At an early age he was attracted to Giovanni Pico whose life and ideals had a profound influence on him.[52] Introduced to Pico's writings by Colet, More translated his biography, together with a selection of his works and letters, from the original Latin into English. Though the area of agreement between them on certain intellectual matters may have been small, More was so impressed by Pico's fervour and his attachment to orthodox Christianity that he adopted him as his ideal of Christian life in the world. In the words of Stapleton, 'He determined . . . to put before his eyes the example of some prominent layman, on which he might model his life. He called to mind all who at that period, either at home or abroad, enjoyed the reputation of learning and piety, and finally fixed upon John Pico, Earl of Mirandula, who was renowned in the highest degree throughout the whole of Europe for his encyclopedic knowledge, and no less esteemed for his sanctity of life'.[53] By choosing to make a thorough study of Pico's life and writings More declared his support of the new learning and made it clear that he took Colet's side against those who opposed him. In the biography, written by Pico's nephew, he read of the Italian scholar's search for truth in the pages of the Bible, his indefatigable study of the original languages, and through them, of the Scriptures.[54] Writing to a friend, who had urged him to abandon his contemplative and studious life, Pico mentions the pleasure he has in his books and claims that he is currently studying Hebrew, Aramaic and Arabic.[55] In an exposition of Psalm 16, which More in his anthology placed between the biography and the letters, Pico seeks to demonstrate how his knowledge of Hebrew helps him to understand the meaning of the text.[56] By the time he had completed his translations More was quickly becoming a firm adherent of Christian humanism with great veneration for Giovanni Pico.

Further evidence of More's positive attitude towards the revival of letters may be gleaned from his correspondence. Writing to Martin Dorp in 1515 he speaks with approval of Reuchlin and defends him vigorously against his many opponents: 'Good heavens, what a man! Extremely learned, prudent, and honest, while his rivals, utterly ignorant, stupid and worthless liars, attacked him with such monstrous injustice that had he revenged himself with his fists, it would have seemed proper to pardon him'.[57] In a letter addressed to the Vice-Chancellor and proctors of Oxford in March 1518 he pleads for an enlightened and tolerant attitude on the part of the university authorities towards the new learning. He had heard that many senior and junior members were violently opposed to the introduction of Greek into the curriculum and that the more conservative students had formed a Trojan Society with the intention of making their protest more effective. The matter had caused much comment, and fuel had been added to the fire by an academic who had 'chosen during Lent to babble in a sermon against not only Greek but Roman literature, and finally against all polite learning, liberally berating all the liberal arts'.[58] More castigates such crass ignorance and is adamant that more than a knowledge of English is required for the study of Theology. Referring to the preacher he writes:

This fellow declares than only theology should be studied; but if he admits even that, I don't see how he can accomplish his aim without some knowledge of languages, whether Hebrew or Greek or Latin; unless, of course, the elegant gentleman has convinced himself that there is enough theology written in English or that all theology can be squeezed into the limits of those (late scholastic) "questions" which he likes to pose and answer, for which a modicum of Latin would, I admit, suffice. But really, I cannot admit that theology, that august queen of heaven, can be thus confined. Does she not dwell and abide in Holy Scripture? Does she not pursue her pilgrim way through the cells of the Holy Fathers: Augustine and Jerome; Ambrose and Cyprian; Chrysostom, Gregory, Basil, and their like? . . . Anyone who boasts that he can understand the works of the Fathers without an uncommon acquaintance with the languages of each and all of them will in his ignorance boast for a long time before the learned trust his judgement.[59]

He then contrasts the situation at Cambridge where 'those who are *not* studying Greek are so moved by common interest in their university that they are actually making large individual contributions to the salary of the Greek professor', and concludes by enlisting royal and ecclesiastical support for the proposed reform. The whole letter is typical of the humanistic critique of a society dominated by obscurantist churchmen and is written in the same vein as his defence of Erasmus whose work was being criticised by members of the religious orders. In a lengthy letter to a monk who had attacked Erasmus' edition of the Greek New Testament, More cites with approval the example of the early Fathers who wrote in Greek, and in particular of Jerome who applied himself diligently to the study of Hebrew.[60]

In spite of his insistence on the importance of mastering the original languages and his admiration for those who had done so, More does not appear to have learned Hebrew. In a busy life, he lacked the time, and perhaps even the appetite, since for the Christian the Old Testament was of far less importance than the New. However, he does go beyond the Vulgate, not only to the Septuagint, but also to the Hebrew original whenever he has 'a trusty guide'.[61] The 'guides' on whom he depended for his interpretation of the Scriptures were the early Church Fathers, whose opinions he would have found summarised in the *Glossa ordinaria* and in the writings of Nicholas of Lyra. The latter's commentaries were intoned in More's house at lunchtime each day.[62] Although Nicholas' *Postillae* would have acquainted him with the writings of Mediaeval Jewish exegetes and demonstrated the value of their comments for a clearer understanding of the literal meaning of the Old Testament, it is almost certain that More would not have known any Jews personally. In his *Dialogue Concerning Heresies* he tells us that it is on the authority of others, possibly Italian correspondents, that he has learned of the great respect the Jews had for their Bible and of the way in which they read it.[63]

For most of his life Thomas More gave the new learning his whole-hearted and powerful support. After his appointment as one of Henry VIII's councillors in 1517 he appears as the connecting link between the court and the university, fostering the desire for learning in circles where hitherto it had received but scant recognition, and exerting considerable influence on the king in educational matters. Erasmus, in a letter to Mosellanus, claims that as a result of More's criticism of the authorities at Oxford for refusing to provide for instruction in Greek, the king himself 'gave orders that those wishing and approving it should embrace Greek letters'.[64] That John Fisher recognised More's standing at the royal court is obvious from the appeal he makes to him on behalf of a Cambridge student who was in need of financial assistance:

I beg that through your good offices with our Most Gracious King, we at Cambridge may have some hope that our young men may receive encouragement to learning from the bounty of so noble a Prince. We have very few friends at Court who have the will and the power to commend our interest to the King's Majesty, and among them we reckon you the chief; for hitherto, even when you were of lower rank, you have always shown the greatest favour to us. We rejoice that now you are raised to the dignity of Knighthood and become so intimate with the King, and we offer you our heartiest congratulations, for we know that you will continue to show us the same favour. Please now give your help to this young man, who is well versed in theology, and a zealous preacher to the people. He puts his hopes in your influence with our noble King and in your willingness to accept my recommendation.[65]

The Bishop of Rochester is not disappointed, for More replies that the king is prepared to support the student by giving him a prebend, and adds that whatever influence he has with Henry is as freely available to Fisher or his scholar as a house is to its owner.[66]

But in spite of his tireless campaign for the advancement of humanistic studies in England More, like Tunstall, was above all else loyal to the Church of Rome. During the three year period of his chancellorship of the realm (1529–1532) he made every effort to keep the religion of England Catholic and to stem the growth of Protestantism. He objected to Tyndale's English translation of the Scriptures, not because he was opposed to translations in principle, but because the version had not been approved by the Church; a new translation could signify a break with tradition, and this More would not sanction. His dedication to Roman Catholicism has appeared to some Protestant historians as an eventual retreat from the humanism he once espoused. 'More,' writes W. A. Clebsch, 'once the friend of foreign humanists and leader of the new learning at home, found himself pressed by events to turn against the very enlightenment for which he had laboured. . . . His writings from 1529 until his death evidence a drift and then a march from the ideal of *libertas humanitatis* towards the ideal of personal and intellectual security on the bosom of Mother Church.'[67] Whatever his views during the final years of his life, there can be no doubt that More's patronage of letters while he was a member of the king's council was an important factor in the gradual acceptance of Hebrew and Greek as subjects worthy of inclusion in the university curriculum.

More's close friend and colleague was Richard Pace, cleric and diplomat, and one of the few English Renaissance humanists who was actually proficient in Hebrew. Pace owed much of his success as a diplomat and his recognition as a scholar to his patron and mentor Thomas Langton, Bishop of Winchester. Langton, who had been among the many English travellers to Italy during the second half of the fifteenth century, appointed the young Pace as his secretary, but recognising his academic ability sent him to Italy in 1498 to complete his education. In an essay on the benefits of a liberal education written in 1517 Pace records his debt to the bishop:

When I was a page in his household, Thomas Langton . . . noted that I was talented in music far beyond my years . . . and said, "The boy's bright; he was born for greater things". A few days later, he sent me to Italy to study liberal arts at the University of Padua, which was then in its prime, and kindly paid the expenses since he encouraged all learning and acted the part of another Mycenas for his age.[68]

Pace stayed on in Italy and spent several years at different universities obtaining a thorough grounding in the humanities and becoming acquainted with those who were in the forefront of Renaissance scholarship. At Padua his teachers included Cuthbert Tunstall and William Latimer and he soon made a name for himself as an able promoter of the new learning. He had been in close touch with many foreign humanists who had consulted him and taken his advice on the work in which they were engaged. He was admired and respected by them.[69]

In a long and brilliant career as royal secretary and foreign emissary Pace found time to pursue and support linguistic studies. In 1504 he is reported to have made an oration in Venice in favour of learning Greek. His ability had so impressed Erasmus that he referred to him in a letter to Mountjoy in 1508 as 'a young man so well versed in knowledge of Greek and Latin letters that his intellect would enable him unaided to bring fame to the whole of England'.[70] In April 1520 his skill in languages was officially recognised when he was invited to become lecturer in Greek at Cambridge, but he declined to take up the post. Testimony to his knowledge of Hebrew comes from Gasparo Spinelli, secretary to the Venetian ambassador in London, who had visited Pace at the monastery of Syon where he had retired through ill health. Writing to his brother on 30 July 1527 Spinelli says:

I went to Sion to visit the Reverend Richard Pace who leads a blessed life in that beautiful place. . . . He has rendered himself an excellent Hebrew and Chaldean scholar, and now, through his knowledge of those languages, has commenced correcting the *Old Testament*, in which, as likewise in the *Psalms*, he found a stupendous amount of errors. He has also corrected the whole of *Ecclesiastes*, and in a few days will publish them. He is now occupied with the *Prophets*, and the book will assuredly prove most meritorious, and render him immortal. When the first part is printed I will endeavour to obtain it.[71]

Despite Spinelli's promise that Pace's work would soon appear in print the only published evidence of his interest in the Old Testament is an Introduction to the text of Ecclesiastes.[72] The existence of this preface suggests that a larger work was forthcoming. His intention was to discover the correct meaning of Ecclesiastes by comparing four independent versions of the text, namely the Hebrew, Vulgate, Septuagint and a Hebrew translation of the Septuagint. He claims in the preface that a similar treatment of Job was already complete, and, as Spinelli states, he was planning to go through the entire Old Testament in the same way. He makes a strong plea to all students of the Bible to go to 'the most pure sources' of the Hebrew original. There are a few references to the works of Kimchi, and at one point he criticises the Vulgate for mistranslating the Hebrew abstract noun *yeshu'ah* as a proper noun. Apart from Spinelli's letter we have also Robert Wakefield's claim, made in April 1524, that he had taught Pace Hebrew, Arabic and Aramaic all within a period of three months, and Wegg points to the fact that he had made a translation of the Psalms from the original in 1525.[73] There can be no doubt that Pace was well versed in Hebrew long before he retired from a busy public life, but at Syon he had the leisure to perfect his knowledge of it.

In 1505 the chancellorship of the University of Oxford was given to William Warham, Archbishop of Canterbury, who continued in office for an unprecedented term of twenty-six years. Warham was firmly committed to the humanist cause. Like many of his brother bishops he was a recognised supporter of the new learning and someone in whom the leading English scholars of the day found a protector and patron.[74] Linacre, Grocyn, William Latimer and Colet all owed their ecclesiastical preferment to him, and Erasmus, whose life work would have been impossible without the support of wealthy patrons, was especially grateful to him for financial help during his stay in England. In a letter sent to Antoon van Bergen in February 1512 he writes:

If you have any desire to hear how I am, your Erasmus is now almost entirely transformed into an Englishman, so extremely kind have many persons been to me, including especially the Archbishop of Canterbury. . . . Great heavens, how well-endowed and fertile his mind is! What skill he shows in the conduct of highly important business and how distinguished his scholarship! At the same time his demeanour towards everyone is uniquely affable; he has the pleasantest manner in the world towards those he meets, so that he never leaves anyone depressed in spirit on departing, which is a truly royal trait. Besides, his generosity is lavish and prompt; and lastly, for all the eminence of his station and his rank, he has not a trace of arrogance, so that he gives the impression of being the only person who is unaware of his greatness. No one stands up for his friends more loyally or more stoutly. In a word, he is the primate indeed, not only in rank, but in all praiseworthy qualities. When I have him on my side, ought I not to consider myself exceptionally lucky, even if that were all?[75]

It is unfortunate that Warham, like several other prominent humanists, left no writings by which his scholarship could be judged, but a perusal of the bequest of almost a hundred theological books which he made to All Souls College indicates a lively interest in humanistic studies.[76]

Although Warham held the office of Chancellor of Oxford for over a quarter of a century, from about 1515 onwards his influence in the university was secondary to that of Thomas Wolsey, the Cardinal Archbishop of York. Whereas Wolsey, unlike Warham, could make no claim to scholarship, he was widely recognised as a competent educator and as a patron of letters. He had no hesitation in harnessing the new learning to the service of the state, and made a determined effort to reform the process of education in both school and university. In his native Ipswich he founded a grammar school to prepare boys for further academic training or for a possible career in the service of the king. It was in this connection that he published his *Rudimenta grammatices* (1529), a manual of instruction in the technique of education intended for those who were to teach at his school. It is perhaps significant that the only book he ever wrote was concerned with teaching methods, a prime example of his practical approach to educational matters. As a benefactor Wolsey was generous. At no expense to the university he established seven public lectureships at Oxford, one of which was in Greek. In 1525, spurred on almost certainly by the example of Richard Fox, he founded Cardinal College to which he brought a group of Cambridge graduates 'scholars of ripe wits and abilities', with the express intention of promoting the spread of humanist learning. His munificence is recognised by the Spanish scholar Juan Luis Vives who was appointed by Wolsey to a university lectureship in rhetoric at Oxford in 1523. Vives claims that the Cardinal was a man from whom he had 'never come away empty-handed and whose kindness and goodwill to students are incredible'.[77] In *The Benefit of a Liberal Education* Richard Pace reminds English students of Wolsey's 'love for all learned men'. 'He patronises them so admirably that he seems to have no greater care than to advance them to high places. And he deserves the best from these men, for he values learning so much that he thinks nothing should be preferred to it.'[78]

Although he declined an invitation by the University of Cambridge in 1514 to become its Chancellor, Wolsey did accede to the request made by Oxford four years later to reform its statutes. His reformation, if it was actually carried out, had no perceptible impact, but the very fact that the authorities invited him to help them suggests that he was regarded as an educational reformer. While his influence with Henry VIII lasted, the cause of higher learning had a powerful advocate at the royal court in the person of Thomas Wolsey.[79]

It seems justifiable to conclude that these early English humanists are to be credited with providing their contemporaries with the intellectual climate in which Hebrew studies could begin to flourish. Though they did not share the enthusiasm of Pico and Reuchlin for the Kabbalah and other post-biblical Jewish writings, many of them were influenced by these two prominent continental scholars and saw clearly the significance of the Hebrew language for a proper understanding of the Old Testament. It must be recognised, however, that their prevailing concern was not with the revival of learning *per se*, but with the reform of the Church, which they tried to bring about by raising the educational standards of the clergy. Education was considered to be the panacea for every ecclesiastical malady, with the result that the reform of the university had to precede the reform of the Church. Thus the primary motive for promoting the study of the biblical languages on the eve of the Reformation in England was the renewal of the Christian life. Because these Catholic reformers were convinced that the Church could be purged of its abuses only by the methodical study of the Bible in the spirit of Savonarola, they urged teachers and preachers to strive for an informed piety by becoming well-versed in the Scriptures. To this end the English Reuchlinists introduced a new technique of biblical interpretation based on the study of the original texts and stressed the philological basis of exegesis. They put their theories into practice, not necessarily by becoming proficient linguists themselves, but by securing the patronage of the royal court for the new learning and by providing for the study of Hebrew and Greek at the universities on the pattern of the trilingual colleges at Alcalá and Louvain. Although such sweeping reforms of a well established educational system did not go unopposed, it is difficult to believe that the resistance to change was either effective or deep rooted. Higher learning had friends on the bench of bishops and at the court, men of influence and vision who were anxious to promote educational reform and secure a place for the study of the biblical languages in the university curriculum. It was through the combined efforts of scholar and patron that Hebrew was rediscovered in sixteenth-century England.

Notes

1   *The English Traveller to Italy*, Rome 1954, vol. I, pp. 490ff. See also L. Einstein, *The Italian Renaissance in England*, New York 1902 (reprinted 1970); A. Hyma, 'The origins of English humanism', *Huntington Lib. Qtly.*, vol. IV, No. 1, 1940, pp. 1ff.
2   J. K. McConica, *English Humanists and Reformation Politics*, Oxford 1961, p. 74.
3   *Epistolae Obscurorum Virorum*, p. xxxviii.
4   *CWE*, vol. 4, Letter 471, p. 85.
5   *Humanism in England during the Fifteenth Century*, 3rd ed. Oxford 1967, ch. 12.
6   *CWE*, vol. 1, Letter 118, p. 235; Huizinga, *Erasmus of Rotterdam*, Eng. trans. by F. Hopman, New York 1924 (reprinted London 1952), p. 30. See also C. A. L. Jarrott, 'Erasmus' biblical humanism', *Studies in the*

Renaissance, vol. 17, 1970, pp. 119ff.

7   'John Colet of Cambridge', *Archiv für Reformationsgeschichte*, vol. 65, 1974, pp. 6ff. If the author is correct in regarding fifteenth-century Cambridge as providing the source and stimulus for Colet's biblical lectures, his thesis points to the need for a re-evaluation of the view that Cambridge lagged far behind Oxford as a centre of English humanism.

8   F. Seebohm, *The Oxford Reformers of 1498*, 3rd ed. London 1896, p. 17.

9   S. Jayne, *John Colet and Marsilio Ficino*, Oxford 1963, p. 20.

10   For Colet's general attitude to the new learning and his knowledge and use of Patristics see P. A. Duhamel, 'The Oxford lectures of John Colet', *JHI*, vol. 14, No. 4, 1953, p. 498. Also L. Miles, 'John Colet: an appreciation', *Moreana*, vol. 6, No. 23, 1969, pp. 5ff.

11   E. H. Harbison, *The Christian Scholar in the Age of the Reformation*, New York 1956, p. 70.

12   *CWE*, vol. 3, Letter 423, pp. 311ff.

13   *Letters to Radulphus on the Mosaic Account of Creation together with Other Treatises*, Eng. trans. with intro. and notes by J. H. Lupton, London 1876 (reprinted by Gregg International, 2nd impr. 1968), Letter I, p. 3.

14   See C. G. Nauert Jr., *Agrippa and the Crisis of Renaissance Thought*, Urbana, Ill. 1965, ch. 6.

15   'Expostulatio contra Catilinetum' *Operum Pars Posterior*, Lugdunum, n.d., p. 494, 'contorqueam sacras literas ad artes haereticas et thalmuth Iudaeorum'. *Ibid.*, 'nec mors nec vita separabit me a fide Christi, Christianosque doctores omnibus praefero, tamen Iudaeorum rabinos non contemno'.

16   C. G. Nauert Jr., *op. cit.*, p. 31.

17   J. H. Lupton, *The Life of John Colet D.D.*, 2nd ed. London 1909, p. 225. See also *CWE*, vol. 4, Letter 593, p. 398.

18   *Two Treatises on the Hierarchies of Dionysius*, Eng. trans. with intro. and notes by J. H. Lupton, London 1869 (reprinted by Gregg International, 2nd impr. 1968), pp. 111f.

19   C. Zika, *op. cit.*, *Journal of Religious History*, vol. 9, 1977, p. 243.

20   H. W. Charless Davis, *A History of Balliol College*, 2nd ed. Davis and Hunt, Oxford 1963, p. 58.

21   *Letters of Richard Fox 1486–1527*, ed. P. S. and H. M. Allen, Oxford 1929, p. xiv. For a full account of the part played by Oldham see R. Holinshed, *Chronicles of England, Scotland and Ireland*, London 1808, vol. III, pp. 839–40.

22   A. A. Mumford, *Hugh Oldham 1452(?)–1519*, London 1936, p. 105.

23   *The Foundation Statutes of Bishop Fox for Corpus Christi College in the University of Oxford*, Eng. trans. with a life of the founder by G. R. M. Ward, London 1843, p. 101.

24   *Ibid.*, p. 104.

25   *Opus Epistolarum*, vol. III, Letter 990, p. 620.

26   Listed by H. O. Coxe, *Catalogus Codicum MSS qui in Colegiis Aulisque Oxoniensibus*, Oxford 1852, Part II, Nos. V–X.

27 Preface to *De veritate corporis et sanguinis Christi in eucharista*, Cologne 1527.

28 *Humanism in England during the Fifteenth Century*, p. 164.

29 *CWE*, vol. 4, Letter 471, p. 87.

30 *CWE*, vol. 4, Letter 520, pp. 201f.

31 See Eng. trans. by P. E. Hallett, London 1935, pp. 46, 50, 62, 80, 105.

32 *Ibid.*, pp. 70ff. For a full discussion of Fisher's knowledge and use of Greek and Hebrew see E. Surtz, *The Works and Days of John Fisher*, Cambridge, Mass. 1967, ch. VIII.

33 *CWE*, vol. 4, Letter 457, p. 55.

34 J. Rouschausse, *Erasmus and Fisher: their Correspondence 1511–1524*, Paris 1968, Letter 3, p. 45.

35 J. E. B. Mayor, *Early Statutes of St. John's College, Cambridge*, Cambridge 1859, p. 375.

36 *Ibid.*, p. 313.

37 *Ibid.*, p. 250.

38 For the reforms undertaken by Ximénez see M. Bataillon, *Erasme et l'Espagne*, Paris 1937, pp. 1–82; B. Hall, 'The Trilingual College of San Ildefonso and the making of the Complutensian Polyglot Bible', *Studies in Church History*, ed. G. J. Cuming, Leiden 1969, vol. 5, pp. 114ff.

39 See further F. Pérez Castro, *El Manuscrito Apologetico de Alfonso de Zamora*, Madrid, 1950, pp. xxviiiff. Though the teaching of Hebrew was introduced with the appointment of Zamora, a fully trilingual college was not set up at Alcalá until 1528, see D. Benito Hernando y Espinosa, 'Cisneros y la fundación de la universidade de Alcalá', in *Boletin de la Institución libre de Enseñanza*, 31 December 1898, p. 358. J. von Hefele, *Life and Times of Cardinal Ximénez*, Eng. trans. J. Dalton, London 1885, refers to a College of the Three Languages which had thirty students and was dedicated to St Jerome. He quotes as his authority E. de Robles, *Compendio de la Vida y Hazañas del Cardenal Fray Francisco Ximénez de Cisneros*, Toldeo 1604.

40 See H. de Vocht, *Jerome Busleyden, Founder of the Louvain Collegium Trilingue: his life and writings*, Turnhout 1950, p. 91.

41 *CWE*, vol. 5, Letter 836, pp. 413f.

42 *Opus Epistolarum*, vol. III, Letter 877, p. 416, 'Hebreus triumphat, et nihil illi non succedit'. See further H. de Vocht, *History of the Foundation and the Rise of the Collegium Trilingue Lovaniense 1517–1550*, Louvain 1951–55, Part I, p. 369.

43 *An Answer to Sir Thomas More's Dialogue*, Parker Soc. 1885, p. 75.

44 *De pronunciatione graecae*, Basle 1555, p. 47.

45 This is the view of J. J. Scarisbrick, *Henry VIII*, London 1968, p. 516. Contrast that of E. M. G. Routh, *Sir Thomas More and his Friends 1477–1535*, London 1934, p. 89: 'At this period of his reign (1517–18), King Henry VIII delighted to surround himself with men of note and learning; Humanist scholars found a cordial welcome from him and from the Queen'. Even at a later date it is difficult to believe that the founder of Christ Church, Oxford and Trinity College, Cambridge had no interest whatever in higher education.

46 See E. Hawkins, A. W. Franks and H. A. Grueber, *Medallic Illustrations of the History of Great Britain and Ireland*, London 1885, (reprinted 1969), vol. I, pp. 48ff. Also S. Singer, 'Jews and coronations', *TJHSE*, vol. V, 1902–05, pp. 113ff.

47 *The Life and Illustrious Martyrdom of Sir Thomas More*, Douai 1588, Eng. trans. by P. E. Hallett, London 1928, edited and annotated by E. E. Reynolds, London 1966, p. 44.

48 *CWE*, vol. 4, Letter 540, p. 259. In another letter he claims that Tunstall is 'as good a scholar in the humanities as anyone we have'. *CWE*, vol. 3, Letter 388, p. 235.

49 *A Catalogue of the Bishops of England*, London 1615, p. 669.

50 Quoted in translation by C. Sturge, *Cuthbert Tunstal: Churchman, Scholar, Statesman, Administrator*, London 1938, p. 28. See also D. Hay, *Polydore Vergil: Renaissance Historian and Man of Letters*, Oxford 1952, p. 30.

51 Sturge, *op. cit.*, ch. 28.

52 V. Gabrieli, 'Giovanni Pico and Thomas More', *Moreana*, vol. 4, No. 15, 1967, pp. 46f.

53 *The Life . . . of Sir Thomas More*, p. 9. For a critique of the view that More saw in Pico the ideal layman see B. Basset, *Born for Friendship: the Spirit of Sir Thomas More*, London 1965, p. 57.

54 *The English Works of Sir Thomas More*, ed. W. E. Campbell, London 1931, vol. I, pp. 347ff.

55 *Ibid.*, p. 370.

56 *Ibid.*, p. 377.

57 *St. Thomas More: Selected Letters*, ed. E. F. Rogers, New Haven, Conn. 1961, p. 61.

58 *Ibid.*, p. 97.

59 *Ibid.*, p. 99.

60 *The Correspondence of Sir Thomas More*, ed. E. F. Rogers, Princeton, N.J. 1947, p. 173.

61 G. Marc'Hadour, *The Bible in the Works of St. Thomas More*, Nieuwkoop 1971, Part IV, p. 37.

62 R. W. Chambers, *Thomas More*, London, 1935, p. 170. On More's use of the works of the Fathers see R. C. Marius, 'Thomas More and the early Church Fathers', *Traditio*, vol. 24, 1968, pp. 379ff.

63 *The Workes of Sir Thomas More*, London 1557, p. 246c.

64 *Opus Epistolarum*, vol. III, Letter 948, p. 547, 'At Rex, ut non indoctus ipse, ita bonis literis favens, qui tum forte in propinquo erat, re per Morum et Paceum cognita, denunciavit ut volentes ac lubentes Graecanicam literaturam amplecterentur. Ita rabulis illis impositum est silentium'.

65 Stapleton, *The Life . . . of Sir Thomas More*, pp. 43f.

66 *Ibid.*, p. 44.

67 *England's Earliest Protestants 1520–1535*, New Haven, Conn. 1964, pp. 299f. See also H. A. Enno van Gelder, *The Two Reformations of the Sixteenth Century*, Netherlands 1961, p. 175.

68 *De fructu qui ex doctrina percipitur* (*The Benefit of a Liberal*

Education), ed. and trans. by F. Manley and R. S. Sylvester (Renaissance Texts Series, II), New York 1967, p. 39.

69 See J. Wegg, *Richard Pace: a Tudor Diplomatist*, London 1932 (reprinted 1971), p. 117.

70 *CWE*, vol. 2, Letter 211, pp. 141f.

71 *Calendar of State Papers and Manuscripts relating to English Affairs existing in the Archives and Collections of Venice*, ed. Rawdon Brown, London 1871, vol. IV, p. 78.

72 *Praefatio*, Ḍ. Ricardi Pacei in Ecclesiasten recognitum ad Hebraicam veritatem, et collatum cum translatione lxx interpretum et manifesta explicatione causarum ubicunque incidit, R. Pynson, (?) 1526.

73 See R. Wakefield, *Oratio de laudibus et utilitate trium linguarum Arabicae, Hebraicae, Chaldaicae*, W. de Worde, 1529, sig. Eii; Wegg, *op. cit.*, p. 274.

74 For the support given by the English Bishops to the new learning see R. Masek, 'The humanistic interests of the early Tudor episcopate', *Church History*, vol. 39, No. 1, 1970, pp. 5ff.

75 *CWE*, vol. 2, Letter 252, pp. 213ff.

76 See N. R. Ker, *Records of All Souls College Library 1437–1600*, Oxford Biblio. Soc. N.S. XVI, Oxford 1971, pp. 24ff.

77 *Vives: On Education*, ed. F. Watson, Cambridge 1913, p. lxxviii. Erasmus also writes of Wolsey's 'very great good will' towards him while he was in England, *CWE*, vol. 4, Letter 577, p. 345.

78 *De fructu* (*The Benefit of a Liberal Education*), p. 141.

79 For a full discussion of Wolsey's role as patron of letters see W. G. Zeeveld, *Foundations of Tudor Policy*, Cambridge, Mass. 1948, ch. 2; J. Simon, *Education and Society in Tudor England*, Cambridge 1966, ch. 4.

V

The Bible in English

The exponents of the new learning during the early years of the sixteenth century in England were conspicuously orthodox. Although they dissociated themselves from the Schoolmen and the obscurantists and frowned on corruption in high places, they had no intention of seceding from the Church to instigate a reformation from the outside. Without leaving the broad tradition of mediaeval Catholicism they demanded a simplification of doctrine and reform of practice. True Christianity should be able to transform an individual's life without subverting ecclesiastical authority. Men like Colet, Fisher, Fox, More and Tunstall did much to secure a footing for humanistic studies in the official university curriculum by stressing the importance of Hebrew and Greek for all students of the Bible. Yet, they had no desire to challenge the authority of the Vulgate, and thereby the authority of Rome, by producing a vernacular version of the Scriptures. At a time when the Bible was being translated into many European languages, Archbishop Warham and his fellow clergy were singularly unenthusiastic about producing an English version. Although they stressed the importance of the study of the Scriptures for a right understanding of the Christian faith, they would not have admitted that England was a 'Bible thirsty land'. They felt that an English translation would confuse rather than edify the faithful, and in any case, had not Lollardy underlined the dangers of having the Bible in the language of the people? Whatever the strength of the opposition to official Church policy, it is noteworthy that when a translation was eventually made under the auspices of the ecclesiastical authorities, royal injunctions were necessary to ensure its circulation.

William Tyndale

There was, however, in the humanist camp one protesting voice on the issue of scriptural translation, that of Erasmus.

I totally dissent [he wrote in the preface to his edition of the Greek New Testament in 1516] from those who are unwilling that the sacred Scriptures, translated into the vulgar tongue, should be read by the unlearned, as if Christ had taught such subtle doctrines that they can with difficulty be understood by a very few theologians, or as if the strength of the Christian religion lay in men's ignorance of it. The mysteries of Kings it were perhaps better to conceal, but Christ wishes his mysteries to be published as widely as possible. I could wish even all women to read the Gospels and the Epistles of St Paul. . . . and that the farmer may sing parts of them at his work, that the weaver may chant them when engaged at his shuttle, that the traveller with their stories beguile the weariness of the journey.[1]

The leaders of the English Church must have pondered these words deeply, but they were not swift to act upon them. It was left to William Tyndale to take Erasmus' plea seriously and to apply himself to making an English version of much of the Bible. Faced by hostility to his plans, especially from Cuthbert Tunstall on whose support he had originally relied, Tyndale left his native land in April 1524 never to return. It was on the Continent that he produced his translation of the New Testament in 1526, the Pentateuch in 1530 and the Book of Jonah in 1531. He issued a revised edition of Genesis in 1534, but his version of Judges to II Chronicles was only in manuscript at the time of his death. It is traditionally maintained that this last section was incorporated by John Rogers into the Matthew's Bible.

The significance of Tyndale's translation is that it became the basis of later official versions. Butterworth's claim that in the lineage of the English Bible the 'chief place of honour' belongs undoubtedly to Tyndale has been supported by other scholars.[2] But while there can be no doubt regarding Tyndale's literary ability, his originality as a translator has been a matter of dispute. To what extent did his zeal for translating motivate his efforts to learn Hebrew? Was he a skilled linguist capable of translating from the original languages, or was he only an amateur who relied heavily on the Vulgate and on Luther's German Bible for his rendering of parts of the Old Testament? Did he ever become a competent Hebraist who could translate directly from the Massoretic Text, or was he dependent on the Latin version of Pagninus for his understanding of obscure Hebrew words? If he is to be regarded as 'the father of English Hebraists', as some have claimed, where and from whom did he learn Hebrew? The answers to such questions are hard to find. They must be sought by following his scholastic career, a difficult task in itself since Tyndale seems to have been remarkably successful in covering his tracks, and by examining his translation of Old Testament books.

One of the earliest testimonies to his linguistic ability is that of Hermann Buschius, a member of the group of German humanists which included Reuchlin and Ulrich von Hutten. Buschius is reputed to have told Spalatin, secretary to the Elector of Saxony, at a supper party in August 1526 that Tyndale was 'so skilled in seven languages, Hebrew, Greek, Latin, Italian, Spanish, English, French, that whichever he spoke you would suppose it his native tongue'.[3] Though this is a patent exaggeration, there can be little doubt that Tyndale had learned some Greek and Hebrew before he began to translate. Even his avowed opponent, George Joye can speak of his 'high learning in his Hebrew, Greek and Latin'.[4] It is probable that he studied Greek in England, for he received his early education at Magdalen Hall, Oxford, at a time when the influence of William Latimer, Linacre and Grocyn was still strongly felt there. After taking his Oxford M.A. in 1515 it is believed that he spent some time in Cambridge, where Erasmus and Fisher had been enthusiastically pioneering the teaching of Greek. There is a possibility that he could have learned the elements of Hebrew also at Cambridge during this same period, but it is more likely that he did so in Germany where by now the language had established itself as an academic subject. If we are to believe a tradition that goes back to Thomas More, the first year of his exile was spent in Wittenberg.[5] Here he would have profited from the educational reforms carried out by Luther and possibly received instruction in Hebrew from Matthew Aurogallus. It is tempting to think that at Worms, where his translation of the New Testament was published in 1526 and where he stayed for almost two years, he came into contact with Jews and had first hand experience of the Hebraic tradition. Worms had been an important centre for German Jewry since the time of Rashi.

Despite the lack of concrete evidence, it is unanimously accepted by those who have examined his Old Testament translation that Tyndale wasted no time in availing himself of the opportunities offered in Germany for learning Hebrew. There is, however, a difference of opinion with regard to his competence as a Hebraist. Some scholars maintain that he had only a very basic knowledge of the language and that he relied heavily on previous translations when he turned to the Hebrew Scriptures. Almost a century ago J. I. Mombert drew attention to the close correspondence between Tyndale's translation of the Pentateuch, completed in 1530, and that made by Luther seven years previously. He concluded that Tyndale was to a large measure, though not entirely, dependent on Luther.[6] This judgement is echoed by W. A. Clebsch, who asserts that Tyndale's 'great facility as a translator hardly argues freedom from enormous debt to Luther's German Bible'.[7] Such dependence must be recognised. A clear instance of it is to be found in Genesis 49:22 where Tyndale translates the difficult Hebrew phrase *banoth tsa'dhah 'le shur* as 'the daughters come forth to bear rule'. He makes no attempt to give an independent version of the original, but chooses to follow Luther verbatim. The result is a rendering which makes no sense in the context, since both translators fail to realise that the Hebrew word for daughters is to be understood figuratively to denote branches. Joseph is described as a thriving young vine 'with branches climbing over the wall' (N.E.B.).

Tyndale's originality as a translator and his knowledge of the Hebrew language is called into question also by Dahlia M. Karpman in an analysis of Exodus 1–6 in his version. Not only does Karpman seek to show that when Tyndale strays from the Massoretic Text he is following either the Vulgate or Luther, she also notes several 'mistranslations' of simple Hebrew words and phrases in these six chapters alone. Because of these mistakes she questions his fluency in Hebrew and concludes that it is 'likely that the Hebrew Bible wasn't Tyndale's primary version and was only consulted on some points'.[8] While such a conclusion goes beyond the evidence supplied by the examples of alleged errors, no one would wish to deny that Tyndale did have constant recourse to earlier translations. Like every translator in every age he used to his advantage the versions of his predecessors. Those of Jerome and Luther were far too important to be neglected. To these two may be added a third, not mentioned by Karpman, that of Sanctes Pagninus, published at Lyons in 1528 while Tyndale was still working on the Pentateuch. A detailed comparison of Tyndale's translation with that of the learned Dominican has yet to be made. But even a cursory examination, at points of lexicographical or exegetical difficulty, does provide further evidence of the translator's reliance on others for his understanding of the original text. Three examples from the Book of Genesis are offered here of Tyndale's unmistakable dependence on Pagninus, and through him on traditional Jewish exegesis.

The A.V. translates the first clause of Genesis 6:3 as 'and the Lord said, My spirit shall not always strive with man'. But the verb *yadhon*, rendered here as 'strive', has caused problems for translators and exegetes alike. There have been two traditional interpretations. The Septuagint, Vulgate, Syriac and Targum Onkelos all take it to mean 'stay', an understanding which is supported by Ibn Ezra who suggests a connection with the word *nadhan*, 'sheath', taking the human body to be like a sheath in which the spirit of God dwells. The Greek version of Symmachus and Targum Jonathan assume the word to be derived from the root *din* and translate it as 'judge'. Luther follows suit and in a lengthy note on this verse in his Genesis commentary states why he prefers this rendering.[9] Pagninus, however, rejects both these translations and in his version gives 'non disceptabit [strive] spiritus meus cum homine'. In his *Thesaurus* he justifies his translation by referring to Rashi and Joseph Kimchi, both of whom understand the verse as a promise on God's part not to be displeased with mankind for ever.[10] Tyndale follows Pagninus word for word at the expense of the Vulgate and Luther by translating 'my spirit shall not always strive with man', a rendering which found its way into the authorised English Bible.

The different renderings offered for the word *'abrech* in Genesis 41:43 testify to the difficulty felt by the translators. There is no agreement among the ancient versions as to what the Egyptians shouted when Joseph rode in the second chariot with Pharaoh. The Septuagint takes it to be an Egyptian term for 'herald', whereas the Syriac renders it as 'father and ruler'. The A.V. translates with an imperative 'bow the knee', but, recognising the difficulty, adds in the margin 'or *Tender father*: Heb. Abrech'. In the text it follows the Greek version of Aquila and Luther, but in the margin it notes the interpretation of Targum Pseudo-Jonathan. Pagninus, although he refers in his *Thesaurus*[11] to Kimchi's *Book of Roots* in support of the meaning 'bow the knee', in his version chooses to reproduce the word without translating it: 'clamabant ante eum, Abrech'. Once more in his translation Tyndale follows Pagninus exactly by saying, 'and they cried before him, Abrech', whereas in his list of difficult words found in the Book of Genesis he explains it as 'Tender father, or, as some will, Bow the knee'.[12]

Although the word *nazir*, which is used in Genesis 49:26 to represent Joseph's supremacy over all the other tribes, is common enough, the Vulgate's rendering of it by 'Nazirite' is anachronistic and therefore unsuitable in this context. The suggestion of the Septuagint that it refers to Joseph as 'the one who was the leader of his brothers' makes more sense. Luther follows the Vulgate with 'Nasarer'. But

Pagninus, by rendering it 'separatus', reproduces a Jewish explanation and in his *Thesaurus* acknowledges his sources as Rashi's commentary and Kimchi's *Book of Roots*.[13] They in turn are dependent on Targum Onkelos. Tyndale again ignores Luther and the Vulgate, choosing to follow Pagninus by translating 'he who was separate' from his brothers, thereby preserving yet another ancient Jewish explanation which was adopted by the translators of the A.V.

But the existence in his Old Testament of renderings adduced from previous translations must not be allowed to obscure the fact that Tyndale was capable of tackling the original text himself. His competence in Hebrew has not gone unrecognised. J. R. Slater, after making a careful study of Tyndale's Pentateuch and noting what he considered to be the marked influence of Luther's German version of 1523, can still regard him as 'the father of Hebrew scholarship among Englishmen, and the author of the first version in English made from the Hebrew'.[14] This assessment of Tyndale's achievement is endorsed by J. F. Mozley, who takes twenty-seven examples from the translation of Jonah and finds that Tyndale 'either stands alone or agrees with only one of the four versions which he is at all likely to have known'. Mozley feels that Slater overstates the case for Tyndale's dependence on Luther and concludes that 'in essential accuracy to the Hebrew he is superior to Luther, the Vulgate and the LXX and not inferior to Pagninus'.[15] L. J. Trinterud has claimed that Tyndale's greatest debt was first to Christian humanism and then to the German-Swiss Reformers of Zurich and Basle. While 'his dependence upon Luther's translation of the Old Testament can be demonstrated ... his independence of, and difference from Luther is much more significant'.[16] C. H. Williams is of the opinion that 'when he came to work on his Old Testament' Tyndale was 'a respectable Hebrew scholar' in his own right, a view which has been adequately substantiated recently by Gerald Hammond.[17]

Evidence of such scholarly independence with regard to the Hebrew Bible has been presented by Mozley in his study of Tyndale's translation of Jonah and by Hammond in his detailed examination of the Pentateuch; it need not be repeated here. There are, however, three general points concerning his response to the Hebraic tradition which may be noted. The first is based on his assertion that Hebrew can be translated far more easily into English than into Latin. It appears in the preface to *The Obedience of a Christian Man* where he defends the principle of having the Bible in the vernacular. Those who claim that the original text of the Old and New Testaments cannot be rendered into English because it is such a 'rude' language are branded as 'false liars', for as a matter of fact

the properties of the Hebrew tongue agree a thousand times more with the English than with the Latin. The manner of speaking is both one; so that in a thousand places thou needest not but to translate into the English, word for word; when thou must seek a compass in the Latin, and yet shall have much work to translate it well-favouredly, so that it have the same grace and sweetness, sense and pure understanding with it in the Latin as it hath in the Hebrew. A thousand parts better may it be translated into the English than into the Latin.[18]

The claim that it is easier 'a thousand times' to translate Hebrew into English than into Latin is a deliberate exaggeration put forward for purposes of propaganda. Its primary intention was to defend the vernacular against those who lost no opportunity to disparage it. Well into the sixteenth century the English language was the butt of many derogatory remarks. Its 'barbarous simplicity' was contrasted unfavourably with the rich literary qualities of Latin. Englishmen found it impossible to write eloquently in their native tongue. Few gave it praise. Tyndale's defence of it was therefore quite uncharacteristic.[19] But the above quotation bears testimony not only to Tyndale's positive attitude towards English but also to his grasp of Hebrew. Written during the summer of 1528, a full two years before the Pentateuch appeared in print, it suggests a first hand knowledge of the Hebrew Bible. It indicates that Tyndale was already familiar with the simplicity and directness of Semitic literary style, a simplicity which he endeavoured to reproduce in his translation. It demonstrates an awareness that the short Hebrew sentences, with few subordinate clauses and linked together with the simple conjunction *we* (and), can be accommodated more readily in the terse pointed sentences which are a feature of Tyndale's English style than in the long cumulative sentences of Latin.

Another indication that Tyndale had studied the Hebrew Scriptures and was familiar with Hebrew grammar is to be found in the prologue to his translation of Matthew's Gospel. This prologue was included in the 1534 revision of the English New Testament to explain what some might regard as imperfect renderings of the original Greek and as changes for the worse from the first edition. Tyndale advises the reader that these alterations must be attributed to the Semitic background of the New Testament writings:

If aught seemed changed, or not altogether agreeing with the Greek, let the
finder of the fault consider the Hebrew phrase or manner of speech, left in the
Greek words; whose preterperfect tense and present tense are oft both one,
and the future tense is the optative mood also, and the future tense oft the
imperative mood in the active voice and in the passive ever. Likewise person
for person, number for number, and interrogation for conditional, and such
like, is with the Hebrews a common usage.[20]

Here Tyndale demonstrates his familiarity with Hebrew idiom and
with the peculiarities of the Hebrew verbal system. He claims,
correctly, that the thought patterns and many of the expressions found
in the Greek New Testament can be understood only with reference to
Hebrew usage. Later in the same prologue he justifies his choice of
'repentance' rather than 'penance' for the Greek *metanoia* on the basis
of the Hebrew word *shub*, to return, which can also mean 'to repent',
as for example in Ezekiel 14:6.[21]

Finally, three Tables expounding certain obscure words in Genesis,
Exodus and Deuteronomy would suggest that Tyndale's text was the
original Hebrew at which he laboured with the aid of any dictionaries
available to him.[22] His explanation of 'Belial' as 'wicked, or
wickedness; he that hath cast the yoke of God off his neck' agrees
almost verbatim with that given by Münster in his Hebrew lexicon of
1524.[23] Likewise, Münster's interpretation of *'emim* in Deuteronomy
2:10 as 'populi terribiles' seems to be the basis of Tyndale's definition of
the same word: 'a kind of giants, so called because they were terrible
and cruel; for *Emim* signifieth terribleness'.[24] He derives the word
'awwim from the root *'awah* and concludes that it refers to a race of
giants who were 'crooked, unright, or wicked', a definition found in
Pagninus' *Thesaurus*.[25]

An examination of his English version of the Pentateuch and Jonah
with their appended annotations shows that Tyndale's knowledge of
Hebrew and his sensitive response to Hebraic style and idiom, is no
longer open to question. That he worked from a Hebrew original
admits of no doubt, and the fact that he made liberal use of all the aids
available to him in translations, grammars and dictionaries, does not
detract in any way from his greatness as a biblical scholar. He may be
justly regarded as the father of English Hebraists. His love of the
language and his desire to perfect himself in it emerge from one of the
last letters he ever wrote. Addressing the governor of the prison of
Vilvorde a few months before his execution in 1536 he requested warm
clothing to help him survive the rigours of winter, and added, 'Most of

all I earnestly entreat and implore you to ask the officer to allow me my Hebrew Bible, Hebrew Grammar and Hebrew Dictionary, so that I may spend my time in those studies'.[26] Until his dying day William Tyndale remained an ardent student of Hebrew, spurred on by his desire to provide the English people with a copy of the Bible in their own language.

Miles Coverdale and John Rogers

Despite Tyndale's skill as a translator, his New Testament was never given official recognition. As soon as it appeared in 1526 it was proscribed and consigned to the flames by Archbishop Warham at the express command of the king. Yet, within eight years the Convocation of Canterbury was petitioning the Crown for an official English version of the Scriptures. The request was granted and the task of producing the first complete English Bible was given to Miles Coverdale. The translator must have worked quickly and diligently for on 4 October 1535 'Coverdale's Bible' came off the press.

Coverdale, a former Augustinian friar, knew no Hebrew and had only a slender knowledge of Greek. In his dedicatory letter to the king he openly admits that he is incapable of translating from the original languages and mentions 'five sundry interpreters' on whose assistance he relied. Traditionally these have been identified as Jerome, Tyndale, Pagninus, Luther and the group of Zurich divines led by Zwingli. Of these Pagninus alone would have introduced him directly to the explanations of mediaeval Jewish authors and suggested alternative renderings of perplexing words, based on the exegesis of the rabbis. A detailed examination of Coverdale's translation of the Book of Daniel shows that he consulted this version at points of philological difficulty or ambiguity and, occasionally, preferred it to the Vulgate and Luther. Here are three examples. In Daniel 4:24 (Aramaic, English 27) Coverdale translates the final phrase 'for such things shall prolong thy peace', a rendering which is traceable by way of Pagninus ('prolongatio paci tuae') to the commentaries of Rashi and Pseudo-Saadia. In 5:5 he again follows Pagninus by translating the Aramaic *pas yeda'* as 'the palm of the hand', an explanation offered by Gersonides as an alternative to Ibn Ezra's 'the part of the hand' that wrote. In 11:8 the word *nesikhim* can be taken in two ways. Jerome translates it as 'molten images', on the assumption that it is derived from the verb *nasakh*, 'to pour out'. But the rabbis unanimously derive it from another meaning of the same root, namely 'to install, set up', which then gives *nasikh*, 'prince'. This is reproduced by Pagninus, who in turn is followed by Coverdale. In each of these three examples Luther and the Zurich translators side with the Vulgate and reject Pagninus, thereby disregarding Jewish explanations. But Coverdale, though no great Hebraist himself, ensured that the Hebraic tradition found a place in the earliest English Bible by giving preference to Pagninus over his other 'interpreters'.[27]

Coverdale's Bible was hardly two years old when another version appeared which claimed to have been 'truly and purely translated into English by Thomas Matthew'. Printed at Antwerp, it was received enthusiastically by Cranmer and Cromwell and immediately given royal sanction. 'Thomas Matthew' the translator, or to be more precise, the editor, was in reality John Rogers, the first of the Marian martyrs. Educated at Cambridge in the 1520s, where he may have learned some Hebrew, Rogers went to Antwerp in 1534 as chaplain to the English community. He remained there for six years and became friendly with Tyndale and Coverdale under whose guidance he trained as a translator. Later he moved to Wittenberg where he impressed Melanchthon with his scholarship.[28]

Rogers was essentially an editor. His 'translation' contained little that was original. For the Pentateuch he accepted Tyndale's version, and for the section from Ezra to Malachi that of Coverdale, both of which he reproduced with only minor revisions. From Joshua to II Chronicles it is believed that he made use of Tyndale's unpublished manuscript. Of greater significance in the present context, however, is his dependence on the French Bible of Calvin's cousin Robert Olivetan. Like Calvin, Olivetan had been a humanist lawyer before he became a theologian. Thus, when he fled from France to Strasbourg in 1528 Bucer and Capito had no difficulty in persuading him to study Greek and Hebrew. His linguistic training bore fruit in a translation of the Bible into French from the original languages published at Neuchâtel in 1535. Like those of the bridge builders mentioned in an earlier chapter this version is noted for its preservation of the Hebraic tradition in the translation of the Old Testament and in the appended annotations. The source of much of this was Pagninus, whose version Olivetan used freely, though not slavishly. The marginal notes demonstrate that he was capable of referring at first hand to the Massoretic Text, the Targum and rabbinic commentaries. In a detailed critique E. Reuss gives the work high praise and draws attention to the Jewish sources employed by the translator.

> I have no hesitation in declaring that Olivetan's Old Testament is not only an erudite and excellent work but a real masterpiece, especially when one considers the literary and philological resources which exegesis had at its disposal during this period. . . . Olivetan had read the rabbis, the great Jewish commentators of the twelfth and thirteenth centuries. In addition to those rabbis, and almost as frequently, Olivetan quotes . . . the Targums.[29]

It was this version which Rogers used as the source of many of his notes and as the basis of his revision of the earlier translations.

But in spite of his reliance on other translators, Rogers was himself a proficient linguist. His travels on the Continent ensured fluency in German and French, while a sound knowledge of Latin may be taken for granted. J. F. Mozley adduces evidence from the translation and the annotations to the Old Testament which points to at least some familiarity with Greek, Aramaic and Hebrew. References to the Septuagint and quotations from the Targum which do not appear in any of his sources suggest a basic knowledge of Greek and Aramaic. The commentaries of Pellican, Oecolampadius and Bucer, which he frequently cites, would have been of assistance to him only if he had enough Hebrew to appreciate their detailed discussions of specific words. At times he makes an original comment on individual Hebrew words or phrases, and on rare occasions demonstrates an acquaintance with rabbinic literature. In a note on Proverbs 9:8 he identifies 'the scorner' by quoting verbatim from David Kimchi.[30] Though none of his usual interpreters refer to this explanation, the fact that Rogers quotes it need not be taken to imply that he could read post-biblical Hebrew. It is most probable that he knew Kimchi only in translation.

With the printing of Rogers' translation in 1537 there were now in circulation two versions of the Bible, both appearing 'with the king's most gracious licence'. For different reasons both were unsatisfactory. Coverdale's version was based on other translations rather than the original languages. That of Rogers was doctrinally suspect. Its dependence on Tyndale and its propensity to endorse the teaching of the Reformers in its marginal notes rendered it unacceptable to many. Thomas Cromwell, accordingly, invited Coverdale to prepare yet another edition which was to be based on the original texts. Coverdale complied and in April 1539 produced the Great Bible which claimed on its title-page to have been 'truly translated after the verity of the Hebrew and Greek texts by the diligent study of diverse excellent learned men expert in the aforesaid tongues'. In order to placate conservative clerics all annotations and glosses were compulsorily omitted, much to Coverdale's disappointment. The translation was a success and immediately became the 'authorised version' of its day. It held its ground until 1560.

Although Coverdale states in the preface that he followed 'the standing text of the Hebrew with the interpretation of the Chaldee and Greek', all of which would have been available in the Complutensian Polyglot, it is doubtful whether he knew any more Hebrew in 1538 than he did three years previously. But he did have an invaluable aid. By the time he had started to work on his translation the 1535 Hebrew–Latin version of Sebastian Münster, with its copious explanatory notes on difficult and obscure words, was at his disposal. For his revision of Matthew's Old Testament he relied entirely on Münster and thereby incorporated traditional Jewish interpretations into the English Bible. Since this dependence has been adequately demonstrated by both B. F. Westcott and J. F. Mozley[31] it is unnecessary to elaborate upon it here save in one respect. For our purposes it is of interest to note instances of rabbinic influence in the text of the Great Bible which are directly attributable to Münster. Two examples are offered of the way in which Coverdale altered his original translation of 1535 as a result of consulting Münster.

The name given by Moses to the altar which he built after defeating the Amalekites (Exodus 17:15) was *Jehovah nissi*. In his translation Münster disregards both the Septuagint and Vulgate and renders these two words as 'Dominus miraculum meum', the explanation found in Rashi. Coverdale follows suit by translating 'the Lord is he that worketh miracles for me' in the Great Bible, whereas the Matthew's Bible simply transliterates the Hebrew (cf. A.V.). In Ezekiel 16:36 the rendering of *nechoshet* as 'bronze' by the Septuagint and Vulgate makes tolerable sense, the reference being to the spending of money on idols. Yet in the Jewish tradition it was understood quite differently. Kimchi, on the basis of parallelism with the following phrase 'your nakedness is uncovered', takes the word to signify 'lower parts'. Münster adopts this interpretation and translates 'quia prostituitur pubes tua'. Coverdale accepts this and changes his original version from 'thou has spent thy money' (1535) to 'thou hast set forth thy youth to whoredom' (1539).[32]

It is not possible to credit Coverdale and Rogers with the same interest in Hebrew as Tyndale. Yet their desire to produce the best possible English translations of the Bible led them to recognise the importance of Hebrew and the value of rabbinic exegetical works. They themselves may not have read the rabbis, but by opting to follow Pagninus and Münster at points of difficulty they ensured that traditional Jewish renderings found a permanent place in the English Bible.

The Geneva Bible

On the accession of Mary Tudor to the English throne in 1553 many prominent Protestants either fled or chose to emigrate to the continent of Europe, where they came into close contact with the Reformed Churches of Switzerland and Germany. A small group of them, after a short but not uneventful stay at Frankfurt, moved to Geneva where they founded an English church in 1555. Here these Marian exiles found themselves in congenial and scholarly surroundings. In addition to printing, much attention was being paid to the study and translation of the Bible, for Geneva was regarded as an important centre for biblical textual scholarship. William Whittingham, in his preface to the 1557 edition of the English New Testament, speaks of 'the store of heavenly learning, which so aboundeth in this city of Geneva, that justly it may be called the patron and mirror of true religion and godliness'.

When the exiles arrived, John Calvin was daily expounding the Scriptures to scores of enthusiastic listeners. The emphasis was on making the Bible comprehensible, especially by means of vernacular versions. The Latin and Greek New Testament of Theodore Beza, with its extensive notes and critical apparatus, was becoming the basis of many another translation. The French Bible of Robert Olivetan was being reprinted and receiving careful revision. Italian expatriates were engaged in Bible translation, and the Spanish version of the New Testament had just been produced. Yet the English were using a Bible printed some fifteen years previously. So they decided to make another translation which would take advantage of the most recent scholarship and help to circulate their own theological ideas. Westcott claims that it was essentially a revision of the Great Bible. 'In the Old Testament', he writes, 'they took the Great Bible as their basis and corrected its text, without ever substituting for it a new translation. Even where the changes are greatest the original foundation can still be traced, and the new work fairly harmonises with the old'.[33] Though this observation may be true in general, there are several instances where the Geneva Bible is much closer to the original Hebrew than its predecessor, especially on points of philological difficulty. This is perhaps not surprising when we remember that the translation of 1560, in marked contrast to that of 1539, was the product of a team of scholars who could pool their resources when faced with a perplexing passage.

The list of translators comes originally from the manuscript of the *Life* of Whittingham where we read that 'after some two or three years, the learned that were at Geneva, as Bishop Coverdale, Mr. Goodman, Mr. Gilby, Mr. Sampson, Dr. Cole, and Mr. Whittingham (and who else I cannot relate) did undertake the translation of the Geneva Bible'.[34] It is not easy to decide who was responsible for the major part of the work. Charles Martin highlights the problem and suggests that the leading role was taken by 'Whittingham together with Anthony Gilby, known for his Hebrew learning and the author of commentaries on Micah and Malachi. They received continuous help from William Cole, William Kethe and John Baron, and intermittently from Goodman and the venerable Miles Coverdale'.[35] Martin adds Kethe and Baron to the existing list, but omits Sampson on the grounds that he could have contributed little or nothing to the translation because he was not there long enough. This conclusion is based on letters written by Sampson to Peter Martyr, for although he came to Geneva in 1556 he says in a letter from Strasbourg dated 17 December 1558, 'I shall shortly move towards England'.[36] He writes again to Martyr from England on 6 January 1560 claiming that he has 'now been in England one year'.[37] He must therefore have left Geneva in December 1558 not long after the translators had begun their work. Coverdale, likewise, did not spend much time in Geneva. He arrived in October 1558 when the work had already started, but on 12 November 1559 he was preaching in London, having left Switzerland in August. Goodman left Geneva for Scotland in September 1559 at the request of John Knox. Little is known of Baron's connection with the translators. C. H. Garrett suggests that he might have been associated with the printing of the version.[38] Kethe, chiefly remembered for his metrical psalms, remained in Geneva until 1561.[39] Gilby and Cole may have stayed to complete the translation, but the responsibility of publishing the finished article was left to Whittingham. Whatever the part played by the others, it would appear that the main promoters of the Geneva Bible were Gilby and Whittingham.

To what extent can the translators be described as competent Hebraists? In Pocock's view, writing in 1882, it seemed improbable that they 'had any considerable knowledge of Hebrew or Greek'.[40] Admittedly there is nothing to indicate that Baron, Kethe, Cole and Goodman were familiar with Hebrew, and it is unlikely that Coverdale would have been of much assistance in this field either. Thomas Sampson, however, had a reputation for sound learning. In a communication to Queen Elizabeth on his election to the deanery of Christ Church after his return to England from the Continent, twenty men of letters claimed that 'it was very doubtful whether there was a better man, a greater linguist, a more complete scholar, or profound divine'.[41] Furthermore, he was a close friend of Tremellius. Whittingham also was without doubt a good linguist. After graduating from Oxford he spent several years (1550–1553) travelling in Europe in order to increase the scope of his linguistic studies. B. Hall describes him as 'skilled in many languages, a master of Hebrew and Greek'.[42] Although there is no definite statement in the manuscript of his *Life* to the effect that he was proficient in Hebrew, we do know that he was Senior Student of Christ Church from 1546 to 1550 and that he became a friend of Thomas Harding, the Regius Professor of Hebrew, an association which in all probability contributed to his knowledge of the language. In any case, it is difficult to believe that, in the then climate of opinion, he would have undertaken such a major task as Bible translation without an adequate knowledge of Hebrew.

Anthony Gilby, who graduated B.A. from Cambridge in 1531, was educated at Christ's College, 'where he acquired an exact knowledge of the Latin, Greek, and Hebrew languages'.[43] We are not told who his teachers were, but John Watson, the Master of Christ's in Gilby's day, would have been in sympathy with such linguistic pursuits. Watson was a humanist, a friend of Erasmus and a person of some culture who encouraged his students to study Greek and substituted a classical education for the scholastic subtleties.[44] The young Gilby may well have benefited from Watson's humanistic interests, for in his commentary on Micah (1547) he demonstrates considerable ability as a Hebraist. He makes several explicit references to the original text and frequently discusses the interpretation of individual words and phrases. In Micah 2:1, for example, he comments on the phrase *ki yesh le'el yadham*. He disagrees with Coverdale's rendering (which follows the Septuagint and Vulgate) 'for their power is against God', and suggests instead 'because power is in their hands'. In his note he explains that 'the Hebrew hath *El*, and divers have translated the same, God, and have thereby encumbered themselves with diversity of interpretations. But as it is taken by the best learned in the Hebrew tongue it signifieth in this place, power, as Gen. xxi and Proverb. iii'. Münster's translation reads at this point 'quia est potentia in manu eorum', and he adds in the margin that this is the interpretation favoured by leading Hebrew scholars; *'el* must be taken to signify 'strength', not 'God', in this instance. This is precisely the explanation offered by the Targum, Kimchi and Ibn Ezra, and which appears in Gilby almost certainly by way of Münster.[45]

Gilby apart, there is no conclusive evidence to show that the translators were accomplished Hebraists. Nevertheless, it may be confidently asserted that they worked directly from the Hebrew text. The preface to the translation testifies to their interest in Hebrew and indicates their concern for sound biblical scholarship based on the original languages. They assure 'the brethren of England, Scotland and Ireland' that they appreciate the work done by those who have already rendered the Bible into English. 'Yet considering the infancy of those times and imperfect knowledge of the tongues, in respect of this ripe age and clear light which God hath now revealed, the translations required greatly to be perused and reformed'. The labours of Tyndale, Rogers and Coverdale are duly recognised, but the time has come for Matthew's Bible and the Great Bible to be revised. In order to compensate for the deficiencies of the earlier versions the Geneva translators claim 'in every point and word' to have faithfully rendered the text, 'and in all hard places most sincerely expounded the same'. In many instances they deliberately preserved the Hebrew phrases, 'notwithstanding that they may seem somewhat hard in their ears that are not well practised and also delight in the sweet sounding phrases of the holy Scriptures'. To clarify the meaning of certain verses and to justify the new translation, literal renderings of Hebrew idioms were printed in italics in the margin and prefaced by the letters *Ebr.* Genesis, with one hundred and twenty-seven, has by far the lion's share, while the twelve prophets (Hosea–Malachi) have only three between them, an indication, perhaps, that enthusiasm for this particular exercise waned as the work progressed. Four examples, taken from the Book of Ezekiel, will serve to illustrate the translators' grasp of Hebrew. In 2:3 'impudent' children are, literally, those who are 'hard of face', while in 3:5 people 'of an unknown tongue' are people with 'deep lips'. In 43:26 'consecrate' is rendered in the margin as 'fill his hand', and in 44:5 'mark well' is the English equivalent of the Hebrew 'set thine heart'. In each case the Hebrew phrase is translated word for word into English.

Like the many other scholars resident at Geneva during this period, Gilby and his companions were surrounded by the best critical apparatus of their time. For first hand knowledge of Jewish commentaries on the biblical text they had Bomberg's Rabbinic Bible of 1517. Grammars and dictionaries compiled by eminent Christian Hebraists were readily available. Those whose knowledge of the original languages was not as thorough as it might have been were able to use with advantage the many independent Latin translations published during the previous thirty years. The versions of Münster and Leo Jud were highly prized, whereas that of Pagninus appeared in a new and revised edition published at Geneva by Robert Estienne in 1557. Since all three consciously drew on Jewish exegesis in their search for the plain meaning of the text it is hardly surprising that echoes of the Hebraic tradition abound in the Geneva Bible.[46]

During their stay in Geneva, Gilby and his colleagues were closely associated with John Calvin. In a discussion of the relationship between the Reformer and the expatriate English, W. M. Southgate claims that, though it was one of a number of influences, that of Calvin was 'probably the strongest single influence' on their thinking.[47] This conclusion is substantiated by the fact that the Calvinistic tone of the new translation's marginal notes has been widely recognised.[48] But in addition to elucidating doctrinal and exegetical matters, is it not possible that Calvin could also have helped the translators to solve many a problem in the text itself? That his advice on points of philology and translation was sought is suggested in a letter sent by Coverdale to Cole in Geneva in February 1560, two months before the work was completed. Cole, in a previous letter, has obviously alluded to Calvin, and in reply Coverdale writes, 'I thoroughly approve of your proposal to await the opinion of your kind preceptor, Master Calvin, on the remaining chapters of Daniel also'.[49] 'The opinion' which Cole and his fellow translators awaited was given by Calvin in a course of lectures on the Book of Daniel delivered during 1559 and 1560.

From this brief examination of the background against which the Geneva Bible was produced, the conclusion is justified that points of Jewish exegesis found their way, if only indirectly, into the version. S. L. Greenslade suggests that those responsible for it 'were sufficiently good Hebraists to form their own judgement and were perhaps the earliest English translators to make first hand use of Rabbi David Kimchi's commentary, though they may have known him only through Pagninus'.[50] One might add 'and Münster'. But in addition to these mediators of Jewish scholarship, the exiles were afforded help and encouragement from John Calvin who, whatever his views on rabbinic exegesis, was no mean Hebraist.

The Bishops' Bible

The wide popularity enjoyed by the Geneva Bible in Elizabethan England had two important consequences. It undermined the authority of the Great Bible, the version 'appointed to the use of the churches', and it caused Archbishop Parker to try to supersede it by yet another translation in a bid to gain uniformity. Because of its superiority in terms of scholarship to the Great Bible, that of Geneva soon had a wide readership, especially among the early Puritans. Within a very short time the first impression was sold out. The lengthy marginal notes appended to difficult words were a novelty for the English, but they were appreciated inasmuch as they made the complexities of the text easier to understand. For the convenience of the reader each chapter in the new Bible was divided into verses, and a useful apparatus of maps and tables was provided. Last but not least, the finished article was less expensive and less bulky than the Great Bible.

In spite of its excellent qualities, however, the translation of the Marian exiles was not viewed with favour in some Anglican circles. Since, as was explicitly stated in the preface, its purpose was to eradicate all false doctrine and to implant in English Christians a thorough knowledge of the Word of God, it was regarded by many as 'an instrument of Puritan propaganda'.[51] Its dependence on the French Bible of Olivetan, which had been revised by Calvin himself, had not gone unnoticed. In certain quarters the Protestant bias of its annotations was keenly felt. For some they may have been 'spectacles for weak eyes'; for others they were no more than 'pestilent glosses'. In his letter to the queen accompanying the first edition of the Bishop's Bible, Parker refers to the Geneva version as 'having interspersed diverse prejudicial notes which might have been also well spared'.[52] The archbishop himself did not despise the Geneva Bible, but it was clear, in view of the opposition of the Catholic party, that it could not be given the sanction of the Church and appointed to be read to English congregations. Parker, therefore, at the suggestion of Richard Cox, Bishop of Ely, launched yet another version. He formed a panel of translators, chiefly from among his fellow bishops, and sent each member a portion of the text together with instructions on how to proceed. Although the avowed purpose of this new Bible was to supply a text which would be a more faithful representation of the original Hebrew than the Great Bible had been, Coverdale's efforts were not to be despised. In his instructions Parker urged his colleagues 'to follow the common English translation used in churches and not to recede from it but where it varies manifestly from the Hebrew or Greek original'.[53] While he was anxious to return to the sources, the archbishop also made a determined effort to conciliate those with Catholic sympathies. The revisers 'were to make no bitter notes on the text, or yet to set down any determination in places of controversy'. Thus the more pronounced expressions of Calvinistic doctrine, as well as the open antagonism to Roman dogma and practice which appear in the Geneva version, were omitted.

Despite its alleged intention of following the original texts more closely, the Hebrew scholarship of some of those responsible for the Bishops' Bible is not immediately apparent. Pocock maintains that it is unnecessary to provide 'elaborate proof of the ignorance of Hebrew that prevailed among English Bishops'.[54] Hence, presumably, Parker's instructions that those chosen for the work were 'for the verity of the Hebrew to follow the said Pagninus and Münster especially, and generally others learned in the tongues'.[55] These independent Latin versions would help those with only a slender knowledge of Hebrew to render a faithful translation of the original. But Pocock's pessimism is not entirely justified, for there is some evidence of Hebrew learning among Parker's men.

William Alley, who followed Coverdale as Bishop of Exeter, was a prominent member of the group. According to one source he revised the last three books of the Pentateuch; according to another he was responsible for Deuteronomy only.[56] Alley was a contemporary of Anthony Gilby at Cambridge, matriculating at King's in 1528. Who kindled his interest in Hebrew will never be known. There is, however, ample proof of his knowledge of the language and of his appreciation of Jewish exegetes in his only published work *The Poor Man's Library*, printed in London by John Day in 1565. The first part of this two-volume work consists of observations on controversial questions relating to the Scriptures and to the authority of the Church. The second part contains a series of expositions of the First Letter of Peter which the author delivered when he was a canon of St Paul's. Interspersed throughout the work, as the title-page informs us, are 'certain fruitful annotations which may properly be called *Miscellanea*'. These notes deal with 'diverse and sundry things, and therefore needeth the more men's judgements and helps'.[57]

The 'helps' to whom Alley refers his readers in cases of textual, and sometimes doctrinal difficulty, include mediaeval rabbis and noted Christian Hebraists. Nicholas of Lyra, Petrus Galatinus, Münster, Reuchlin and Förster are all mentioned many times. It is clear that he held Nicholas in high esteem, often relying on him for the comments of Jewish exegetes. Nicholas, we are told, 'being instructed of the rabbis from his childhood in the Hebrew letters, had that holy tongue at his fingers' ends. . . . Truly he did more good in Scripture than any other at that time'. Galatinus' scholarship is also recognised, and he is quoted as an authority on the date of the writing of the Talmud. But despite his debt to these two scholars, Alley does not hesitate to take them to task on certain doctrinal issues for which they claim rabbinic support, and at times to criticise them for their lack of attention to linguistic detail. In a lengthy discussion on Psalm 72:16, 'May there be abundance of grain in the land; on the tops of the mountains may it wave', he criticises mediaeval Christian sources for misconstruing rabbinic arguments. 'I will show you how fondly, yea rather how stretchedly Petrus Galatinus doth allege and bring some of the Hebrew rabbis to confirm by this text in this psalm the sacrifice of the Mass and the elevation of the host'. Galatinus apparently quotes several rabbinic authorities and the Targum of Jonathan in support of the eucharistic doctrine of his Church. Such exegesis is the symptom of 'four fold, nay forty fold blindness and ignorance. . . . To draw this verse unto a cake above the priest's head . . . is an allegory, not so far set as foolish'.

Though he made substantial use of the works of intermediaries, it is possible that Alley had recourse to rabbinic writings himself. On several occasions he appears to be quoting directly from Jewish sources. He agrees with the 'Talmudists' in their interpretation of the phrase 'I am who I am' in Exodus 3:14, and refers to Ibn Ezra on the identification of the place to which Enoch was translated. He alludes to Kimchi's explanation of 'the land of the living' in Psalm 27:13 as 'the state of the life to come'. When discussing the identity of Isaiah he quotes with approval Kimchi's opinion that the prophet's father was the brother of King Amaziah. In reply to the argument that the priest offers the Son of God in the form of bread and wine at the Eucharist, just as Melchizedek 'offered' bread and wine in Genesis 14:18, he cites Rashi in support of the literal meaning of the verse. The rabbinic view, however, is not accepted in every instance. Rashi's explanation of the material out of which the two stone tables of the Law were made and his interpretation of the command given to Moses to cut new ones after the first were destroyed (Exodus 34:1) are rejected as being 'both fained and false'.

Of all those engaged in the translation, Alley is the only one who has left any indication of his expertise in Hebrew. But there were others who, though they did not publish anything, were acclaimed as Hebraists by their contemporaries. Robert Horne, Bishop of Winchester, revised Isaiah, Jeremiah and Lamentations. Educated at St John's, Cambridge, he had served as Hebrew lecturer for his college in 1544–45. During Mary's reign he found refuge at Frankfurt where he became a prominent member of the 'Prayer Book party' of English exiles. For a short time he taught Hebrew at the college established in the city by Richard Cox to cater for the needs of the community.[58] It is unfortunate that someone who was twice elected to lecture in Hebrew left no trace of his knowledge of the language. The only evidence we have of his interest in the Hebraic tradition is a thirteenth-century manuscript of Rashi's commentary on the Bible apart from the Pentateuch, which he presented to his college.[59] A fellow exile with Horne at Cox's academy was Richard Davies, later Bishop of St David's. He was invited by the archbishop to revise the prose books from Joshua to II Samuel. Testimony to Davies' competence in Hebrew comes from William Salesbury, with whom he collaborated to produce the first translation of the New Testament into Welsh. Writing to Parker in 1565 Salesbury refers to Davies' thorough knowledge of German, Latin, Greek and Hebrew.[60]

In order to encourage the translators to be diligent, and to ensure that they were answerable for their work, Parker directed each one to append his initials to whatever part of the Bible he had revised. The initials of Thomas Bentham appear at the end of Ezekiel and Daniel. One time fellow of Magdalen College, Oxford, Bentham commenced as M.A. in 1547 and, in the words of a contemporary, 'about that time did solely addict his mind to the study of theology and to the learning of the Hebrew language, in which last he was most excellent'.[61] After spending his exile in Zurich, Basle and Geneva he became Bishop of

Lichfield, and immediately appointed Peter Morwyn, a friend of his student days, as his private chaplain, and later to a canonry in the cathedral. In Morwyn the bishop had not only a trusted adviser but also an able scholar who had already demonstrated his skill as a Hebraist in a venture undertaken in conjunction with the printer Richard Jugge.

In response to a growing interest in the history of the Jews after the end of the Old Testament period, Jugge decided to publish an English version of the *Sefer Yosippon* (*The Book of Joseph Ben Gorion*) which contained an account of the fortunes of the Jewish people in post-biblical times. He invited Morwyn to undertake the task of translating, and printed the first edition in 1558. Münster, however, had already rendered Abraham ibn Daud's abbreviated version of the *Sefer Yosippon* into Latin in 1529, and the first five books of the original work in 1541. This has led Lucien Wolf to doubt whether Morwyn did in fact translate from the original, and to claim that the book was a literal translation of Münster's version, although the author pretended to have made it directly from the Hebrew.[62] But faith in Morwyn's Hebrew scholarship has been restored by J. Reiner, who after a close study of the original document and the translations, claims that 'we can, without hesitation, conclude that a Hebrew text of the *Yosippon* was translated by Morwyn'. There are indications which suggest that he did in fact make use of the Hebrew text of the abbreviated version, but there is no reason to suspect that he used Münster's Latin translation of Ibn Daud's text.[63]

Jugge's venture was obviously a great success, for in less than fifty years ten different editions of the English translation of the history were issued. It answered a need felt by Christians for further information about the Jews. As Morwyn states in his 'Epistle to the Reader', his object in acceding to Jugge's request was to supply a 'history of the Jews, to the intent that as there is amongst us already in our native tongue, the original beginning of that nation, and the continuance for a long space, in the Bible . . . so there might be likewise an understanding and declaration to all men in the English tongue, as well as in other, of the destruction of so famous a commonweal'. In the words of Lucien Wolf 'it supplied the first connecting link in the Gentile mind between the Bible and the Ghetto'.[64] Although such a statement ignores the attitude of the Franciscan and Dominican Hebraists of the thirteenth century, who had made the same equation mentally, this disinterested attitude on the part of Christians towards the Jews and their literature was new in practice. It provides evidence of another, and more worthy motive for Hebraic studies in sixteenth-century England. The translator was the Bishop of Lichfield's right hand man. Bentham was in close touch with one who had, to some extent, understood the intricacies of post-biblical Hebrew. The chaplain may well have been called upon to solve some of the textual problems found in the books allocated by Parker to the bishop.

The canonical Wisdom Literature was shared between Andrew Perne, Master of Peterhouse and Dean of Ely, and Andrew Pearson, a canon of Canterbury. Both were eminent scholars, but there is nothing in their literary remains to suggest that they were noted Hebraists. It is, however, significant that among the two and a half thousand volumes which Perne had in his personal library there are no fewer than fifty-five Hebrew and Aramaic books. (For the full list see Appendix III, pp. 288f). In addition to copies of the Rabbinic Bible and Targum Onkelos, there are several dictionaries, grammars and commentaries by eminent Christian Hebraists. Admittedly, none of them are well-thumbed or annotated, so that one is prompted to think that Perne was more of a bibliophile than a scholar. Yet, the very existence of such books in his library indicates a sympathy for the Hebraic tradition. If the Dean of Ely never made much progress in Hebrew it was not because he lacked the requisite tools. The books of Kings and Chronicles were given to Edwin Sandys, Bishop of Worcester, who felt that he knew enough Hebrew to criticise even Sebastian Münster. The Great Bible, in Sandys' opinion, was deficient because its translators were too anxious to follow Münster 'who doubtless was a very negligent man in his doings, and often swerved very much from the Hebrew'.[65] Edmund Grindal, Bishop of London, was assigned the Minor Prophets. Though his most recent biography can tell us nothing of his life as a student in Cambridge, or subsequently as a scholar,[66] there are indications that Grindal knew Hebrew and was anxious to develop his skill in it. During Mary's reign he was a member of a group of prominent Englishmen at Strasbourg who attended Peter Martyr's lectures on the Book of Judges.[67] When we recall Martyr's own description of the Old Testament lectures which he gave at Strasbourg a decade earlier, it may be assumed that his exposition of Judges would be based on the Hebrew text. Whatever his own proficiency in Hebrew, Grindal's interest in the language had been awakened on the Continent. Within six months of returning to England in January 1559 he wrote to Konrad Hubert, Rector of St

Thomas' Church, Strasbourg, asking him to look for a capable young man who could be persuaded to act as his secretary. He specifies that whoever is chosen should have a legible hand, a good command of Latin, 'be somewhat acquainted with Greek, and especially with Hebrew and should take a delight in the study of the holy Scriptures'. He is confident that such a person will be found, for 'all these qualifications are generally to be met with' in Strasbourg students.[68] Why Grindal stresses the importance of having a Hebraist as his personal assistant is not clear. Perhaps he felt the need of further tuition in Hebrew, as he did in German. At all events, Dielthem Blaurer must have had the requisite qualifications for he responded to the invitation and worked harmoniously with the bishop for three years. Among the books which Grindal left to The Queen's College, Oxford, five testify to an interest in Semitics: the Syriac and Latin New Testament of Tremellius, Fagius' annotated Latin translation of Targum Onkelos on the Pentateuch, Pagninus' Latin Bible and Lexicon, and a Hebrew Concordance which, although listed in the bequest, is apparently no longer in the library.[69] The Hebrew–Latin lexicon (*Thesaurus*) of Pagninus is the 1577 edition which Grindal must have purchased only a few years before his death in 1583, a fact which points to his continuing interest in Hebrew even though burdened with archiepiscopal duties.

On 5 October 1568 Parker sent a presentation copy of the Bible to the queen with a letter for her secretary, William Cecil, containing a list of the revisers of the various books. Curiously, he does not include the Psalter. According to the *Parker Correspondence*[70] the book had been assigned originally to Edmund Guest, Bishop of Rochester. In the Bible itself, however, there are indications that things had not gone as planned, for the translator of the Psalms signs himself as 'T.B.'. Strype, and others after him, maintain that these letters stand for Thomas Becon, a canon of Canterbury. But this is unlikely since Becon, though a prolific writer on devotional and controversial matters, was not a prominent biblical scholar. On his own admission he knew but little Greek. In explanation of foreign words which sometimes appear in his writings he says, 'You shall find in diverse parts of my books Greek words made English, as "encomion" for "praise", "mnemosinon" for "a remembrance", and such other monstrous words for the reader to wonder at, and written only by me for vainglory to make the reader understand that I were learned in the Greek tongue, wherein I confess plainly I am not learned at all'.[71]

Since his knowledge of Greek was not what it might have been, it is improbable that he knew Hebrew and is therefore an unlikely candidate for the task which the archbishop had in mind. The suggestion of W. Aldis Wright, that the initials are those of Thomas Bickley, the Archdeacon of Stafford, and later Bishop of Chichester, is more plausible.[72] A contemporary of Bentham at Magdalen College, Oxford, Bickley fled to the Continent in 1553 and there 'improved himself much in learning'.[73] But of his competence in Hebrew there is no concrete evidence.

In the list of names sent to Cecil, Matthew Parker himself appears as the translator of Genesis and Exodus. In the Bible his initials stand under the title of each book. Although there is nothing in his academic record or his published works to suggest that Parker was a Hebraist, it would be surprising if he had not gained some knowledge of the language during his student days. He was at Cambridge in the 1520s, at a time when the revival of learning was beginning to make an impact on the university. In 1519 Richard Croke had delivered his inaugural lecture as a reader in Greek, and the following decade was to witness the first determined effort at teaching Hebrew. Parker's vast personal library, which he bequeathed to the college of which he was once master, Corpus Christi, Cambridge, contains evidence of an interest in Hebrew and the Hebraic tradition.[74] In addition to the works of Reuchlin and a *Cabalisticarum selectiora* of Pico, he had Pagninus' Bible and *Thesaurus*, Fagius' translation of the Targum, an Aramaic dictionary, the Latin Bible of Vatable and a selection of Old Testament commentaries by Luther, Zwingli, Oecolampadius and Pellican, all of which make frequent reference to the Hebrew text. A manuscript edition of the Hebrew Psalter which once belonged to Parker is now in the Bodleian Library. But his own attainments in Hebrew apart, it is clear from his patronage of other scholars that the archbishop was anxious to promote the study of the language in every possible way. His friendship with Immanuel Tremellius has already been noted. Later, in 1574, when he was Chancellor of Cambridge, he felt that the annual salary paid to the Regius Professor of Hebrew was too low and proposed that it should be augmented.

The fruit of Parker's labours must be regarded as a work of uneven merit. Since each reviser acted independently of his colleagues, one book, or group of books, cannot be taken as representative of another. In many cases the versions of Coverdale and Geneva are followed exactly, with little attempt at originality. But while there is no positive proof that all the revisers of the Old Testament were Hebraists, we may surely assume that Parker would have expected his assistants to have some skill in the language. Furthermore, anyone who hoped to make use of Münster's annotations, 'for the verity of the Hebrew', would have to be familiar with the Bible in the original.

The pursuit of a perfect English translation of the Scriptures, based on the original languages, continued throughout the sixteenth century, and with it went a deepening appreciation of the Hebraic tradition. Influenced by the teachings of the continental Reformers, and encouraged by their example, the English translators from Tyndale onwards recognised the importance of Hebrew for the task in which they were engaged. Some were capable Hebraists who could cope adequately with the Hebrew text. Those with a limited knowledge of the language relied on intermediaries, with the result that the works of Pagninus, Münster and Leo Jud became an indispensable part of their equipment. But proficient Hebraists or not, the desire to produce the definitive vernacular version of the Old Testament led, both directly and indirectly, to the *hebraica veritas*. The Elizabethan Church Settlement, however, and the subsequent flowering of the Puritan movement with its strong biblical emphasis and its penchant for controversy, provided yet another stimulus for the study of Hebrew. This, together with the motive for studying the Kabbalah which arose out of a preoccupation in some quarters with occult philosophy, will be the subject of the next chapter.

Notes

1 *Erasmus' Prefaces 1505–1536*, ed. with Eng. trans. by R. Peters, Menton 1970, pp. 205f.

2 C. C. Butterworth, *The Literary Lineage of the King James Bible, 1340–1611*, Philadelphia, Pa. 1941, p. 233.

3 Quoted by R. Demaus, *William Tyndale: a Biography*, 2nd ed. rev. R. Lovett, London 1886 (reprinted Amsterdam 1971), p. 130.

4 *An apologye made . . . to satisfy W. Tindale*, J. Bydell, 1535.

5 For the view that he was registered under an assumed name at Wittenberg on 27 May 1534 and became friendly with Luther see P. Smith, 'Englishmen at Wittenberg in the sixteenth century', *EHR*, vol. 36, No. 143, 1921, p. 422; L. F. Gruber, *The First English New Testament and Luther*, Burlington, Iowa 1928, pp. 29ff; C. H. Williams, *William Tyndale*, London 1969, p. 16. For the contrary point of view see

E. G. Rupp, *Six Makers of English Religion*, London 1957, p. 18, who thinks it probable that Tyndale 'did not go to Wittenberg, but stayed in the Rhineland'.

6   *William Tyndale's Five Books of Moses called the Pentateuch*, (verbatim reprint of 1530 ed.) ed. J. I. Mombert, 1884, new ed. F. F. Bruce, Centaur Press, Arundel 1971, introduction and text *passim*.

7   *England's Earliest Protestants 1520–1535*, p. 138. See also S. L. Greenslade ed., *The Work of William Tindale*, London 1938, p. 30; H. Bluhm, *Martin Luther: Creative Translator*, St Louis, Miss. 1965, p. 180.

8   'William Tyndale's response to the Hebraic tradition', *Studies in the Renaissance*, vol. 14, 1967, p. 115.

9   *Luther's Works*, vol. 2, pp. 13–32.

10 Col. 485.

11 Cols. 328f.

12 *The Work of William Tyndale*, ed. G. E. Duffield, Courtenay Reformation Classics I, Appleford 1964, p. 43.

13 Col. 1569.

14 *The Sources of Tyndale's Version of the Pentateuch*, Chicago, Ill. 1906, p. 54. Judged from the standpoint of Tyndale's dependence on Luther, Slater's study is rendered useless by his failure to realise that he was quoting from a revision of Luther's 1523 version issued several years after Tyndale had completed his translation.

15 'Tyndale's knowledge of Hebrew', *JTS*, vol. 36, 1935, p. 396.

16 'A reappraisal of William Tyndale's debt to Martin Luther', *Church History*, vol. 31, No. 1, 1962, p. 33.

17 C. H. Williams, *William Tyndale*, p. 69; G. Hammond, 'William Tyndale's Pentateuch: its relation to Luther's German Bible and the Hebrew original', *Renaissance Quarterly*, vol. 33, No. 3, 1980. Hammond's article is by far the most detailed assessment to date of Tyndale as a Hebraist. By showing how, among other things, the style of the translation is influenced by that of the original, the author makes out a very plausible case for regarding Tyndale as a competent Hebrew scholar.

18 *The Work of William Tyndale*, ed. Duffield, p. 326.

19 On the status of English during this period see R. F. Jones, *The Triumph of the English Language*, Oxford 1951, ch. 1.

20 *The Work of William Tyndale*, ed. Duffield, p. 104.

21 *Ibid.*, p. 113.

22 *Ibid.*, pp. 43ff., 57f., 83f.

23 *Ibid.*, p. 83. Cf. Münster, *Dictionarium Hebraicum*, Basle 1525, *s.v.*

24 *The Work of William Tyndale*, ed. Duffield, p. 83.

25 *Ibid.*, p. 83. Cf. Pagninus, *Thesaurus, s.v.*

26 *The Work of William Tyndale*, ed. Duffield, p. 401.

27 Further examples of the acceptance of traditional Jewish renderings by Coverdale in his translation of Daniel appear also in 2:1; 4:5; 8:2; 11:8. H. Bluhm in ' "Five Sundry Interpreters": the sources of the first printed English Bible', *Huntingdon Library Qtly.*, vol. 34, 1975–6, pp.

107ff rejects the view that Coverdale used Pagninus for his translation of the N.T. While this may be so, there is much to suggest that he consulted him regularly over the O.T.

28 For the details of Rogers' early career see J. L. Chester, *John Rogers*, London 1861, ch. 1.

29 'Fragments littéraires et critiques relatifs à l'histoire de la Bible française', *Revue de Théologie*, vol. IV, 3e. série, Strasbourg 1865–6, p. 302.

30 'Scorners' are those who are 'subtle and crafty to hurt others and to open and tell secrets and so to break concord and unity'. Thus the marginal note on Prov. 9:8 in Matthew's Bible where reference is made to Kimchi.

31 Westcott, *A General View of the History of the English Bible*, 3rd ed. W. Aldis Wright, London 1905, pp. 181ff; Mozley, *Coverdale and His Bibles*, London 1953, ch. 12.

32 Further examples of the influence of Münster on the Great Bible may be found in G. Lloyd Jones, 'Jewish exegesis and the English Bible', *ASTI*, vol. VII, 1968–9, pp. 53ff.

33 *A General View of the History of the English Bible*, p. 222.

34 *MS of the Life and Death of William Whittingham Deane of Durham*, ed. M. A. E. Green, Camden Soc. 1870, pp. 9f.

35 *Les Protestants Anglais réfugiés à Genève au temps de Calvin*, Genève 1915, p. 241.

36 *The Zurich Letters 1558–1579*, Parker Soc. 1842, First Series, p. 2.

37 *Ibid.*, p. 62.

38 *The Marian Exiles*, Cambridge 1938, p. 81.

39 *Ibid.*, p. 205.

40 'Some notices of the Genevan Bible', *The Bibliographer*, 1882, vol. III, p. 37.

41 Quoted by C. Anderson, *Annals of the English Bible*, London 1845, vol. II, p. 322, n. 6.

42 *The Genevan Version of the English Bible*, London 1957, p. 4.

43 C. H. Cooper, *Athenae Cantabrigienses*, Cambridge 1858, vol. I, p. 517.

44 J. Peile, *Christ's College*, Cambridge 1900, p. 43.

45 For other references to the original Hebrew see his comments on Micah 1:5; 2:6, 8; 5:2, 5; 6:11.

46 For further evidence of this specifically Hebraic influence see the present author's study of 'The influence of mediaeval Jewish exegetes on biblical scholarship in sixteenth-century England: with special reference to the Book of Daniel', unpublished Ph.D. thesis, London 1974, Pt. II, ch. 5.

47 'The Marian Exiles and their influence on John Calvin', *History*, vol. 27, 1942, p. 148. Cf. L. Lupton, *History of the Geneva Bible*, London 1973, vol. V, p. 108, 'As soon as one turns to Calvin's commentary on Genesis and compares his remarks on the Hebrew text and spelling with the Geneva Bible it is immediately clear that no further search for the source of the exiles' Hebrew scholarship is necessary'.

48 See H. Craig, 'The Geneva Bible as a political document', *Pacific Historical Review*, vol. 7, 1938.

49 See J. F. Mozley, *Coverdale and His Bibles*, p. 316, for the Latin

original.

50   *CHB*, vol. 3, p. 157. The note appended in the Geneva Bible to Exodus 38:8, where Kimchi is quoted, presumably prompted this remark.

51   B. Hall, *The Genevan Version of the English Bible*, p. 9.

52   A. W. Pollard, ed. *Records of the English Bible*, London 1911 (reprinted 1974), p. 295.

53   Pollard, ed. *Records of the English Bible*, p. 297.

54   *The Bibliographer*, March 1882, p. iii.

55   Pollard, ed. *Records of the English Bible*, p. 297.

56   The initials 'W.E.' (William Exon:) appear at the end of Deuteronomy. Since Leviticus and Numbers are not initialled it is possible that Alley was responsible for these also, not just for Deuteronomy.

57   Preface to the Reader, *The Poor Man's Library*, vol. I, p. 11. The following quotations from this work are taken from vol. I unless stated otherwise.

58   In *A Brief Discourse of the Troubles begun at Frankfort*, ed. J. Petheram, London 1846, p. 60, the author states with reference to the exiles, 'They have set up an university to repair again their estimation by maintenance of learning'. But although provision was made for the maintenance of lectureships in Latin, Greek and Hebrew nothing further is known of the activities of this college.

59   M. R. James, *A Descriptive Catalogue of the Manuscripts in the Library of St John's College, Cambridge*, Cambridge 1913, pp. 1ff.

60   G. Williams, *Bywyd ac Amserau'r Esgob Richard Davies*, Cardiff 1953, p. 105.

61   *DNB*, *s.v.* quoting Laurence Humphrey in his *Life of Jewell*, London 1573.

62   ' "Yosippon" in England', *TJHSE*, vol. VI, 1908–10, p. 279.

63   'The English Yosippon', *JQR*, N.S. vol. 58, 1967–8, pp. 134, 136.

64   *Op. cit.*, *TJHSE*, vol. VI, pp. 282f.

65   *Correspondence of Matthew Parker*, Parker Soc. 1853, p. 257.

66   P. Collinson, *Archbishop Grindal 1519–1583*, London 1979, p. 35.

67   R. Churton, *The Life of Alexander Nowell*, Oxford 1809, p. 23.

68   *The Zurich Letters*, Parker Soc. 1845, Second Series, p. 23.

69   The Queen's College, Oxford, MS. 556.

70   *The Correspondence of Matthew Parker*, Parker Soc. 1853, p. 250.

71   T. Becon, *Early Works*, Parker Soc., 1843, p. 192.

72   Westcott, *A General View of the History of the English Bible*, 3rd ed., p. 99, n. 3.

73   Anthony Wood, *Athenae Oxonienses*, 3rd ed. rev., London 1813–20, vol. II, col. 840.

74   Corpus Christi College, Cambridge, MS. 575.

VI

Disputations and controversies

The reign of Elizabeth witnessed many bitter disputes between Puritans and Catholics. Scripture and tradition alike provided both sides with highly controversial issues which were the subject of fierce debate. During the same period an interest in magic led to the adoption of kabbalistic ideas and techniques. For different reasons, both Puritan and magus had recourse to the Hebraic tradition. Their writings offer further examples of the motives from which English scholars turned to the study of Hebrew.

Learned Puritans

For many Englishmen the combination of Catholic ritual and Protestant doctrine which characterised the Elizabethan Settlement was intolerable. The returning Marian exiles had strong links with Zurich and Geneva; for them any kind of compromise with Catholicism was unacceptable. Bent on 'rooting out the weeds of popery', they sought to combat the teachings of Rome with the best theological weapons at their disposal. If they were to succeed, a well educated ministry capable of refuting the Catholics and of instructing the laity was essential. In their view, learning was the handmaid of religion. Like earlier advocates of reform, they believed that the best remedy for a corrupt Church was education. A 'Supplication' addressed to Queen Elizabeth in 'the third year of her reign or thereabouts' begs the sovereign to ensure that only suitably qualified men be allowed to enter the ministry. The suppliants complain of clergymen who are ignorant of the Scriptures; dumb dogs and idle shepherds unable and unwilling to help their congregations. Such unlettered and careless pastors are the cause of the pervading 'popish blindness' with which the common people are afflicted. Ignorance is the enemy of true religion; it can be overcome only by educated preachers capable of expounding God's Word to the nation.[1]

Unlike the Erasmian humanists of a previous generation, these early Puritans did not have much interest in scholarship *per se*, but where they saw it as a means to an acceptable end they pursued it with vigour. In an attempt to educate the parish clergy in the Scriptures and to help them improve their preaching they instituted prophesyings on the Zurich pattern at various centres. Their interest in the reform of doctrine led some of them to see the value of a degree in theology, and consequently to become prominent members of Oxford and Cambridge colleges. They came to regard the universities as nurseries for the clergy, turning to them for informed and well trained recruits. One of their main sources of supply was Emmanuel College, founded in 1584 by Sir Walter Mildmay, financier and philanthropist. Mildmay was a zealous Puritan, anxious to promote the reformed religion in every possible way. Already, in 1569, he had demonstrated his concern for higher education by making an annual grant of twenty pounds to Christ's College to support, among other things, a lectureship in Greek. A bequest of books to the college at about the same time is further testimony to his interest in the humanist scholarship pioneered at Cambridge by Fisher and Erasmus. But Mildmay was determined to make an even greater contribution to the cause of learning. Since the study of divinity was, in his own words, 'much decayed' in the university, he decided to establish a college which would cater to the needs of a learned preaching ministry and become a 'seed-bed' of the English Church. The statutes of Emmanuel, which were based on those of Christ's and Trinity, indicate clearly the level of scholarly attainment which the founder expected of the members. Besides being 'professors of pure religion, contrary to Popery and other heresies' the fellows had to be 'skilled in the three tongues, Greek, Latin and Hebrew'.[2] In order to maintain such high linguistic standards every candidate for a fellowship had to pass an examination in Greek and Hebrew before being admitted.

To ensure that his intentions were carried out Mildmay chose as the master of his new college Laurence Chaderton, formerly a fellow and tutor of Christ's. Converted from Catholicism during his student days, Chaderton had made a name for himself as a defender of Calvinistic orthodoxy. He is described by Collinson as 'the pope of Cambridge puritanism', for in the second half of the century he made both Christ's and Emmanuel Puritan seminaries in all but name.[3] But Chaderton was not just an ardent Puritan preacher. Long before he went to Emmanuel he had established a reputation as a theologian and linguist. Since his printed works amount to no more than two sermons preached at Paul's Cross, an evaluation of his Hebrew scholarship and of his attitude to the Hebraic tradition based on his own writings is impossible. The only monument to his interest in rabbinic exegesis is his copy of the Bomberg Bible (Venice 1546–48) which he donated to the college library. But in spite of the lack of evidence, a comment made by Walter Dillingham, his seventeenth-century biographer, suggests that he was an ardent Hebraist who continued to study the language up to the end of his life. Remarking on the fact that Chaderton retained all his faculties, even in advanced old age, Dillingham claims to have been told 'by trustworthy people that in his Hebrew Bible the smallest point did not escape his sight'.[4] His competence in the language is also indicated by his inclusion in the group of eight Cambridge Hebraists appointed to translate the Old Testament from I Chronicles to the Song of Songs for the Authorised Version of 1611.

In appointing Chaderton as the first master, Mildmay secured the services of one who could be guaranteed to impress upon his students the importance of the biblical languages. One of his earliest protégés was William Bedell who matriculated in 1584 at the age of thirteen. A typical product of the college, Bedell soon became a competent linguist. 'The Greek Fathers and Historians he read in Greek; going to the fountain-head, and not beholding to translations. He attained also no mean skill in the Syriac, Arabic and Hebrew tongues. . . . He had this rare faculty, that whatsoever art or language he would set himself to acquire, he would reduce it into a body or method of his own contrivance: and of languages he would usually draw up a Grammar'.[5] As a preacher he applied his linguistic knowledge to difficult texts and never failed to comment on the precise meaning of Greek and Hebrew words. A brief period as chaplain to the British Embassy in Venice brought him into close contact with many Italian Jews whose company he greatly valued and at whose feet he deepened his knowledge of Semitic languages. It was at Venice too that he purchased the beautiful manuscript copy of the Hebrew Bible which can still be seen in Emmanuel College library.

The 'conferences' organised by Chaderton and some of his Cambridge colleagues provide an insight into one of the methods adopted by these early Puritans to achieve their educational aims. They also serve as a good example of how seriously Hebrew was taken in certain quarters during the final decades of the sixteenth century. As the academic form of 'the exercise of prophesying' the weekly conference was a class for the intensive study of Scripture. It was the intention of the participants that once every two years the whole Bible should be read, studied and expounded. A glimpse of what took place in this scholarly gathering is given by Samuel Clarke in his biography of John Carter of Clare Hall who

held constant meetings with divers of his famous contemporaries, and that every week, as with Doctor Chaderton, Doctor Andrewes (afterwards Bishop of Ely), Master Culverwell, Master Knewstub and diverse others. . . . At their meetings they had constant exercises: first, they began with prayer, and then applied themselves to the study of the Scriptures; one was for the original languages; another's task was for the grammatical interpretation; another's for the logical analysis; another's for the true sense and meaning of the text; another gathered the doctrines. Thus they carried on their several employments till at last they went out, like Apollos, eloquent men and mighty in the Scriptures.[6]

Apart from Chaderton, this particular group included at least two other Hebraists: John Knewstubb of St John's, who had been Hebrew lecturer at his college in 1572–73, and the youthful Lancelot Andrewes, fellow and later Master of Pembroke Hall. Andrewes' linguistic abilities are eulogised in his funeral oration preached by John Buckeridge, his successor as Bishop of Ely. On coming to Pembroke in 1575 'he was admitted one of Dr Watts' scholars; a noble grammarian, well entered in the Latin, Greek and Hebrew tongues'.[7] Before election the Watts' scholars had to demonstrate a knowledge of the three languages, a fact which suggests that Andrewes had learned some Hebrew at the Merchant Taylors' School where he had been a pupil prior to his coming to Cambridge. At the university he made rapid progress, and in time became proficient in fifteen languages, a feat which prompts Thomas Fuller to remark that he was 'so skilled in all, especially Oriental languages that some conceive he might (if then living) almost have served as an interpreter-general at the confusion of tongues'.[8]

The claim that Andrewes had mastered over a dozen languages may be debatable, but of his expertise in Hebrew there can be no doubt. Although he makes little use of it in his sermons and theological writings, he was sufficiently familiar with the language to pray in it. A manuscript copy of his personal devotions, the *Preces privatae*, which he presented to Laud in 1626 shortly before his death, contains prayers for daily use written in Latin, Greek and Hebrew, the languages of the cross. Such was his attachment to this prayerbook that towards the end of his life he was seldom seen in private without it. Its tattered condition testified to constant use. 'Had you seen the original manuscript', writes an eyewitness, 'happy in the glorious deformity thereof, being slubbered with his pious hands and watered with his penitential tears, you would have been forced to confess, that book belongs to no other than pure and primitive devotion'.[9] The whole work is a 'mosaic of quotations' in which the author draws freely on the Bible, the Church Fathers, early Christian liturgies and Jewish writings. For the psalms he uses the Septuagint, but frequently corrects the text by referring to the Hebrew original. In addition to the Hebrew Bible, he finds a place in his devotions for the Targum, and is especially attracted to the prayers of the Synagogue. Admittedly, Hebrew passages form only a small part of the whole, but whenever a quotation is made from post-biblical Jewish literature, the original language is preserved. He quotes verbatim morning and evening prayers and parts of the Sabbath liturgy according to the Sephardic rite. Of particular interest is the use he makes of the ancient Jewish prayer based on the description of God found in Exodus 34:6f.

The Lord, the Lord God,
full of compassion and gracious,
slow to anger and abounding in mercy and truth,
keeping mercy for thousands,
forgiving iniquity, transgression and sin:
but He will by no means clear the guilty,
visiting the iniquity of the fathers upon the children.

These thirteen 'divine attributes' or 'qualities of mercy' had been an essential element in Jewish penitential prayers since talmudic times. For centuries they had formed a part of the liturgy of the Synagogue for fast days, the New Year season and the Day of Atonement.[10] In his private devotions Andrewes includes them in morning prayer on Mondays.

The existence of this collection of prayers, compiled from different sources and written in the ancient languages, is indicative of two things. The first is the compiler's catholicity. Andrewes realised the value of extra-biblical material for private devotion, a realisation which led him not only to the Christian Fathers but also to the Hebraic tradition. The second is his love of the biblical languages. Greek and Hebrew do not of necessity belong only to the study or the lecture room; they can also be used as vehicles of prayer by those who have taken the trouble to learn them.

By compiling his prayer-book in this way Andrewes was consciously opposing a point of view expressed by contemporary left-wing Puritans. In 1582 Robert Browne, the early Congregationalist leader, had criticised current preaching methods. He could find no justification whatever for quoting Latin, Greek and Hebrew in the pulpit. These 'maidens of the bishops', as he calls the languages, are used by preachers only to give the impression of profound scholarship; they are of no value at all in the saving of souls.[11] Andrewes' disapproval of such an attitude is evident from a sermon preached at St Giles, Cripplegate in 1592 in which he condemns the Separatists for their narrow-minded and anti-scholarly views. Those who will listen to 'no Latin, nor Greek; no, though it be interpreted', who will have 'none of the Apocrypha cited', and who will accept nothing 'out of the Jews' Talmud', are utterly misguided in their opinions.[12] Not only does the saintly bishop quote from the devotional literature of the Jews, he also says his prayers in their language.

Andrewes' eminence as a Hebrew scholar led to his election as the chairman of the Westminster group which was responsible for translating Genesis to II Kings in the Authorised Version. But as well as being a keen student of Semitic languages himself, in later life he actively promoted them at Oxford and Cambridge by urging foreign teachers to settle in this country. 'He was a lover and encourager of learning and learned men which appeared in his liberality and bounty to Master Casaubon, Master Cluverius, Master Vossius, Master Grotius, and Master Erpenius whom he attempted with the offer of a very large stipend out of his own purse to draw into England, to have read and taught the Oriental tongues here.'[13] The seeds of this lifelong interest in Semitics had been sown at Merchant Taylors' and nurtured in Elizabethan Cambridge during the heyday of Puritan scholarship.

However much they may have valued their weekly conference as a forum for discussion and debate, the main concern of these Cambridge Puritans was not for an eclectic band of scholars. They were anxious that as many ordinary clergymen as possible should be enabled to defend what they considered to be right doctrine. This could be achieved only by applying scholarly rigour to the minutiae of biblical exegesis. In a manuscript ascribed to 'Mr. Chaderton of Cambridge' we find 'An Order to be used for the training up and exercising of students in Divinity, whereby they may be made fit and meet to discharge the duties belonging to that profession'.[14] Here we are given a glimpse of how these conferences were conducted. Because every minister was expected to be able 'to teach sound doctrine by the true interpretation of the Word, and to confute all contrary errors', his training had to have two basic ingredients: Bible study and skill in disputation. Before coming to such a conference the participants were required to do some homework. They must 'diligently search out by themselves the true sense and meaning of the text appointed, using the help of all these gifts following'. The first of six 'gifts' is a knowledge of the biblical languages. Through Hebrew and Greek 'God hath revealed and written his will and testament by his prophets and apostles, and therefore hath given this gift to his church, for the better understanding of the etymology, true construction, proper signification, phrase and use of all those words wherein his will is expressed'. Mastery of the languages was considered to be of prime importance, for it was only when he had fully grasped the meaning of Scripture in its original sense that a student could proceed to disputation which was vital 'for defence of the truth and confutation of error'.[15] Some of the disputes which punctuate the closing decades of the sixteenth century testify to the thoroughness of Puritan educational methods and to the use of Jewish literature by English scholars to uphold certain standpoints.

Disputations on Holy Scripture

One of the main religious issues of the Elizabethan period was concerned with the source of religious authority. Was it the Church or the Bible which had the last word in matters of doctrine and belief? Since the Puritans stressed the sufficiency of Scripture for all doctrinal questions and claimed that only the written Word could provide a secure source of revelation, they had to be prepared to defend their understanding of certain key texts. Since they also insisted that the Bible in the language of the people was a basic requirement, they had to demonstrate that the pure oracles of God had not been distorted, intentionally or unintentionally, in translation. 'Whereas men in the early sixteenth century felt themselves to be rediscovering the original Christian Gospel ... later Protestant theologians in Elizabethan England were set the task of defending the rediscovered and now systematised Gospel by proving, in terms of detailed textual and linguistic scholarship, its sound basis in pure texts and faithful translations.'[16] Their opponents were those who could see no possible advantage in having vernacular versions of the Scripture and were determined to discredit those who had made them.

In 1582 a reader in divinity in the English College at Rheims published a book entitled '*A Discoverie* of the manifold corruptions of the Holy Scriptures by the heretics of our days, especially the English Sectaries, and of their foul dealing herein, by partial and false translations to the advantage of their heresies, in their English Bibles used and authorised since the schism'. The author was an English Catholic, Gregory Martin, who had fled to France in 1570 to escape persecution. One of the original scholars of St John's College, Oxford, Martin was considered by his contemporaries to be an excellent linguist. He served as Greek lecturer for his college from 1564 to 1568. On one occasion when the Duke of Norfolk visited the university he was welcomed by a member of St John's who, referring to Martin, said 'Thou hast, O illustrious Duke, our Hebraist, our Grecian, our poet, our honour and glory'. In France Martin attended the college opened at Douai in 1568 by Cardinal Allen for Catholics exiled from England and was ordained priest in 1573. He soon joined the faculty as a teacher of Hebrew and in 1578 moved with the college to Rheims where he became one of the principal translators of the Rheims Bible.

The Catholic scholar was equally matched on the Protestant side by William Fulke, Master of Pembroke Hall, Cambridge and Vice-Chancellor of the university. A member of St John's College, Fulke graduated B.A. at Cambridge in 1558 before proceeding to one of the Inns of Chancery in accordance with his father's wishes. But he soon discovered that the legal profession was not for him, and within a few years he had returned to his old college to read theology and Oriental languages. In 1566 he was appointed lecturer in Hebrew at the college, a post which he held for three years. It is safe to assume that he had started his Hebrew studies while he was still an undergraduate in Marian Cambridge, for by 1560 he was beginning to make use of the language in his publications. Fulke has the distinction of being the first Englishman of the Tudor period to pen a formal attack on astrology. His *Antiprognosticon* (London 1560), as the English translation made in the same year states on the title-page, was an 'invective against the vain and unprofitable predictions of the astrologians'. Compared with continental polemics of a similar kind it contained little that was new, yet it became one of the most important documents in the war against astrology. Twice in the course of this short book Fulke demonstrates his familiarity with the original Hebrew version of the biblical account of the creation of the world and uses it in support of his arguments.

It is, however, as a protagonist of the Puritan cause that Fulke is best known. Samuel Clarke states that he had frequent meetings with Puritan scholars at Cambridge for the study of the Scriptures; a reference without doubt to the conferences.[17] Among his close friends were Laurence Chaderton, William Whitaker and Thomas Cartwright. He was passionate in his defence of reformed doctrine. His vehemence in disputations with Catholics earned him the title of 'acerrimus papamastix', and by the late 1570s he had become a staunch defender of the Protestant cause. Within a period of three years he produced over a dozen anti-papal works in reply to various recusant publications. In 1583 he published 'A *Defence* of the sincere and true translations of the Holy Scriptures into the English tongue, against the manifold cavils, frivolous quarrels, and impudent slanders of Gregory Martin',[18] in which Martin's attack on the vernacular translations is answered point for point. Why, asks Fulke, should one follow the Vulgate when its unreliability is well known and widely attested? 'Where so many of your own popish writers do accuse your vulgar Latin text of innumerable corruptions, what reason is there that we should follow that translation only; especially seeing God hath given us knowledge of the tongues, that we may resort to the fountains themselves'.[19] No theologian worth his salt will neglect Hebrew and Greek. If he does, he will command but little respect from his colleagues. 'He which shall profess to be an absolute learned divine without the knowledge of the three tongues at the least, may think well of himself; but hardly he shall get and retain the credit he seeketh among learned men in this learned age.'[20]

Martin's main contention throughout his *Discoverie* is that 'the English heretics' purposely mistranslate the text of Scripture in favour of their own erroneous teachings. He seeks to prove that the doctrinal claims of Protestants rest on a deliberately false translation of the original. The argument begins with a criticism of vernacular translations in general, but quickly develops into a detailed discussion of doctrinal issues with an attempt to clarify the meaning of key biblical words before engaging in interpretation. This has to be done because the Protestants 'in translating places of controversy flee from the Hebrew and the Greek; . . . a most certain argument of wilful corruption'.[21] The preface and thirteen out of twenty-two chapters contain comments on Hebrew words or phrases and frequent references to post-biblical Jewish literature.

The discussion of the doctrine of purgatory provides a good example of how Fulke, in his disagreement with Martin over the meaning of specific words, utilises his knowledge of Hebrew and rabbinic literature to defend his own beliefs.[22] Martin opens the debate by criticising the Protestant understanding of the Hebrew word *she'ol* as 'grave'. Rather, it should be taken to refer to the place where the patriarchs went before their deliverance was effected by Christ, 'the bosom of Abraham' or '*limbus patrum*'. He takes Theodore Beza as a representative of the non-Catholic position and challenges his statement that 'among the Hebrews the word signifieth nothing else but the grave'. 'I would gladly know', says Martin, 'what are those Hebrews. Doth not the Hebrew text of the Holy Scripture best tell us the use of this word? Do not themselves translate it 'hell' very often? Do not the Septuaginta always? If any Hebrew in the world were asked how he would turn these words into Hebrew *Similes estis sepulchris dealbatis*, "You are like to whited graves", would he . . . translate it by this Hebrew word which Beza saith among the Hebrews signifieth nothing else but 'grave'?'

At this point Fulke enters the discussion in support of Beza's rendering and refers to Rashi's comment on the phrase 'I shall go down to Sheol to my son' in Genesis 37:35: 'Rabbi Solomon . . . saith plainly that the true and proper interpretation of Sheol is Keber'. In his commentary on Genesis Rashi does in fact say that 'according to the simple sense *she'ol* means "grave"', but he goes on to give the alternative explanation that 'according to the Midrash it means "gehenna"'. Fulke, however, does not mention the midrashic explanation here, he returns to it later. But Martin is suspicious of these 'later rabbis . . . which falsely interpret all the holy scriptures against Our Saviour Christ's . . . descending into hell, which those Jewish rabbis deny, because they look for another Messiah that shall not die at all, and consequently shall not after his death go down into hell and deliver the fathers expecting his coming, as Our Saviour Christ did'. He laments that the English translators 'join themselves with such companions, being the sworn enemies of Our Saviour Christ'. Fulke springs to the defence of the rabbis as grammarians and asks, 'As for the Jewish rabbis, what reason is there why we should not credit them in the interpretation of words of their own tongue, rather than any ancient Christians ignorant of the Hebrew tongue? And although they do sometimes frowardly contend about the signification of a word or two, against the truth of the gospel, that is no sufficient

cause why they should be discredited in all words'. He does not
advocate following the Jews in their exposition of the Scriptures, but
it is 'no more unlawful to learn Hebrew of the Hebrew rabbis than
Latin of Quintilian'.

The debate continues, with Martin, despite his protestations, using
the Jewish authorities to his own advantage and quoting the Targum
and the rabbinic commentaries on verses from the Psalms, Proverbs,
Job and Jonah, whenever they take *she'ol* to mean 'gehenna'. He cites
the targumic rendering of Psalm 49:16 in support of this meaning. But
Fulke replies by quoting Kimchi on the same verse who explains *she'ol*
by *geber*, 'grave'. Rashi makes no helpful comment here, but it is clear
from his exegesis of Genesis 37:35 that he understands the word to
mean 'grave' in its primary sense, 'although', says Fulke, 'after
figurative and sometimes fond expositions, it was interpreted for
'hell' '. (A reference to the midrashic explanation of the verse.)
Similarly Kimchi interprets the phrase 'the wicked shall return to
Sheol' in Psalm 9:18 (Heb.) as referring to their going back to the
grave. In Job 14:13 and 17:13 the Targum translates *she'ol* as 'grave',
a rendering for which Fulke also claims the support of the Italian
Jewish commentator Abraham Farissol whose exposition of Job had
been printed in the Bomberg Bible of 1518. He admits that Ibn Ezra in
his note on Jonah 2:3 (Heb.) explains *she'ol* as 'a deep place opposite to
heaven'. But he is quick to point to the same rabbi's comment on the
phrase 'I will ransom them from the power of Sheol' in Hosea 13:14
which contains no suggestion of a place like gehenna, an interpretation
which is supported also by Rashi and Kimchi *ad loc*. The discussion
then moves into the New Testament, but not before Fulke has
castigated his opponent for showing scant respect for the opinion of
eminent Hebraists, Jewish, Catholic and Protestant, who also
translate *she'ol* as 'grave':

In the margin you tell us, that such catholics as have translated the word
she'ol for a 'grave', have also done amiss. Pardon us, M. Martin; we take you
for no such learned Hebrician, that you should control Pagninus, Isidorus
Clarius, and all other Hebricians of this time upon such slender sleeveless
reasons as you have brought hitherto. And you show an intolerable proud
stomach, that being a man so little seen in the Hebrew tongue (as you show
yourself to be), you should condemn such grave and learned persons of your
own side, of rashness or ignorance. . . . You may in time to come, if you apply
your study, prove learned in that language, wherein as yet you are but a
smatterer, not worthy to be heard against so many, so learned, so famous
professors of the Hebrew tongue, Jews and Christians, protestants and

papists, authors of grammars, dictionaries, and translations.

As in this discussion on Purgatory so in those on the priesthood, devotion to the saints, the use of sacred images, and many others, the disputants quote freely from the Hebrew Bible and from post-biblical Jewish writings. Both Fulke and Martin evince a sound knowledge of the language and refer to a wide range of rabbinic commentaries. Christian Hebraists such as Pagninus, Münster, Montano and Clarius are regarded as important channels of the Hebraic tradition. Martin at times appears suspicious of Jewish explanations. But Fulke, although he views the rabbis unfavourably as theologians, stresses their importance as guides in matters of grammar and exegesis, especially when their explanations offer confirmation of Protestant doctrines.

Within five years of the publication of Fulke's *Defence* another leading Cambridge Puritan was taking up the issue of the authoritative version of the Bible with equal vigour. In his *Disputation on Holy Scripture against the Papists* (1588) William Whitaker, Regius Professor of Divinity and Master of St John's College, takes to task those Catholic theologians who maintain that the Vulgate, rather than the Hebrew or Greek original, is the authentic text of Scripture. He points out that the Council of Trent had stated categorically that 'the Old Latin Vulgate edition should be held for authentic in public lectures, disputations, preachings and expositions, and that no man shall dare or presume to reject it under any pretext whatsoever'.[23] From this, certain Catholic scholars had deduced that in disputation no reference could be made to the Hebrew or Greek, and that in matters of faith and morals the Vulgate must not be corrected from the original texts. Protestants are in fundamental disagreement with these views:

Our churches, on the contrary, determine that this Latin edition is very generally and miserably corrupt, is false and not authentic; and that the Hebrew of the Old Testament, and the Greek of the New, is the sincere and authentic Scripture of God; and that, consequently, all questions are to be determined by these originals, and versions only so far approved as they agree with these originals.[24]

In order to demonstrate the superiority of the Hebrew over the Latin he combs the Vulgate for erroneous renderings. The forty-three instances of mistranslations which he finds in the Book of Genesis alone point unmistakably, in his opinion, to 'the infinite perversity of that version'.[25] He gives further instances from the Psalter when he defends Calvin's critique of the Vulgate against the criticisms of the Jesuit Robert Bellarmine.[26]

While Whitaker was a capable Hebraist who made constant reference to the Massoretic Text in the course of his disputation, he was not as familiar as Fulke with the works of Jewish commentators. For his knowledge of rabbinic exegesis he depended entirely on continental Christian Hebraists. Pagninus, Génébrard, Vatable, Montano and Tremellius figure prominently throughout the dispute as guides to the Hebraic tradition.

A younger and less eminent contemporary of Fulke and Whitaker was Nicholas Gibbens of Clare Hall, Cambridge. Although he never held an academic post, Gibbens' knowledge of Hebrew and his appreciation of rabbinic literature was equal to that of any other Puritan divine at the turn of the century. His one surviving publication demonstrates how ready he was to use it in defence of the Protestant cause. On the title-page of *Questions and Disputations concerning Holy Scripture* (1601) he declares that his intention is to free 'the everlasting truth of the Word of God . . . from the errors and slanders of atheists, Papists, philosophers and all heretics'. His method is to provide 'brief, faithful and sound expositions' of the most difficult texts in the first fourteen chapters of Genesis. In the preface, addressed to the Bishop of Durham, he voices his concern over the influence which Catholicism is exercising in England:

Our church and commonwealth is continually assaulted by the adversaries, either by open insinuation or secret immission of lurking spies, . . . priests, Jesuits, solicitors for the Church of Rome, remaining in every corner of this land; who through the power of darkness, do work into the hearts of men, by false suggestions and coloured hypocrisy. It is the duty of ministers to labour with watchfulness and wisdom to bridle the fury of such enterprisers.

In his exposition Gibbens aims to help his fellow clergy to combat the claims of Rome by providing them with what he considers to be the correct interpretation of problematic passages.

The keynote of the work is the author's defence of the integrity of the Hebrew text of the Old Testament. Roman Catholic scholars persistently maintain that the original is corrupt, and will accept nothing but the Vulgate as the authoritative version of the Bible. In support of the *hebraica veritas* Gibbens notes the contradiction that exists in Genesis 8:7 between the extant Hebrew text and the Greek and Latin translations. Whereas the Hebrew reads 'and the raven went out and returned until the waters had dried up', the Septuagint and

Vulgate render the phrase as 'and the raven went out and returned not until the waters had dried up'. Since, according to certain authorities, Jerome claims that the second of these two versions was to be found in the Hebrew original during his day, some argue that the Jews have wilfully corrupted the text extant in the fifth century A.D. This Gibbens vigorously denies. 'The Scriptures in the Hebrew tongue are pure and unspotted of all corruption', and Rome errs in preferring the Vulgate to the Hebrew fountain 'which the singular providence of God hath hitherto preserved pure'. In Gibbens' view, the 'not' in the above quotation from Genesis was inserted by the Catholics because they followed conjecture instead of the truth. Inasmuch as it is not expressly stated that Noah received back the raven, as he did the dove, they wrongly concluded that it did not return. It is the Vulgate, not the Hebrew, which is corrupt. To add weight to his argument, he demonstrates that 'the Rabbis and Jewish interpreters do with one consent expound it so, which argues that the same is to be reverenced and received as having the authority of the Word'.

Whenever he encounters a difficulty in a particular verse he brings to bear upon it all the rabbinic solutions known to him. He discusses points of grammar by referring to Rashi, David Kimchi, Ibn Ezra and 'diverse Jewish doctors', including Abraham Seba and Isaac Karo. But since he rarely quotes the original, either in Hebrew or in translation, it is difficult to determine whether he was familiar with these authorities at first hand or simply relied on other Christian Hebraists. Several references in the marginal notes to commentators such as Nicholas of Lyra, Paul of Burgos and Génébrard, indicate a certain amount of dependence on the works of intermediaries. Even so, Gibbens' attainments as a Hebraist are impressive, and what is more, he adopts a tolerant attitude towards contemporary Judaism.

Doctrinal controversies

Although Cambridge has usually been regarded as the power-house of Elizabethan Puritanism, Oxford's contribution to the growth of the movement should not be underestimated. Men who made no secret of their sympathies towards the more radical Reformers were as active and influential at Oxford as Chaderton and his colleagues were at the other place. The Chancellor of the university from 1564 to 1588 was none other than Robert Dudley, Earl of Leicester, that 'cherisher and patron-general' of the Puritans. The membership of such Puritan colleges as Exeter, Queen's, Brasenose, Magdalen and Christ Church increased considerably during Elizabeth's reign. Heads of Houses, in particular Laurence Humphrey of Magdalen and Thomas Sampson of Christ Church, ensured that their colleges produced well-educated ministers and enthusiastic laymen.

Sampson's Puritan leanings have already been noted in connection with the Geneva Bible. Humphrey is of particular interest, both for his views on the education of the laity and for his knowledge of Hebrew. As a Marian exile he had visited Basle, Zurich and Geneva, and had been suitably impressed by the pioneering work of John Sturm in Strasbourg. On his return to England he was appointed Regius Professor of Divinity at Oxford. He served as President of Magdalen from 1561 to 1589 and as Vice-Chancellor of the university on several occasions. For thirty years he dominated the Oxford scene and exercised a profound influence on scores of students. 'He stocked his college', writes Anthony Wood, 'with a generation of nonconformists, which could not be rooted out in many years after his decease, but sowed also in the divinity school such seeds of Calvinism, and laboured to create in the younger sort hatred against the Papists, as if nothing but divine truths were to be found in the one, and nothing but abominations were to be seen in the other.'[27] Humphrey was as anxious as his Cambridge counterparts to promote Puritanism by means of a sound education. He made public his aims and ideals in a book entitled *The Nobles, or Of Nobility* written in Latin in 1559 and issued in English four years later.

As the title suggests, this was a blueprint for the education of the gentry. Laity, as well as clergy, should be schooled in the Christian virtues. However rich, wise and learned a gentleman might be, he would receive no respect unless he was good and godly. 'For with God is no account or respect, either of stock, honour or person, either of desert or dignity, but through Christ Jesus.' Christ was to be the model, 'the pillar, crest and perfection of all nobility'.[28] But the imitation of Christ could be practised only by those who were grounded in the Bible, for 'the sound and only proof of true religion is the conference and examining of divine Scriptures'. To be effective such an examination requires a knowledge of the biblical languages which, because of their difficulty, should be mastered at an early age:

Be the hardest first imprinted. For growing riper in years and knowledge, they lightly neglect them as trifles. Therefore, not little helpeth it, even at first, to learn them Greek and Hebrew. Preposterously do all universities, schools and teachers that contrary it. For about the bush run they to arts who understand not the original tongues. . . . In these harder tongues much availeth the trusty, plain and learned explication of a painful teacher.[29]

Humphrey, like Chaderton, placed the Bible before the Classics, and by stressing the supreme importance of Scripture tried to include Hebrew in the educational pattern not only of the clergyman but also of the godly gentleman. As a professor of divinity he undoubtedly made a contribution towards the teaching of the language himself. His proficiency in it is demonstrated from a treatise on the best method of translating and expounding the works of sacred and profane authors, published in Basle in 1559 under the title *Interpretatio linguarum*. After discussing the importance of Hebrew for the biblical exegete he takes the prophecy of Obadiah as an example, first reproducing it in the original and then providing the reader with a translation and exposition of the text. While his indebtedness to Pagninus and Münster is obvious, one may conclude from his exegetical comments that Humphrey was a competent Hebraist in his own right. The only other extant testimony to his linguistic ability is three short laudatory poems written in Hebrew and appended to the preface of Peter Baro's sermons on the book of Jonah (London 1579).

The Oxford equivalent of William Fulke was John Rainolds, President of Corpus Christi College and a prominent member of the Hampton Court Conference. A protégé of Leicester, Rainolds was a notable theologian and preacher whose erudition was widely recognised. Edward Leigh, writing in the preface to an edition of Rainolds' sermons on the Book of Haggai, claims that he resembled 'a well furnished library, full of all faculties, of all studies, of all learning: the memory, the reading of the man were near a miracle'.[30] Rainolds' unequivocal attitude towards the study of Hebrew emerges from a letter written to a friend on 4 July 1577, in which he offers advice on how to study divinity. Because Hebrew and Greek are indispensable for a proper understanding of the Bible, Rainolds urges his correspondent to persevere:

I wish that you also join Hebrew to your Greek, though peradventure you have once began it and given it over. For in that you may follow me . . . who myself, when I was first Master of Arts began the study of it, and being weary left it: the next year, perceiving the necessary use of it, I set again upon it, and I thank God, since continued a student in it. Wherefore the Word of God, and that, if it may be, out of the very well-spring, not out of the brooks of translations ... must be diligently read.[31]

His writings show that Rainolds was the first to take his own advice with regard to Hebrew studies. What appear to have been his own lecture notes are preserved in manuscript (MS. 352) in the library of The Queen's College, Oxford. In them he outlines some elementary grammatical rules, describes the use of accents and provides a word list of certain psalms, giving the root, the meaning, and in some cases the Greek equivalent of the Hebrew words. One such list is entitled 'Expositio verborum in preci nocturna habitorum'. Collections of sermons on Obadiah and Haggai, his only published works on biblical books, display a much deeper knowledge of the language and contain several references to the Massoretic Text and to the Talmud. In a comment on Obadiah 9 he translates the phrase *'ish mehar 'esau* as 'the valiant of the mount of Esau'. He rejects the rendering found in the Geneva Bible and in Tremellius ('every one of the mount of Esau') on the grounds that 'the Hebrew word *'ish* signifieth a valiant man differing from *'adam* as *vir* doth from *homo'*.[32] It is possible that he took this point from Jerome or Münster, both of whom read 'vir de monte Esau', but it is equally possible that he was familiar with Rashi's explanation *ad loc.* of *'ish* as *gibbor*, 'hero', or 'warrior'. In other writings, of a polemical rather than exegetical nature, Rainolds makes direct references to rabbis and Christian Hebraists. In his debate with Bellarmine he is often dependent on rabbinic authorities for the elucidation of textual or lexicographical difficulties. For example, when discussing the correct spelling and meaning of *lahatehem* ('their enchantments') in Exodus 7:11 he refers the reader to David Kimchi's *Book of Roots* for a possible explanation.[33] Ibn Ezra, whom he describes as 'the most learned of all the rabbis', proves to be of assistance in making sense of the strange title given to Nehemiah in Nehemiah 8:9.[34]

Rainolds' insistence on the importance of the Hebrew text of the Old Testament as the basis of any exegetical work is nowhere more clearly seen than in the discussion which he had with the Jesuit scholar John Hart in 1584. Hart was one of the many priests trained at Douai who, on their return to England as missionaries, were apprehended by the authorities and forced to defend their beliefs against Protestant theologians.[35] At such conferences notes were taken and these were sometimes published in support of the Protestant cause. This particular debate, conducted in the Tower, lasted for many weeks and was reported in a volume of over seven hundred pages entitled *The Sum of the Conference between John Rainolds and John Hart: Touching the Head and the Faith of the Church* (1598). Several doctrinal issues were raised, one of which was the Catholic belief in the supremacy of the Pope.[36] When Rainolds inquires how this doctrine can be gleaned from Deuteronomy 17:8–12, as stated in a decree of Innocent III, Hart replies:

By a reason which I ground upon the likeness and proportion of the Church of Christ to the children of Israel. For if the Israelites had a high Priest to be their judge in matters of difficulty and doubt . . . why should not we semblably have a high Priest to be the judge of our causes? . . . Here [Deut. 17:8–12] the high Priest is made the chief judge, to hear and determine hard and doubtful causes amongst the people of God. And who amongst Christians is such a Priest and Judge but the Pope only.

Rainolds immediately objects that the mystical interpretation of the passage is being put forward at the expense of the literal. 'For the literal sense of that in Deuteronomy doth concern the Jews. . . . Now, how dangerous it is to build, as upon Scripture, things which are not grounded upon the literal sense thereof'. Because Innocent III takes it in the mystical sense his interpretation of these verses is entirely misleading. Furthermore, Rainolds denies that the High Priest is also a judge to whom the Jews are to go for a decision on difficult questions. 'This the Scripture saith not; but maketh a difference between the judge and the Priest. For it giveth sentence of death upon him who refuseth to hearken to the Priest or to the judge [Deut. 17:12]. Wherein, by divisioning the Priest from the judge, it declareth plainly that the Priest was not the same as the judge.' Hart rejects this explanation on the basis of the text of the Vulgate. 'Our common edition in Latin doth not read it so: but in this sort: he that shall presumptuously refuse to obey . . . the commandment of the Priest, by the decree of the judge shall that man die. You see it is here, the commandment of the Priest: and the decree of the judge is another point. It is not, as you cite it, the Priest or the judge.' Rainolds replies by going beyond the Vulgate to the original, 'It is not so in your Latin which man hath translated. But it is so in the Hebrew, written by the spirit of God'. Hart then appeals to the decree of the Council of Trent which stressed the authority of the Vulgate. 'No man may dare or presume to reject it [the Vulgate] under any pretence', not even 'under pretence of the Hebrew text. And that for great reason. For the Hebrew Bibles, which are extant now, are shamefully corrupted in

many places by the Jews, of spite and malice against Christians'. He
then quotes Lindanus, Bishop of Ghent and one of the foremost
sixteenth-century Catholic apologists, in support of this statement.
But Rainolds springs to the defence of the Hebrew texts' condemning
Lindanus' view as a 'shameful slander brewed by Satan'. He suggests
that the correct answer would be found in the writings of

three of the learnedest and fittest judges of this matter that your church hath,
even Isaac Levita, Arias Montanus and Payua Andradius. Of whom the first,
being Lindanus' own master, and professor of the Hebrew tongue in the
University of Cologne, hath written three books in defence of the Hebrew
truth against the cavils of this scholar. The next, for his rare skill of tongues
and arts, was put in trust by King Philip to set forth the Bible in Hebrew,
Greek, Chaldee and Latin: wherein he hath reproved that treatise of
Lindanus and disclosed his folly. The last was the chiefest of the Divines and
Doctors at the Council of Trent. The decrees whereof, though he have
defended, and namely that which you mention, yet . . . he hath confuted them
who say that the Jews have corrupted the Hebrew text.

Hart, however, is still not persuaded. He admits that he has not read
these men; but whatever they say they will not be able to prove that the
Jews did not corrupt the text of the Bible. In a final bid to convince his
opponent Rainolds quotes the Targum and the Septuagint, both of
which reproduce the Hebrew of Deuteronomy 17:12 faithfully. But to
no avail. Hart insists on the priority of the Vulgate: 'I appeal still unto
our Latin, and will not forsake it under any pretext'.

These examples, to which many more could be added, demonstrate
the use made by Rainolds of the works of Christian Hebraists and
Jewish exegetes to support what he considered to be the true meaning
of the biblical text.[37] Not only could the rabbis be called on to elucidate
difficult grammatical points, they could also be enlisted on the
Protestant side in almost any argument. But in spite of his frequent
recourse to rabbinic literature, it would be a mistake to think that
Rainolds adopted a wholly uncritical attitude towards Jews and
Judaism. The mediaeval Christian hatred of the Jews which Luther,
and to a lesser extent Calvin, so successfully perpetuated, occasionally
comes to the surface. There are times when his fervent belief in the
uniqueness of Christ leads him to speak in the most derogatory way of
the work of those rabbis to whom he often turned for help. In terms
reminiscent of leading anti-Jewish propagandists he warns his fellow
Christians of the pitfalls of rabbinic exegesis. The Jews are

stricken with madness and with blindness and with astonishment of heart, since they have shut their eyes against the sun of righteousness. And the plague which God did threaten them is come upon them: Thou shalt grope at noonday as the blind doth grope in darkness. The tokens hereof are rife in their Rabbis' handling of the Scriptures. Who (beside the filth of many other follies wherewith they do soil them) are wont . . . to piece out their glosses with brain sick dreams and sottish fables. [e.g.] In Genesis 49:7 it is prophesied of Simeon and Levi, I will divide them in Jacob and scatter them in Israel. In Joshua it is showed how this prophecy was performed both in Simeon and Levi. Rabbi Solomon [Rashi], not perceiving it, surmised that the tribe of Simeon must be scattered in the same sort as was the tribe of Levi. Wherefore as the Levites were scattered throughout Israel to teach the whole Church, so he had a fancy that the Simeonites were to teach little children. With this did he travail, and he brought it forth: he thought it might be: he liked it should be: he wrote it was so.[38]

Yet, in spite of such charges, Rainolds found much that was of value in the rabbis and was quite prepared to utilise their arguments whenever it suited him to do so.

From the frequent references he makes to Jewish writings it is clear that Rainolds had a firm grasp of biblical and post-biblical Hebrew. Mastery of the language, coupled with the part which he played in the Hampton Court Conference, led to his appointment as a member of the Oxford group of translators for the Authorised Version. His death in May 1607, just as the work was gathering momentum, must have been a severe blow to his colleagues. All who knew him would have echoed the words of Sir Isaac Wake in his funeral oration, that in John Rainolds' passing the university had lost a person who 'far outshined the rest of her sons in the exact skill of diverse languages'.[39]

The apocalyptic tradition

The second half of the sixteenth century saw the formation of the Protestant apocalyptic tradition with its emphasis on chronology and its obsessive fear of the antichrist. As in ancient Judaism, the message of apocalyptic was delivered in a time of crisis to encourage perseverance among the faithful. The Elizabethan Church, at times feeling threatened by the might of Rome, turned readily to a way of thinking which had its roots in persecution and martyrdom. Introduced by a minority, which had experienced exile during the reign of Mary, apocalyptic ideas were soon propagated throughout the society. They became not just one facet of Elizabethan religious thought, but a vital issue.[40] They contained two prominent elements. Coupled with the attempt to identify the antichrist of the Letters of John went a consuming interest in chronology and calculation of the future. While the exact date of the end of the world was something which had to be worked out from the Scriptures, many English Protestants had no hesitation in equating antichrist with the Pope. This, not unnaturally, brought a response from the Jesuits who immediately challenged the Protestant interpretation of key apocalyptic texts. In an attempt to defend their own understanding of the Bible and to bring what they considered to be the true message of apocalyptic to their fellow-countrymen, some English Protestant scholars looked for support within the Hebraic tradition. The work of Hugh Broughton is typical of this approach.

Broughton (1549–1612), a protégé of Bernard Gilpin, matriculated at Cambridge in 1569 as a member of Magdalene College. After holding fellowships at St John's and Christ's, he was appointed to teach divinity at Durham and to a canonry at the cathedral. But he did not remain there long. He was a difficult man to work with, and as a result of a disagreement with the university authorities, he moved to London. There he was given lodgings in the house of a friend, William Cotton, in exchange for which he acted as tutor to Rowland, his host's son. In 1589 a difference of opinion with Archbishop Whitgift encouraged him to flee to the Continent, where he was destined to stay for most of his life. He finally returned to England in 1612, terminally ill with consumption.

It is clear from his writings that Broughton was an accomplished Hebrew scholar. Daiches describes him as 'perhaps the most profound of all the English Hebraists of the period'.[41] He had studied the language at Cambridge, though there is no record that he had taught it in an official capacity at either of the colleges where he was a fellow. On the Continent he developed close associations with Jews and with such eminent Christian Hebraists as Scaliger, Junius and Raphaelengius; these connections were a significant factor in his Hebrew attainments. Not only was he capable of dealing with the Old Testament in the original, he was familiar at first hand with a wide range of post-biblical Jewish literature. His contribution to Old Testament studies includes an English version of the Book of Job, a commentary on Ecclesiastes, an English rendering of Lamentations and a translation of Daniel into English and Latin with explanatory notes and comments. In all four works the predominating feature is the author's extensive use and citation of rabbinic sources. In addition to Targum and Talmud, he insists that other Jewish writings must be regarded as indispensable to anyone engaged in translating the Bible. Even 'ungracious Barbinel [Isaac Abravanel] . . . helpeth such as will not be deceived, and can judge when he saith well. And Jarchi [Rashi] and Aben Ezra, and David Kimchi, and Rambam and Menachem, and Bochai and Ben Arama, and Isaac Caro, and many yet unprinted. . . . Those Hebrews are all profitable, and he that cannot use them should not translate'.[42] In a footnote to his *Treatise of Melchisedek* he lists no fewer than twenty-two Jewish sources which the serious student of the Hebrew Scriptures might consult to his advantage.[43] Elsewhere he refers to David Kimchi as 'the king of grammarians'.[44] Furthermore, he shared the rabbinic attitude towards the vocalisation of the Hebrew Bible by the Massoretes. In what became known as 'the battle of the vowel points' he sided with the Jews and argued against the Catholics that the vowels were a part of the original text, not a late invention of the rabbis and therefore untrustworthy.[45] Yet, in spite of his constant references to rabbinic writings, he warns that they must not be used indiscriminately. The rabbis are to be quoted as authorities only when they support the christological interpretation of a given word or phrase. 'When the Jews speak for Christianity', he writes, 'then we should cite them; and not cite our enemies against oneself. There is neither Christianity nor wit in that dealing.'[46] Abravanel is 'a rabbi of great pains and wit, but not of grace, and only to be followed when he is on our side'.[47] This use of Jewish writings for the confirmation of the Christian point of view leads him to modify his scholarship to conform to his prejudices.

Although he has an unusual grasp of rabbinics for an Elizabethan scholar, Broughton frequently has recourse to the works of other Christian Hebraists. He is quick to praise several prominent intermediaries who helped diffuse Jewish learning among sixteenth-century Christians. Pagninus' skill in Hebrew 'giveth place to none Italian, former nor later. . . . Montanus, whose like if Spain had bred many, the Pope should have been closely bitten to the heart'. As for the translation of Tremellius, it 'giveth place to none'.[48] But he finds little to commend in the Hebrew studies of those responsible for the Bishops' Bible, a version full of 'traps and pitfalls'. Such was his contempt of the efforts of the bishops that in 1597 he was pressing for a fresh translation so that the reader would 'in no place be snared by the translator'.[49] Four years previously, in June 1593, he had written to

Sir William Cecil requesting financial support for the promotion of a new and better English version of the Scriptures. He claimed that 'sundry lords, and amongst them some bishops, besides doctors and other inferiors of all sorts' had asked him to undertake 'a clearing of the Bible's translation'. All of them 'judged rightly that it must be amended', and in response to their request he was proposing to invite five other scholars, 'the longest students in the tongues' to join him in the enterprise.[50] But Cecil had not approved of the venture, with the result that Broughton's generous proposal came to nothing.

Cecil's refusal to co-operate is not altogether surprising. On account of his cantankerous nature and controversial writings Broughton won little recognition in scholarly circles. It was for this reason that he was excluded from the group of linguists responsible for the A.V. However, his ability as a Hebraist is not to be disparaged. It must also be recognised that his zeal for all things Hebraic was implanted in scholars of the following generation. Summing up what he considers to be Broughton's contribution to scholarship, Samuel Clarke writes:

In his writings the serious and impartial reader will find these two things. First, as much light given to the Scriptures, especially into the most difficult passages of it, as is to be found in any one author whatsoever; nay, it may be, in all authors together. Secondly, a winning and inciting enforcement to the reading of the Scriptures, with a greater seriousness, and more than ordinary searching into them. Among those that have studied his books, many might be named that have grown to be proficients, so far as that they have attained to a most singular, and almost incredible skill ... in the understanding of the Bible, though otherwise unlearned men. Yea, some such there were, that being excited and stirred up by his books, applied themselves to the study of the Hebrew tongue and attained to a great measure of skill and knowledge therein. Nay, a woman might be named who did it.[51]

He does not choose to tell us who she was.

As an enthusiastic exponent of apocalyptic ideas, Broughton was motivated to delve deeply into the Hebraic tradition and to perfect his knowledge of the Hebrew language. For him, and for many of his Protestant contemporaries, the motives for studying Hebrew were implicit in the study of apocalyptic. He applied his linguistic training to two issues in particular which were of interest to apocalyptists: chronology and the conversion of the Jews. The first book he ever published was concerned with calculations of the end of the world, and as such it was an important contribution to the development of the apocalyptic tradition in England. *A Concent of Scripture* (1588), his 'little book of great pains' as he called it, is in essence a statement of his belief about the nature of the biblical record. Though full of charts and tables, it makes the point that the Bible contains all truth. On matters of chronology, each book agrees with the other; the whole Bible must therefore be regarded as authoritative. It is infinitely superior to pagan sources, which are to be disregarded whenever they contradict the pure Word of God. To unravel its mysteries one needs to make a thorough study of the Hebrew text and to take note of traditional Jewish exegesis. His interest in the rabbinic *Seder 'Olam* is typical of his approach to Jewish learning; he even adopted it as the title of one of his chronological works.

In apocalyptic thought the question of the time of the end was closely linked to the hope that the Jews would turn to Christ. Based on such texts as Matthew 24:14 and Romans 11:26, the belief that the consummation of all things would be preceded by the conversion of the Jews was not uncommon in the sixteenth century. Among its early proponents were Bale, Bucer, Martyr and Musculus.[52] By the last two decades of the century it had become very popular in England. In 1587 William Perkins published *A Fruitful Dialogue between the Christian and the Worldling, concerning the end of the World* in which 'Worldling' asks 'Christian' how he can be sure that the end of all things is not yet. In reply 'Christian' lists six scriptural signs which must be fulfilled before Christ comes. The final one is 'the conversion of the Jews unto that religion which they hate, as appeareth in the 11 to the Romans'.[53] Since this has not yet taken place, it must be concluded that the end, though certain, cannot be imminent. Two other leading English apocalyptists, Thomas Brightman and Henry Finch, also voiced the conviction that the Jews would accept Christ.[54] Broughton's views were those of his contemporaries. But not only did he stress the apocalyptic importance of the conversion of the Jews, he tried to take positive steps to effect it. By seeking to provide the Jews with Christian literature in their own language, he hoped to hasten their conversion. He planned to write a treatise in Hebrew proving that Christ fulfilled the messianic prophecies found in the Old Testament. In 1609 he petitioned James I for a sum of money of between £500 and £1000 a year to support his projected translation of the New Testament into Hebrew. Two years later he presented the king with another petition, this time seeking authority to expound the Book of Revelation in Hebrew and Greek in order to show both Jews and gentiles that Rome 'in caesars and pope is therein still damned'.

Although Broughton's scheme came to nothing, it must be recognised that he made an effort to bring his Hebrew expertise to bear on what, for apocalyptists, was an issue of some importance.

The practical Kabbalah

It took the Christian Kabbalah, as propounded by Pico and Reuchlin, several decades to make any appreciable impact on the English mind. Although the study of it had made considerable progress on the Continent, and commended itself to enthusiasts for Catholic reform, it had failed to take root in England. The connections of English scholars with Italy and the Florentine circle had ensured that it was not unknown on this side of the Channel, but it was not given a rapturous welcome. Despite their admiration for Pico and Reuchlin, the early English humanists did not become fervent Kabbalists. Colet, Fisher and More, though not entirely unsympathetic, felt that they could reform the Church without the help of Jewish mysticism. As far as they were concerned, the Kabbalah was a blind alley. Whereas they regarded the study of Hebrew and Jewish exegesis as being of unquestionable value, the exposition of kabbalistic doctrines by Christians represented doubtful scholarship. In this they had the powerful support of Erasmus.

However, soon after the accession of Elizabeth, the Kabbalah suddenly became popular among those interested in the occult. Within seven years of John Fisher's execution, a youth of Welsh extraction, who was destined to become a keen exponent of the Kabbalah, entered St John's College, Cambridge. John Dee first saw the light of day in London in 1527. Although he was born into a poor family, his father found the means to send him to Cambridge, where he matriculated in 1542. At St John's Dee would have been exposed to the new learning. In addition to the trivium, quadrivium and philosophy, he would have been instructed in the two biblical languages, Hebrew and Greek. But his passion for science and mathematics led him to the allied subjects of alchemy and Kabbalah, so that by the time he left Cambridge for Louvain in 1548, on one of his many trips abroad, he was already familiar with kabbalistic teachings.[55]

It is not my intention to discuss Dee's importance as a late Renaissance scholar; this has been done admirably by those who have made his life and writings their special province.[56] I simply offer him as an example of a sixteenth-century English Christian who took an active interest in one particular element of the Hebraic tradition and used it to support his own brand of Christianity.

Dee's actual competence in Hebrew defies any realistic assessment. Though his biographers pay tribute to his linguistic expertise, his skill as a Hebraist is not singled out for special mention by any of them. However, the contents of his personal library suggest that even if he was not very well acquainted with the language, he was certainly interested in it and anxious to promote the study of it. Shortly before his departure for Poland in September 1583, he compiled a catalogue of the books and manuscripts in his possession. Two autographed copies of this catalogue are extant; one is in the British Library and the other in the library of Trinity College, Cambridge. In them he lists one hundred and seventy manuscripts and two thousand five hundred printed volumes, many of which contain more than one work. Perusal of the catalogue gives some notion of the astonishing breadth of Dee's interests. Although he is chiefly remembered as an occult philosopher, scientist and geographer, his library was by no means narrowly scientific. Indeed, 'the whole Renaissance is in this library'.[57] But while literary and historical material is to be found next to works of science and philosophy, the core of Dee's collection consists of books on magic and Kabbalah. The kabbalistic works of Lull, Pico, Reuchlin, Agrippa and the Venetian friar Francesco Giorgi are all catalogued, and we can be sure that they had been carefully studied. If he had so desired, Dee could have gained a fairly detailed knowledge of Jewish mysticism by doing no more than reading the Latin treatise of these intermediaries. A smattering of Hebrew and Aramaic would have been useful, but not absolutely essential. However, there is every indication that he took Semitic studies seriously. In a section of the catalogue devoted to Hebrew and Aramaic works he lists almost sixty items which are directly related to linguistic study. He lists three more in the rest of the catalogue. He owned 'tables' and 'alphabets' suitable for beginners, several Hebrew grammars by eminent continental scholars, the Hebrew–Latin dictionaries of Reuchlin, Münster, Pagninus and Förster, Elias Levita's Aramaic lexicon, David Kimchi's commentary on the Psalter and his *Michlol*, a copy of the Rabbinic Bible printed by Bomberg in Venice, and various individual portions of the Hebrew Scriptures such as the Pentateuch, the Psalms and the Book of Proverbs.[58] In sum, he had all the apparatus one would expect to find on the shelves of a dedicated Hebraist. The fact that friends and

students were encouraged to use his library probably accounts for the
many copies of grammars and dictionaries which he had. If, as seems
probable, he had been introduced to Hebrew at St John's, we may
surely assume that he was not unfamiliar with the contents of at least
one of his many Hebrew manuals and that he was capable of
consulting the Old Testament in the original should the need arise.

In his study of the Kabbalah, Dee was dependent on the
contributions of earlier Christian Kabbalists whose works he
possessed. He was influenced not only by Lull, Pico and Reuchlin, but
also by Agrippa and Giorgi. Cornelius Agrippa wrote the first version
of his *De occulta philosophia* in *c.* 1510, at about the time of his visit to
John Colet in London. In the third part of this work Agrippa relies
heavily on Pico's *Conclusiones*. He seeks to reach the spirit world by
magical means and by manipulating the numerical value of the letters
of the Hebrew alphabet in true kabbalistic fashion. For him, as for
Pico, the climax is reached when it can be demonstrated that the name
of Jesus is to be found in the Kabbalah; it is only in this name that a
Kabbalist, whether he be Jew or Christian, can now operate.[59] Dee
had three editions of Agrippa's book in his library, one of which, on his
own admission, was always open in front of him when he was dealing
with kabbalistic themes. Like those of Agrippa, Francesco Giorgi's
kabbalistic studies were also inspired by Pico. In company with his
eminent Florentine contemporary, Giorgi believed that the Kabbalah
proved the truth of Christianity. He made his views known in *De
harmonia mundi*, the first edition of which appeared in 1525. Besides
being the leading Renaissance textbook on cosmic harmony, this work
of Giorgi was also an important channel for transmitting the Christian
Kabbalah. It may be presumed that Dee turned to it often, but one
wonders how well he coped with the many Hebrew quotations
interspersed with the Latin text. The existence of the works of several
prominent lexicographers on his shelves suggests that he regarded a
reliable dictionary as an useful vade-mecum in such circumstances.

The influence of Agrippa and Giorgi on Dee's kabbalistic writings
has been clearly demonstrated by Josten, Yates and French; it need not
therefore concern us here. We may simply note that Dee was an
enthusiastic proponent of kabbalistic techniques which can be traced,
by way of Reuchlin and Pico, to the mediaeval Jewish mystics. In the
words of the seventeenth-century classical scholar Meric Casaubon,
'he was a Kabbalist up to the ears'.[60] But he was also a pious Christian.
What, then, was the motive behind his study of the Kabbalah? What

did he hope to achieve by following the methods advocated by the Jewish mystics? Wherein lay the appeal of the Hebraic tradition? At the risk of oversimplifying what is an exceedingly complex subject, a few brief observations may be made in this connection.

The first concerns the belief in the efficacy of the Hebrew alphabet for making contact with the spirits, and through them with God. Since, according to the first chapter of Genesis, Hebrew was the language of God, the very letters were considered sacred. In order to overcome the difficulties posed by the doctrine of God's transcendence, the early Jewish Kabbalists, as we have already noted, developed an emanation theory. In this the alphabet played a prominent part. The mystics taught that the universe was divided into ten angelic spheres, each one governed by an intermediary or emanation of the divine. There were seventy-two inferior angels through whom these intermediaries could be approached. By means of the magical power with which the characters of the sacred alphabet was invested, these supercelestial beings could be contacted and their help sought. The names of angels not found in the Bible were created by the Kabbalists themselves, written in Hebrew on seals and used in invocations. Thus a way was opened to God. But the sacred letters could be used also in another fashion to achieve the same end. According to a system called *Gematria* the letters of the Hebrew alphabet represented numbers. By manipulating the numerical value assigned to each letter, the mystic believed that he was able to break through into the spirit world and tap the powers of the angels. This particular branch of the Kabbalah, used in a practical as opposed to a speculative sense, appealed to Dee's mathematical mind. For him, the ability to summon the spirits was all important. Not only did he regard his angelic communications as the pinnacle of his career, he also believed that this was a legitimate method of approaching God. In his own words:

The science of the alphabet contains great mysteries, since He, who is the only Author of all mysteries, has compared Himself to the first and last letter (which is to be understood not only for the Greek language, but also for the Hebrew and Latin ones, as can in various ways be proved by that art). How great, then, must be the mysteries of the intermediate [letters]? And it is not surprising that this [mystery] should be so constituted in letters; for all things, visible and invisible, manifest and most occult things, emanating (through [the medium of] nature or art) from God Himself, are to be most diligently explored in our wanderings, so that thereby we may proclaim and celebrate His goodness, His wisdom, and His power.[61]

The ancient Hebrew 'science of the alphabet' is to be commended, for it helps mortals to understand the nature of the Godhead. Through it the mystic comes to a greater spiritual awareness and draws near to the Creator himself. This can be achieved only when Hebrew characters are used to write the names of the angels.

This Jewish mysticism could also be employed to provide protection from harmful influences. Since it had the power to summon angels, the practical Kabbalah was regarded by its Christian practitioners as an indispensable supplement to natural magic. Pico had taught in his *Conclusiones* that Hermetic magic was weak and ineffective unless it was reinforced by the Kabbalah, a conclusion which was developed further by Reuchlin. Agrippa spoke of 'purifying' natural magic by linking it to the religious magic of the Kabbalah. The use of kabbalistic techniques made natural magic not only more effective but safer. There were good and bad spirits. In practising his art the magus might unwittingly summon the powers of evil and do harm to himself. But if he used the Kabbalah he would be protected against such a mishap, for the Kabbalah ensured that only good and beneficial spirits responded to the invocations of men. The holy magic of the Jewish mystics rendered the demons harmless. With this Dee heartily concurred. Given his preoccupation with angel-invocation, it was in his interests to be able to practise it successfully and safely.

There is yet another way in which the practical Kabbalah appealed to John Dee. It served to reinforce his tolerant and ecumenical outlook. His experience of prejudice and hatred led him to preach a universal religion of peace and love in which Catholic and Protestant would be united. He could not accept that Christendom must always be divided. Even the Jew could be included in this worldwide brotherhood, if only he would accept that 'the same most benevolent God is not only [the God] of the Jews, but of all peoples, nations and languages'.[62] It has been suggested that Dee derived his ideas about a common religion suitable for all men from the sect known as the Family of Love.[63] Originally from the Netherlands, the Familists, as they were called, had a considerable following in Elizabethan England. Their teachings were characterised by a mystic pantheism and were distinctly antinomian. Although they did not deny biblical doctrines, in practice they ignored them, regarding them only as a preparation for the age of universal love which would soon arrive. Whether he was associated with this sect or not, Dee sympathised with some of their beliefs, and in particular with their desire to see charity breaking down the barriers between one Christian and another. To reach this state of tolerance, men could do nothing better than heed the angelic visions of universal religion which Dee had received through the Kabbalah. The angels, he claimed, had perpetually exhorted him and his companion Edward Kelley 'to a betterment of our life, to piety, and to the practising of peace and charity towards our neighbours'.[64] One of them had directed that there should be no sects, denominations or dogmas:

Whosoever wishes to be wise may look neither to the right nor to the left; neither towards this man who is called a catholic, nor towards that one who is called a heretic (for thus you are called); but he may look up to the God of heaven and earth and to his son, Jesus Christ, Who has given the Spirit of His abundant and multifarious graces to those who live a natural life in purity and a life of grace in their works.[65]

With this Dee wholeheartedly agreed. His desire to see a reformed and reunited Christian Church was linked closely with the angel-magic of practical Kabbalah.

However, despite his consuming interest in a universal religion there was an evangelical missionary streak in Dee's make-up. He was a Christian Kabbalist 'with leanings towards evangelicalism and Erasmian reform'.[66] It is indicative that one of the several works to come from his pen, though never published, was entitled *De modo Evangelii Iesu Christi publicandi . . . inter infideles*. But there was no conflict between his study of Jewish mysticism and his desire to bring members of other faiths to Christ. The Kabbalah could be used as a missionary instrument, for it confirmed the gospel story. Its adoption into Christianity might bring about the conversion of the Jews. Faced with arguments taken from their own literature the Jews could not fail to recognise the truth of the Christian faith. Here again he was following Pico and Agrippa. In the seventh of his *Conclusiones cabalisticae* Pico had declared that 'No Hebrew Kabbalist can deny that the name IESU, if interpreted on kabbalistic principles, signifies the Son of God'.[67]

Recent research has shown that John Dee cannot be dismissed simply as a conjurer and sorcerer, as he was by some of his contemporaries when the reaction to occultism set in towards the end of the sixteenth century. His immense erudition appealed to the learned world of his day and earned him a place at the royal court. He was clearly an influential figure in Elizabethan England, despite his controversial ideas and his failure to initiate a religious reform. As a faithful disciple of Pico and Reuchlin he was responsible for developing and propagating their views concerning the Hebraic tradition. For him, as for them, the Kabbalah was the solution to every religious problem. The interest which he generated in it is reflected in the works of several seventeenth-century writers, notably the Rosicrucian Robert Fludd. To describe this fascination for Jewish mystical teachings as 'an intellectual fad' which 'flamed, flickered, and finally faded', is not entirely justified.[68] That it eventually faded out after enjoying considerable popularity, especially among continental Christians, is not disputed; it was rejected because Christians feared the judaising of their religion. But for John Dee it was not just a fad.

If the Renaissance provided the initial impetus for the study of Hebrew in England, the Reformation provided the energy and enthusiasm necessary for its development. Many of the early Puritans may be regarded as capable Hebraists. Motivated by a strong desire to see an educated clergy well-versed in the Bible, they placed considerable emphasis on the original languages and regarded them as an integral part of any course of theological training. They were sceptical of doctrines affirmed by ecclesiastical tradition but not supported by a correct interpretation of the original texts of the Scriptures. In justifying their rejection of the Vulgate and their support of vernacular translations, they made it their business to become thoroughly acquainted with the *hebraica veritas*. Their attempt to defend the Protestant position on some of the burning doctrinal issues of the day led them to the Hebraic tradition. To counter what they considered to be erroneous explanations of key Old Testament texts, they utilised rabbinic writings to the extent that post-biblical Jewish literature touched, and in some cases influenced their thoughts on textual and doctrinal matters. The followers of Pico and Reuchlin also had cause to turn to the Hebraic tradition. The Christian Kabbalah was not without its devotees in Elizabethan England.

Notes

1 A. Peel ed., *The Seconde Parte of a Register*, Cambridge 1915, vol. I, pp. 50f. Peel notes that although the document is dated *c*. 1561 'the supplication seems to be more in line with those of twenty years later'.
2 I am indebted to Dr F. H. Stubbings, Fellow and Librarian of Emmanuel, for allowing me to quote from his hitherto unpublished Eng. trans. of the original statutes of Emmanuel College, ch. XVII, 'Of the

Qualification of the Fellows', p. 28. For the foundation of Emmanuel see S. E. Lehmberg, *Sir Walter Mildmay and Tudor Government*, Austin, Tex. 1964, ch. 14.

3   P. Collinson, *The Elizabethan Puritan Movement*, London 1967, p. 125. For a full assessment of Chaderton's contribution to the Puritan movement see P. G. Lake, 'Laurence Chaderton and the Cambridge Moderate Puritan Tradition, 1570–1604', unpublished Ph.D. thesis, Cambridge 1978.

4   E. S. Shuckburgh, ed., *Laurence Chaderton, D.D.: Translated from a Latin Memoir of Dr. Dillingham*, Cambridge 1884, p. 22.

5   T. W. Jones, ed., *A True Relation of the Life and Death of . . . William Bedell*, Camden Society, New Series IV, 1872, pp. 3f.

6   *The Lives of Thirty-two English Divines*, London 1677, p. 133. The life of Carter printed here was originally written by his son, John Carter junior.

7   'A Sermon Preached at the Funeral of . . . Lancelot, Late Lord Bishop of Winchester', *Ninety-six Sermons*, ed. J. Bliss, Library of Anglo Catholic Theology 1843, vol. V, p. 291. Thomas Watts, Archdeacon of Middlesex and a canon of Westminster, founded seven Greek scholarships in 1571.

8   *Church History*, London 1655, Bk. XI, p. 126.

9   The description of Richard Drake, the first translator of the *Preces* into English, quoted by R. L. Ottley, *Lancelot Andrewes*, 2nd ed. rev., London 1905, p. 179.

10 See *The Authorized Selichot for the Whole Year*, ed. A. Rosenfeld, London 1956, *passim*. I am indebted to Dr S. C. Reif of the Cambridge University Library for this information. For the use which Andrewes made of this prayer see *The Preces Privatae of Lancelot Andrewes*, Eng. trans. by F. E. Brightman, London 1903, pp. 62f.

11 *The Writings of Robert Harrison and Robert Browne*, ed. A. Peel and L. H. Carlson, London 1953, p. 173.

12 *Ninety-six Sermons*, vol. V, p. 61.

13 J. Buckeridge, *ibid.*, vol. I, p. 293.

14 Dr Williams' Library, Morrice Collection MSS. 'A', Old Loose Papers, fol. 191. Reproduced in H. C. Porter, *Puritanism in Tudor England*, London 1970, pp. 195ff. Partial transcript in A. Peel, *The Seconde Parte of a Register*, vol. I, pp. 133f. It has been suggested that the 'Mr. Chaderton' mentioned here was William Chaderton, Bishop of Chester. But he could well have been Laurence Chaderton.

15 Cf. L. Kukenheim's remark with reference to the use of Hebrew by the continental Reformers, 'Les Réformateurs avaient besoin de cette science dans leur polémique contre l'Eglise catholoque', *Contributions à l'histoire de la Grammaire Grecque, Latine et Hébrïque à l'époque de la Renaissance*, Leiden 1951, p. 127.

16 R. J. Bauckham, 'The career and thought of Doctor William Fulke (1537–1589)', unpublished Ph.D. thesis, Cambridge 1972, p. 325. I am indebted to Dr Bauckham for drawing my attention to several bibliographical items in connection with this chapter.

17 *The Lives of Thirty-two English Divines*, p. 169.

18　Printed alternately with Martin's *Discoverie* in the Parker Soc. volume ed. Cf. H. Hartshorne, Cambridge 1843.

19　*A Defence*, Parker Soc., p. 78.

20　*Ibid.*, p. 509.

21　*A Discoverie*, Parker Soc., p. 99.

22　The following paragraphs contain a synopsis of the debate found on pp. 278–319 of the Parker Soc. volume.

23　Parker Soc. edition of the *Disputation*, trans. and ed. W. Fitzgerald, Cambridge 1849, p. 111.

24　*Ibid.*

25　*Ibid.*, pp. 174ff.

26　*Ibid.*, pp. 179–92.

27　*Athenae Oxonienses*, 3rd ed. rev., vol. I, col. 559.

28　*The Nobles* (reprinted Amsterdam, 1973; The English Experience, No. 234), Bk. I, n.p.

29　*Ibid.*, Bk. III.

30　*The Prophecy of Haggai interpreted and applied in Sundry Sermons*, London 1649.

31　*Motives to Godly Knowledge*, London 1613, sigs. A5f.

32　*The Prophecy of Obadiah opened and applied in sundry learned and gracious Sermons*, Oxford 1613. For further evidence of his acquaintance with rabbinic sources and of the use he made of them in his sermons, see his notes on Obadiah vv. 10, 15, 20; Haggai 1:8; 2:9.

33　*Censura librorum Apocryphorum Veteris Testamenti adversum Pontifices imprimis Robertum Bellarminum*, London 1611, vol. II, col. 1088.

34　*Ibid.*, vol. I, col. 1462.

35　For the details of his career see G. Anstruther, *The Seminary Priests*, Ushaw 1968, vol. I, pp. 153ff.

36　For the following discussion see *The Sum of the Conference*, pp. 195ff.

37　See also the discussion on the temporal power of the Pope, *ibid.*, pp. 341ff, and that on Scripture and tradition, *ibid.*, pp. 391ff.

38　*Ibid.*, p. 271.

39　C. Barksdale, *A Remembrancer of Excellent Men*, London 1670, p. 5.

40　See further P. Christianson, *Reformers and Babylon*, Toronto 1978; R. Bauckham, *Tudor Apocalypse*, Appleford 1978; K. R. Firth, *The Apocalyptic Tradition in Reformation Britain 1530–1645*, Oxford 1979.

41　*The King James Version of the English Bible*, p. 155.

42　'Advertisement how to examine the translation now in hand', *The Works of Hugh Broughton*, ed. J. Lightfoot, Bk. III, p. 700.

43　*Works*, Bk. II, p. 246.

44　*An Epistle to the Learned Nobility of England* (1597) (reprinted in The English Experience, Amsterdam 1977), p. 12.

45　See J. Bowman, 'A forgotten controversy', *Evangelical Qtly*, vol. 20, 1948.

46　*Works*, Bk. III, p. 588.

47　*Ibid.*, Bk. II, p. 215.

48   *Ibid.*, Bk. I, p. 257.
49   *An Epistle to the Learned Nobility of England*, p. 3.
50   See British Library, MS. Harleian 7031.
51   *The Lives of Divers Eminent Divines of this Later Age*, London 1683, p. 8.
52   J. Bale, *The Image of bothe Churches after the most wonderfull and heavenly Revelacion of Sainct John the Evangelist*, London 1548, sigs. Oiiif; for Bucer see W. Nijenhuis, *Ecclesia Reformata*, ch. 3; P. Martyr, *Most learned and fruitfull commentaries upon the Epistle of S. Paul to the Romanes*, Eng. trans. London 1568, fol. 360; W. Musculus, *Common Places*, Eng. trans. London 1563, fols. 450r, 451v.
53   *The Workes*, Cambridge 1618, vol. III, p. 470.
54   'Exposition . . . of the Prophecie of Daniel' (1614) in *The Workes of That Famous, Reverend, and Learned Divine, Mr Tho: Brightman*, London 1644, p. 954. Though published originally in 1614, Brightman's commentary on Daniel was written during the final decade of the sixteenth century. H. Finch, *Worlds Great Restauration, or The Calling of the Jewes*, London 1621, pp. 59f.
55   C. H. Josten, 'A translation of John Dee's "Monas Hieroglyphica" (Antwerp 1564), with an introduction and annotations', *Ambix*, vol. XII, 1964, p. 86.
56   See e.g. P. J. French, *John Dee: the World of an Elizabethan Magus*, London 1972; Frances A. Yates, *The Occult Philosophy in the Elizabethan Age*, London 1979.
57   Frances A. Yates, *Theatre of the World*, London 1969, p. 12. For a description of the library and further bibliography see also P. J. French, *John Dee*, ch. 3, 'Elizabethan England's greatest library'.
58   See British Library, MS. Harleian 1879, fols. 66r–68v.
59   For a description of the *De occulta philosophia* see Frances A. Yates, *Giordano Bruno and the Hermetic Tradition*, pp. 130ff.
60   *A true and Faithful Relation of what passed for many years between Dr John Dee . . . and some Spirits*, London 1659, Preface.
61   Introduction to the *Monas Hieroglyphica*, Eng. trans. C. H. Josten, *Ambix*, vol. XII, 1964, p. 125. The square brackets are those of the translator.
62   *Ibid.*, p. 133.
63   See P. J. French, *John Dee*, p. 124, n. 2.
64   C. H. Josten, 'An unknown chapter in the life of John Dee', *JWCI*, vol. XXVIII, 1965, p. 234.
65   *Ibid.*, p. 245.
66   Frances A. Yates, *The Occult Philosophy*, p. 86.
67   *Johannes Picus Mirandulanus: Opera Omnia*, ed. E. Garin, vol. I, p. 108.
68   J. Blau, *The Christian Interpretation of the Cabala*, p. 16.

Part three

Opportunities

VII
At the universities

The impetus for the study of Hebrew and the Hebraic tradition in Tudor England came originally from the Continent, under the combined influence of Renaissance and Reformation. Christian humanists, such as Colet, More and Fisher, following the lead given by Pico, Reuchlin and Erasmus, hoped to purge the Church of its abuses by encouraging the serious study of Scripture in its original languages. Through the scholarly endeavours of men like Pagninus, Münster, Leo Jud and Tremellius, the significance of the rabbinic contribution to biblical study became increasingly apparent. The English reformers, influenced by their European counterparts, produced several versions of the Bible in the vernacular and duly emphasised the importance of Hebrew and Greek. The Puritans insisted that Hebrew should be part of the equipment of their disputants in their confessional battles with Roman Catholics. Gradually there evolved a genuine interest in the history of the Jews during the post-biblical period, and perforce in Jewish writings and in the language in which they were written. The obsession with apocalyptic ideas, which was so characteristic of Elizabethan religious thought, led a few English theologians to explore the Hebraic tradition. For some the Kabbalah held particular fascination.

The motives for learning Hebrew and the influences which were brought to bear on English scholars are not difficult to discover. But what opportunities existed for those Englishmen, who had the ability and were so inclined, to study the language? What provision was made for the teaching of Hebrew in school and university? Who were the teachers during the period when Jews were officially excluded from England? What books were available to help the conscientious student to become a proficient Hebraist? It is with such questions as these that we shall be concerned in the remaining chapters. We begin by considering the diffusion of Hebrew scholarship within the universities from the second decade of the century onwards. Our chief concern will be the contribution of some of the more prominent scholars whose names have not appeared hitherto, but we shall also take into account those whose reputation as Hebraists rests entirely on the testimony of their contemporaries with no support from published or unpublished works.

The pioneers

The first Hebraist worthy of the name in sixteenth-century England was the Yorkshireman Robert Wakefield.[1] One of the first students to matriculate at St John's College, Cambridge, he graduated in liberal arts in 1514, and then proceeded to canon law. In 1516 he was elected a fellow of Clare Hall, but he cannot have stayed there long for the autumn of 1518 found him enrolled at the trilingual college in Louvain as a student of philosophy and languages. Through his close association with Fisher at Cambridge he would have become acquainted with Erasmus, a fact which in all probability influenced his decision to go to Louvain. It is possible that he was the 'young man' mentioned by a Benedictine from Liège in a letter to Erasmus dated 17 September 1517. The monk refers to the bearer of the letter and says, 'This young man who has brought you my greetings is a most agreeable person and has a very kindly disposition. He has been staying with us for almost a whole month, during which time he has conscientiously taught me the rudiments of Hebrew. . . . I commend to you my Hebrew teacher who is going to Louvain in order to see you'.[2] If, as P. S. Allen suggests, this passage does refer to Wakefield, then we must assume that he had learned enough Hebrew to teach elementary grammar to others since his departure from Cambridge. Between September 1517 and November of the following year we lose track of him, but when he finally settled in Louvain he made further progress in his linguistic studies through his association with the celebrated Hebraist Matthew Adrianus. Although Adrianus was not officially elected professor of Hebrew until July 1518, he had arrived at the trilingual college nine months previously. But after one year in office he resigned the chair and was succeeded by Wakefield on 1 August 1519. The annals of the college provide no information about the courses offered by the new professor from England, nor why he, too, relinquished his post after only a few months. At the beginning of December he resigned. Early in 1520 he was back in his native country, and within a short time had been appointed to a fellowship at his old college in Cambridge. Nothing is known of him for the next two years, but it may be presumed that he continued his study of Semitics and made some pupils. He may have paid another visit to the Continent during this period for according to the few autobiographical details available to us he had, at some time, studied in Germany under Gaspar Amman, a student of Reuchlin and Hebrew teacher to Capito, Oecolampadius and Münster. In 1522 he was certainly back in Louvain visiting a former student, and from there he went to Hagenau to have discussions with a publisher. While he was at Hagenau in June of that year Reuchlin died at Tübingen and Wakefield was appointed to replace him. 'Your Robert', says Erasmus to Fisher in a letter of 1 September 1522, 'is teaching Greek and Hebrew at Tübingen for a fairly high salary.'[3] But again his tenure of office was brief. Although he had successfully introduced Syriac and Arabic into the curriculum, he was persuaded to leave Germany in the early spring of 1523 and accept a post as lecturer in Hebrew at Cambridge. He returned to England via Paris where he taught for a few months before commencing his duties as the first official university lecturer in Hebrew. In 1530, as a result of a disagreement with Fisher over Henry's divorce from Catherine of Aragon, Wakefield moved to Oxford. Originally he had opposed the annulment of the marriage, but was apparently 'converted by fair promises to change his mind'.[4] In a letter to Henry he undertook to defend him in this delicate matter by referring not only to the Scriptures and the works of the Church Fathers, but also to 'the best learned and most excellent authors of the interpreters of the Hebrews'. He assured the king that support for his action would be forthcoming from rabbinic sources. Furthermore, he promised to answer the criticisms of the Bishop of Rochester in the hope that he would 'be ashamed to wade or meddle any further in the matter'.[5] Since relationships between scholar and patron were now obviously strained, Wakefield probably welcomed the opportunity to go to Oxford. After an initial period of probation, during which he made a very favourable impression on his listeners, the university petitioned the king to allow him to stay there permanently. The request was granted and he was made a canon of Henry VIII's College (previously Cardinal College) in 1532 and in the same year was incorporated B.D. He remained at Oxford for the rest of his life.

Wakefield's contemporaries are divided in their opinion of his proficiency as a Hebraist and his skill as a teacher. The physician Wolfgang Rychard of Ulm, writing to Luther from Tübingen shortly after Reuchlin's death, claims that the new professor is teaching

Hebrew so badly that he is beginning to make everybody sick.[6] On the other hand, a letter written by the Rector of Tübingen University to the Chancellor of Cambridge in a fruitless attempt to retain Wakefield's services, describes him as 'a most illustrious man ... remarkably learned and well-informed in Syriac and Hebrew'. In some respects the rector regards him as being superior even to Reuchlin.[7] Writing in a similar vein Ferdinand, the brother of Charles V, appeals to the King of England to allow 'that excellent scholar Wakefield' to stay a little longer in Germany.[8] Richard Pace has the same high opinion of Wakefield's scholarship. When he advises the king on the matter of the divorce, Pace recommends his teacher to Henry as a man 'of excellent learning as well in divinity as in wonderful knowledge of many and diverse tongues'.[9] Fisher's estimation of him is couched in similar terms.[10] Oxford University, in its letter to the king in 1530 requesting Wakefield's transfer from Cambridge, is no less enthusiastic. From the lectures he had already given as a visitor it was clear that he was a most proficient Hebraist, and second to none in his command of Syriac and Arabic. If the king would allow him to remain permanently at Oxford, then not only the university, but also the whole realm, would be brought to a better understanding of the Scriptures.[11]

The extant published works from which Wakefield's contribution to Hebraic studies may be measured are four. On taking up his appointment at Cambridge in 1524 he delivered an oration in praise of Semitic studies which was immediately printed under the title *Oratio de laudibus et utilitate trium linguarum, Arabicae, Chaldaicae et Hebraicae*. Although Arabic and Aramaic are included in the title, the author devoted himself mainly to Hebrew. Six years later, at Oxford, he produced his *Syntagma de hebraeorum codicum incorruptione*. This was a companion volume to the *Oratio* but could not be produced sooner, according to the author, because of the lack of Hebrew type in England. In *Kotser codicis* (?1528) he published his comments on a catena of quotations from the Old Testament in opposition to the royal divorce; he was to change his mind later. Finally, he made a synopsis of the Book of Ecclesiastes, *Paraphrasis in librum Koheleth* (?1536), in which he summarised the contents of the book chapter by chapter. In the preface he describes his paraphrase as succinct, clear, and faithful to the original; throughout the work he will adhere as closely to the Hebrew as the Latin idiom will allow.

Of these four publications the *Oratio* is by far the most significant for our present purpose, and since the *Syntagma* covers much of the same ground it will be considered together with it.[12] The *Oratio* opens with a dedicatory letter to Henry VIII which is immediately followed by the author's apologia for composing the speech. First, he wishes to prove his competence as a Hebraist and to show that he is a capable teacher. Secondly, he wants to demonstrate the relationship which exists between Hebrew, Aramaic and Arabic. Thirdly, he is anxious to refute those who oppose the study of Semitics. Finally, he wants his speech to be taken as a mark of respect for Cambridge, whose scholars delight in new things.[13] From a perusal of the *Oratio* and the *Syntagma* some salient points emerge. The primacy of Hebrew and the significance of the Hebraic tradition for the Christian are paramount; they are stressed repeatedly throughout both works. In words reminiscent of Roger Bacon, Wakefield insists that a knowledge of Hebrew is an absolute necessity for every theologian. He is severely critical of those who hinder its study by giving it low priority. Surely it is more important for divines to concern themselves with the language 'which leads men to eternal salvation' than with the sale of holy relics. In company with Pico and Reuchlin he believes that a knowledge of Hebrew by Christians is essential for the successful propagation of the faith. Since the Old Testament is the source of Christianity, the language in which it was originally written must be mastered if the Christian is to understand his own religion and be an effective apologist. There is no substitute for the original text. The Vulgate cannot be accepted as authoritative because it is so very corrupt. Christians should by-pass it and drink, not from the streams, but from the spring itself.

But in spite of this stress on the theologian's need of Hebrew, it is not Wakefield's intention to produce a handbook for beginners. As the titles of both works suggest, they are meant to encourage rather than to instruct. By extolling the virtues of Hebrew and demonstrating its usefulness, the author seeks to persuade students to take up the challenge posed by this little-known tongue. They must not be faint-hearted, for with a good teacher and a propensity for hard work the grammar is easily mastered and success assured. Pico and Pace are cited as examples of those who have learned Hebrew in a matter of months. Origen, Reuchlin and Erasmus commenced their study of it when they had already reached manhood. Nicholas of Lyra busied himself with Hebrew literature even though he was hampered by the debilities of old age. The purpose of such references is to give the student the assurance of success. But the careful reader will also learn something of the structure of the language in the pages of the *Oratio* and the *Syntagma*, for interspersed with eulogistic remarks in praise of Hebrew are discussions of grammatical and lexicographical points. The author describes the formation of nouns and adjectives, and illustrates the difference between singular and plural. He enumerates the various conjugations of the Hebrew verb and shows how Greek and Latin words, such as 'sakkos', 'balsamum', 'myrrha' and others, are derived from Hebrew roots. He draws attention to the difference in meaning between the *Qal* and the *Pi'el* forms of the Hebrew verb. He also detects the influence of Arabic on Hebrew rhyme and metre and notes the Hebraic practice of using the letters of the alphabet as numerals.

Throughout the *Oratio* and the *Syntagma* the author's debt to Jewish sources and to mediaeval Christian Hebraists is very apparent. He quotes from the Mechilta, the Talmud, the works of Maimonides and from kabbalistic writings. He shows great respect for the opinions of the rabbinic exegetes. In his discussion of the names of God, the identification of Melchizedek and the plural form of the world *'elohim* (God), he invariably consults the 'rabbini' whose comments he quotes with approval. In particular he venerates David Kimchi whom he describes as 'the chief of grammarians', and whose *Michlol* and *Book of Roots* he regards as indispensable aids for the study of grammar and lexicography. But despite his frequent allusions, it must not be assumed that Wakefield had read all these Jewish works in the original. For many of his references he relied on such intermediaries as Nicholas of Lyra, Johann Reuchlin, Petrus Galatinus and Paul of Burgos.

When he turns to consider the merits of learning Aramaic, Wakefield wastes no time in making a scathing attack upon Luther. The Reformer's disparaging remarks about the Targumim of Onkelos and Jonathan may be rejected out of hand. Properly appreciated, these Aramaic versions of the Bible can be of great value to the Christian who wishes to study the Old Testament. Indeed, most Jewish commentators unfailingly refer to them in matters of textual difficulty. They regard anyone who cannot read them through ignorance of the language as a very poor Hebraist, for Aramaic and Hebrew have much in common. Luther's peremptory dismissal of these early translations of the Hebrew scriptures shows clearly that he has not given them the attention they deserve. Had he studied them thoroughly he would have avoided several howlers in his translation of the Old Testament. To render *chalak* in Deuteronomy 4:19 as 'to appease' rather than 'to apportion', and *shanan* in Deuteronomy 6:7 as 'to sharpen' rather than 'to instil' or 'to repeat' is decidedly wrong-headed. The double meaning of both verbs, though attested by several Jewish authors, has obviously escaped Luther. Such ignorance, coupled with prejudice, leads Wakefield to conclude that Luther has 'no more than an elementary knowledge of Hebrew, and rashly judges what he does not know'. Let him make his pronouncements on Jewish writings when he is intellectually equipped to do so.

The *Oratio* and *Syntagma* are important Renaissance texts, not only because they offer evidence of one man's positive attitude towards Hebrew scholarship, but also because they mention other Englishmen who were drawn to study the language during the first quarter of the sixteenth century. Some of these were Wakefield's own pupils, others were contemporary scholars whose linguistic competence was generally recognised. John Taylor, orator to the king, Jacob Bullein, possibly a relative of Thomas Boleyn the Earl of Wiltshire and Wakefield's patron, John Frisel prior of Rochester, Cuthbert Tunstall and a Dr Lovel are all listed in the *Oratio* as students of Hebrew. Thomas Hurskey, the English Provincial of the Gilbertine order, was possibly the first to receive instruction from Wakefield. In the *Syntagma* Wakefield states that he had given Hurskey lessons in Hebrew eighteen years previously.[14] If we are correct in dating the publication of this work as 1530, and if the author's memory is reliable, then Hurskey learned Hebrew while his mentor was still a student at Cambridge. But Hurskey was the exception rather than the rule, for it was only after he had studied on the Continent and taught at Louvain that Wakefield became recognised in England as a competent teacher. In 1520, on his return to Cambridge as a fellow of St John's, Henry VIII asked him to teach Hebrew to Reginald Pole. The king took considerable interest in the education of his young nephew who was by inclination much better suited to the life of a scholar than that of an ecclesiastical statesman. How much progress Pole actually made as a Hebraist cannot be determined, but Wakefield takes pride in recording his illustrious pupil's awareness of the advantages of linguistic study for understanding the Scriptures.[15]

The name of John Stokesley, Tunstall's successor as Bishop of London, also appears in the *Oratio*.[16] Stokesley was a close friend of Wakefield; it was at his house that the latter had lodged between leaving Louvain and taking up his fellowship at Cambridge. But Stokesley's Hebrew attainments, to which Wakefield refers, had been recognised many years previously by other eminent scholars. In April 1517 Pace could describe him as a 'brilliant theologian and excellent philosopher – completely admirable – who not only knows Greek and Latin, but also something about Hebrew'.[17] Erasmus was even more enthusiastic. In a letter of 1518 he rated him as second to none in scholastic theology and described him as someone who was 'exceptionally well-acquainted with Latin, Greek and Hebrew'.[18] Richard Croke, in the course of his inaugural lecture as reader in Greek at Cambridge in 1519, referred to 'the threefold linguistic learning of Stokesley' as an example of Oxford's determination to equal Cambridge in the study of the languages.[19] But where Stokesley had learned enough Hebrew to impress Pace by 1517 remains a mystery. The Oxford of his student days (*c.* 1500) would have afforded him no opportunity to learn it and there is nothing to indicate that he studied on the Continent.

Though not mentioned by Wakefield, there were others who had a reputation for being Hebrew scholars. John Helyar, an Oxford man, enjoyed the patronage of Wolsey who, according to Anthony Wood, held him in high esteem 'for his extraordinary sufficiencies in the Latin, Greek and Hebrew tongues'.[20] John Caius is remembered chiefly for his attainments in medical science, but he was also a gifted linguist. When he matriculated at Cambridge in 1529 his main interest was theology, and it is probable that at one stage in his career he had contemplated ordination. Evidence of at least an elementary knowledge of Hebrew is to be found in a manuscript copy of the Hebrew Bible apart from the Pentateuch which he presented to Gonville and Caius College in 1557. At the beginning there are two pages of notes in his hand 'concerning the canonical books of the Old Testament' in which he gives the Hebrew names of the various parts of Scripture, and concludes with the words 'written by the young Caius, a student of the Hebrew language at Cambridge'.[21] This presumably refers to his early student days, before he became interested in medicine, and suggests that he might have been a pupil of Wakefield.

Another contemporary of Wakefield in the Cambridge of the 1520s was George Stafford, a fellow of Pembroke College from 1513 until his early death in 1529. Appointed to the Lady Margaret chair in divinity at the university in 1523, he followed the example of Colet at Oxford by concentrating on the Scriptures instead of the *Sentences*. His lectures aroused much enthusiasm, for Thomas Becon, writing during the reign of Edward VI recalls the saying which was popular during his student days, 'when Master Stafford read and Master Latimer preached then was Cambridge blessed'. Becon describes his teacher as one who was 'approvedly learned in the Hebrew, Greek and Latin tongues'.[22] Perhaps it was the application of his linguistic knowledge to the Bible that made Stafford's lectures so memorable. At his death he bequeathed to his college library a copy of the Complutensian Polyglot and a Hebrew Bible containing the Targum.[23] Richard Reynolds, a monk of Syon monastery where Pace lived during the final years of his life, was another Hebraist of note. A fellow of Corpus Christi College, Cambridge, Reynolds entered Syon in 1513 after taking his B.D. He was described by Cardinal Pole as a scholar who always went *ad fontes* and as the only English monk of his time who was 'well-versed in the three principal languages'.[24] Such a description is well-attested by the contents of the monastery library, though the actual number of Hebrew books is small.[25] Lancelot Ridley of Clare Hall commenced M.A. in 1527 and was 'deeply skilled in theology and in the Latin, Greek and Hebrew languages'.[26] His only extant contribution to Old Testament studies is a commentary on the Book of Joshua published in 1537 in which he annotates Coverdale's translation. According to the *Short Title Catalogue* the one remaining copy is in the New York public library; an examination of it might give some indication of his Hebrew scholarship.[27] Bryan Rowe was Vice-Provost of King's College when he died in 1521. His library contained two Hebrew works, an alphabet and a grammar, which bear witness to an incipient interest in the language.[28] It is possible that he had received instruction at the hands of Wakefield.

On his departure from the Collegium Trilingue at the beginning of December 1519 Wakefield was immediately replaced by another Englishman, one Robert Shirwood. Erasmus, who was in Louvain at the time, stated in a letter that he was incapable of judging the suitability of any candidate for the vacant chair but that he would consult those who were.[29] He was true to his word, and on Wakefield's recommendation, suggested to the college authorities that they should offer Shirwood a provisional appointment as professor of Hebrew. The young scholar had the good fortune of being in the right place at the right time. After spending some years at Oxford, where he had applied himself successfully to Greek and Hebrew, he had travelled abroad to further his knowledge of Oriental languages, and attracted by the presence of Wakefield, had settled in Louvain.[30] By the end of 1519 he was considered to be a Hebraist of sufficient calibre to take the place of his teacher. But although he accepted the post with alacrity, for some unknown reason he soon became disillusioned and resigned after only a month in office. Perhaps he was dissatisfied with the conditions of service; his salary was half that of Wakefield. On his return to England some years later he became parish priest of Dirham in Gloucestershire where he remained for the rest of his life.

Shirwood is credited with making a Latin translation of the whole Old Testament from the original Hebrew. But the work was never printed, and since the manuscript is no longer extant it cannot offer any help in evaluating the scholarship of the translator. From this version, however, one biblical book has survived, that of Ecclesiastes. It was published, together with annotations drawn from rabbinic commentaries, at Antwerp in 1523.[31] In the preface the author introduces his work and gives his reasons for undertaking it. He emphasises that his translation is not a paraphrase but a word for word rendering which, in order to ensure complete accuracy, is based on a careful comparison of the Vulgate with the Massoretic Text. Difficult words and phrases are explained by the help of the Targum and the comments of the rabbis. His intention in producing a rival translation to the Vulgate is not so that he can censure the version commonly used by the Church, but in order to rectify errors and omissions and make the meaning of the text that much plainer. He believes that students of Hebrew will find his translation particularly helpful because of its extreme literalness when compared with the Vulgate. Above all, he is anxious to rescue the Book of Ecclesiastes from the obscurity into which it had apparently fallen. Judging from the sudden popularity of the book among scholars connected with Louvain, his efforts met with immediate success, for within the next few years Wakefield, Pace and Jean Campensis, Shirwood's successor at the trilingual college, all made a study of it. But this new annotated translation did not serve simply as an encouragement to others to take the book seriously, it was greatly valued by later scholars as an important contribution to biblical studies. In 1620 the Jesuit scholar Johannes de Pineda published a lengthy commentary on Ecclesiastes. As well as offering an exposition, this volume contained also a polyglot edition of the book comprising several different Latin translations. That of Shirwood was included alongside the version of Jerome, the Septuagint and the Targum, on the grounds that it was true to the Hebrew original.[32]

Three examples from chapter twelve of his version demonstrate how Shirwood utilised the Hebraic tradition to explain the obscurities of Ecclesiastes. In a marginal note he expounds the 'evil days' of 12:1 as a reference to the debility of old age and cites 'the Hebrews' in support of his interpretation. His sources were the mediaeval rabbis. Rashi's explanation is that these are 'days of senility and weakness', and Ibn Ezra writes that this is the time of old age and terminal illness. Both commentators reproduce the explanation offered by Jewish exegetes since talmudic times. The word *masmeroth*, which is used in 12:11 to describe the teachings of a faithful pastor, is translated correctly as 'nails' by both the Septuagint and the Vulgate. Shirwood preserves this translation in his version, but in an attempt to provide a better parallel to 'goad' in the first part of the verse he notes that David Kimchi claims that the word means 'a fork'. The final phrase of 12:13 states the reason why God should be feared and his commandments kept. Rendered literally it reads 'for this is every man'. Most modern versions regard it as a pregnant idiom and translate 'for this is the whole duty of man'. But Shirwood, prefacing his comment with the words 'the rabbis give this explanation', paraphrases it as 'for this purpose was every man created'. In doing so he quotes Rashi verbatim.

The notes provided by Shirwood for the guidance of the reader reveal a competent Hebraist who is not unfamiliar with the rabbinic commentaries. At least six years before Pagninus had published his translation, Shirwood had recognised the relevance of the Jewish exegetical tradition for a proper understanding of the Old Testament. Though, as far as is known, he never taught Hebrew in his native land, Shirwood deserves mention as one of the earliest English scholars to appreciate post-biblical Jewish writings.

The king's readers

As a result of Henry's break with the Roman Catholic Church the English universities came increasingly under royal control. The king, anxious to abrogate the power of Rome, took steps to ensure that the academic community gave him its undivided loyalty. He placed the matter in the capable hands of Thomas Cromwell, his Secretary of State, whom he had appointed Chancellor of Cambridge in place of Fisher. Cromwell lost no time in putting the king's plan into action. In 1535 he promulgated a set of injunctions which brought about sweeping changes at Oxford and Cambridge, and which had far-reaching consequences for higher education. Under the new regulations the universities were required, in the first place, to change their ecclesiastical allegiance; henceforth homage was to be paid to the crown rather than to Rome. Secondly, the syllabus was to be revised. In the interest of humanistic learning the study of civil law was to be substituted for that of canon law, the Scriptures for the Sentences, Melanchthon for Duns Scotus. Two daily public lectures, one in Greek and the other in Latin, were to be inaugurated and were to be maintained by the colleges. In a word, it was decreed that, 'all ceremonies, constitutions and observances that hindered polite learning should be abolished', and any university or college statute 'repugnant to these articles and injunctions should be void'.[33]

In many colleges these royal injunctions were carried out immediately. The official visitors sent to monitor the proceedings at Oxford noted that the new learning was now gaining ground in the university. In a letter to Cromwell commissioner Robert Layton reported with evident satisfaction that scholasticism was on its last legs. 'We have set Dunce in Bocardo [the university prison] and have utterly banished him from Oxford for ever, with all his blind glosses, and is now made a common servant to every man, fast nailed up upon posts in all common houses of easement.' During his inspection of New College he had been gratified to see the quad 'full of the leaves of Dunce, the wind blowing them in every corner'.[34] At Cambridge, Layton's colleague, Thomas Leigh, made two significant additions to the original injunctions. He ordered the university to hand over its chattels, to supply the crown with an inventory of its property and to institute, at its own expense, a public lecture in either Hebrew or Greek. In order to conciliate those who would find such recommendations irksome, he suggested to Cromwell that the tax levied on the university during the previous year should be abolished in the interests of both students and colleges. Cromwell complied. By an act of parliament passed early in 1536 both universities were relieved of the tax. But exemption was granted only on one condition: that the universities should establish a public lecture, named after the king and provided for out of their own funds:

In consideration of which his most gracious pardon and release of the said first fruits and tenths, and for increase of learning in the said universities, His Grace's pleasure is that it be enacted by authority of this present parliament that all the colleges, houses, and halls corporate in either of the said

universities shall perpetually from henceforth, at their own proper cost and
charges, find . . . one discreet and learned personage to read one open and
public lecture . . . in any such science or tongue as the king's majesty shall
assign or appoint to be most profitable for the students in either of the said
universities, every which lecture shall be called perpetually King Henry the
eighth his lecture.

In a preamble to the act the king specified 'the seven liberal sciences
and the three tongues of Latin, Greek and Hebrew' as subjects to be
catered for by the lectureship.[35] Thus, at both Oxford and Cambridge
a permanent teaching position was created. It was to be held by a
person appointed and paid by the university to lecture in a subject
selected by the king. This was the germ of the Regius professorships.

Although the royal lecture was intended as a permanent
arrangement, it existed in its original form for only four years. In
1540, much to the relief of the universities, the financial responsibility
for the post was shifted to the cathedral church of Westminster. At the
same time the number of lectureships at each university was increased
to five. Greek, Hebrew, divinity, civil law and medicine were now to be
taught by a qualified teacher lecturing in the Schools for a salary of
£40 a year. Westminster was therefore obliged to provide £400
annually to support ten lectureships. This phase lasted until 1546
when Trinity College was founded at Cambridge and Christ Church at
Oxford. From now on the endowments given to these new foundations
were to be used to pay three out of the five lecturers, those in Greek,
Hebrew and divinity, while the other two were to be supported by the
state. The Regius professorships were thereby confirmed, and they
were administered according to this pattern until Hanoverian times.
According to the statutes of 1549 the professor was to lecture for five
hours per week on Scripture and grammar. In 1564 his commitments
were reduced by one hour, an arrangement which was reaffirmed in
1576.

The establishment of these chairs marked an important watershed
in the history of the universities and introduced new principles into
higher education. First and foremost it was a triumph for humanism.
What had been attempted in the past by persuasion had now been done
by force. Not that scholasticism was completely ousted. We know that
by the early seventeenth century it was once more finding a place in the
curriculum.[36] But such an innovation did possess all the marks of early
humanist thinking on educational matters. By its action the crown
demonstrated its endorsement of the new learning and its

determination to support the advocates of university reform, especially with regard to linguistic study. The foundation of these five lectureships at both universities underlined the significance of divinity, Greek, and Hebrew. These three subjects were 'three pillars in the edifice of the new learning. Their place was special'.[37] But the study of these vital subjects was not left, as in the past, to the whim of individual colleges. The university as a whole was now called upon to teach them, and every college was expected to play its part in the dissemination of fresh ideals. Secondly, the permanence afforded by the endowments ensured that the subjects could be taught more effectively. The guarantee of a regular salary meant that the universities would no longer be dependent on voluntary teachers, regent masters who had to maintain themselves by other means, but could employ recognised experts on a full-time basis. It also meant that the lectures could be 'open and public' in the sense that students would be permitted to attend them free of charge.

The universities quickly implemented the statute of 1536 and found the means to support a royal lecturer. At Oxford the chosen subject was divinity; at Cambridge it was Hebrew. Since the appointment of Richard Croke regular instruction in Greek had been provided in Cambridge, but with Robert Wakefield's departure to Oxford in 1530 the study of Hebrew had suffered. This state of affairs, coupled with Thomas Leigh's recommendation, may well have influenced the crown's choice of subject for the lectureship.

In all probability the person chosen as Hebrew lecturer at Cambridge in 1536 was Thomas Wakefield, the younger brother of Robert. On 9 November 1540 he was elected to the newly created Regius chair, a post which he held in name if not in practice until his death in 1575.[38] According to Cooper 'others were appointed readers of the Hebrew tongue whilst he held the endowed professorship' because of his adherence to Roman Catholicism.[39] Of his career prior to his appointment to the chair very little is known. He graduated B.A. at Cambridge in 1523, and is presumed to be the Wakefield granted leave of absence with pay from St John's College by Fisher in 1523–24 so that he could continue his studies abroad. Writing to the Master of St John's, Fisher expresses the hope that by going 'beyond the sea' Wakefield would become 'the more expolite and perfect in the tongue of Hebrew' and on his return would be able 'to perfect others in the same learning and do honour both to your college and to the whole realm'.[40] As far as is known he published nothing. His only extant work is an examination of phrases in the New Testament which have an obvious Hebrew background; dated 1544 and dedicated to the king, it is preserved in manuscript at the British Library. The only other clue to his Hebrew scholarship is to be found in the marginalia of the books he possessed.[41] He had inherited his brother's excellent library, much of which had come from the monasteries at the dissolution. His copy of Felix Pratensis' Latin Psalter translated from the Hebrew original is heavily annotated. In the margin of Sebastian Münster's Hebrew version of the Gospel of Matthew, he identifies the source of the translator's note on a particular word as David Kimchi's *Book of Roots*. While Reuchlin's *De arte cabbalistica* was also on his shelves, it is not as well thumbed as the Hebrew version of *The Book of Joseph Ben Gorion*. His close perusal of the first three chapters of this latter work indicates considerable competence in post-biblical Hebrew. Thomas Wakefield's Hebrew books were no mere ornaments. They were read and studied with care by one who was capable of criticising their contents.

When Wakefield died the professorship passed to Edward Lively, a scholar and later fellow of Trinity College. In the course of a distinguished scholastic career, during which he was chosen to lead the Cambridge group of translators of the A.V., Lively produced several learned works dealing with the Old Testament. All of them indicate an excellent grasp of Hebrew and an uncommon familiarity with rabbinic writings. The letters which passed between James Usher, later Archbishop of Armagh, and his friends early in the seventeenth century testify to the eagerness with which these works were awaited, and to the respect in which the author was held as a Hebraist by biblical scholars of his own day.[42] Lively was also a competent teacher. The oration delivered at his funeral in 1605 by Thomas Playfere, Lady Margaret Professor of Divinity at Cambridge, demonstrates how successfully he had communicated his love of Hebrew and his interest in rabbinic literature to his contemporaries. Referring to Hebrew, Playfere says:

Which tongue, howsoever some account of it, yet ought to be preferred above all the rest. For it is the ancientest, the shortest, the plainest of all . . . When any man hath found the Hebrew etymology, then he need seek no further. . . . The rabbis themselves, though they have no small number of fables and lies in them, yet diverse things they have notwithstanding fit for the opening of the Old Testament. Therefore though a man cannot read the rabbis, yet unless he can understand handsomely well the Hebrew text, he is counted but a maimed, or as it were half a divine, especially in this learned age.[43]

The valuable assessment by Erwin Rosenthal of Lively as a Semitic scholar renders superfluous a lengthy examination of his works.[44] We shall confine ourselves to his commentary on Daniel's Seventy Weeks (Daniel 9:24–27), that 'dismal swamp of Old Testament criticism' which was the subject of fierce debate among sixteenth-century scholars. Entitled *A True Chronologie of the Times of the Persian Monarchy and after to the destruction of Jerusalem by the Romans* (London 1597) the book runs into two hundred and fifty-eight octavo pages, and offers ample evidence of the author's breadth of scholarship and of his attitude towards the Hebraic tradition.

In his exposition of the Seventy Weeks, Lively takes other commentators, both Protestant and Roman Catholic, to task for their erroneous explanations. On the title-page he plainly states that he is expounding 'the Angel Gabriel's message to Daniel ... against the frivolous conceits of Matthew Beroald', a French Protestant writer and friend of Vatable. During the course of the discussion he also criticises the Spanish Jesuit Benedict Pereira for his exegesis of Gabriel's speech in his *Commentariorum in Danielem prophetam libri XVI* (1586). Even Joseph Scaliger, 'a man of rare gifts, a great light of this age: one whom the Church of God for his pains is much beholding to', does not escape Lively's judgement for the views he expressed in *De emendatione temporum* (1583).[45] The *True Chronologie*, however, is not simply a refutation of other opinions. In it Lively presents an ordered and well-argued case for his own explanation of the passage. His exegetical principles, on which he expands in a lengthy introduction, are twofold, 'the one is a just account of the times; the other, a true interpretation of the words in the original tongue. If we fail in either of these, there is no hope to know what Daniel meant by his weeks'.[46] In his search for the true interpretation he turns constantly to the 'judgement of cunning linguists, and sound divines',[47] with the result that the comments of Classical authors, Church Fathers and Jewish exegetes are blended together and harnessed to the task of biblical exposition.

Classical learning, in which Lively himself was steeped, is to be recommended to all those aspiring to understand the Scriptures. With examples from Pliny, Horace, Homer, Sophocles, Herodotus and a host of others, he stresses the contribution made by non-Christian writers to the understanding of God's Word. Classical authors 'for many parts of Scripture are diligently to be sought unto, and not as some rash brains imagine, to be cast away as unprofitable in the Lord's schoolhouse; but especially for Daniel above all. In other places they may seem profitable, but here they are necessary even by Jerome's judgement'.[48] It was this reliance on the Classics for help in difficult places that displeased Richard Simon and led him to criticise Lively for parading his learning and 'adorning his discourse with unnecessary authorities'.[49] Simon represents a later generation of biblical scholars who rarely illustrated any points by referring to Classical authors, and certainly did not accept them as authoritative. But in Lively's view these 'profane writers' were important sources for the illumination of the Word of God.

In addition to the Classics, Lively displays great familiarity with the writings of the Church Fathers whose opinions he respected because they had the weight of tradition. Jerome, Eusebius, and Theodoret feature prominently throughout his exposition of the Seventy Weeks. Tertullian's judgement on an obscure point should be heeded for he 'was one of the Latin Fathers most ancient, and very near the Apostles'.[50] Clement of Alexandria was 'a man for great knowledge rare, and as ancient, if not more than Tertullian'.[51] Sulpicius Severus is of similar standing with Augustine, Epiphanius, and Chrysostom; his comments on Daniel are more illuminating than those of any other ancient writer.

Lively's third and constant court of appeal when wrestling with the obscurities of Gabriel's message is the works of post-biblical Jewish historians, exegetes and grammarians. As well as Targum and Talmud, and the principal commentators of the Late Middle Ages, he makes use of David Kimchi's *Book of Roots* and the *Tishbi* of Elias Levita whenever he is confronted with a lexicographical problem. On questions related to Jewish history and chronology he introduces us to two new sources: the two versions of the *Seder 'Olam* and Abraham ibn Daud's *Book of Tradition*. The *Seder 'Olam Rabbah*, a chronicle of the history of Jews from Adam to Bar Kochba, is ascribed to the second century tanna Jose ben Halafta. It was acknowledged by Jewish tradition as authoritative and used by later commentators as a basis for exegesis. During the Early Middle Ages a shorter version, the *Seder 'Olam Zuta*, was produced by an anonymous author whose intention was to show that the Babylonian exilarchs were of Davidic descent. Both were translated into Latin by the French Hebraist Gilbert Génébrard in 1577. Abraham ibn Daud produced his *Book of Tradition* during the twelfth century in response to the Karaite attack on Rabbinic Judaism. In it he surveys Jewish history from the reign of

Alexander the Great up to his own time, but in the prologue gives notice of the apologetic nature of the work:

The purpose of this Book of Tradition is to provide students with the evidence that all the teachings of our rabbis of blessed memory, namely, the sages of the Mishna and the Talmud, have been transmitted: each great sage and righteous man having received them from a great sage and righteous man, each head of an academy and his school having received them from the head of an academy and his school, as far back as the men of the Great Assembly, who received them from the prophets, of blessed memory all. Never did the sages of the Talmud, and certainly not the sages of the Mishna, teach anything, however trivial, of their own invention, except for the enactments which were made by universal agreement in order to make a hedge about the Torah.[52]

The first abridgement of this important work was published by Sebastian Münster together with a Latin version in 1527. A second and larger abridgement with a new Latin translation appeared in Génébrard's *Hebraeorum breve chronicon* (1572).

Lively refers to the whole range of Jewish writings in his discussion of Daniel 9:24–27. But there is one notable omission, namely the *Ma'yenei Ha-Yeshu'ah* (*The Wells of Salvation*) of Isaac Abravanel. This commentary on Daniel by one of mediaeval Jewry's outstanding sons was published in Naples in 1497 and again at Ferrara in 1551, but it does not seem to have entered into Lively's calculations. In the whole of the *True Chronologie* there is not one explicit reference to it. This is all the more surprising when we remember the interest which Abravanel's writings generated among Christians. 'Theologians and Bible critics, orientalists and historians, bibliographers and encyclopaedists, belonging to a variety of Christian camps, diligently studied Abravanel's writings, investigated his life, wrote in defence or in refutation of his theories, and, above all, translated large parts of his works into Latin.'[53] Despite such popularity, his views on Daniel's Seventy Weeks attract little, if any, support among Christians. The reason for this must be sought in his motive for writing *The Wells of Salvation*. The fifteenth century saw the fortunes of Jewry at a very low ebb. Harassed by the attacks of Christian polemicists and disillusioned by the unfulfilled hopes of a redeemer, many Jews were turning their back on the faith of their fathers. Abravanel sensed this mood of defeatism and in his messianic trilogy, of which *The Wells of Salvation* is the first part, he set out to restore the self-confidence of his people and to reject the Christian claim that the Messiah had come in the person of Jesus of Nazareth. This task inevitably led to a careful

examination of Daniel's prophecies, and, as can be expected, to a
passionate refutation of the Christian interpretation of crucial
passages. His spirited defence of Judaism earned Abravanel the
disapproval of Calvin, as we have already noted, and in all probability
it is for the same reason that Lively omits him from his list of rabbinic
authors.

On the whole, however, Lively is favourably disposed towards post-
biblical Jewish works and states categorically that rabbinic writings
are of value and significance for the Christian biblical scholar. 'The
Church of God ... is much beholding to the Hebrew rabbis, being
great helps unto us for understanding holy scripture in many places, as
well of the New Testament as the Old.'[54] Only once in the *True
Chronologie* does he reject rabbinic interpretation and agree with the
criticisms of Pereira and Temporarius. On the subject of the
identification of the Persian kings and the length of their reign the
Jewish commentators lose their credibility on two counts: their failure
to agree among themselves on major questions and their refusal to
consult Classical writers.

This is the rabbinical stuff of the chief masters of the Hebrews, being at odds
betwixt themselves, and differing from others, and therefore not without
cause doth Pererius in his commentaries upon Daniel (speaking of this
chronology of theirs) say that it is false, fained, full of faults, toys, ignorance,
absurdity and inconstancy, and altogether ridiculous as it is indeed.
Temporarius is more sharp and bitter against them. The Talmudists,
Cabbalists and Rabbis, (saith he) are blind in the Persian times, and the
writings of the Jews herein plain proofs of pitiful ignorance in them: who can
read the chronologies of the Rabbis, their *Seder Olam Rabba*, their *Seder
Olam Zota*, their *Historical Cabbala* without laughing? Therefore the
knowledge of times is not to be fetched from the dotings of these men being
more blind than moles ... Touching the knowledge of the Persian Empire,
wherein they should have been most cunning, they were as blind as beetles, no
light herein amongst them for knowledge to be seen, but darkness for
ignorance enough and too much. The reason whereof is, that they wanted the
key as it were of profane histories, and secular learning, to unlock the shut
and hid meaning of Daniel's oracles, without the which by Scripture alone it
can never be opened. Some of them not disdaining to read the Latin and
Greek Histories, by the direction of these guides went not so far astray.[55]

This justified, if intemperate, criticism stems from the fact that the
Seder 'Olam Rabbah, contrary to the historical record, allows only
thirty-four years for the Persian period of Jewish history.[56] The rabbis
are of value in elucidating many complex questions, but on specifically
chronological issues their comments must be treated with

circumspection.

By his linguistic expertise and his appreciation of rabbinic sources Cambridge's second Regius professor played a major part in furthering Hebrew studies in Elizabethan England. Most of his writings reflect contemporary controversies about the Scriptures. Like Fulke, he firmly supported the Protestant stand on vernacular translations of the Bible and was critical of Rome's stubborn adherence to the Vulgate. In defence of his views he made extensive use of Jewish sources, and on the whole adopted an unbiased attitude towards the Jews.

Between them, Wakefield and Lively held the Regius chair of Hebrew at Cambridge for sixty-five years (1540–1605). During the same period Oxford had seven professors.[57] On Robert Wakefield's death in 1537 the teaching of Hebrew was undertaken by John Shepreve who, for the past seven years had been fellow and lecturer in Greek at Corpus Christi College. But his appointment was not confirmed until April 1542 when the university gave him permission to expound the book of Genesis in Hebrew at the Schools 'provided that he lectured in a pious and catholic manner'.[58] He was in office for only three months, but in the absence of any definite information it may be assumed that he was the first Regius professor. Though he was considered at the time to be 'one of the most skilful linguists' Oxford had ever seen, there is little evidence of such ability in his writings. The only testimony to his Semitic expertise is a Hebrew translation, extant in manuscript, of the New Testament letters of James and Jude from the Greek. Prefaced by a Latin dedication to Henry VIII, the translation is executed in good classical Hebrew and the semi-cursive Sephardic script is clear and well-formed. The overall impression gained from reading it is of one who was a practised Hebraist, familiar with post-biblical Hebraic idioms and modes of expression.[59] One of Shepreve's earliest pupils at Corpus Christi was George Etheridge who later became Regius Professor of Greek at Oxford but who was also a recognised Hebrew scholar.

Thomas Harding, a fellow of New College, succeeded Shepreve in 1542. He too was acclaimed 'a knowing person in the tongues', though no evidence of his ability as a Hebraist survives. Under Edward VI he staunchly upheld the Protestant cause, but when Mary came to the throne he 'wheeled about', and as a protagonist of Roman orthodoxy devoted his energies to supporting the Counter-Reformation. In 1561 he fled to the Continent, finding refuge at Louvain where he soon became an influential member of the faculty. It was here that he spent the rest of his life, promoting the study of Greek and Hebrew and lecturing at the house of study which had been opened especially for the benefit of exiled English students. His library, sold by auction after his death in 1572, contained the lexicons of Pagninus and Münster, David Kimchi's *Book of Roots*, and grammatical treatises by the two famous Louvain Hebraists, Clenardus and Campensis.[60]

Harding did not remain long as King's Reader at Oxford. In 1547 he resigned in favour of Richard Bruerne of Lincoln College, who, according to Cox in a letter to Peter Martyr, was an 'excellent Hebraist'.[61] The only known extant work to come from Bruerne's pen is an unpublished Hebrew translation of the Letter to the Hebrews. The autographed manuscript, presented by the author to Henry VIII, is now in the library of Hebrew Union College, Cincinnati (MS. 24.1). Written in clear, square characters, it is fully vocalised throughout, and apart from a grammatical howler in the opening verses of the first chapter, appears to be a faithful rendering of the original Greek into classical Hebrew prose. But despite such competence, Bruerne did little to fire his students with enthusiasm for things hebraic, and as a result almost lost his job through the interference of Cardinal Pole. The cardinal could see no future for Semitics at Oxford and in 1555 proposed that a lectureship in scholastic theology be substituted for the Hebrew professorship, because the Hebrew lecture 'had few, if any, auditors'.[62] The proposal came to nothing, but the precarious state of Hebrew studies was recognised and deputies were appointed to teach the language while Bruerne was either suspended or unavoidably absent. The Salamanca educated Dominican, Peter de Soto, together with John Whyte and Nicholas Saunders, both of New College, all helped to provide some kind of instruction in Hebrew during the final years of Bruerne's tenure.[63] Thomas Neale, another fellow of New College, was appointed to succeed Bruerne in 1559. Although he retired from university life ten years later, afraid that his adherence to Catholicism would be called into question, Neale is one of the few Regius professors in sixteenth-century Oxford who left direct evidence of his familiarity with biblical and post-biblical Hebrew. His published works include a Latin translation of Kimchi's commentaries on the twelve minor prophets, and a speech of thirteen lines and a poem of five stanzas written in Hebrew to honour Queen Elizabeth on her visit to Oxford in 1566. Though they contain some orthographical oddities both the speech and poem, which are extant in manuscript (MS.

Bodleian 13), bear witness to Neale's proficiency as a Hebraist. They contain several phrases and idioms peculiar to rabbinic Hebrew. Thomas Kingsmill of Magdalen College followed Neale and was professor for twenty-two years, though for much of the time he appears to have done little if any teaching on account of a serious mental illness. From 1579 to 1584 his place was taken by Richard Hooker, and in 1585 by Edward Gellibrand who was given leave to discontinue his theological lectures at Magdalen so that he could deputise for his colleague in the university. Whereas Kingsmill was appointed for life, his two immediate successors were to hold the professorship only at the queen's pleasure. John Harding, later to become President of Magdalen and leader of the Oxford group of translators for the A.V., served from 1591 to 1598. The final name on the list is that of yet another fellow of New College, William Thorne, a scholar held in great esteem as an Orientalist both in England and on the Continent, 'a most noted linguist and rabbi of his time'.[64] Unfortunately, none of these last three left any literary remains which would serve as an illustration of anything more than an elementary knowledge of Hebrew.

Strangers and exiles

'English youths have come over to us in great numbers within these few days, partly from Oxford, and partly from Cambridge, whom many godly merchants are bringing up to learning, that should it please God to restore religion to its former state in that kingdom, they may be of some benefit to the church of England.' So wrote Peter Martyr to Henry Bullinger from Strasbourg on 24 February 1554.[65] English students, anxious to benefit from the educational legacy of the continental Reformers and financed by wealthy business men, were crossing the Channel in ever increasing numbers. But it was not only undergraduates who made their way to Strasbourg. Prominent churchmen and senior members of both universities found refuge there during the reign of Mary Tudor. John Jewel, Edwin Sandys, Christopher Goodman, Thomas Sampson and Edmund Grindal were among the many English exiles who passed through the city during the 1550s. How many of them actually attended lectures on the Scriptures must remain an open question. But had they wished to improve their Hebrew and familiarise themselves with the Hebraic tradition, there would have been ample opportunity for them to do so. Martyr organised what Thomas Fuller describes as a 'petty college' in his own house with Jewel as 'vice-master'.[66] It was here that Martyr delivered his lectures on the Hebrew text of the book of Judges. Girolamo Zanchi, a gifted Hebraist, who like Martyr had fled Italy in the face of persecution, was also expounding the Old Testament. From 1553 to 1560 he lectured on the prophecies of Isaiah and Hosea, paying particular attention to the rabbinic interpretation. His list of recommended books for those attending his courses included the Bibles of Pagninus, Münster and Leo Jud, Münster's Dictionary and Kimchi's commentary on the minor prophets.[67]

If Martyr and his colleagues had their hands full in Strasbourg, the successors of Zwingli were equally busy in Zurich. For several decades they gave generous hospitality to a constant stream of visitors. From the late 1530s onwards, the letters which passed between London and Zurich indicate the respect in which English students held their Swiss teachers. The names of Bullinger, Bibliander, Leo Jud and Pellican, all of whom were competent Hebrew scholars, feature prominently in the correspondence.[68] Bullinger has always been overshadowed by Zwingli, yet it was he who developed and established the latter's work at Zurich. He organised the first part of the exercise of 'prophesying' on a more formal basis, moving it from the choir of the Great Minster to a nearby lecture room, and arranged for systematic instruction in the biblical languages to be given to the participants. He was in Zurich for over forty years, welcoming scholars and diplomats from all over Europe and from every confession to his home. Although he never travelled abroad, by writing and teaching he exercised considerable influence on the English Church.[69] Since 1525 the teaching of Hebrew at the Zurich seminary had been supervised by Konrad Pellican, who was succeeded in 1556 by Peter Martyr. Bibliander, like Leo Jud, was noted for his appreciation of Jewish exegetical writings. Such was the group of scholars at whose feet the English visitors sat. John Hooper, later Bishop of Gloucester, learned Hebrew from Pellican, though he was fast approaching middle age. Laurence Humphrey and Thomas Bentham, whatever their proficiency in Hebrew before they arrived, must have developed their skill in the language at Zurich.

At Basle and Geneva the story was the same. Here too English scholars were welcomed and encouraged to participate in the university courses. But the traffic was not all one way. By 1550 the debt to these continental centres of learning was being repaid by

English hospitality to foreign students. During the reign of Edward VI, Protestants began looking to England as a place of refuge in the face of persecution. Some considered Oxford and Cambridge as suitable places of education for their children. In 1571 Rudolph Gualter, Zwingli's grandson, came to Cambridge where he was supported by Parkhurst, Bishop of Norwich. Reporting to Gualter senior on his son's progress, Parkhurst writes: 'our Rudolph lives, is well, hebraises'.[70] The universities also attracted eminent scholars as well as students. Merton College, through its generosity to religious refugees, provided at least two gifted Hebrew teachers for its members. John Drusius, seeking refuge from religious persecution in the Netherlands, fled with his parents to London from where he went to Cambridge to continue his study of Semitic languages. He had formerly studied at the trilingual college in Louvain. Dissuaded from returning across the Channel by the Bartholomew Day massacre of 1572, he settled at Oxford where he was given rooms in Merton and paid forty shillings a year to read the Hebrew lecture for the college.[71] At the request of Laurence Humphrey he was also employed at Magdalen College from 1572 to 1576 to teach Syriac, Aramaic and Hebrew.[72] In 1574 the Earl of Leicester acted on his behalf and secured for him the post of Syriac lecturer in the university, but two years later he left England to become Hebrew professor at Leiden. The other foreigner befriended by Merton was Benseris of Caen whose services were retained by the college 'to lecture on Hebrew to its students, at a salary of £3. 6s. 8d. a year, when great efforts were being made to recall him to his own country'.[73] We know nothing of Benseris' accomplishments as a scholar, but the esteem in which he was held by his own university is evident from the contents of a letter sent to Oxford from Caen on 18 July 1576. 'Peace is at last restored in France. We have written to our pastor, M. de la Benseris, asking him to return with all speed to his pastoral charge. We thank you for your kindness in receiving him, helping him with money, and giving him a place among your "theologiae professores". We now ask you to send him back; because you have plenty of good men, we have not.'[74]

Continental Hebraists were prominent in Cambridge during the time of Thomas Wakefield. Although Wakefield had been appointed Regius professor for life in 1540, there were occasions, as we have noted, when he was barred from lecturing and had to rely on others to take his place. The first substitute for him was Paul Fagius who came to England in the company of Martin Bucer as a result of the persecution of Protestants in Germany. An Italian by birth, Fagius learned Hebrew from Elias Levita and established a press for the printing of Hebrew books at Ferrara. Faced with opposition in his native land, he fled to Strasbourg where he continued his studies under Wolfgang Capito. He quickly became a proficient Hebraist and succeeded his teacher as professor for three years. On his arrival in England he was invited, on Cranmer's instigation, to teach Hebrew at Cambridge, and with the co-operation of Bucer, to make a new translation of the Bible. Within weeks of his being appointed, however, Fagius died and his place was taken by Immanuel Tremellius.

Under Mary, Wakefield was reinstated and permitted to read the Hebrew lecture until 1569 when he was again suspended. On this occasion he was replaced by Anthony Rudolph Chevallier, a pupil of Vatable and formerly professor at the Geneva Academy. While on a brief visit to England in search of aid for the Huguenots, Chevallier was persuaded by Parker and Sandys to act as Wakefield's deputy. He accordingly arrived at Cambridge during May 1569 bearing a letter of recommendation signed by the two prelates. Addressing the Vice-Chancellor and the university authorities, Parker and Sandys commend Chevallier as a teacher of Hebrew. They write with conviction for he was a scholar whom they had 'aforetime not only known in the same university, but also have seen good testimony of his learning in the said tongue; and having more experience of his good zeal to exercise his said talent towards all such as be desirous to be partakers of the same'.[75] As the letter suggests, this was not the first time Chevallier had taught at Cambridge. In *c.* 1550–1553 he had lectured free of charge for Immanuel Tremellius, and it appears that his erudition and generosity had impressed his contemporaries. During this second visit he was given a room in Peterhouse and appointed Hebrew lecturer for the college, a post which he held from 1569 until he left England in 1572. His services were obviously appreciated, for in 1570 his salary of six shillings a year was doubled.[76] King's College was more generous. During the same period (1569–1572) it paid him three pounds a year for delivering the Hebrew lecture.[77] St John's also employed him to succeed William Fulke as Hebrew lecturer in 1569. Chevallier's son, Emmanuel, was at Cambridge with his father and was incorporated B.A. from Heidelberg in 1569. He too was employed to teach Hebrew. In 1570 Corpus Christi College elected him to a fellowship with the title of Hebrew lecturer.[78]

Anthony's ability as a teacher is recognised by his students. Hugh Broughton, who is not often given to flattery, considered him to be 'a very learned man' from whom one would learn more in a month 'than others could teach in ten years'.[79] Similar sentiments are expressed by Rudolph Zwingli in a letter to Edwin Sandys dated 26 January 1572. Zwingli reports that he is enjoying student life at Cambridge, especially since he has had the opportunity of attending Chevallier's lectures. He is full of admiration for 'that most famous and learned man, master Anthony Chevallier, to whom our Germany can scarce produce an equal in the knowledge of Hebrew, or one who can bear a comparison with him, except Immanuel Tremellius'.[80] It was the good fortune of Cambridge undergraduates to have this generous scholar at hand to teach them Hebrew. He died, loved and revered, on the island of Guernsey in 1572.

Another of Wakefield's many deputies was Philip Bignon whose father had fled to England in *c.* 1550. As a member of Corpus Christi College Bignon may well have learned his Hebrew from Emmanuel Chevallier. When the Regius chair finally became vacant in 1575, the Chancellor of the university suggested that Bignon be appointed. But despite pressure from Andrew Perne and the Master of Corpus, he was not acceptable. The statutes required the professor of Hebrew to be at least an M.A., and since Bignon had no degree whatever he was not eligible for election. The chair went to Edward Lively. After his rejection by Cambridge Bignon went to Oxford and from 1577 to 1580 taught Hebrew at Magdalen College.[81]

One of Bignon's contemporaries at Cambridge was Peter Baro, another French Protestant who had found refuge in England after the massacre of St Bartholomew. A graduate in law from the University of Bourges, he later turned to theology and in 1560 was ordained by Calvin in Geneva. On his arrival in Cambridge he was received by Peterhouse and elected a fellow-commoner of the college in April 1573. For the next twenty-five years he and his family lived in a house belonging to Peterhouse. Since he was a competent Hebraist he must surely have been persuaded by Andrew Perne to teach Hebrew for the college in place of Anthony Chevallier; but no record of such an arrangement exists. In 1576 he was appointed by Goad, the Provost of King's, to read a Hebrew lecture daily to all Kingsmen studying divinity. At first he read publicly in the college chapel and then privately in the Provost's lodgings. How long this arrangement continued is not known. The lectures were obviously popular, for

Goad refers with satisfaction to the Hebrew lecture to which 'diverse also of the company, both of the seniors and young masters of art, did usually resort'.[82] Baro's excellence as a teacher of Hebrew was to be quoted in his defence twenty years later when, as Lady Margaret Professor of Divinity, he was accused of teaching doctrines which were 'agreeable to the errors of popery'. As a result of the dispute Baro's re-election to the professorship was called into question. But Archbishop Whitgift supported him and wrote to the Vice-Chancellor, Jegon, the Master of Corpus, appealing for a fair election. Although Thomas Playfere of St John's was in fact appointed to the chair, Jegon was not entirely unsympathetic to Baro. If he disagreed with his theology, he appreciated his skill as a teacher and recognised his proficiency in Hebrew. On 4 December 1596, in a letter to Whitgift, he expressed his hope that Baro could be persuaded to return to Cambridge to teach Hebrew and that an adequate stipend would be found for him:

I easily perceive by letters from your Grace your good opinion and gracious meaning to that reverend old man Dr Baro, who hath been here a long time, a painful teacher of Hebrew and Divinity to myself and others. To whom I am (as I have always been) very willing to show my thankful mind. But he hath lately found some heavy friends among us, to the prejudice of his former credit and his present re-election. But if he returns, and please to take pains in reading Hebrew lectures in private houses, I doubt but to his good credit, there may be raised as great a stipend.[83]

But Baro did not return. He died in London in 1599 at the age of sixty-five. Cambridge had lost both a saintly man and a scholar.

Philip Ferdinand, a baptised Jew of Polish origin, was yet another foreign scholar who taught Hebrew in Tudor England. Little is known of his life. According to Wood he arrived at Oxford in a state of penury, but through the good offices of John Rainolds found employment in several colleges as an instructor in Hebrew.[84] In 1596 he moved to Cambridge and was attached to Peterhouse, where he received forty shillings a year from the Perne Foundation in exchange for giving Hebrew lessons.[85] It was in Cambridge that he published his one and only book, *Haec sunt verba Dei* (1597). This was an anthology of post-biblical Jewish writings, including a commentary on the six hundred and thirteen commandments, the hermeneutic rules of Rabbi Ishmael, and Maimonides' Thirteen Articles of Faith. Its publication gives him the distinction of being the first to introduce English scholars to certain parts of rabbinic literature.[86] Ferdinand was probably more successful as a writer than as a teacher, for although he dedicated his

book to his students, his lectures were not well attended. Thomas
Gouge writes that his father, William Gouge of King's College, went to
listen to Ferdinand, as many others did. But the lecturer did not
inspire his auditors, for 'most of them soon grew weary and left him,
only the said Master Gouge kept close to him as long as he tarried. But
when he was gone, those who before had lost the opportunity, now
seeing their own folly, they came to Master Gouge, and entreated him
to instruct them in the grounds of the said language, which he
accordingly did and thereby himself became an excellent Hebrician'.[87]
William Eyre of Emmanuel College was another of Ferdinand's
faithful disciples. Writing to James Usher, Eyre regretted the
departure of his teacher from Cambridge, for while he lectured, there
was a hope, however slight, that Hebrew would be kept alive in the
university.[88] Ferdinand had left in 1598 to take up a professorship at
Leiden, but died within months of accepting the appointment. In
letters to his friends, the eminent Orientalist Joseph Scaliger mourned
his passing. Writing to Drusius in 1599, he fights to conceal his grief.
Three years later, in a letter to Isaac Casaubon, he laments the loss of
such an excellent teacher in Talmud, and complains that Ferdinand's
death has left his studies 'barren and desolate'.[89]

   Generosity towards the victims of religious persecution played a
significant part in securing competent instructors in Hebrew for
English students. Coupled with this was the determination of leading
humanist scholars at both universities that Hebrew should form a
recognised part of the curriculum, and that adequate financial
provision should be made for those teaching it. Fagius, Tremellius,
Anthony and Emmanuel Chevallier, Drusius, Benseris, Bignon, Baro
and Ferdinand were among those who enjoyed the hospitality of
Oxford and Cambridge colleges. Such was the respect in which they
were held and the readiness with which they were accepted, that Foster
Watson is surely correct when he claims that it was 'these foreign
refugees who established the teaching of Hebrew in England' during
the second half of the sixteenth century.[90]

Collegiate instruction

The establishment of salaried professorships at Oxford and Cambridge
was undoubtedly an important factor in promoting Hebrew studies.
Though some of those appointed to the chairs appear to have made

little or no impact on the scholarly world, the universities were now committed to providing regular instruction in the Schools. From 1540 onwards Hebrew was a recognised part of the curriculum. Even so, the burden of undergraduate education rested on individual colleges. It was the responsibility of each college to supplement the public lectures and to make fuller academic provision for its members. This it did by means of college lectureships. If any college felt that the university was not providing adequate facilities for the teaching of the biblical languages, it was free to appoint a lecturer. This supplementing of university teaching with collegiate instruction was one of the most significant developments of the Tudor period. By the end of the sixteenth century endowed college lectureships had become a permanent feature of higher education.

J. B. Mullinger supposed the lectureship to have been an innovation made by the Countess of Richmond, under the influence of Fisher, in her statutes for Christ's College drawn up in 1506. In reality it goes back to the middle of the previous century. As early as 1451 William Byngham had instituted some type of lectureship for Godshouse in Cambridge.[91] The statutes of Magdalen College, Oxford, written in 1479, provided for two college lecturers, one in philosophy and the other in theology. The King's Hall, Cambridge, appointed a lecturer in canon law in 1492. With the revival of learning these lectureships assumed greater significance as a form of academic instruction. They suited the college system and proved to be more efficient than public lectures in dealing with new subjects. In response to the demand for educational reform, collegiate teaching was more flexible than that found within the official university curriculum. It could adapt itself more easily and more quickly to new ways. It was this flexibility which made the lectureship an important vehicle in the advancement of Hebrew studies.

The first college to employ a Hebrew lecturer was St John's, Cambridge. It is likely that Robert Wakefield had given instruction in the language while he held a college fellowship in 1520–21. If he did, there is nothing to suggest that anyone succeeded him when he returned to the Continent. It is possible that his brother did some teaching for the college at a later date, but official recognition of the need to establish a lectureship came only in 1530 with Fisher's revision of the statutes. But despite the provision of a salary of five pounds a year, no one was found to fill the post for four years. As far as one can judge from the college records, the first to be appointed was John

Redman who served from 1534 to 1535. Educated at Oxford and Paris, Redman took his B.A. at Cambridge in 1525 and became a fellow of St John's a few years later. He was almost certainly a pupil of Robert Wakefield. In 1542 he was invited with five others 'well skilled in Latin, Greek, Hebrew and English', to produce a new version of the Old Testament in a projected revision of the Great Bible.[92] The scheme was shortlived, but the appointment of Redman suggests that he was regarded as a competent Hebraist. It is not clear whether or not he had an immediate successor at St John's, but from 1544 onwards the college records are more or less complete. The Hebrew lecture was delivered by men who were to become eminent scholars and churchmen. Robert Horne, William Fulke, Andrew Downes later Regius Professor of Greek, Thomas Playfere later Lady Margaret Professor of Divinity, and Robert Spalding who followed Lively in the Regius Chair of Hebrew are among those who taught successive generations of Johnians to appreciate the Old Testament in its original language.[93]

It was not long before The King's Hall followed the example set by St John's. Alert to the educational challenge of humanism, this fourteenth-century foundation actively promoted the new learning within the university.[94] From 1535 until the last extant bursar's account in 1543–44, before its amalgamation with Michaelhouse to form Trinity College, the hall employed someone to teach Hebrew. During the final year the lecture was given by John Young, a fellow of St John's, but who his predecessors were is not known. The establishment of this lectureship by the hall coincides with the visit of Thomas Leigh to Cambridge in October 1535. In order to carry out his investigations of the curriculum Leigh used The King's Hall as a base from which to operate, and in the circumstances, the master and fellows had no option but to respond enthusiastically to the commissioner's recommendations for educational reform. However, instead of instituting lectureships in Latin and Greek, as all colleges and halls were bidden to do, they followed the injunction given to the university, thereby appointing lecturers in Hebrew and Greek to give public instruction in the Schools at the hall's expense.

From 1576 Christ's College had the financial means to provide Hebrew lessons for its members, though whether it actually did so as early as this is not clear. In that year Nicholas Ashton, a former fellow, made a bequest to the college out of which £2 13s 4d was to be used to pay a Hebrew lecturer and catechist.[95] But the bursar's records do not mention payments being made specifically to a teacher of Hebrew until March 1592 when John Wentworth, who is described as a cultured and broad-minded Puritan, made provision for a salary of four pounds *per annum* to be paid to the Hebrew lecturer.[96] The first to hold the office was Richard Clarke, a fellow of the college since 1583. Clarke's knowledge of Hebrew did not go unrecognised by his contemporaries. The early seventeenth-century expositor Andrew Willet, in a dedicatory letter to the college, described him as 'an expert in the three languages'. Charles White, the editor of a collection of Clarke's sermons, writes that 'he thoroughly understood . . . Latin, Greek and Hebrew', as his Hebrew lectures in the college testified.[97] Clarke's expertise was also acknowledged by the Crown when it appointed him to the panel of Old Testament translators for the Authorised Version. The only direct evidence of his Semitic scholarship, however, is to be found in his sermons where quotations from the Hebrew Bible abound. Clarke held the lectureship for six years (1592–1598), but who his immediate successor was is not recorded. From 1601 to 1604 Hebrew instruction was given by Thomas Taylor, another fellow of the college and in all probability one of Clarke's pupils.

Those who became members of Gonville and Caius from 1586 onwards were to benefit from the generosity of Mrs Joyce Frankland, a noted philanthropist whose portrait hangs in the college Combination Room. She bequeathed four pounds a year to support a Hebrew lectureship at Caius. The records are incomplete, but the names of George Estey, Anthony Disberowe and Oliver Naylor appear in the bursar's accounts between 1594 and 1603 as having received payment for teaching Hebrew. By the turn of the century the college clearly regarded Hebrew as an important subject which was to be assigned to all members, for an order dated 16 October 1601 states that no one could be admitted to the B.A. degree if he had not attended the Hebrew lecture for at least a year. Furthermore, instruction in the language was to continue after graduation. As long as this regulation was enforced, every member would have received Hebrew lessons for several years, since students usually resided in the college until they commenced M.A.[98] A Jesuit priest, Charles Yelverton, who was at the college from *c.* 1590 to 1597, writes later of the time he spent at Cambridge: 'Sometimes I applied myself to the humanities; sometimes to philosophy; and as it is the fashion everywhere, I was at one time eager to learn Greek, and at another Hebrew'.[99]

The stress placed by Chaderton at Emmanuel on proficiency in

Hebrew has already been noted. Yet, although every fellow had to be able to cope with the language, there is no record of a Hebrew lecturer being appointed by the college in the sixteenth century. Sidney Sussex, another Puritan foundation, dating from 1596, likewise expected all fellows to pass an examination in Latin, Greek and Hebrew before being admitted. The first master, James Montagu, secured the services of a former scholar of St John's, Thomas Gataker, to teach for the college for a few months in 1596 and again from 1598 to 1600. From Samuel Clarke's account of Gataker's life, it may be presumed that he taught Hebrew, for when he left Sidney in December 1600 to take up residence in London, Montagu tried to persuade him to return to the college to read the Hebrew lecture 'which had a salary annexed to it by Lord Harrington'.[100] But Gataker chose to stay in London and became Preacher at Lincoln's Inn. Since the earliest recorded list of annual college officers is dated October 1604, there is no way of knowing whom Montagu appointed instead of him. A former student, John Pocklington, is named as the 'Hebraeus Lector' employed by the college in that year.[101]

The earliest record of a college lectureship in Hebrew at Oxford is to be found at Magdalen during the presidency of Laurence Humphrey. In a letter to the college in 1566, the visitor, Robert Horne, Bishop of Winchester, directed that 'the divines and chaplains there resort to the Hebrew lesson within the college, and the bachelors to that and Greek also'.[102] Horne's intention was to encourage attendance at the Hebrew lecture which had already been instituted, for according to the college register it was given from 1565 to 1569 by Thomas Kingsmill.[103] When Kingsmill was appointed to the Regius chair in 1569 he had no immediate successor, but in 1571–72 Thomas Brasbridge, a friend and almost certainly a pupil of Peter Morwyn, is mentioned as being in receipt of the salary of three pounds a year which was allocated to the lecturer. A fellow of the college since 1562, Brasbridge's appointment was for one year only; in 1572 he was replaced by Drusius, who in turn was succeeded by Bignon. For the first half of the next decade the college records are deficient, but in 1586 the Hebrew lecturer is named as Mr Pye. This could have been Thomas Pye, chaplain of Merton who took his B.D. in 1585 and, according to Wood, was 'accounted an eminent linguist'.[104] Four years later the lectureship passed to a Mr Cooke and in 1596 to John Wilkinson, who held it until 1620. Apart from Kingsmill, none of these lecturers at Magdalen distinguished themselves as Hebraists. However, the very existence of an official lectureship suggests that the college was taking the study of the language seriously. It was, in fact, the only Oxford college to do so in the sixteenth century.

In addition to official lecturers, several colleges had other senior members who were sympathetic to the cause of Hebrew and capable of teaching the language. Those elected to the Lady Margaret and Regius chairs of divinity could, by reason of their executive posts, exert a positive influence on the propagation of Hebraic learning within the universities. Of the twenty-two theologians who served as Lady Margaret professors at Cambridge during the sixteenth century, four were recognised Hebrew scholars.[105] John Redman (1538–1542 and 1549–1554) and Thomas Playfere (1596–1609) had both been Hebrew lecturers at St John's. Peter Baro (1574–1596) taught Hebrew for various colleges while he held the professorship. Thomas Cartwright, a fellow of Trinity, was dismissed by the Vice-Chancellor after holding office for only twelve months (1569–70). But while his views on Church government were unacceptable to many, his skill in Hebrew was recognised by at least one of his contemporaries. When Anthony Chevallier left Cambridge in 1572 Edward Dering, a fellow of Christ's, wrote to the Chancellor requesting that Cartwright be appointed to take his place as deputy to the Regius Professor of Hebrew who was currently out of favour.[106] The request, however, went unheeded and Cartwright eventually left England to become the pastor of expatriate English congregations on the Continent. Of the Regius professors, Martin Bucer (1549–1551), William Whitaker (1580–1596) and John Overall (1596–1607) were Hebrew scholars.

At Oxford, three of the early Regius professors of divinity were conspicuous for their Hebrew learning. Two of them have already been mentioned: Peter Martyr, professor from 1549 to 1553, and Laurence Humphrey, who combined the professorship with the presidency of Magdalen for twenty-nine years. Though Martyr was engaged in doctrinal disputes during his time in England, he was a competent linguist who would have supported Hebraic studies enthusiastically. In 1589 Humphrey was succeeded in the Regius chair by Thomas Holland, a fellow of New College. Holland published little, but occasional citations in his writings and in one of his sermons, together with a short Hebrew poem, substantiate the reputation which he had for 'skill in the tongues'. The poem, composed in simple classical Hebrew but without vowels, is printed in *Funebria . . . Henrici Untoni* (Oxford 1596), a collection of poems written in memory of the diplomatist and soldier Sir Henry Unton. His references to the Targum serve as examples of his positive attitude towards post-biblical Hebrew literature. Though, like his contemporaries, he drew on Nicholas of Lyra for his knowledge of Jewish exegesis, at times he appears to go directly to the Hebrew original. In a preface to a sermon preached at St Paul's in 1599 on 'the peregrinations of the Queen of the South' (Matthew 12:24), he refers in passing to the exposition of Song of Songs 3:7f found in the Targum. In a long appendix to the same sermon, addressed to Richard Bancroft, Bishop of London, in which he deals with the text in detail, he quotes the Targum again. Commenting on I Kings 10:1, he reproduces the Hebrew text together with a translation of Targum Jonathan on the verse. He also quotes the targumic explanation of the name 'Sheba' in the queen's title.[107]

For the anniversary of Queen Elizabeth's coronation on 17 November 1599 Holland penned an 'apologetical discourse' which was meant as 'a defence of the church and commonwealth' against the cavils of Rome. In support of an annual celebration of the coronation he quotes Psalm 20 (Hebrew 21). He admits that many, such as Jerome and Augustine, 'expound this psalm only of Christ our saviour', but he points to the Jewish understanding of it in terms of King David, citing Rashi as his source. In the course of a lengthy attempt to justify the ringing of bells to mark the anniversary, he supports his standpoint by referring to Elias Levita's Hebrew lexicon (*Tishbi*), and a little further on quotes Kimchi on why the tabernacle in the wilderness was called a 'tent of meeting'. He notes Ibn Ezra's opinion in a discussion of the significance of the Sabbath.[108]

For a sixteenth-century Oxford college to have a Hebrew lecturer or a fellow who was a competent Hebraist was the exception rather than the rule. Yet, despite the lack of official provision, several foundations were supportive of Hebrew studies. Corpus Christi provided the university with its first Regius Professor of Hebrew and could boast of a keen and able Hebraist in John Rainolds, its president from 1598 to 1607. The letters patent for Jesus College, issued on 27 July 1571, stated that the primary purpose of the college was to provide its members with a thorough grounding in theology by teaching them Hebrew, Greek and Latin. According to the statutes, students had to speak one of the three ancient languages in the dining hall and in the lecture rooms, unless they were entertaining guests.[109] St John's, founded in the reign of Mary Tudor, was not unsympathetic to the new learning. The aim of the founder was to educate prospective clergymen so that they could defend the orthodox faith and hold their own with Lutherans and Calvinists. Though lack of money prevented the college from appointing a Hebrew lecturer, students were encouraged to learn the language by attending lectures at the Schools. James Whitelocke relates in his diary that when he went up to St John's from Merchant Taylors' in 1588, he continued his study of logic and the arts and 'laboured much in the Hebrew and Greek tongues'.[110] The Queen's College adopted a similar attitude. A letter written by Christopher Brayne, the Vicar of Kerry in Montgomeryshire, to the provost in 1637–38 suggests that the college authorities in his student days were not averse to the learning of Hebrew. Brayne took his B.A. at Queen's in 1598 and forty years later was anxious to make a bequest to his college. He proposed to endow a Hebrew lectureship and stated thus his reasons for doing do.

> I am a lover of that language and well willer to all which study it and think it most necessary for a divine, and the greater skill therein the greater gift of God. And though I studied not the holy tongue in the holy land, yet had I the happiness to be instructed in the same in the country by one who was skilful in that language, a man famous for many good parts, one who had been sometime chaplain in our college, Mr Christopher Harvey (quem honoris causa nomino), a man highly esteemed by those two worthies Dr Rainolds and Dr Robinson. . . . And when I was bachelor of arts, being to declaim in the hall, I then made an oration in commendation of the Hebrew tongue, and by my means many divers were incited to study that language.[111]

Though the college did not employ a Hebrew lecturer in the 1590s, the reputation of the former chaplain, Christopher Harvey, as a Hebraist was well-established. From Brayne's remarks it must be presumed that at the end of the century he was living outside Oxford, but offering tuition in Hebrew for those who wanted it. He clearly made a favourable impression on at least one of his pupils.

Tudor England witnessed a determined effort by humanist scholars to make Hebrew an integral part of theological studies. Though only a few of those who were appointed professors or lecturers became eminent Hebraists, they did provide their students with the opportunity to study the rudiments of the language. The English counterpart of Germany's Reuchlin was Robert Wakefield, the pioneer of Hebraic studies at both Oxford and Cambridge. His students turned to him, not only for instruction but also for inspiration and stimulus, for in his *Oratio* he transmitted to Christian scholars a love and understanding of Hebrew and Jewish literature which, for that period, was remarkable. But it was not until the establishment of the Regius chairs that the opportunities for studying Hebrew really blossomed. If, however, the elected professors proved to be inefficient, or were suspended from lecturing for religious reasons, the promoters of the new learning sought to provide alternative teaching. Magdalen (Oxford), Merton, Peterhouse, King's and Corpus (Cambridge), because of their sympathy for the revival of letters and their generosity towards foreign refugees, employed talented continental scholars to teach their students. Those Englishmen who chose to live abroad before and during the reign of Mary, resided at centres of learning where the greatest emphasis was placed on studying the Bible in its original languages. Many of them returned to their native land enthusiastic supporters of this linguistic approach to the Scriptures. By the end of the century other colleges had followed the example of St John's, Cambridge and instituted Hebrew lectureships to supplement the teaching given in the Schools. This form of instruction eventually proved to be a most effective method of promoting the study of Hebrew within the universities.

Notes

1 For details of his career see his *Oratio de laudibus, passim*, and H. de Vocht, *History of the . . . Collegium Trilingue Lovaniense 1517–1550*, Part I, pp. 379ff.
2 *Opus Epistolarum*, vol. III, Letter 674, pp. 96f.
3 J. Rouschausse, *Erasmus and Fisher: their Correspondence*, Letter 17, p. 81.
4 Wood, *Athenae Oxonienses*, 3rd ed. rev., vol. I, col. 102.
5 See S. Knight, *The Life of Erasmus*, Cambridge 1726, Appendix p. xxviii.
6 L. Geiger, *Johann Reuchlin: sein Leben und seine Werke*, p. 473.
7 Letter printed with Wakefield's *Oratio*, n.p.
8 *Ibid.*
9 S. Knight, *The Life of Erasmus*, Appendix p. xxv.
10 *L and P*, vol. IV, Pt. 3, 5730.
11 *Syntagma de hebraeorum codicum incorruptione*, 1530, sig. Eiii.
12 For a brief description of these two works see F. Rosenthal, 'Robert Wakefield and the beginnings of biblical study in Tudor England', *Crozer Qtly.*, vol. 29, 1952, pp. 173ff. For a fuller treatment see A. Schper, 'Christian Hebraists in sixteenth-century England',

unpublished Ph.D. thesis, London 1944, pp. 19ff. John Bale in *Illustrium Maioris Britanniae Scriptorum Catalogus*, London 1548, p. 225, lists Wakefield as the author of *Institutiones hebraicas*. In his *Syntagma* Wakefield himself claims to have written an Aramaic dictionary which was stolen from him.

13   *Oratio*, sig. Bi.
14   sig. Aiii.
15   *Oratio*, sig. Bi.
16   sig. Cii.
17   *De fructu (The Benefit of a Liberal Education)*, p. 127.
18   *Opus Epistolarum*, vol. III, Letter 855, p. 357.
19   See J. B. Mullinger, *The University of Cambridge*, Cambridge 1873, vol. I, p. 535.
20   *Athenae Oxonienses*, 3rd ed. rev., vol. I, col. 107.
21   Gonville and Caius College, MS. 404. See also J. Venn, *The Works of John Caius . . . with a Memoir of his Life*, Cambridge 1912, p. 5.
22   *The Catechism of Thomas Becon with Other Pieces*, Parker Soc. 1854, p. 425.
23   M. Wren in his *Catalogus* (1617), p. 21, lists these two books, though at the present time neither of them is in the college library. The Hebrew Bible with the Targum is presumably that of Bomberg.
24   Quoted by A. Hamilton, *The Angel of Syon*, London 1905, p. 26.
25   For the latest study of Syon library see N. B. Tait, 'The Brigittine Monastery of Syon (Middlesex) with special reference to its Monastic Usages', unpublished D.Phil. thesis, Oxford 1975, pp. 286ff.
26   C. H. Cooper, *Athenae Cantabrigienses*, Cambridge 1858, vol. I, p. 354.
27   *STC*, 2nd ed. 1976, vol. II, p. 227.
28   F. J. Norton, 'The library of Bryan Rowe, Vice-Provost of King's College', *TCBS*, vol. II, 1954, pp. 350f.
29   *Opus Epistolarum*, vol. IV, Letter 1046, p. 133.
30   Wood, *Athenae Oxonienses*, 3rd ed. rev., vol. I, col. 58, claims that at Oxford he 'made a considerable progress in logicals, but more by far in the Hebrew and Greek languages'. But who taught him Hebrew in the Oxford of *c*. 1512 is not known. For further details of his career see H. de Vocht, *History of the . . . Collegium Trilingue Lovaniense 1517–1550*, Part I, pp. 500ff.
31   See J. Lelong and C. F. Boerner, *Bibliotheca Sacra*, Leipzig 1709, Pt. I, p. 675, quoting Jacob Tirinus, 'versionem Bibliorum ex Hebraeo Latinam confecit anno 1520'. In a later edition of this work (1783) A. G. Masch adds, 'Vetus Testamentum integrum ex Hebraeo Latine reddidit, sed solus Ecclesiastes cum commentariolo in publicum exiit', vol. III, Pt. II, p. 548. The full title of the commentary reads, *Ecclesiastes Latine ad veritatem hebraicam recognitus, cum nonnullis annotationibus chaldaicis et quorundam Rabbinorum sententiis, textos obscuros aliquot interaliter explanantibus.*
32   *Commentarii in Ecclesiasten*, p. 38, col. 1.
33   J. Heywood, *Collection of Statutes for the University and Colleges of*

Cambridge, London 1840, p. 198. The record of the injunctions for Oxford has not survived; it is presumed that they were identical with those made for Cambridge.

34 *Three Chapters of Letters relating to the Suppression of the Monasteries*, ed. T. Wright, Camden Soc. 1843, p. 70.

35 27 Henry VIII c 42, 4, *Statutes*, eds. A. Luders *et al.*, London 1810–28, vol. III, p. 600.

36 See W. T. Costello, *The Scholastic Curriculum at Early Seventeenth-Century Cambridge*, Cambridge, Mass. 1958.

37 F. D. Logan, 'The origins of the so-called Regius Professorships: an aspect of the Renaissance in Oxford and Cambridge', *Studies in Church History*, vol. 14, ed. D. Baker, Oxford 1977, p. 277.

38 No deed of foundation for the Regius chairs exists; the only direct evidence comes from the Letters Patent of Henry VIII. See J. W. Clarke, *Endowments of the University of Cambridge*, Cambridge 1904, p. 156.

39 *Athenae Cantabrigienses*, vol. I, p. 338.

40 See T. Baker, *History of the College of St. John the Evangelist Cambridge*, vol. I, p. 358.

41 Some of these are now in the Lambeth Palace Library. See S. R. Maitland, *A List of Some of the Early Printed Books in the Archiepiscopal Library at Lambeth*, London 1843, pp. 354ff.

42 For references to Lively in the letters of his contemporaries see R. Parr, *The Life of the Most Reverend Father in God James Usher Archbishop of Armagh*, London 1686, Pt. II, pp. 2, 3, 369, 378, 599.

43 *Collection of Tracts*, Cambridge 1609, vol. I, p. 57.

44 'Edward Lively: Cambridge Hebraist', *Essays and Studies presented to S. A. Cook*, ed. D. W. Thomas, London 1950, pp. 95ff (reprinted in *Studia Semitica*, vol. I, pp. 147ff).

45 *A True Chronologie* p. 83.

46 *Ibid.*, p. 27.

47 *Ibid.*, Preface p. 44.

48 *Ibid.*, p. 22.

49 *Histoire Critique du Vieux Testament* (Eng. trans.), Bk. III, p. 110.

50 *A True Chronologie*, p. 221.

51 *Ibid.*, p. 225.

52 Abraham ibn Daud, *The Book of Tradition*, ed. with Eng. trans. G. D. Cohen, London 1967, p. 3.

53 See B. Netanyahu, *Don Isaac Abravanel*, p. 251.

54 *A True Chronologie*, p. 36.

55 *Ibid.*, p. 35.

56 See the text of *Seder 'Olam Rabbah*, ed. A. Neubauer, *Mediaeval Jewish Chronicles and Chronological Notes*, Anecdota Oxoniensia, Semitic Series, Oxford 1887, vol. I, p. 166.

57 For a list of those who served as professors at Oxford during the sixteenth century see the forthcoming History of the university.

58 See A. B. Emden, *A Biographical Register of the University of Oxford A.D. 1501 to 1540*, Oxford 1974, p. 513.

59 British Library, Royal MS. 16. A.2.
60 On Harding see H. de Vocht, 'Thomas Harding', *EHR*, vol. 35, 1920, pp. 233ff.
61 *The Zurich Letters*, Parker Soc. 1842, First Series, p. 66.
62 *Calendar of State Papers: Venetian*, ed. R. Brown, London 1877, vol. VI, Pt. I, pp. 226f.
63 A. Wood, *The History and Antiquities of the University of Oxford*, Eng. trans. by J. Gutch, Oxford 1786, vol. II, Pt. II, p. 849.
64 A. Wood, *Athenae Oxonienses*, 3rd ed. rev., vol. II, col. 480.
65 *Original Letters Relative to the English Reformation*, Parker Soc. 1847, vol. II, p. 514.
66 *The Church History of Britain*, ed. J. S. Brewer, Oxford 1845, vol. IV, Bk. VII, p. 230. See also R. Faerber, 'La Communauté anglaise à Strasbourg pendant le règne de Marie (1553–1558)', in *Strasbourg au coeur religieux du XVIe siècle*, eds. G. Livet and F. Rapp, Strasbourg 1977, pp. 432ff.
67 For Zanchi as an Old Testament scholar see G. J. Burchill, 'Girolamo Zanchi in Strasbourg 1553–1563', unpublished Ph.D. thesis, Cambridge 1979.
68 *Original Letters*, vol. II, Letters 279–81, 286–92. See also Th. Vetter, *Relations between England and Zurich during the Reformation*, London 1904; O. Chadwick, 'The sixteenth century' in *The English Church and the Continent*, London 1959, pp. 60ff.
69 See further F. J. Smithen, *Continental Protestantism and the English Reformation*, London 1927, p. 23; D. J. Keep, 'Henry Bullinger and the Elizabethan Church', unpublished Ph.D. thesis, Sheffield 1970.
70 G. D. Gorham, *Gleanings . . . of the Reformation in England*, p. 458. On the popularity of Oxford and Cambridge among continental scholars see further C. Cross, 'Continental students and the Protestant Reformation in England in the sixteenth century', in *Reform and Reformation: England and the Continent c1500–c1750*, *Studies in Church History*, Subsidia 2, ed. D. Baker, Blackwell, Oxford 1979, pp. 35ff.
71 *Registrum Annalium Collegii Mertonensis 1567–1603*, ed. J. M. Fletcher, Oxford Hist. Soc., N.S., Oxford 1976, vol. XXIV, p. 43.
72 Magdalen College, Oxford, *Libri Computi*, 1559–1580, fol. 217v.
73 C. Broderick, *Memorials of Merton College*, Oxford 1885, p. 57. See also *Registrum . . . Mertonensis 1567–1603*, pp. 247, 250.
74 Quoted by A. Clark, *Register of the University of Oxford*, Oxford 1887, vol. II, Pt. I, p. 375.
75 J. Strype, *Annals of the Reformation*, Oxford 1824, vol. I, Pt. 2, p. 552.
76 T. A. Walker, *A Biographical Register of Peterhouse Men*, Cambridge 1927, Pt. I, p. 280. I am indebted to Dr R. W. Lovatt of Peterhouse for drawing my attention to this reference.
77 A. E. B. Owen, Archivist to King's College, kindly supplied me with this information taken from the bursar's accounts.
78 J. and J. A. Venn, *Alumni Cantabrigienses*, Cambridge 1922, vol. I, p. 331.

79 *The Works of Hugh Broughton*, ed. J. Lightfoot, Preface.

80 *The Zurich Letters*, Parker Soc. 1845, Second Series, p. 190.

81 See J. Strype, *The Life . . . of Matthew Parker*, vol. II, p. 379; Macray, *A Register . . . of Magdalen College, Oxford*, vol. III, p. 5.

82 Cooper, *Athenae Cantabrigienses*, vol. II, p. 274.

83 R. Masters, *Memoirs of the Life and Writings of the Late Rev. Thomas Baker*, Cambridge 1784, p. 130.

84 *Athenae Oxonienses*, 3rd ed. rev., vol. I, cols. 607f.

85 T. A. Walker, *A Biographical Register of Peterhouse Men*, Pt. II, p. 182.

86 For an examination of this work see S. Stein, 'Philippus Ferdinandus Polonus: a sixteenth-century hebraist in England', in *Essays in Honour of J. H. Hertz, Chief Rabbi*, pp. 397ff.

87 S. Clarke, *The Lives of Thirty-two English Divines*, London 1677, p. 397.

88 Parr, *The Life . . . of James Usher . . .*, Letters, p. 4.

89 J. Scaliger, *Epistolae*, Leiden 1627, pp. 208, 594.

90 'Notes and materials on religious refugees in their relation to education in England before the revocation of the Edict of Nantes, 1685', *Proceedings of the Huguenot Society of London*, vol. IX, No. 3, 1911, p. 317.

91 Mullinger, *The University of Cambridge*, vol. I, p. 459. But see A. H. Lloyd, *Early History of Christ's College*, Cambridge 1934, pp. 131ff. Byngham initiated a movement which eventually spread to other colleges with important consequences. On lectureships in general see M. H. Curtis, *Oxford and Cambridge in Transition 1558–1642*, Oxford 1959, pp. 101ff.; W. A. Pantin, 'The conception of the universities in England in the period of the Renaissance', in *Les Universités Européennes du XIVe au XVIIIe siècle: aspects et problèmes*, Geneva 1967, p. 109.

92 D. Wilkins, *Concilia Magnae Britanniae et Hiberniae*, London 1737, vol. III, p. 860.

93 For a partial list of the Hebrew lecturers at St John's during the sixteenth century see Appendix I p. 274.

94 See A. B. Cobban, *The King's Hall within the University of Cambridge in the Later Middle Ages*, Cambridge 1969, ch. 2.

95 J. Peile, *A Biographical Register of Christ's College 1505–1905*, Cambridge 1910, vol. I, p. 22.

96 *Ibid.*, p. 192.

97 *Sermons preached by that Reverend and Learned Divine Richard Clarke*, London 1637, Preface.

98 *The Annals of Gonville and Caius College by John Caius*, ed. J. Venn, Cambridge 1904, p. 192; J. Venn, *A Biographical History of Gonville and Caius College 1349–1901*, Cambridge 1901, vol. III, pp. 246f.

99 See J. Foley, *Records of the English Province of the Society of Jesus*, London 1877, vol. I, p. 145.

100 *The Lives of Sundry Eminent Persons in this later Age*, London 1683, p. 251.

101   See Sidney Sussex *Acta Collegii*, pp. 5, 9. I am grateful to Dr R. C. Smail of Sidney Sussex College for this reference.

102   W. D. Macray, *A Register of . . . Magdalen College, Oxford*, vol. II, p. 39.

103   The names and dates of the lecturers are taken from the college's *Libri Computi*. I am grateful to Mr C. M. Woolgar of Magdalen College for his help at this point.

104   *Athenae Oxonienses*, 3rd ed. rev., vol. II, col. 59.

105   For a full list of the Regius and Lady Margaret professors see H. R. Luard, *Graduati Cantabrigienses*, Cambridge 1873, pp. 481ff.

106   *Calendar of State Papers Domestic 1547–1580*, p. 439.

107   *A Sermon Preached at Pauls in London*, Oxford 1601, sig. E2b.

108   *The Apology or Defence of the Church and Commonwealth of England for their annual celebration of Q. Elizabeth's coronation day the 17th of November*, n.p., n.d., sigs. K1a, O3b, P4b, Q1b.

109   *Statutes of the Colleges of Oxford*, London 1853, 'Statutes of Jesus College', p. 5.

110   *Liber Famelicus of Sir James Whitelocke*, ed. J. Bruce, Camden Society 1858, p. 13.

111   The Queen's College, MS. 2 T 89. I am grateful to Mr J. M. Kaye of The Queen's College for drawing my attention to this letter.

VIII

Schools and tutors

In the preface to *The Benefit of a Liberal Education* (1517) Richard
Pace explains to John Colet why he wrote and published a book with
such a title. The explanation takes the form of what is by now a well-
known story. On a return visit to England from Rome in 1514, Pace
claims that he had attended a banquet where he was unknown to most
of those present. Half-way through the meal one of the guests began to
discuss the kind of education which he considered suitable for his
children. 'He thought first of all that he should find them a good
teacher and that they should by all means attend school and not have a
tutor.' Seated nearby was a nobleman, one of those 'who always carry
horns hanging down their backs as though they were going to hunt
while they ate'. When he heard his companions praising education he
became very annoyed and demanded to know what possible use book
learning was to any right-minded person. Education led to nothing but
penury. 'Scholars', he expostulated, 'are a bunch of beggars. Even
Erasmus is a pauper, and I hear he's the smartest of them all. . . . I'd
rather see my son hanged than be a student. Sons of the nobility ought
to blow the horn properly, hunt like experts, and train and carry a
hawk gracefully. Studies, by God, ought to be left to country boys.'[1]
Such crass ignorance and hostility to learning induced Pace to put pen
to paper immediately. His reaction to what was regarded as a long-
standing problem is typical of other Tudor humanists. J. H. Hexter
reminds us that 'ignorance and indifference to letters in the aristocracy
was not new in the sixteenth century; what was new and radical was
the suggestion that things should be otherwise'.[2] The controversial
question of how far this criticism of the well-born by supporters of the
new learning was justified cannot be considered here; suffice it to note
the advice given by some of the leading English humanist writers in
their attempt to persuade the gentry to apply themselves to scholarly
pursuits.

It is within the general context of the education of the aristocracy
that we shall examine further the facilities for learning Hebrew in
sixteenth-century England. We must seek to determine the role of

Hebraic studies within the courtly tradition, and the status of Hebrew in grammar schools and Tudor households. Let it be said at the outset that it is much easier to discover what certain people thought this role should be than to provide concrete evidence of what it was in practice. Nevertheless, it is possible to demonstrate that some were given the opportunity of studying the essentials of Hebrew grammar before proceeding to university.

A learned aristocracy

Although humanist scholars still found it necessary at the beginning of the seventeenth century to criticise the gentry for their idleness, the situation had improved markedly since the time of Pace. On his return to Italy from England in 1551 the Florentine scholar Petrucchio Ubaldini reported that 'the rich cause their sons and daughters to learn Latin, Greek and Hebrew, for since this storm of heresy has invaded the land they hold it useful to read the scriptures in the original tongues'.[3] By 1600 the sons of the well-born were to be found in ever increasing numbers at the universities, having been prepared for matriculation either at school or by a private tutor. Foreign travel was as popular as it had been a hundred years previously.

This striving for intellectual attainment was, in large measure, engendered by eminent educational theorists who wrote with the aristocracy in mind. The earliest Renaissance treatise on education to be written in English was *The Book named the Governor* (1531). In this seminal work Thomas Elyot attempts to provide what he considers to be 'the best form of education or bringing up of noble children from their nativity in such a manner as they may be found worthy and also able to be governors of a public weal'.[4] He was anxious that his book should be regarded as a guide for all those appointed by the king to any position of importance in the state. As a keen student of the humanities Elyot emphasised the role of education, giving priority to languages and literature. After receiving a thorough grounding from his tutor in Latin and Greek, the pupil could proceed to the Classical texts. Only a rigorous educational programme, in which linguistic study was a prominent feature, would provide the Crown with efficient and responsible servants possessing the requisite qualifications. *The Governor* was the first in a long line of books concerned with the intellectual training of Tudor gentlemen. In 1561 Thomas Hoby published an English translation of Castiglione's *Il Cortegiano*. This sketch of the ideal courtier was first printed in Italy in 1528. Though placed on the Roman Catholic *Index* of forbidden books in 1590, *The Courtier* enjoyed great popularity in England. Here again the importance of scholarship was stressed. Since he was responsible for guiding and instructing the prince in statecraft, the courtier had to be a man of learning as well as a man of arms. 'In letters I would have the courtier more than moderately instructed, especially in what they style polite literature, and to understand not only the Latin tongue but the Greek'.[5] That the training of the gentry was to be carried out in conformity with humanistic principles is affirmed also by Roger Ascham in *The Schoolmaster*. Published in 1570, soon after the author's death, the subtitle indicates that it was 'specially purposed for the private bringing-up of youth in gentlemen's and noblemen's houses'. Although he admits that efforts are being made to educate the sons of the aristocracy, Ascham feels that there is still a long way to go. 'From seven to seventeen young gentlemen commonly be carefully brought up, but from seventeen to seven-and-twenty (the most dangerous time of all a man's life and most slippery to stay well in) they have commonly the rein of all licence in their own hand, and specially such as do live in the court.' He has heard of some who are even ashamed 'to be counted learned'.[6] Faced with such apathy, he took it upon himself to fashion an educational programme designed to regenerate the decadent nobility of England. As one would expect from a former lecturer in Greek at Cambridge, he gave considerable prominence to the Classics. The only way to learn English was by studying Latin and Greek.

While they saw the significance of linguistic studies for sons of the gentry, neither Elyot nor Ascham made any reference to Hebrew in their schemes of training. There were, however, those who did. It will be remembered how Laurence Humphrey recommended that Hebrew lessons should be included in the curriculum. In his *The Nobles, or Of Nobility* he urged that the children of noblemen be introduced to the language at an early age.[7] The reasons for such insistence were religious. Since the Bible, not the Classics, was his textbook, and the quarry for his models of perfect nobility, the young nobleman must be encouraged to read it. Furthermore, sound instruction in the true faith as revealed in Scripture was the Puritan's only defence against Roman Catholicism. Admittedly, it was now available in translation, but for a proper understanding of its message a knowledge of the original languages was essential. In this particular blueprint for a 'gentle education' one detects the influence of the Reformation rather than the Renaissance, of the Swiss city states which sheltered the Marian exiles rather than the Italian courts.

Shortly after the publication of Ascham's *Schoolmaster*, a plan for the education of royal wards was put forward by the famous explorer Humphrey Gilbert. The lack of educational facilities for these orphans who were now the responsibility of the court had long been recognised. As early as 1536 Thomas Starkey had suggested that guardians should pay more attention to the intellectual development of their wards than to the collection of rents and revenues.[8] More recently the cause had been espoused by Nicholas Bacon. On his retirement from acting as attorney to the court of wards in 1561 Bacon wrote to William Cecil, master of the court, in an attempt to remedy the situation. He proposed that all royal wards, whose lands had an annual value of over a hundred marks, should be educated from the age of nine in a special academy. Under the supervision of qualified teachers they would receive formal instruction, not only in the courtly arts, but also in languages, law and music.[9] But in spite of Bacon's enthusiasm the plan failed, only to be resurrected by Gilbert a few years later. Like Pace, Elyot, Starkey and Ascham, Gilbert was shocked by the indifference displayed by the upper classes towards intellectual pursuits. He complained that the orphaned children of noblemen were brought up 'to no small grief of their friends, in idleness and lascivious pastimes, estranged from all serviceable virtues to their prince and country'. Since they tended to drift to London, there was surely a strong case for establishing an academy in the capital for boys of twelve years old and over. Such a scheme would ensure that 'there shall be hereafter . . . no gentleman within this realm but good for somewhat, whereas now the most part of them are good for nothing'.[10]

Gilbert's proposal was more ambitious than that of Bacon. In addition to what he calls 'matters of action meet for present practice, both of peace and war', the wards were to be taught a whole range of subjects including law, philosophy, mathematics, divinity, modern languages and, surprisingly, Hebrew. For a salary of fifty pounds a year the academy was to hire 'one who shall read and teach the Hebrew tongue'. In common with his colleagues employed to teach other languages, the Hebrew instructor's duties were to involve more than just the giving of lessons. 'Every one of those which shall publicly teach any of the languages as aforesaid, shall once every three years publish in print some translation into the English tongue of some good work, as near as may be for the advancing of those things which shall be practised in the said academy.'[11] Clearly Gilbert was confident that a proficient Hebraist could be found who would not only ensure that the language was taught but also make a substantial contribution to scholarship. The salary was attractive, set at £66 13s 4d per annum. This figure, however, was crossed out by Gilbert himself in the original manuscript and emended to £50, but even this lower sum compared very favourably with the £26 allocated to each of the teachers in French, Spanish, Italian and Dutch. Although he does not tell us in so many words, Gilbert's motive for including Hebrew in the curriculum of his academy was religious. Like Humphrey, he had Puritan sympathies. He hoped that by means of his proposed scheme 'all the best sort shall be trained up in the knowledge of God's word, . . . who otherwise, through evil teachers, might be corrupted with papistry'.[12] But despite his conviction that such a school would benefit the realm and ensure a place of honour for England and her queen among all the nations of the world, the plan was destined to remain on paper.

Richard Mulcaster (*c*. 1531–1611) is chiefly remembered as an educational reformer who tried to improve the lot of those entering the teaching profession by providing adequate facilities for their training.[13] The same pragmatic approach is discernible in the advice he offers parents on the upbringing of their children. It was not until he had spent twenty years as headmaster of Merchant Taylors' School that he put his ideas on paper, thus making a notable contribution to the debate on education. Throughout the *Positions* (1581) his declared aim is to provide the aristocracy with a blueprint for the training of their offspring. He wants 'young gentlemen to be better than the common in the best kind of learning'.[14] Though he devotes much space to physical exercise and stresses the importance of attaining a high standard in English before embarking on Latin and Greek, he attaches due weight to proficiency in languages. England should 'have her youth well directed in the tongues, which are the ways to wisdom, the lodges of learning, the harbours of humanity, the deliverers of divinity'. He even recommends the establishment of a college devoted only to languages. The grammar-school master, in Mulcaster's scheme, will be a linguist and will even know some Hebrew. 'Besides having skill in exercising and training of the body, he must be able to teach the three learned tongues, the Latin, the Greek, the Hebrew, if the place require so much, if not, so much as is required'.[15] Such a condition of appointment stems from Mulcaster's own high regard for Hebrew and reflects his reputed skill in the language. No less a scholar than Hugh Broughton considered him to be 'one of the best Hebrew scholars of his age'.[16] But of such erudition there is no proof. While his sympathy for Hebraic studies is unambiguous, for the linguistic expertise which so impressed his contemporaries we must trust the voice of fame.

The first grammar schools

Educational theorists were not the only ones to press for the introduction of Hebrew lessons into English schools. Among those responsible for drawing up the statutes of new foundations and actually shaping the curricula, there were enlightened scholars anxious to give the language a recognised place in the syllabus. Almost twenty years before Humphrey included Hebrew in his pattern of learning for well-born youth, two English archbishops had tried to ensure that it would become a school subject. It is Thomas Cranmer who must be recognised as the first to legislate for the teaching of Hebrew grammar in the schoolroom. He was followed closely by Robert Holgate.

On 27 November 1539 Thomas Cromwell sent Cranmer a letter enclosing a plan for the re-constituting of the cathedral church at Canterbury.[17] The proposal, submitted to the archbishop for his approval, was occasioned by an act of parliament which legalised the appropriation of the money received from the dissolution of the monasteries. Several of the items listed in the new scheme concerned the school which was to be attached to the cathedral. In addition to a provost, twelve prebendaries and six preachers, there was to be a schoolmaster, an usher or assistant teacher and five readers. The schoolmaster was to be responsible for teaching sixty scholars 'both grammar and logic in Hebrew, Greek and Latin'. The reader in divinity also was expected to give lectures in Hebrew at a salary of thirty pounds per annum, but his audience was not specified. If this 'device', as Cranmer calls it, did not actually come from Cromwell himself, it was drawn up with his blessing. It is of interest in that it testifies to the willingness of the Secretary of State to support Hebraic studies, a testimony which is strengthened by another letter written in the same year by one Thomas Coventry. Addressing Cromwell,

Coventry voiced his concern at the dissolution of Evesham abbey. Hitherto the monastery had provided him with an exhibition to further his studies, but since such financial assistance would no longer be available he appealed to Cromwell for a pension. He was encouraged to make such an appeal by Cromwell's positive attitude towards the humanities. 'Your Lordship's favour towards the teaching of holy letters encourages me to hope that the pains I have taken in studying Hebrew, Greek and Latin, of which Mr Morysyne can inform you, may not be without profit. I studied these tongues to enable me to refute papistical sophistry.'[18]

In his reply to Cromwell's letter Cranmer endorsed the scheme and expressed the conviction that, if implemented, it would produce 'a very substantial and godly foundation'. But he had one major reservation. He could find no good reason for the appointment of prebendaries, and therefore suggested that they should be excluded from the plan. Since the 'said sect of prebendaries have not only spent their time in much idleness, and their substance in superfluous belly cheer, I think it not to be a convenient state or degree to be maintained and established, considering first, that commonly a prebendary is neither a learner, nor teacher, but a good viander'. In place of these twelve dignitaries Cranmer proposed that the foundation should provide maintenance grants for sixty students — twenty in divinity and forty in 'the tongues, and sciences, and French'. This provision would increase the complement of the school to one hundred and twenty and ensure an audience for the five readers,

for if such a number be not there resident, to what intent should so many readers be there? And surely it were great pity that so many good lectures should there be read in vain: for as for your prebendaries, they cannot attend to apply lectures, for making of good cheer. And as for your sixty children in grammar, their master and their usher be daily otherwise occupied in the rudiments of grammar, than that they may have space and time to hear the lectures: so that to these good lectures is prepared no convenient auditory. And therefore, my lord, I pray you let it be considered what a great loss it will be to have so many good lectures read without profit to any, saving to the six preachers.

Cranmer's intention was that the cathedral revenues should be used to further the new learning. In order to achieve his purpose he was ready to support a scheme which included Hebrew in the school curriculum. Such provision was not confined to Canterbury. Foster Watson detects the archbishop's hand behind a document entitled *King Henry VIII's*

Scheme of Bishoprics which contained proposals for the re-founding of several other cathedral schools.[19] According to this plan all schools were to offer Latin and Greek, and Rochester, Westminster, St Albans, Peterborough, Durham and Canterbury were required to teach Hebrew as well. The scheme has been described as 'the first modern suggestion for a systematic provision of secondary education'. It contains 'a forecast of the subjects which were to become the aim of masters to include in the grammar schools of the future – viz. Latin and Greek literature, and where possible, the elements of Hebrew'.[20] In practice, however, the plan to introduce Hebrew came to nothing. As finally constituted in 1541 the school at Canterbury had only fifty students with a master and usher. The statutes make no reference to Hebrew.

Cranmer's opposite number at York was Robert Holgate who was translated from Llandaff in 1544.[21] Originally a Gilbertine monk, Holgate developed strong academic interests, spending many years at his order's house of studies in Cambridge, first as a student and then as a teacher. He took his B.D. in 1523–24. At York he proved to be a staunch upholder of humanistic principles, to which he had been introduced in the Cambridge of the 1520s. He modernised the minster library, stocking it with books which he considered essential if the new learning was to flourish. He stressed the place of preaching within the context of worship and realised the importance of having the Bible in the vernacular. But his most significant action was the foundation of three grammar schools in his archdiocese. By the authority of letters patent issued on 24 October 1546, York, Hemsworth and Old Malton were all to have a new school, each one a separate corporation with a master and usher. They were intended 'for the education of the boys of England as well in good manners as in grammar and other liberal sciences'.[22] The archbishop himself wrote the foundation deeds. He stipulated that in each of the three schools Hebrew, Greek and Latin were to be taught free of charge to every suitable student. In the sixth clause of the deed for York school he states with reference to the master: 'I will and ordain that the said schoolmaster shall be conveniently seen and have understanding in the Hebrew, Greek and Latin tongues and shall teach and inform the same to such scholars . . . as shall be most meet and apt for the same according to the discretion of the same schoolmaster'.[23]

Holgate's archdiocese included the parish of East Retford in Nottinghamshire. By letters patent, issued in 1551 'on the petition as well of the bailiffs and burgesses of East Retford as of very many others of the whole country round, the king granted that there should be a grammar school at East Retford to be called the Free Grammar School of King Edward VI'. The staff was to consist of a master and usher, and the school was to continue for ever. The statutes, drawn up by Holgate in April 1552, are among the fullest Edwardian school statutes now extant. Of special interest is the curriculum which is described in some detail. In the fourth form, to which a boy graduated at the age of twelve or thirteen, the master is to teach the scholars 'the Greek Grammar and also the Hebrew Grammar, if he be expert in the same'.[24] The inclusion of this final qualifying clause may well reflect the difficulties already encountered by Holgate in trying to find masters proficient in Hebrew to serve in his Yorkshire schools. Since, according to the letters patent, the staff at York and its sister foundations were to be appointed by the archbishop, it may be presumed that he looked for men capable of teaching basic grammar, if nothing else. There is, however, no indication that Thomas Swann, York's first headmaster, or any of his successors during the Tudor period taught Hebrew. But even if the archbishop failed to find qualified Hebraists for the institutions with which he was associated, he must be commended for seeking to provide English schoolboys with an elementary knowledge of the language. Though not a recognised Hebrew scholar, he had in all probability mastered the rudiments during his time at Cambridge. He graduated B.D. in the year that Robert Wakefield delivered his famous 'oratio de laudibus et utilitate trium linguarum'.

In time, other schools were to show the same enthusiasm for Renaissance ideals as did those which came under the influence of Holgate. The reorganisation of the cathedral school at Ely in *c.* 1562 brought with it the recommendation that the students should be acquainted with Hebrew. With reference to the twenty-four poor boys who were to be supported by the foundation, the statutes given by Henry VIII in 1544 state: 'We will that these boys shall be maintained at the expense of our church, until they shall be moderately skilled in the knowledge of the Latin grammar, and shall have learned to speak in Latin, and write in Greek'. Under Elizabeth proficiency in music and in Hebrew grammar was also expected of them.[25] Joyce Frankland's support for a Hebrew lectureship at Gonville and Caius has been noted above. In 1588 she left a bequest for the founding of a grammar school at Newport, Essex, in memory of her son. The statutes, drawn up by Thomas Legge, Master of Caius, decreed that Hebrew should be taught.[26] This provision reflects Legge's own interest in Hebraic studies, for though he was never Regius Professor of Hebrew, as has been claimed, he was no mean linguist. The statutes of Blackburn grammar school were approved in December 1597. They stipulated that 'some Hebrew grammar of [sic] Splalter' should be taught 'if any be willing and fit thereunto'.[27] By a statute of c. 1600 the master at Heath grammar school was expected to teach his pupils Hebrew grammar.[28] In all these establishments there is nothing to show that instruction in Hebrew was anything but the pious hope of the founder, for the statutes of schools, like those of the realm, were not always observed to the letter. There were, however, a few schools where lessons were actually given. To these we now turn.

The statutes of Merchant Taylors' School, approved by the governors in 1561, stated that the headmaster must be proficient in Latin and Greek, 'if such may be gotten'. There is no mention of Hebrew. Such an omission may be explained by the difficulty in finding anyone capable of satisfying the requirement, or by the dependence of the statutes on those drawn up by Colet for St Paul's School fifty years previously. But despite the lack of statutory provision, it is certain that instruction in Hebrew was offered at Merchant Taylors' almost from the beginning. The first three headmasters, Richard Mulcaster, Henry Wilkinson and Edmund Smith, were all capable of giving it, and there is contemporary evidence that at least one of them did so. On 10 June 1572 an entrance examination to St John's College, Oxford, was held at the school. Two senior boys were to be elected. The examiners included Nowell, Dean of St Paul's, Watts, Archdeacon of Middlesex and Horne, Bishop of Winchester. 'Before this venerable assembly the head scholars of the school presented themselves for examination and after one of them had briefly enumerated the several books they were learning in Latin, Greek and Hebrew, the examination began.'[29] They were examined by Nowell and Watts in Classics, and by Horne in the Hebrew Psalter. Among the four finalists selected on this occasion was Thomas Harrison who was appointed in 1604 to the panel of Old Testament translators for the Authorised Version. Though he was turned down by St John's, he was accepted at Cambridge where he soon made his mark as a capable linguist. Such, we are told, was his knowledge of Hebrew and Greek that he was chosen by the university to be 'one of the chief examiners of those who wished to excel in these languages'.[30]

He had Mulcaster to thank for his Hebrew.

Sir James Whitelocke, who later became Justice of the Common Pleas, also refers to Hebrew at Merchant Taylors' in his family history. One of four boys, James was born in November 1570, three weeks after his father's death. Although his mother remarried, her husband took no interest whatever in the welfare of his stepchildren. The boys' upbringing was left entirely to their mother. Fortunately she was an enlightened woman and was determined to educate them

> in as good sort as any gentleman in England would do, as in singing, dancing, playing on the lute and other instruments, the Latin, Greek, Hebrew and French, and to write fair: every one of them to that he was likeliest to do good in, but all were by her appointed and directed to the best course, that is of learning, and to have been professed scholars, but some took one way some another, yet she still persisted her care in continuing them in this costly education.[31]

The phrase 'as any gentleman in England would do' is noteworthy. Is the author guilty of false reminiscence here or are we to understand that Hebrew did form a recognised part of an English gentleman's education? Whatever the answer, the Whitelocke children were introduced to Hebrew at an early age, and two of them were to continue studying it at Merchant Taylors'. The eldest brother Edmund became one of 'Mr Mulcaster's children' in *c.* 1573. Eight years later he went to Christ's College, Cambridge, 'where having been well grounded in the liberal sciences, and much farthered in his knowledge of the Latin, Greek and Hebrew tongues, in which he was well instructed in the grammar school, he left the university and came to Lincoln's Inn to study the common law'. James followed his brother to Merchant Taylors' in *c.* 1579. 'I was brought up at school by Mr Mulcaster, in the famous school of the Merchant Taylors' in London, where I continued until I was well instructed in the Hebrew, Greek and Latin tongues'. But Mulcaster was not Whitelocke's only teacher of Hebrew during his London schooldays. He goes on to tell us that at St John's College, Oxford, he

> laboured much in the Hebrew and Greek tongues, for I had heard a reader of the Hebrew tongue at London that was reputed the most famous in that language about the town. His name was Hopkinson, he dwelt in Grub Street, an obscure and simple man for worldly affairs, but expert in all the lefthand tongues, as Hebrew, Chaldee, Syriac, Arabic, and wrote them very fair; he had at that time great learned men that consulted him in those languages, and especially Dr Andrewes that is now bishop of Chichester. He read unto me all Job, and twenty Psalms, and a part of Genesis, and after I had taken my

lecture from him, which was after five of the clock that I went from school, I would duly, after supper, make a praxis of that I had heard, and set it down in writing.

The learned Hopkinson has disappeared without trace, but his readiness to supplement the Hebrew teaching given at Merchant Taylors' has been gratefully recorded.

The earliest known complete curriculum for St Paul's School belongs to the last quarter of the seventeenth century. According to this, the eighth form had lessons in Hebrew grammar. For how long this had been the accepted practice it is impossible to tell. Since the early curriculum of Merchant Taylors' was modelled on that of St Paul's, T. W. Baldwin concludes that Hebrew was already being taught at St Paul's in the 1560s.[32] But of this there is no proof. It is more likely that the language was first taught by Mulcaster while he was headmaster from 1596 to 1608. Alexander Gill, Mulcaster's immediate successor, is represented in a piece of doggerel as censuring his son and namesake for not applying himself to his lessons. Alexander junior, who was a pupil at the school in *c.* 1610, is chided by his father

for thy faults not few
in tongue Hebrew
for which a grove of birch is due.[33]

Evidently Hebrew was regarded as part of the scheme of study at St Paul's by this time. If it was not introduced by Gill himself, the credit must go to Mulcaster.

By the mid 1570s boys in the seventh form at Westminster School were expected to attend a lesson in Hebrew grammar between the hours of 4 and 5 p.m. each day.[34] The prescribed text was the Psalter, which was to be studied in both Greek and Hebrew. However, it was only when Lancelot Andrewes became dean in 1601 that the study of the language really blossomed. Andrewes had laid the foundation of his own Hebrew scholarship under Mulcaster at Merchant Taylors', and during his vacations from Cambridge had paid regular visits to Hopkinson in Grub Street. Old Westminsters testify to the interest he took in the education of the senior boys and to the efforts he made to teach them the ancient languages. John Hacket, one of his first pupils and later Bishop of Lichfield, relates how Andrewes often took the place of the master and usher for a whole week. Even when he was not officially deputising for a member of staff, he would spend much of his spare time giving the boys extra lessons. 'Sometimes thrice in a week, sometimes oftener, he sent for the uppermost scholars to his lodgings at night, and kept them with him from eight until eleven, unfolding to them the best rudiments of the Greek tongue, and the elements of the Hebrew grammar'. Hacket adds gratefully, 'He was the first that planted me in my tender studies, and watered them continually with his bounty'.[35] Another eminent alumnus who came under Andrewes' stimulating influence was Brian Duppa, Bishop of Winchester. His epitaph in Westminster Abbey records his attendance at the school 'where he was instructed in Hebrew by the then dean, Lancelot Andrewes'.[36] The extra tuition provided by Andrewes suggests that the language was not being taught as efficiently as it might have been. If this was indeed the case, a marked improvement was discernible by 1660 when Charles Hoole could describe Westminster as the school where 'the eastern languages are now become familiar to the highest sort of scholars'. Not only had the pupils mastered elementary grammar, they could even write Hebrew speeches and poems. 'It is no small ornament and commendation to a school, (as Westminster School at present can evidence) that scholars are able to make orations and verses in Hebrew, Arabic, or other Oriental tongues, to the amazement of most of their hearers, who are angry at their own ignorance, because they know not well what is then said or written.'[37]

It was during the long incumbency of Andrewes' immediate predecessor that Hebrew began to feature as a possible option in the Westminster syllabus. Gabriel Goodman, who served as dean from 1561 to 1601, was another Cambridge man, though whether as a member of Christ's or of St John's is unclear. A period as a fellow of Jesus College preceded his appointment to Westminster at the age of thirty-two. That he took an active interest in education is obvious from several quarters. Shortly after graduation he found employment in the household of William Cecil as a tutor to his children. For many years while he was at Westminster he helped to examine those boys from Merchant Taylors' who were selected to apply for a place at St John's, Oxford. As one of the executors of the will of Lady Frances Sidney, he was closely connected with the founding of Sidney Sussex College. In 1598 he produced a set of statutes for the grammar school in his native Ruthin. While there is nothing in his writings to indicate that he was a Hebrew scholar, it may be safely assumed, on the basis of the contents of his library, that he had some knowledge of the language and that he would have encouraged others to learn it. He owned several Hebrew books. In his will he left a Complutensian Polyglot Bible to Sidney Sussex, a Hebrew Bible to St John's, Cambridge, and to Thomas Bodley, for use in his newly founded library, an Aramaic lexicon and 'Albatu: in Hebrew', whatever that may have been. To Ruthin School he bequeathed one hundred and twenty-one volumes. Among them was a parallel Old Testament in Latin, Greek and Hebrew, a Hebrew-Latin version of the historical books and the three major prophets, Förster's Hebrew dictionary, and commentaries on Old Testament books by such authors as Pellican, Martyr, Mercer and Musculus, all of which contain frequent allusions to the Hebrew text.[38] His literary interests would suggest that the effort to bring Hebrew into the curriculum at Westminster met with the dean's approval.

There is no indication in the official history of Bedford School by Sargeaunt and Hockliffe that Hebrew was taught in the upper forms during the sixteenth century. However, a letter sent to John Wynn of Gwydir, a member of a leading North Wales family, indicates that it was. Wynn proposed to educate the eldest of his ten sons at Bedford. On 14 April 1597 Thomas Martyn, a London lawyer and friend of the family, reported that he and Ellis Wynn, John's brother, had visited the school and had discussed the curriculum with Mr Paget the headmaster. In his opinion, the school provided an excellent education at very reasonable cost. He specified that in addition to music, French, Italian, Latin and Greek, the pupils were also taught the rudiments of Hebrew.[39]

A discussion of the place of Hebrew in Elizabethan schools would not be complete without mentioning the contribution of two eminent teachers, William Kempe and John Brinsley. Contemporaries at Cambridge, they graduated in 1584, Kempe from Trinity Hall and Brinsley from Christ's College. While Kempe became headmaster of Plymouth Grammar School, Brinsley was appointed to the school founded by the Earl of Huntingdon at Ashby de la Zouch where he remained from 1590 to 1620. Tribute to Brinsley's extraordinary skill as a teacher is paid by one of his pupils, the seventeenth-century astrologer William Lilly. In his autobiography Lilly tells how his father sent him to Ashby when he was eleven years old to be instructed by Brinsley, 'one in those times of great abilities for instruction of youth in the Latin and Greek tongues. He was very severe in his life and conversation, and did breed up many scholars for the universities'. Lilly goes on to say that he was introduced to Hebrew grammar at Brinsley's school soon after he was enrolled in 1613.[40]

Both Kempe and Brinsley regarded Hebrew as a school subject. In *The Education of Children* (1588) Kempe offers a clear and systematic presentation of his scheme of study. He does not claim originality for it, but admits that the principles by which he works are those accepted by 'many learned men' who have preceded him. He is particularly indebted to Sturm, Ramus and Ascham. In a nine-year curriculum, divided into eight forms, Kempe takes a boy from the age of seven to sixteen. He recommends that the pupil, 'if he will be a Hebraist', should be introduced to elementary Hebrew in the fifth form at the age of twelve. In the higher forms he would gain a 'more perfect understanding of the grammar and knowledge of the tongues'.[41] Brinsley published the fruit of several years' research into educational methods in two books, the *Ludus literarius, or Grammar School* (1612) and *A consolation for our Grammar Schools* (1622). Though written in the early Jacobean period, both these works reflect the author's Tudor inheritance and indicate what was regarded, in some quarters, as the normative scheme of education for a grammar school. Of the two books, the first is the longer and the more significant. It is an account of a schoolmaster's job presented in the form of a dialogue between two teachers who have not met since they were students at the university. Spoudeus finds his chosen profession to be sheer drudgery. He complains that he spends his time 'in a fruitless, wearisome and unthankful office' at a poor rural school.[42] His friend Philoponus, however, is a very successful teacher who likes his work and is ready to share the secret of his success. Thus, in the guise of Philoponus, Brinsley sets out what he believes to be the most efficient method of teaching and lists what should be included in the curriculum of every grammar school. The *Consolation* continues in a similar vein. Addressed to educators and potential patrons, it is written, according to the title-page, in order to encourage learning in schools 'of the inferior sort' and to suggest ways of laying a firm intellectual foundation in 'all ruder countries and places', such as Wales, Ireland and Virginia. A lengthy annotated bibliography, in which there is a section on Hebrew books, is appended to the text.

Since Brinsley's intention in both books is to help smaller country schools rather than prestigious urban ones, the prominent position occupied by Hebrew in his system is significant. In chapter 21 of the *Ludus literarius* Philoponus responds to his colleague's request for guidance on the teaching of 'that most sacred tongue, the Hebrew'. He begins by stating why the basic essentials of the language can be grasped easily and quickly. The principal roots are few; nouns do not decline; the only text is the Old Testament, which is already familiar to the student in English; literal Latin versions of the original, which 'beat out the propriety, force and sense of every word and phrase', simplify the task of translating. Having convinced his pupil that a working knowledge of the language is not beyond his capabilities, the teacher should take him through three stages. First, there must be a grounding in grammar, so that the rules governing the conjugation of the verbs and the use of prepositions and suffixes are clearly understood. This is to be followed by memorising the roots, a certain number to be learned every day. The less common ones may be underlined 'with a black lead pen'. An hour a day for twelve months or less would be enough to get all the roots by heart, and once learned they are easily kept 'by oft repetition, running over the hardest being marked out'. Familiarity with the roots is important because Hebrew is 'the mother tongue of all tongues, and was the only tongue until the confounding of the tongues at Babel'. Many words in other languages are derived from, or at least are similar to, a Hebrew original. Finally, there must be translation, both from Hebrew into Latin and from Latin into Hebrew. For the beginner, the historical books such as Samuel and Kings, or Psalm 119, are to be recommended. In any difficulty he will find 'the perfect verbal translation' of Arias Montano most helpful. It will make him 'most cunning in the text, and in the very order of the words of the Holy Ghost, without danger of any way depraving, corrupting or inverting one jot or tittle'. He emphasises in the *Consolation* also that the practice of translating portions of the Bible back into Hebrew will make students 'both very cunning in the tongues, and also perfect in the texts of the originals themselves, if it be observed constantly'.[43]

Household education

Attendance at one of the many grammar schools which had been founded in England by 1600 was not the only way of preparing young men for a place in the university. The Tudor family was regarded as an educational institution equal in importance to any school. There is no lack of evidence to show that progressive parents provided instruction at home for their children. Although the emphasis, in many cases, was on the courtly arts, there were some notable households where children were given a Classical education, and occasionally taught the elements of Hebrew. One of the earliest examples of an interest being taken by the aristocracy in Hebrew is recorded in the case of Francis Willoughby, a cousin of Lady Jane Grey. On the death of their father in 1549 Francis and his sister Margaret were put in the care of their uncle, George Medley, whose record of household expenses gives some indication of how the two children were educated. The accounts for 12 July 1550 state that Francis was provided with twenty-pence-worth of sweets 'to make him learn his book'.[44] But in 1552 no such inducements to learning are mentioned when 'a Greek and a Hebrew grammar' was purchased for two shillings and fourpence.[45] While Margaret got an inkhorn, some counters and 'a little Bible', Francis, at about six years of age, was expected to start Greek and Hebrew. Though we are told nothing further about his Hebrew studies at home or at Trinity College, Cambridge, where he went in 1558, we may presume that he persevered, for in *c.* 1575 he wrote an epitaph for his father in English, Latin, Greek and Hebrew.[46]

As a rule, household instruction was given by a qualified tutor, but sometimes by the head of the family. John Bois (1563–1643) is a good example of a distinguished linguist who received his early education at the hands of his own father.[47] Bois is remembered chiefly for the part he played in the Authorised Version of the Bible. Together with six other Cambridge scholars he was appointed by James I to translate the Apocrypha. For the four years he was engaged in the work he left his parish of Boxworth each Monday morning and travelled to Cambridge, where he was given board and lodging at St John's, his old college. Some of his colleagues found his presence irksome, claiming that 'they needed no help from the country'. But Bois' contribution was not to be deprecated. In his younger days he had taught Greek for his college and had been a lifelong student of the biblical languages. According to his grandson and biographer, Anthony Walker, 'he was a most exact grammarian, having read nearly fifty grammars, Latin, Greek, Hebrew and Syriac'. Even when he had left academic circles, he retained his interest in linguistic study. After resigning his lectureship in favour of a rural living, he journeyed regularly to Cambridge to attend the lectures of Edward Lively.

Membership of St John's (he matriculated in 1580) and the opportunity of listening to Lively would have encouraged Bois, as an undergraduate, to take his Hebrew studies seriously. His knowledge of the basic grammar, however, pre-dated his matriculation at

Cambridge, for he had been introduced to the alphabet at a tender age by his father, William Bois. John recalled his early achievements with pride, and into old age had preserved a record of his first tentative steps in Hebrew. Walker claims that his grandfather had shown him exercises 'which his father had taught him to write very young (unless my memory fails me) by six years old'. He noted that the script was in an exceptionally clear and legible hand. John was fortunate in his tutor, for the elder Bois was, in Walker's words, 'a great scholar, being learned in the Hebrew and Greek excellently well'. A fellow of Michaelhouse, and later of Trinity College, he had attended lectures at St John's where, presumably, he had learned his Hebrew. Under Bucer's influence he became a Protestant, his 'dislike of popery growing with the more perfect knowledge of it'. On Mary's accession his religious convictions led him to relinquish his fellowship and move to Suffolk, where he bought a farm, exercising his ministry by acting as pastor in the parishes of Elmset and West Stow. It was in the seclusion of a Suffolk farmhouse that the young John was taught the elements of Hebrew grammar.

Parents who were less gifted than William Bois appointed tutors to instruct their children in the ancient languages. Consequently, many eminent scholars, Hebraists among them, found sympathetic patrons ready to receive them into their homes. Anthony Gilby, renowned as a linguist for the prominent part he took in the translation of the Geneva Bible, spent the last twenty-five years of his life with the family of the Earl of Huntingdon at Ashby de la Zouch. Such was his enthusiasm for the reformed faith that he 'helped transform the household there into a Protestant seminary in miniature'.[48] We can be sure that lessons in elementary Hebrew formed part of the curriculum for any who were capable of receiving them. Hugh Broughton found similar employment with the Cotton family in London. John Lightfoot touches briefly on the novel and thorough method which this famous Hebraist adopted to teach his pupil, Rowland Cotton, the biblical languages. Daily Bible readings and conversation in Hebrew were regarded as essential. To facilitate matters Broughton drew up a vocabulary for the young student

not in an alphabetical way, as dictionaries and lexicons commonly are. But he first pitched upon a place, or thing more general, and then named all the particulars in it, or belonging to it; as heaven: angels, sun, moon, stars, clouds, etc. So a house: a door, a window, a parlour, a cellar, etc.; a field: grass, a flower, a tree, hedge, furrow, etc. . . . And to complete all, he had him with him very constantly in his study, where he instilled into him the grammar, and then read to him the Bible.[49]

Improbable though it may seem, Lightfoot reports that at the age of seven or eight Rowland could translate almost any chapter of the Bible into English and converse with ease in Hebrew.

When James Montagu, the first Master of Sidney Sussex, appointed Thomas Gataker to teach for the college in 1596, he had acquired a young scholar of considerable promise. From his earliest youth Gataker had been an enthusiastic student. His biographer informs us that even in childhood such was his love of learning that he needed 'a bridle rather than a spur'.[50] At St John's, Cambridge, he pursued his studies with vigour and soon gained a reputation for being a gifted linguist. A poem written shortly after his death in 1654 by Richard Dugard, one-time fellow of Sidney Sussex, contains the following stanza:

His industry long since had treasured
All learning in his comprehensive head;
The crucified three languages spake aloud
His matchless skill, and seemed of him proud.[51]

Gataker learned Greek from John Bois, whose custom it was to give lessons in his rooms at 4 a.m. Together with a few dedicated companions Gataker attended these matutinal sessions regularly, all of them preferring '*antelucana studia* before their rest and ease'.[52] He treasured the notes that he took at these lectures, and when visited by Bois many years later, produced them 'to the no small joy of the good old man who professed himself made some years younger by that entertainment'.[53] Another fellow of the college, Robert Spalding, who succeeded Lively as Regius professor in 1605, gave him his first Hebrew lessons. Gataker describes Spalding as 'an excellent Hebraist to whom I owe my knowledge of the rudiments of the holy tongue'.[54] Since Sidney Sussex was in the process of being built in 1596, Gataker left Cambridge for two years to become tutor to the family of William Ayloffes in Essex. In an autobiographical note he tells us that he was employed by Ayloffes to instruct 'him in Hebrew and his eldest son in the kind of literature suited to his age'. For the benefit of the whole household he expounded 'the prophecies of Isaiah, and a good part of the Book of Job, rendering the text out of the original languages'.[55]

Although Thomas Burgess confidently maintains that 'in the sixteenth century Hebrew made an usual part of female education', he is able to offer but little evidence in support of such a generalisation.[56] That Tudor England had its learned ladies goes without saying. Their patronage of scholarship has already been noted in the previous chapter. It is indeed possible to quote contemporary sources which claim a knowledge of Hebrew on the part of some of them, but whether the language ever formed 'an usual part' of their education is doubtful. According to the Italian scholar Paschali, Queen Elizabeth herself was not unacquainted with Semitic languages. In 1592 he dedicated his translation of the Psalms from Hebrew into Italian verse to the queen, whom he describes as being as proficient in Hebrew and Aramaic as she was in Greek and Latin.[57] When it is remembered that Anthony Chevallier, during his first visit to England, taught French to Elizabeth, it is possible that she learned some basic Hebrew grammar from him. The four eminent daughters of Sir Anthony Cooke were renowned for their learning. Mildred, who married William Cecil, left a copy of the eight-volumed Antwerp Polyglot Bible to St John's, Cambridge, in 1581. The gift was accompanied by a letter in Greek written in the donor's own hand.[58] But only the youngest of the four girls, Katherine, was celebrated for her knowledge of Hebrew.[59] Mary Sidney, sister of Philip and Countess of Pembroke, is credited with having translated Psalms 44 to 150 from the original Hebrew into English verse between 1593 and 1600. This claim, however, was disputed by the seventeenth-century historian John Harington on the grounds that she would not have received the requisite linguistic training. In his view she was helped with the Hebrew by Gervase Babington, tutor and chaplain to the family at the time, and later Bishop of Worcester. This was the only possible explanation, 'for it was more than a woman's skill to express the sense so right as she hath done in her verse, and more than the English or Latin translation could give her'.[60] But the tradition that she learned Hebrew persisted. While her brother was at Shrewsbury School she was educated at the family home in Ludlow, where she 'became acquainted, not only with the best Latin and Greek authors, but even the Hebrew language'.[61]

In the absence of any concrete contemporary evidence, the Hebrew expertise of the above-mentioned ladies must remain a matter of conjecture. With our two remaining examples, however, we can be more positive. Elizabeth Falkland and Jane Grey did actually learn some Hebrew. The biography of Lady Falkland (1585–1639) was written shortly after her death by one of her four daughters, all of whom became Benedictine nuns. In it we are given some interesting details of her early life. The only child of Judge Lawrence Tanfield of Burford Priory, she turned for company to the books in the family library. Her father encouraged such scholarly pursuits, giving her a copy of Calvin's *Institutes* when she was barely eleven. Her mother was more concerned about her daughter's health than her grasp of Protestant theology, and tried to dissuade her from constant study. There was no question of being allowed to read in bed at night. But the precocious Elizabeth bribed the servants to give her candles. By the age of twelve she had gone through eight hundred of them, for which she owed the maids £100. She repaid the debt on her wedding day. Yet, despite the interest in education, not once in the course of the biography is a tutor mentioned. Just as Elizabeth coped with other subjects on her own, so 'Hebrew she likewise about the same time learned with very little teaching; but for many years neglecting it, she lost it much; yet not long before her death, she, again beginning to use it, could in the Bible understand well'.[62] At the end of an active life, during which she converted to Roman Catholicism, she found that the Hebrew grammar learned by candlelight in Burford Priory had not deserted her.

The Marquis of Dorset, Lady Jane Grey's father, was an ardent patron of humane letters. One of his early protégés was the Swiss scholar John of Ulm whom he supported at Oxford. It is from a letter sent by this young student to a former teacher at Zurich that we first learn of Jane Grey's interest in Hebrew. 29 May 1551 was a busy day for John. He had just arrived at Bradgate Manor, the Dorset family home, near Leicester, after spending some weeks with the marquis in Scotland. Despite a long and tiring journey, he found the energy to write two lengthy letters to friends in Switzerland. He had written to Bullinger many times before, but he had never corresponded with Pellican. However, since Pellican was always sending his greetings by means of mutual friends, John felt duty-bound to write to him. But his letter was more than an exchange of pleasantries; it had an ulterior motive. He wanted to acquaint the eminent Hebraist with Jane,

a lady who is well versed in Greek and Latin, and who is now especially desirous of studying Hebrew. I have been staying with her these two days: she is inquiring of me the best method of acquiring that language, and cannot easily discover the path which she may pursue with credit and advantage. She has written to Bullinger upon this subject, but, if I guess right, he will be very willing to transfer the office to you, both because he is always overwhelmed with affairs of greater importance, and because all the world is aware of your perfect knowledge of that language. If therefore you are willing to oblige a powerful and eminent nobleman with honour to yourself, you will by no means refuse this office and duty to his daughter. It is an important and honourable employment, and one too of great use. The young lady is the daughter of the marquis, and is to be married, as I hear, to the king. By your acceding to my request, she will be more easily kept in her distinguished course of learning: the marquis also will be made more steadfast in religion, and I shall appear to be neither unmindful of, nor ungrateful for, the favours conferred by them upon myself . . . Write therefore a letter to her as soon as possible, in which you will briefly point out a method of learning the sacred language, and then honourably consecrate to her name your Latin translation of the Jewish Talmud.[63]

In this appeal to Pellican for advice, John mentions the letter which Jane had addressed to Bullinger on the same topic a few weeks previously. When this earlier letter went unacknowledged, John suspected that it had gone astray, and on 12 July arranged for a copy of it to be sent to Zurich together with a covering letter of his own.[64] From the copy it is clear that Jane already had some knowledge of Hebrew, for in it she quotes Proverbs 11:14 in the original. But she is not satisfied with her progress, and ends by asking for Bullinger's help. 'As I am now beginning to learn Hebrew', she writes, 'if you will point out some way and method of pursuing this study to the greatest advantage, you will confer on me a very great obligation.'[65] John felt that a similar request to Pellican, the doyen of Zurich Hebraists, would do no harm. Once again the couriers proved unreliable and Pellican's reply, dated 5 August 1551, did not arrive in England until February of the following year. John sent back word conveying the delight expressed by Jane on receiving his letter and begging him 'to continue to assist and advance' her studies. He assures the aged professor that his advice on how to learn Hebrew will be carefully heeded, for 'persons do not usually disregard the commendations of distinguished men, especially when they do not seem to be offered lightly, or without sufficient ground; but are rather more vehemently excited by such exhortations to the pursuit of excellence'.[66] The grateful pupil enclosed her own letter of thanks together with that of John, as Pellican noted in his journal: 'On 19 June 1552 I received a Latin letter written with admirable elegance and learning from the noble virgin Jane Grey'.[67]

Although the relevant letters are not extant, it may be confidently asserted that these two eminent scholars gave Henry Grey's fourteen year old daughter good advice on how to proceed with her Hebrew studies. But the credit for teaching her the basic grammar must surely belong to others. Was it Thomas Harding, her first tutor, who introduced her to the language and awakened her interest in it? After resigning the Regius chair of Hebrew at Oxford in 1547 he was employed by the Marquis of Dorset to teach his children and act as chaplain to his household. By the time John of Ulm visited Bradgate in 1551, his place had been taken by John Aylmer (?1521–1594) who taught Jane Latin and Greek. Educated at Oxford at the marquis' expense, Aylmer was a talented linguist. According to Strype, his command of Hebrew so impressed the authorities at the University of Jena that they offered him a chair.[68] Hugh Broughton considered him to be 'the best Hebrician of all the bishops'.[69] The story is also told of him, when he was Bishop of London, that if, during one of his sermons, the congregation became restless, he would regain their attention by reading several verses from the Hebrew Bible, 'whereupon all seemed to listen what would come after such strange words'.[70] In John Aylmer, Lady Jane Grey had a tutor who was in the forefront of humanistic scholarship and a competent Hebraist.

In the annals of English secondary education the sixteenth century is rivalled in importance only by the late nineteenth or early twentieth centuries. In educational endeavours, as in many others, it was a century of beginnings. A study of the main didactic writers proves that it saw the initial formulation of definite aims in education. It witnessed the flowering of humanistic studies and the founding of more schools than any other period in English history. New charters and revised curricula demonstrate the change that was overtaking the educational system. The impact of a small group of theorists who found, in the works of their European counterparts, ideals and principles compatible with their own, was making itself felt. Wealthy patrons, many of whom were learned men and sincere humanists, founded or re-founded schools which were required by statute to promote the new learning. The development of new ideas was reflected in the classroom. The reluctant aristocracy recognised that things were changing and that education was a worthwhile investment. Gradually they adjusted themselves to new ways by sending their children to school or by providing them with tutors.

Although the primary aim of the sixteenth-century teacher was to cultivate in his charges an elegant Latin style, the curriculum of most schools did make provision for Greek. Hebrew was not so popular.

While it did not lack supporters among churchmen, educationists and benefactors, it made little progress as a school subject before the early decades of the seventeenth century. Nevertheless, by the end of Elizabeth's reign it had taken root in some of the leading schools and had even become a part of the educational programme of a few Tudor households. The motive for its study was primarily religious. As Ubaldini observed in 1551, the rich made their children learn Hebrew because the Protestant 'heresy' emphasised the importance not only of having the Bible in the vernacular, but also of being able to read it in the original.

Notes

1 *De fructu (The Benefits of a Liberal Education)*, p. 23.
2 'The education of the aristocracy in the Renaissance', *Journal of Modern History*, vol. XXII, No. 1, 1950, p. 4.
3 Quoted by C. C. Stopes, *Shakespeare's Environment*, London 1914, p. 302.
4 *The Book named The Governor*, ed. S. E. Lehmberg, London, Everyman's Library 1962, p. 12.
5 *The Book of the Courtier*, The Tudor Translations, vol. XXIII, London 1900, p. 85.
6 *The Schoolmaster (1570)*, ed. L. V. Ryan, New York 1967, pp. 40f.
7 See above pp. 158f.
8 *A Dialogue between Reginald Pole and Thomas Lupset*, ed. J. N. Cowper, Early English Text Soc. 1878, Extra Series, vol. XXXII, p. 186.
9 H. E. Bell, *An Introduction to the History and Records of the Court of Wards and Liveries*, Cambridge 1953, pp. 120f; R. Tittler, 'Education and the gentleman in Tudor England: the case of Sir Nicholas Bacon', *History of Education*, vol. 5, No. 1, 1976, pp. 3ff.
10 *Queen Elizabeth's Academy*, ed. F. J. Furnivall, Early English Text Soc. 1868, Extra Series, vol. III, p. 1.
11 *Ibid.*, pp. 2, 9.
12 *Ibid.*, p. 11.
13 See R. L. de Molen, 'Richard Mulcaster and the profession of teaching in sixteenth-century England', *JHI*, vol. 35, No. 1, 1974, pp. 121ff.
14 *Positions*, with appendix by R. H. Quick, London 1888, p. 220. On Mulcaster's interest in the aristocracy see also J. Simon, *Education and Society in Tudor England*, p. 353.
15 *Positions*, pp. 5, 235f.
16 *DNB*, *s.v.* Mulcaster. I have been unable to trace this reference in Broughton's writings.
17 For the text of the plan and Cranmer's reaction see *Miscellaneous writings and letters of Thomas Cranmer*, Parker Soc. 1886, pp. 396ff.

18   *L and P*, Henry VIII, vol. XIV (ii), p. 160.
19   *The Old Grammar Schools*, new imp. London 1968, p. 26; H. Cole, *Henry VIII's Scheme of Bishoprics*, London 1838. Though the scheme is endorsed as coming from Gardiner, Bishop of Winchester, it is very likely that Cranmer played some part in the drafting of it.
20   Watson, *The Old Grammar Schools*, p. 26.
21   For the details of Holgate's life see A. G. Dickens, *Robert Holgate: Archbishop of York and President of the King's Council in the North*, London 1955.
22   *L and P*, Henry VIII, vol. XXI (ii), p. 164.
23   For the statutes of Hemsworth and Old Malton see N. Carlisle, *A Concise Description of the Endowed Grammar Schools of England and Wales*, London 1818, vol. II, pp. 819, 858. For the statutes of York see *Archbishop Holgate Society Record Series I*, 1948; E. N. Jewels, *A History of Archbishop Holgate's Grammar School, York 1546–1946*, York 1963, ch. 2.
24   *VCH, Nottinghamshire*, Vol. II, pp. 240f.
25   Ely Dean and Chapter Records, 1/E/2, cap. 26. I am indebted to Mrs D. M. Owen of Cambridge University Library for this information. For Henry's statutes see R. G. Ikin, *Notes on the history of Ely Cathedral Grammar School*, Cambridge 1931, pp. 20, 24.
26   *VCH, Essex*, vol. II, p. 542.
27   G. A. Stocks, *The Records of Blackburn Grammar School*, Chetham Society 1909, vol. 66, Pt. I, p. 72.
28   Foster Watson, *The English Grammar Schools to 1660: their curriculum and practice*, Cambridge 1908, p. 529.
29   H. B. Wilson, *The History of Merchant-Taylors' School*, London 1812, vol. I, p. 39.
30   C. Dalechamp, *Harrisonus Honoratus*, Cambridge 1632, p. 7.
31   For this and the following references to Whitelocke see *Liber Famelicus of Sir James Whitelocke*, Camden Society 1858, pp. 6–13.
32   *William Shakspere's Small Latine and Lesse Greeke*, Urbana, Ill. 1944, vol. I, p. 421.
33   M. F. J. McDonnell, *A History of St Paul's School*, London 1909, p. 161.
34   T. W. Baldwin, *op. cit.*, vol. I p. 384.
35   J. Hacket, *Memoirs of the Life of Archbishop Williams*, London 1715, p. 45.
36   J. Dart, *Westmonasterium*, London 1742, vol. II, p. 10.
37   *The New Discovery of the old art of Teaching School*, London 1660 (facsimile reprint, London 1973), pp. 194, 220.
38   For Goodman's will see K. M. Thompson, *Ruthin School: the first seven centuries*, Denbigh 1974, pp. 190ff. The books which he left to the school are preserved in the school library.
39   *Calendar of Wynn (of Gwydir) Papers 1515–1690*, Aberystwyth 1926, p. 34. For the family's interest in the new learning see J. Gwynfor Jones, 'Diddordebau Diwylliannol Wyniaid Gwedir', *Llên Cymru*, vol. XI, Nos. 1 & 2, 1970, pp. 95ff; 'The Wynn family and estate of Gwydir: their origins, growth and development up to 1674', unpublished Ph.D. thesis,

Wales 1974, pp. 243ff.

40 _History of his life and times from the year 1602 to 1681_, London 1715, p. 5.

41 _The Education of Children_, London 1588, sig. G.2v.

42 _Ludus literarius_, London 1612 (facsimile reprint, London 1968), p. 1.

43 _A Consolation_, London 1622 (facsimile reprint, Amsterdam 1969), p. 54.

44 _Historical MSS. Commission_, Report on the manuscripts of Lord Middleton, preserved at Wollaton Hall, Notts., Hereford 1911, p. 400.

45 _Ibid._, p. 406.

46 _Ibid._, p. 155.

47 For the details of Bois' career see his _Life_ by Anthony Walker in _Desiderata Curiosa_, ed. F. Peck, London 1779, vol. II, pp. 325ff.

48 C. Cross, _The Puritan Earl: the life of Henry Hastings Third Earl of Huntingdon 1536–1595_, London 1966, p. 24. For his part in the Geneva Bible see above pp. 129–31.

49 _Works_, Preface sig. b.

50 S. Ashe, _Gray hayres crowned with grace_, London 1655, p. 42.

51 _Ibid._, p. 72.

52 _Ibid._, p. 43.

53 _Ibid._

54 T. Gataker, _De novi instrumenti stylo dissertatio_, London 1648, p. 47.

55 _Opera critica_, London 1698, 'Thomas Gatakeri vita propria manu scripta', n.p.

56 _Motives to the study of Hebrew_, 2nd ed. London 1814, p. 93.

57 See _De' Sacri Salmi di Davidde_, Geneva 1592, dedication sig. 2b.

58 For the Greek letter see British Library, MS. Lansdown civ, No. 60. Notice of the Bible is to be found in T. Baker, _History of the College of St John_, vol. I, p. 414.

59 G. Ballard, _Memoirs of several ladies of Great Britain . . . celebrated for their writings or skill in the learned languages, arts and sciences_, Oxford 1752, p. 202.

60 _A brief view of the state of the Church of England . . . to the yeere 1608_, London 1653, p. 128. See also J. C. A. Rathmell, ed., _The Psalms of Sir Philip Sidney and the Countess of Pembroke_, New York 1963, Intro., p. xix. For the contrary view see G. Ballard, _Memoirs of several ladies_, p. 261.

61 H.T.R., 'Lady Mary Sidney and her writings', _The Gentleman's Magazine_, vol. 24, Pt. ii, N.S. 1845, p. 130.

62 _The Lady Falkland: Her Life: from a MS. in the Imperial Archives at Lille_, London 1861, p. 4.

63 _Original letters relative to the English Reformation_, Parker Soc., Pt. II, p. 432.

64 _Ibid._, p. 436.

65 _Ibid._, Pt. I, pp. 5f.

66 _Ibid._, Pt. II, p. 451.

67 _Das Chronicon des Konrad Pellikan_, ed. B. Riggenbach, Basle 1877, p. 182. This letter was not written in Hebrew as stated by M.

Steinschneider in *Zeitschrift für hebräische Bibliographie*, IV, 52, nt. 3.

68 *The life and acts of . . . John Aylmer*, Oxford 1821, p. 11. But cf. C. H. Garrett, *The Marian Exiles*, pp. 76f. who finds insufficient evidence for his travels abroad.

69 *Epistle to the learned nobility of England*, p. 16.

70 J. Harington, *A brief view of the state of the Church of England*, p. 19.

IX

From alphabet to commentary

One of the chief promoters of the new learning was the printed word. Those talented teachers mentioned above would have made little headway had it not been for the invaluable help afforded to them and their students by the invention of printing. The ardour with which this new-found skill was greeted is expressed at the end of the first Hebrew book ever published, Rabbi Jacob ben Asher's compendium of Jewish law, the *Arba'ah Turim* (1475):

> I am the art that is the crown of all the arts. I myself am hidden, but in me all secrets are concealed. Without pens my script is clear to all; without scribes do I create books. In a moment I am dipped in ink. Without rulers, yet my script is evenly formed.[1]

In this chapter we shall consider the availability of the necessary apparatus, in the form of printed books, to those wishing to pursue Hebraic studies in Tudor England. The evidence, which is deliberately selective, is drawn from the following three sources: the library catalogue of John Dee, the earliest catalogue of the Bodleian Library and the inventories of the personal effects of individual scholars and booksellers who died while residing at Oxford and Cambridge. The holdings of college and cathedral libraries are not taken into account here.

Dee's catalogue has already been mentioned in another context.[2] The first Bodleian catalogue was compiled by Thomas James at the request of Thomas Bodley (1545–1613) in 1605, and as such is a useful guide to the books in circulation in England at the end of the Tudor period.[3] The Hebrew books listed by James reflect the founder's love of Semitics. In 1556 the young Bodley had gone with his parents to Geneva where, according to his autobiography, he had attended Chevallier's Hebrew lectures.[4] On his return to England he was 'recommended to the teaching and tuition of Dr. Humphrey', thereupon becoming a member of Magdalen College, Oxford. Later, he was elected to a fellowship at Merton where he formed a close friendship with John Drusius. The interest in Hebrew generated at

Geneva blossomed at Oxford, with the result that Bodley became a proficient Hebraist. The Hebrew poem which he wrote in memory of Jewel shows considerable competence in the language.[5]

The task of discovering which Hebrew books were the most popular among sixteenth-century English scholars is greatly facilitated by a law passed in 1529. This required that the property of deceased persons be inventoried immediately after their death, lest the executors 'be disposed to deal unfaithfully' and purloin some of the goods and chattels left in their charge.[6] Such inventories were to include everything found in a person's house or his college room. The listed items range from beds, tables and chairs to pairs of tongs, candlesticks and bundles of firewood. Of particular significance for the present study are those inventories which contain the personal libraries of dons and students, and the stocks of booksellers. Since the universities had testamentary jurisdiction, appraisers appointed by the authorities were given the task of listing the books of deceased members by title and author. From these lists it is possible for the student of intellectual history to reconstruct the interests of the period. He is able to trace the infiltration of the new learning and discover what books were available in the various disciplines.[7]

The book-lists preserved in the university archives suggest greater enthusiasm for Hebraic studies on the part of English scholars than was once supposed. A number of more obscure persons, non-specialists who rarely feature in any other context, appear to have owned Hebrew books. This is particularly true of Cambridge, where sixty-five extant inventories made between 1539 and 1600 contain one or more Hebrew books. At Oxford, twenty-one lists compiled between 1530 and 1603 testify to a similar interest in Hebrew. Admittedly, ownership of a few Hebrew manuals does not imply an expertise in the language; it does not necessarily indicate that the books concerned had been read, let alone closely studied. The majority of those mentioned in the inventories as being the owners of Hebrew works were not eminent Hebraists. Furthermore, Renaissance England had its fair share of bibliophiles with a penchant for well-stocked libraries. However, it may be presumed that possession of some of the weightier, and therefore more expensive, volumes suggests more than a passing interest in Hebrew scholarship. It indicates at least a rudimentary knowledge of the language and literature of the Jews.

The evidence provided by these inventories and by the list of Hebrew and Aramaic books in the library catalogues of Dee and

Bodley is used to demonstrate the kind of scholarly equipment which was available to English students of Hebrew. It forms the basis of the following remarks.[8]

Learning the rudiments

In the year 1520 the Oxford bookseller, John Dorne, kept a ledger of all the books which he sold and the price he received for them over a period of twelve months. The list, preserved in manuscript at Corpus Christi College, is important because it shows what was really in demand among teachers and pupils early in the sixteenth century.[9] It appears that the writings of the Early Fathers were popular, as were those of Erasmus. Almanacs, novels and medical books were clearly a good investment for any bookseller. The Latin Classics and grammatical works were much sought after. Commentaries on the *Sentences* of Peter Lombard did not have to wait long for a customer. On the 16 April Dorne records that someone came into his shop and bought an *Alphabetum hebraicum* for twopence, the only Hebrew book, out of a total of over eighteen hundred volumes, to be sold during the course of a whole year. Although there is nothing to indicate that instruction in Hebrew was being offered in Oxford at this early date, it appears that someone was anxious to learn. Dorne's customer purchased a basic textbook which would enable him, even without the help of a teacher, to understand the rudiments of the Hebrew language. We are given no clue to the author's identity, as is the case in all these inventories, nor to the place and date of publication, but there are at least three possibilities which may be mentioned.

If Dorne, in compiling his ledger, had abbreviated the title of the only Hebrew book which he sold in 1520, it could have been the *Alphabetum hebraicum et grecum* of Johannes Parvus (Jean Petit), published in Paris about twenty years previously. But our enthusiastic student would have made little headway in Semitics if he had relied on the assistance offered him by Parvus. While fourteen pages are devoted to Greek, only one is devoted to Hebrew; it contains quite literally the alphabet and nothing more. A better bargain would have been that produced a year later at the Venetian press of Aldus Manutius, one of the earliest Italian scholar–publishers.[10] A Classicist by training, Aldus spent two years (1482–1484) at Mirandola as the guest of Pico, during which time he acted as tutor to his host's nephews. The influence of Pico can be detected almost certainly in the preface to the alphabet where Aldus writes: 'Since we judge the Hebrew language to be necessary for understanding the sacred Scriptures, we are now producing the alphabet, combinations of letters and some other things, so that you may become proficient in reading Hebrew'. This attempt at explaining the elements of the language, however, is no more than a trail-blazer. If his efforts meet with the approval of the scholarly world, Aldus promises to publish a grammar, a dictionary and some books of the Bible. But his plans never materialised. Apart from the primer and one or two biblical quotations, the only example of Hebrew printing done at his press is a specimen page of a proposed polyglot Bible.[11]

In sixteen pages, printed from right to left in red and black type, Aldus provides the beginner with what he considers to be the basic essentials of Hebrew grammar. In his own words, it is meant to be 'a most useful introduction for those desirous of learning Hebrew'. He sets out the alphabet, giving the name and value of each letter and drawing attention to the peculiarities of gutturals and labials. For reading practice he produces groups of consonants with vowels attached to them, followed by a Hebrew version of the Lord's Prayer and the title of the cross. In spite of Aldus' claim on the title-page that the primer was his own work, it is doubtful whether he had sufficient command of Hebrew to write a book of this kind. His authorship was, in fact, contested by one of Italy's greatest Jewish publishers, Gershom Soncino. In the preface to his *Introductio ad literas hebraicas*, printed in 1510, Soncino asserts that he had originally written this work when he was a young man, but had given it to someone who was ignorant of Hebrew and who had therefore produced it incorrectly. Though not mentioned by name, Aldus was the butt of this remark, for Soncino wished to demonstrate to the scholarly world that his rival was an incompetent printer of Hebrew books. But Aldus paid no attention to the protest and in 1514 issued the book again under his own name.[12]

Although it left much to the skill of the teacher, or to the imagination of the student, Aldus' alphabet was much more useful than that of Parvus. The best value for money, however, would have been the *Alphabetum hebraicum* of Franciscus Tissardus (*fl. c.* 1505) published by Egidius Gourmontius in Paris in 1508.[13] After spending some time in Italy, the author had come to Paris in 1507 to lecture in Greek. He was a competent Hebraist and obviously indebted to Jewish teachers, for in his manual he uses grammatical terms employed by

Jews. The book is divided into two parts. The first consists of the alphabet and the vowel points, followed by Hebrew and Latin versions of the Lord's Prayer, the Sanctus and the genealogy of the Blessed Virgin Mary. In the second part the definite article, the relative pronoun, the suffixes and the different forms of the verb are explained. The Hebrew words are printed from blocks made from the author's own handwriting, a fact which explains their rather strange appearance. But the attempt to provide Hebrew letters was not sustained, for in the latter part of the book the verbs are conjugated in Latin characters only. Nevertheless, despite its shortcomings, Tissardus' *Alphabetum* was by far the fullest of its kind available to English students early in the sixteenth century. It has the added distinction of being the first Hebrew book to be printed in France.

Alphabets, or tables, as these elementary grammars were also called, retained their popularity as methods of instruction throughout the century. Between 1528 and 1600 no fewer than twenty-six editions were produced at various publishing houses in Paris alone.[14] The renowned French scholar–publisher, Robert Estienne (Stephanus), printed four editions of an *Alphabetum hebraicum* between 1528 and 1554. Of these, the first served as a very basic introduction to the language and as an advertisement for the resources of his press, much as that of Aldus had done. The third edition, revised by Anthony Chevallier and published in 1544, was somewhat expanded and of greater value to the student. In addition to basic information about consonants and vowels, it contained the Ten Commandments in Hebrew, in transliteration and in a Latin translation. These were followed by the Hebrew text of Psalm 79, a guide to the Hebrew accents, the numerical value of the letters of the alphabet, the title of the cross in the three biblical languages, and the Hebrew version of Deuteronomy 27:26. The British Library copy of this book belonged to Christopher Hales, a fellow of St John's, Cambridge, who joined the English exiles at Frankfurt during the reign of Mary. This third edition was re-published in an abridged form by Christopher Plantin at Antwerp in 1569.

In addition to the great scholar–publishers, eminent Christian Hebraists also applied themselves to the task of producing simple introductory grammars uncluttered with detailed regulations. The Louvain educated Nicolas Clenardus (Cleynaerts 1495?–1542) laid down a principle which has often been repeated. He maintained that students should not be introduced to elaborate grammatical rules until they could claim to have a working knowledge of the language. He put theory into practice in his *Tabula in grammaticen hebraicam* (1529), a book which was reprinted thirteen times during the course of the century. It was in sufficient demand for the Cambridge bookseller, Nicholas Pilgrim, to stock several copies of it. When he died in 1544 Pilgrim had three copies for sale in his shop. The copy now in the British Library was once in the possession of Archbishop Thomas Cranmer. Another attempt to provide students with an elementary knowledge of Hebrew in a few easy lessons was that made by Chevallier, who published his own *Alphabetum hebraicum et graecum* (1561) while he was serving as professor of Hebrew at Calvin's Academy in Geneva. It was reproduced four times in fourteen years. In the Hebrew part of the book fifteen pages are devoted to grammar and thirty-one to reading practice. The practice section begins with the Ten Commandments in Hebrew, in Latin and in transliteration. In what is meant to be a more difficult exercise, they are repeated without transliteration. There are several pages of prayers in Hebrew and Latin suitable for various occasions. Sayings of the early rabbis are then reproduced, both in the square script of the Hebrew Bible and in the more cursive script of the mediaeval commentaries.Chevallier was obviously anxious to introduce his readers to post-biblical Hebrew. The work ends with the title of the cross.

The earliest record of an *Alphabetum hebraicum* in an English scholar's private library has already been noted: Brian Rowe, the Vice-Provost of King's, owned both an alphabet and a grammar when he died in 1521. The Oxford student William Woodrofe, whose books were inventoried in 1530 following his disappearance 'after clandestine flight', had copies of a Hebrew alphabet and a primer. In 1527 Richard Pace sent an alphabet to Fox, Bishop of Winchester, to help him understand the controversy surrounding the interpretation of Old Testament texts quoted in the matter of Henry VIII's divorce. The king wanted his marriage to Catherine of Aragon, formerly his brother's widow, annulled so that he could marry Ann Boleyn. On his side was scriptural authority from Leviticus 18:16, where marital relations between a man and the wife of his dead brother are forbidden. In Deuteronomy 25:5, on the other hand, such a union is mandatory if the brother has died childless, so that his name may be perpetuated. To arrive at the proper interpretation of these conflicting passages, it was necessary to go to the original Hebrew and even seek Jewish opinion. Since Jews were officially excluded from England, both sides in the dispute turned to continental rabbinic authorities for support. Though the ensuing arguments became long and involved, the issue did much to enhance Hebraic studies in the eyes of Christians, not least those who were connected to the King of England's court. Pace was anxious that Henry should avail himself of the advice of reputable English scholars, and in his letter recommended Robert Wakefield and Richard Fox. But while Wakefield could cope adequately with the Hebrew Bible and with rabbinic arguments, Fox could do neither. Pace sought to enlighten the ageing prelate by sending him an alphabet by way of the king. In his letter to the sovereign he writes: 'I send unto your Grace herein closed an alphabet in the Hebrew tongue, desiring the same to deliver the said alphabet to Master Fox yourself, with commandment to him to give good diligence for to obtain the intelligence thereof, and to have it promptly without book'.[15] If he applies himself assiduously to the task, Pace assures the king that Fox will obtain sufficient knowledge of the language 'within the space of one month' to be able to compare the Hebrew text of the Old Testament with the Septuagint and Vulgate. But despite possible royal pressure, it is doubtful whether the bishop made any headway. Old and almost totally blind, he is not likely to have regarded a crash-course in Hebrew as a priority, however important the issue.

Although alphabets and tables were the primary sources of the knowledge of Hebrew among Christians, they do not appear as frequently as one might have expected in the libraries of English students. Of grammars, however, there was an abundance. Beginning with the contributions of Konrad Pellican (1504) and Reuchlin (1506), the century witnessed the production of a host of Hebrew grammars by continental scholars, many of which soon found their way to England, as the inventories demonstrate. There were some clear favourites, among them the works of Jews and converts from Judaism. Through his friends and pupils Elias Levita's studies in Hebrew grammar became available to Christians. Jean Campensis, professor at the trilingual college in Louvain from 1519 to 1531, produced a concise and methodical introduction to the Hebrew language based on Levita's writings. On account of its clarity of presentation and freedom from over-emphasis on grammatical minutiae, it became an immediate best-seller. First published in 1520, it was reprinted many times and appears frequently in the inventories where it is referred to as Campensis' *Grammatica hebraica*.[16] Levita's devoted band of disciples also included Sebastian Münster who made a Latin version of his mentor's *Sepher Ha-Dikduk* in 1537. John Dee had his own copy of this translation, as did several others mentioned in the inventories.[17] Another Jewish grammarian whose works found their way onto the shelves of English students was David Kimchi. As in the case of Levita, his major contribution to the study of Hebrew grammar, the *Michlol,* was made available to non-Jews in Latin. Alfonso de Zamora, professor of Hebrew at Alcalá, made a translation of it in 1527 which he presented to Edward Lee, the English ambassador to the Spanish court and later Archbishop of York.[18] Dee possessed a copy of the translation produced by Daniel Bomberg in 1534, and that made by the French scholar Agathias Guidacerius which was first published in Paris in 1540.[19] Sanctes Pagninus, as we have noted above, relied heavily on Kimchi and used the *Michlol* as the basis for his *Institutiones hebraicae* (1549). Assuming that in the inventories the *Grammatica hebraica* of Pagninus is identical to the *Institutiones,* then at least nine Cambridge scholars had access to Kimchi. Dee bought his copy in Louvain in 1562.[20]

The number of accomplished Christian Hebraists whose own grammatical works, as opposed to translations, were to be found in English libraries is noteworthy. With two exceptions they come from the continent of Europe. Pellican, Capito, Bibliander and Bertram from Switzerland, Quinquarboreus (*fl.* 1560) and Martinius (*fl.* 1568) from France, Reuchlin, Münster and Avenarius (1520–1590) from Germany, together with less well-known scholars, are all represented in the inventories. The grammars of Clenardus and Chevallier are also conspicuous; they appear to have been more popular than their earlier elementary works. Until half way through the century English students of Hebrew were dependent on continental scholars to provide the manuals necessary for linguistic study. It was 1550 before a Hebrew grammar was produced by a native Englishman, namely Ralph Baynes (*c.* 1504–1560). Of a Yorkshire Family, Baynes took his B.A. at St John's, Cambridge, in 1517–18, and immediately became a fellow of the college. At St John's he was a contemporary of the Wakefield brothers, and it is tempting to assume that he learned his Hebrew from them. His support for the Catholic cause led to voluntary exile in France, and in 1550 he was elected professor of Hebrew in Paris. Soon after the accession of Mary he returned to England and was appointed to the see of Lichfield in 1554, only to be deposed five years later for refusing to comply with the religious changes brought about by Elizabeth.

Baynes' command of Hebrew and his familiarity with the works of leading Jewish expositors is impressive; it prompted Cooper to describe him as 'one of the chief restorers of Hebrew learning' in England.[21] His commentary on the Hebrew text of the Book of Proverbs was considered by John Pearson to be of sufficient standing to merit inclusion in his *Critici sacri* of 1660. In it can be found ample evidence of his linguistic expertise and of his positive attitude towards mediaeval rabbinic exegesis. He makes plain that he has been helped often 'both by the Hebrew original and by the commentaries of the Jews' in his attempts to unravel something 'which in the Latin version is unclear'.[22] His rabbinic authorities include Rashi, Kimchi, Gersonides and Ibn Ezra. He is especially indebted to the last named whom he describes as the 'most learned of rabbis'. In his notes he invariably draws attention to the rabbinic solution of a particular difficulty; he does not always agree with it, but he never fails to take it into account. He stresses the importance of the Massoretic Text, and on several occasions points to discrepancies between the Vulgate and the original Hebrew. At 31:21 he states outright that the Hebrew must be preferred to the Latin.

Despite the esteem in which his commentary on Proverbs was held, Baynes' chief contribution to the study of the Hebrew language was in the realm of grammar. In 1550 he published his *Prima rudimenta in linguam hebraeam*, a comprehensive introductory manual of seventy-five octavo pages. The preface contains a glowing tribute to David Kimchi. In Baynes' opinion, there is nothing which the author of a basic grammar can say which has not already been said by Kimchi in his *Michlol*. Anyone who wishes to contribute substantially to the study of grammar and syntax must take into account the work of this expert Jewish grammarian. Such was his esteem for the *Michlol* that in 1554 he made a new edition of it, arranged especially for teaching purposes. In the introduction he explains that on account of the unmethodical nature and sheer prolixity of the original, he has not adhered to Kimchi's plan. In the hope that the work would appeal to a wide readership, he admits that he has abbreviated it considerably by leaving out all complex rules and lengthy tables, while at the same time stressing that nothing has been omitted which is necessary for a proper understanding of the language.[23] Though he is certain to have availed himself of the contributions of Alfonso de Zamora, Guidacerius and Pagninus, Baynes' treatment of the *Michlol* suggests a very able

Hebraist equal in every way to his European counterparts. It is ironical that of all the scholars whose books were inventoried at Oxford and Cambridge, only Andrew Perne had a copy of the first Hebrew grammar to be written by an Englishman.

Far into the eighteenth century the language in which these Hebrew manuals were produced was Latin. There is only one extant example of a Hebrew grammar written in English from the whole of the Tudor period. It was the work of the Puritan scholar John Udall (1560?–1592). Originally a student of Christ's College, Cambridge, Udall migrated to Trinity, where he obtained 'a competent knowledge of Hebrew', presumably from Edward Lively.[24] He took his B.A. in 1580–81. Suspected of complicity in the Marprelate Tracts, he was hounded by the authorities, condemned, and spent many months in prison awaiting execution. Although he was finally pardoned, he died soon after his release as a result of incarceration. His grammar, *The Key to the Holy Tongue*, was published posthumously at Leiden in 1593. The book falls into three parts: an elementary introduction to Hebrew grammar, reading practice and a dictionary. The grammar is a word for word translation of Petrus Martinius' *Grammaticae hebraicae libri duo*, 'Englished for the benefit of those that (being ignorant of the Latin) are desirous to learn the holy tongue'.[25] Martinius, professor of Hebrew at a Protestant seminary in La Rochelle, first published his grammar in 1567; he re-issued it, emended and augmented, in 1591. To his translation Udall added the text of three psalms (1, 25, and 68) in order to help the student practise what he had learned. In Psalm 25 every word is examined under the headings of etymology and syntax with chapter, page and line references to the grammar. The other two psalms are treated in less detail. The dictionary contains the principal Hebrew roots with their meanings and the words derived from each root. The whole book runs into one hundred and seventy-four octavo pages.

In spite of Udall's efforts to provide the English student with a Hebrew grammar in his mother tongue, his book is not mentioned specifically by John Brinsley in his *Ludus literarius*.[26] When discussing textbooks which he considers suitable for teaching Hebrew in schools, Brinsley obviously expects the pupils to be able to cope adequately with Latin. It is not until 1622, in the lengthy bibliography appended to *A Consolation*, that he notes Udall's translation and commends it as 'making most things in Martinius very plain'. In the *Ludus* he suggests that the quickest way of grasping the grammatical structure of the

Hebrew language is by using the grammars of Petrus Martinius and Thomas Blebelius (*fl.* 1587). The former's work, especially his *Grammaticae hebraeae technologia*, printed by Plantin in 1611, is to be recommended because it is 'the most used of all the learned, as most methodical and perfect'. Yet, as far as the beginner is concerned, that of Blebelius has more to commend it and will serve as a useful introduction to Martinius. Perusal of both would be most profitable, 'Martinius for method and shortness and Blebelius for resolving and expounding every obscurity'. Blebelius' *Grammaticae hebraeae sanctae linguae institutiones*, first published at Wittenberg in 1587, was singled out by Brinsley because it was tailor-made for the novice. The bulk of the work is presented in catechetical style, dealing with Hebrew etymology and syntax by means of questions and answers in which the rules of grammar are kept to a minimum. One chapter explains the accents, metre and the rudiments of synagogue music. In the final pages the student is instructed in the use of a Hebrew dictionary, and a detailed index helps him to find his way through the four hundred and ninety-six octavo pages of the grammar itself.

These were some of the manuals available to the sixteenth-century English student of Hebrew. Baroway calculates that by 1600 there were one hundred and forty-six published editions of individual grammars.[27] They came from Italian, French, Swiss, Dutch, and above all from German presses.

The Bible in Hebrew

Encouraged by his mastery of the syntax, the student would progress to the biblical text and acquire a copy of the Scriptures in Hebrew. Although the Soncino press had printed the Old Testament with vowels and accents as early as 1488, it was not until the beginning of the following century that Christian scholars began to concern themselves with the text of the Hebrew Bible. Since Aldus Manutius' proposed polyglot never appeared in print, the honour of being the first in this field goes to Cardinal Ximénez. From *c.* 1502 Ximénez and his associates at Alcalá were at work on the Complutensian Polyglot. Though the whole Bible was printed by 1517, it was not issued until 1522, having been authorised by the Vatican for publication only two years previously. The Old Testament covers four out of the six volumes. Each page is divided into three columns. In the centre is the

Vulgate, flanked in the outer column by the Hebrew text, and in the inner column by the Septuagint with an interlinear Latin translation. Throughout the Pentateuch, the Targum of Onkelos, with an accompanying Latin version prepared by Alfonso de Zamora, is printed at the foot of each page. This magnificent monument to Spanish biblical scholarship provided the model for the Royal Polyglot produced by Plantin at Antwerp fifty years later. In preparing the new Bible of 1572 Arias Montano reproduced the Hebrew text of the Complutensian with very few modifications.

In spite of their undoubted merits, these two famous versions do not appear frequently in the inventories of private libraries. Bodley, it is true, had both. But of all the scholars listed in Appendix III below, only two Cambridge men had their own copies. Ambrose Barker (1538) owned a Complutensian Polyglot, and Andrew Perne (1589) had a Royal Polyglot. Most individuals would have found these many-volumed versions far too expensive and would have settled for a simple Hebrew Bible. Editions of the Hebrew Bible and of individual biblical books were produced by several of the leading sixteenth-century scholar-printers. While Ximénez was putting the finishing touches to his polyglot, Daniel Bomberg was seeing the Hebrew Old Testament through his own press at Venice.[28] Of Dutch extraction, Bomberg had come to this 'city of books' in c. 1505. Within a decade he had established a rival press to that of Soncino and obtained from the Senate a privilege for printing Hebrew books. Like many others, he was attracted by the availability of good, cheap paper, and by the opportunities for trade which Venice offered. Referred to by his contemporaries as 'the Aldus in Hebrew books', Bomberg did for Hebrew scholarship what Aldus had done for Greek. He was the first Christian publisher to produce a complete Hebrew Bible. His *Biblia hebraica*, edited with the help of Felix Pratensis, a converted Jew, first appeared in 1517 and was reprinted three times before the press closed in 1549. John Dee had his own copy of it.[29] Froben of Basle published Münster's annotated Hebrew-Latin Bible in 1535. Between 1539 and 1546 Robert Estienne, with the help of Vatable, issued two complete editions of the Hebrew Old Testament. In 1566 Plantin also printed a Hebrew Bible. Although many English scholars had a *Biblia hebraica* on their shelves, only in a few instances is the particular edition identified in the inventories. For obvious financial reasons complete Bibles were not as popular as copies of various biblical books bound separately. Of the many individual books published, the Psalter was in greatest demand, a fact which suggests that it was read as a set text in schools and universities. Proverbs and Genesis rank next in popularity, while Isaiah, Ezekiel, Jeremiah, Hosea, Job, Esther, Ecclesiastes and the Song of Songs are also represented.

For those wishing to make a thorough study of the Scriptures in Hebrew there were several dictionaries, concordances, and even a phrase-book available through English and continental booksellers. The final volume of the Complutensian Polyglot contained a Hebrew and Aramaic dictionary compiled by Alfonso de Zamora. Reuchlin, Pagninus, Münster and Förster all produced popular lexicons. In addition to the Epitome of Pagninus' *Thesaurus*, edited by Raphaelengius and published by Plantin in 1570, John Brinsley recommends the *Liber radicum seu lexicon ebraicum* (1589) of the German Hebraist Johannes Avenarius (Habermann). This was a volume of eight hundred and sixty folio pages, each page divided into four columns. The left-hand column contained the Hebrew root. The second provided examples of different forms of the root by means of biblical verses quoted in Latin. This was followed by the equivalent word in the Septuagint, and in the final column the Hebrew word itself was reproduced in its derived form so that it could be identified without difficulty in the biblical text. The same procedure was followed for nouns derived from the verb. John Dee owned a copy of Rabbi Nathan ben Kalonymus' Hebrew concordance in Antonius Reuchlin's Latin translation published in Basle in 1556.[30] Originally issued by Bomberg at Venice in 1523, the work had been composed at c. 1440 in an attempt to provide Jews with a ready reference to biblical passages for use during polemic discussions with Christians. It became the standard work on which all later Hebrew concordances were based. The *Phrases hebraicae* published by Estienne in 1558 found customers in England. Written in Latin, it listed and explained biblical idioms which might perplex a reader using a French or Latin version of the Bible. A *Concordantiae hebraicae* had been issued by the same press in 1555.[31]

The only English contribution to Hebrew lexicography during the sixteenth century was made by Simon Sturtevant, a member of Christ's College, Cambridge. Entitled *Dibre Adam or Adam's Hebrew Dictionary*, Sturtevant's work was published in London in 1602. To be precise, only the introduction of thirty-two octavo pages was published; whether the dictionary itself ever found its way into print is not known.[32] Addressing the reader, the author demonstrates his enthusiasm for the Hebrew language: 'Most worthy of pre-eminence is this mother tongue, which in very deed is the key of knowledge and the door to happy felicity'.[33] He claims that in order to assist the beginner to pass through this door, he had invented this 'scholastic instrument' twelve years previously, while he was a student at Cambridge. 'Having privately communicated it with approbation to some few of my special friends ... I have now, upon mature judgement, polished and published for the beneficial behoof of all Hebricians'.[34] He names as his collaborators Oliver and William Perkins, Master Williams, Master Hecock and John Downham, all of whom were his contemporaries at Cambridge during the 1580s. Since, in Hebrew, the root is the 'fountain of all rivulets' it is essential that the student should know how to find it quickly. This 'literary engine' is designed to meet this very need.

Post-biblical Jewish literature

Taken as a whole, the inventories suggest that those who bought Hebrew books in Tudor England did so because they were motivated to study the Bible in the original. The focus of their attention was the Word of God as it was to be found in the Hebrew Scriptures. The indications that they were acquainted with post-biblical Jewish writings are few. This is hardly surprising, for only a small minority would have been able to cope successfully with mediaeval Hebrew. But for those who wished to purchase them, rabbinic works were available, either in the original or in a Latin translation. We have already noted how Hugh Broughton, in 1591, compiled a list of twenty-two books by Jewish authors which the zealous student might obtain from Venice or Frankfurt. In addition to the Midrash and the Babylonian Talmud, he refers to the writings of Ibn Ezra, Kimchi, Gersonides, Nachmanides, Abravanel, Maimonides, Isaac ben Arama and several other lesser known Jewish authors.[35] Thomas James' catalogue demonstrates that Bodley's library embraced a wide variety of Hebraica. While most of the manuals and bibles found in the private inventories are represented, the striking feature is the large number of mediaeval Jewish books in both Hebrew and Latin among the library's holdings. As Baroway has shown, it is misleading to speak of only 'a fair number of rabbinical works' in Bodley's collection, in the way that Daiches does.[36] A detailed examination of the catalogue proves that there were far more post-biblical Hebrew books in Oxford's main library by the end of the sixteenth century than was once recognised. Not only were there grammars, bibles and lexicons, but also rabbinic commentaries, legal codes, kabbalistic works and texts from Midrash and Talmud.

Out of a total of sixty-two volumes listed as 'Hebraica et Chaldaica', excluding grammars, dictionaries and works on the Kabbalah, John Dee had six post-biblical Jewish books. Only one, Kimchi's commentary on the Psalter, was in Hebrew; the rest were in Latin translations by Münster, Fagius and Augustinus Justinianus.[37] To help him understand the mediaeval Hebrew of the rabbinic exegetes he had a copy of Génébrard's *Isagoge*, a word by word analysis of Joel 3:1 (English 2:28) based on the text of David Kimchi's commentary. A Cambridge scholar, who must remain anonymous, had a Talmud.[38] Andrew Perne owned a Hebrew copy of *The Book of Joseph ben Gorion*, Nathan ben Kalonymus' Hebrew Concordance (Venice 1523), Levita's commentary on the Song of Songs, commentaries by Kimchi on the Psalter and on Haggai, Zechariah and Malachi, and Bomberg's Rabbinic Bible (*Biblia hebraica cum commentariis hebraicis*). Between 1517 and 1548 Bomberg printed the Rabbinic Bible three times, thus providing those who could read the annotations surrounding the biblical text with the observations of leading Jewish exegetes on every book in the Bible. To help the non-Jewish reader Levita produced two books which were published in a Latin translation by Paul Fagius at his press in Isny in 1541.[39] The *Meturgeman*, an Aramaic dictionary, was intended as a companion to targumic and talmudic studies, whereas the *Tishbi* was a glossary of mediaeval Hebrew. Dee and Perne had purchased copies of both of them. Nicholas Pilgrim, in his Cambridge bookshop, had a copy of the *Tishbi* for sale.

This brief and selective review of the scholarly apparatus available to those studying Hebrew in sixteenth-century England leads to four general conclusions. The first is the obvious dependence of English Hebraists on continental linguists and presses for the books that they required. Without the scores of manuals produced by French, German and Swiss scholars, English students would have made little progress. At a time when Hebrew printing was virtually non-existent in England, the contribution of the great publishing houses of Venice, Basle, Paris, Isny, Wittenberg and Antwerp was all-important. The activity of Europe's learned printers was vital for the development of

Hebraic studies in this country. Secondly, the inventories suggest that, in the main, English Hebrew scholarship was confined to classical grammar and the biblical text. Elementary text-books and dictionaries abound. There were those who advanced from alphabet to rabbinic commentary, but on the whole the complexities of mediaeval Hebrew were beyond the capabilities of most Hebraists. In any case, the contributions of competent translators, such as Fagius and Münster, had made it unnecessary for those who wished to consult the rabbinic sources to struggle with the original. Even with such translations readily available, it is questionable whether Dee and Perne often turned to the post-biblical literature found on their shelves. Thirdly, Bodley's catalogue and the book-lists contained in the inventories demonstrate that Oxford, as well as Cambridge, felt the impact of humanism and the new learning. Admittedly there are fewer lists which contain books extant at Oxford, but there is surely no lack of evidence that the traditional contrast between the conservative scholasticism of Oxford and the progressive humanism of Cambridge is unwarranted.[40] In both universities dons and students were buying Hebrew books. Finally, a study of the inventories indicates the existence of a greater number of Hebrew students in the English universities than was once supposed. Perhaps William Fulke was right, and not just engaged in wishful thinking, when he claimed in 1583 that 'a hundred boys in Cambridge' had a basic knowledge of Hebrew and Aramaic.[41]

Notes

1   I. Zinberg, *A History of Jewish Literature*, vol. VI, p. 49.
2   See Appendix II for the Hebrew books in Dee's catalogue. A facsimile edition of this catalogue with annotations is being prepared for the Bibliographical Society by R. J. Roberts and A. G. Watson.
3   *Catalogus Librorum bibliothecae publicae quam T. Bodleius in academia Oxoniensi nuper instituit*, Oxford 1605.
4   *The Life of Sir Thomas Bodley*, eds. J. C. Dana and H. W. Kent, Chicago, Ill. 1906, p. 35.
5   For the text of the poem see L. Humphrey, *The Life of Jewel*, sig. Nniiii; also C. Roth, 'Thomas Bodley — Hebraist', *Bodleian Library Record*, vol. VII, No. 5, 1966, pp. 242ff. In Roth's opinion the poem demonstrates 'a creditable mastery of the language'.
6   H. Swinburne, *A Treatise of Testaments and Last Wills*, 7th ed., London 1803, vol. II, p. 757. See 21 Henry VIII c 5, *Statutes of the Realm*, eds.

A. Luders *et al.*, vol. III, p. 287.

7   See W. A. Pantin, 'The conception of the universities in England in the period of the Renaissance' in *Les Universités Européennes du XIVe au XVIIIe siècle: aspects et problèmes*, p. 107; Margery H. Smith, 'Some humanist libraries in early Tudor Cambridge', *Sixteenth Century Journal*, vol. V, No. 1, 1974, pp. 15ff; M. H. Curtis, 'Library catalogues in Tudor Oxford and Cambridge', *Studies in the Renaissance*, vol. V, 1958, pp. 111ff.

8   See Appendix III for those dons, students and booksellers in sixteenth-century Oxford and Cambridge the inventories of whose possessions include Hebrew books.

9   *The Day-book of John Dorne*, ed. F. Madan, Oxford Historical Society Collectanea I, Oxford 1885.

10 *Alphabetum Hebraicum*, Venice *c*. 1501 (facsimile reprint, Munich 1927).

11 For a facsimile reprint of this page see A. Renouard, *Annales de l'imprimerie des Alde*, Paris 1825, p. 389.

12 See A. Marx, 'Aldus and the first use of Hebrew type in Venice', *Papers of the Bibliographical Society of America*, vol. 13, 1919, Pt. I, pp. 64ff; M. Marx, 'Gershom (Hieronymus) Soncino's wanderyears in Italy, 1498–1527: Exemplar Judaicae Vitae', *HUCA*, vol. XI, 1936, pp. 455f.

13 See A. E. Cowley, 'Hebrew printing', *Bodleian Qtly Record*, vol. I, No. 8, 1915, pp. 203f.

14 See H. Omont, *Alphabets Grecs et Hébreux publiés à Paris au XVIe siècle*, Paris 1885; F. E. Buisson, *Répertoire des ouvrages pédagogiques du XVIe siècle*, Paris 1886, pp. 2ff.

15 S. Knight, *The Life of Erasmus*, Appendix p. xxvi.

16 The full title is *Ex variis libellis Eliae quidquid ad absolutam grammaticen Hebraicam est necessarium*.

17 See Appendix II, No. 53 for Dee's copy.

18 See F. Perez Castro, *El Manuscrito Apologetico de Alfonso de Zamora*, p. lvii.

19 See Appendix II, Nos. 40 and 56.

20 *Ibid.*, No. 12. This is now in the Bodleian Library.

21 *Athenae Cantabrigienses*, vol. I, p. 202.

22 See introductory comments to Proverbs 22:17 in *Critici sacri*, vol. IV.

23 *Compendium Michlol*, Paris 1554.

24 *DNB*, *s.v.*

25 Title-page of *The Key to the Holy Tongue*, (facsimile reprint, London 1970).

26 See Brinsley, *Ludus Literarius*, ch. 12; *A Consolation*, p. 75; Lilly, *A History of His Life and Times*, p. 5.

27 'Towards understanding Tudor–Jacobean Hebrew studies', *Jewish Social Studies*, vol. 18, No. 1, 1956, p. 15.

28 For an account of Bomberg's press see D. W. Amram, *The Makers of Hebrew Books in Italy*, Philadelphia, Pa. 1909 (reprinted London 1963), chs. VII–IX; J. S. Bloch, *Venetian Printers of Hebrew Books*, New York 1932. A list of the Hebrew books printed by Bomberg is given

in *JE*, vol. III, p. 300.

29 See Appendix II, No. 9.

30 *Ibid.*, No. 1.

31 For Estienne's contribution to Hebrew scholarship see E. Armstrong, *Robert Estienne: Royal Printer*, Cambridge 1954, pp. 117ff.

32 See *STC*, 2nd ed., No. 23409.

33 *Dibre Adam*, Intro., p. 13.

34 *Ibid.*, p. 14.

35 *Works*, Bk. II, p. 246.

36 Baroway, *op. cit.*, *Jewish Social Studies*, vol. 18, No. 1, 1956, pp. 15ff; cf. Daiches, *The King James Version*, p. 166.

37 See Appendix II, Nos. 7, 10, 20, 27, 29, 41.

38 See Appendix III, under Cambridge 1588.

39 For a list of Fagius' own works and the books published by his press, see R. Raubenheimer, *Paul Fagius*, Grünstadt 1957.

40 On the assimilation of continental humanism at Oxford see J. K. McConica, 'Humanism and Aristotle in Tudor Oxford', *EHR*, vol. 94, 1979, pp. 291ff.

41 *A Defence*, Parker Soc., p. 413.

Conclusion

In the past, the place of Hebrew studies in Tudor England has been either neglected or underestimated. On the whole, historians of the Renaissance and Reformation have paid only nominal attention to this particular aspect of their subject. Educationists have shown greater enthusiasm. Yet, their conclusions, when they present them, tend to be negative. Mullinger finds Hebrew to be 'at a very low ebb' in Cambridge, and refers to its 'growing neglect towards the end of the century'.[1] Mallett paints an equally depressing picture of the situation at Oxford during the same period, when he says that Hebrew 'made less headway than scholars might have hoped'.[2] With reference to sixteenth-century England in general, S. A. Hirsch claims that 'apart from a few scholars who achieved great proficiency, Hebrew was only considered a kind of ornamental accomplishment affected by incipient theologians who were, however, quite satisfied with the merest glimpse through the portals of the temple'.[3] The purpose of this study has been to try to redress the balance by taking another look at much of the available evidence. In a final chapter the general conclusions may be restated and emphasised.

The study of Hebrew was not introduced into England in the sixteenth century; it was rediscovered. The tradition of English Hebrew scholarship, which can be traced back into the Middle Ages, may not have been strong, but it did exist. Before it began to flourish, the Tudor period was well under way. The impetus for this sudden interest came initially from humanistic circles on the Continent. The revival of Platonism, with its strong mystical element, at Ficino's academy in Florence, provided a congenial atmosphere for the growth of kabbalistic studies among Christians, which in turn led to Hebrew. Others had preceded Pico in the study of the Kabbalah, but he was the first to explore it in any real depth and to draw from it some startling conclusions with regard to the Christian faith. The task of working out Pico's ideas more fully fell to Reuchlin. His defence of the Hebraic tradition against the attacks of the ignorant and the prejudiced reveals a skilled linguist who was an expert in the esoteric writings of the

Jewish mystics. In his native Germany he was acclaimed as the promoter and protector of Semitic studies. Reuchlin's emphasis on philology was adopted by Pagninus and Münster, whose chief contribution was to integrate rabbinic influence into Christian biblical scholarship on a far greater scale than anyone had done hitherto. Leo Jud and Tremellius were heirs to these two bridge-builders. After the Reformation, Hebrew philology received considerable attention among Protestants as part of the science of theology. Under the influence of Luther, Zwingli, Calvin and other prominent scholars the language was studied assiduously in all the major centres of learning. Some may have had reservations about delving into the works of the rabbis, but of the significance of Hebrew for biblical study there was no doubt.

The intention of the Renaissance humanists, especially those of Germany, was to bring about a 'restitutio christianismi', to use Erasmus' famous phrase. They harnessed the new learning to the task of revitalising the Church. Their demand for renewal was not new in itself; the conciliarists had long since called for 'reform in head and members'. The novel element in this rejection of scholasticism was the rediscovery of the past. Reform could come only through sound learning based on an appeal *ad fontes*. The rediscovery of antiquity led to the Bible, which in turn led to the rediscovery of Hebrew. At the instigation of Italian and German scholars, the pursuit of Hebrew came to be regarded as essential for all serious students of Scripture. This programme of intellectual reform initiated on the Continent had the co-operation of learned Englishmen, whose admiration for Pico, Reuchlin and Erasmus knew no bounds. Although John Colet and his circle were followers of Reuchlin the Hebraist rather than Reuchlin the Kabbalist, they were representative of a group of scholars and statesmen who laid durable foundations for the development of Hebrew studies in this country. They saw the significance of the language for their attempted reform of ecclesiastical abuses. For this reason they sought to promote it in their private correspondence, in the statutes of educational foundations and at the royal court.

While the Renaissance, with its appeal to the sources of Christianity, highlighted the importance of Hebrew for Old Testament studies, the Reformation, with its demand for the Bible in the vernacular, emphasised it further. The Hebrew language led to the Hebraic tradition. Those who produced versions of the Scriptures in English were assisted by Jewish explanations of textual difficulties.

They came to appreciate them either directly through their own knowledge of post-biblical Hebrew or indirectly through the more notable independent Latin translations. The versions of Pagninus, Münster, Leo Jud and Tremellius were prized by English scholars because they were regarded as trusty guides to rabbinic comments, and therefore to the literal sense of the text. Those of Pagninus and Münster in particular were a constant influential factor in every translation from Coverdale onwards. Consequently, the interpretations of the rabbis, which they incorporated, found their way into the English versions. Although this suggests a derived rabbinic scholarship on the part of English Hebraists, their appreciation of Jewish opinion was no less real. In many cases of textual difficulty the ancient versions of Theodotion and Jerome offered no acceptable solution. This made the philological contributions of Jewish scholars towards understanding the Bible all the more valuable in an age when detailed grammatical commentaries by Christians on the literal sense of the Old Testament were still scarce.

The translation of Scripture was not the only motive for learning Hebrew which the Reformation provided for English Protestants. By forcing them to create a new and biblically based doctrinal system, it prompted many to evaluate the Hebraic tradition afresh. In their efforts to maintain a distinctively Protestant position against Catholic dogma, participants in doctrinal disputations with the papal authorities turned to the rabbis. They discovered that mediaeval Jewish commentaries could be consulted with profit, and rabbinic expositions of key scriptural passages quoted in support of their own cause. In their fierce debates with the Church of Rome on matters of doctrine, Fulke, Broughton and Rainolds, and to a lesser extent Alley, Whitaker and Gibbens, found that the Jewish emphasis on the literal-historical sense of the Old Testament could be used to uphold Protestant principles. From this realisation there developed a dogmatic interest in the Hebraic tradition. During the second half of the century there is evidence of a growing awareness among English scholars of the relevance of the rabbinic commentaries for dealing with questions which involved exegesis as well as philology. This becomes apparent when we examine the work of translators and commentators. The Book of Daniel contains numerous examples of the theological issues at stake between Catholics and Protestants. The explanation of the stone cut out of the mountain 'by no human hand' (2:34) as a reference to the virgin birth of Christ was unacceptable to Protestants. For Catholics the fourth beast (7:19ff.) was the Roman Empire; for many Protestants it was the Roman Church. The dominion which is given 'to the people of the saints of the Most High' (7:27) could not, in Protestant opinion, be a prediction of papal supremacy and ecclesiastical authority. In each case Protestant exegetes utilised rabbinic opinion to add weight to their own interpretation.

The fact that many English scholars found rabbinic exegesis to be relevant in their search for the true meaning of Scripture must not be taken to imply that they could unreservedly commend Jewish writings. Although Lively's criticisms of Jewish historiography in the *Seder 'Olam* is based on scholarly rather than dogmatic considerations, his writings do contain a note of caution. Broughton and Rainolds are harsher, and at times express outright hostility towards the Jews. This negative attitude, adopted by men who were otherwise a hundred per cent behind the rediscovery of the Hebraic tradition, can be explained in various ways. In the first place, it is due to the fact that the sixteenth-century Christian theologian was eager to convert the Jew. Even Lively, in spite of his evident partiality to the Jews as philologists and exegetes, asks in his rebuttal of Matthew Beroalde's explanation of the chronology of the Seventy Weeks in Daniel 9: 'What is this else but to make God's word a wax nose to turn which way a man list at his pleasure? How is it possible that by such kind of dealing divine Scripture should be rightly understood? How shall the Jews by such wresting of texts, be made Christians and brought to believe that Christ is come?'[4] The ultimate aim of the exegesis of such passages was to convince the Jew of the error of his ways. Broughton displays a similar missionary motive. If the Jew was to be converted he must be shown the true (i.e. Christian) interpretation of key Old Testament passages. To this end rabbinic arguments must be refuted and rejected. After all, Kimchi and Ibn Ezra were two of Jewry's most gifted and prolific anti-Christian polemicists. Secondly, this negative attitude is due to the dogmatic interest which governed the Christian exegete's attitude to the Old Testament. As a reaction to the allegorical interpretation of the scholastics, Luther had emphasised the importance of the grammatico-historical method of biblical exegesis, whereby the meaning of the verse should be scientifically discovered through a study of the situation out of which it arose. This was his declared exegetical principle. When we turn to his commentaries, however, we are faced, not with Luther the exegete but with Luther the homilist. Despite his exegetical ideal, his interests were basically doctrinal, for in the last anlysis the whole of the Bible was about Christ alone. Calvin adopted the same principle of interpretation, but in his case dogmatic interests did not control his exegesis to the same extent. Nevertheless, for Calvin as for Luther, the Old Testament was a Christian book which had to be approached typologically. This meant that the literal meaning of a passage was superseded by the spiritual. In addition to the *sensus literalis* of the Jewish commentaries, there was the *sensus literalis propheticus* of the New Testament writers. The English Protestants were heirs to this approach to the Bible. In the case of Broughton, and to a lesser extent of Lively, matters of doctrine are always uppermost in their minds, with the result that in such controversial passages as Daniel's Seventy Weeks they are obliged to read the rabbis with circumspection. As exegetes and translators they may have been passionately concerned with the quest for the *hebraica veritas*, but as theologians they could not allow this to over-ride their Christocentric theory of Scripture. Finally, there was the possible fear that Christianity would be contaminated by Judaism. It will be remembered how Erasmus in a letter to Capito in 1517 had expressed his fear of a Jewish revival, if the interest in Judaica generated by Pico and Reuchlin was not checked.[5] By the end of his life Luther had become obsessed with the same idea, and with the threat that it posed to the purity of the faith. Harassed by the rise of Sabbatarianism, he roundly condemned the Jews and advocated their expulsion. It is not unlikely that this fear was felt also by late sixteenth-century English scholars, though not with the same intensity, since contact with actual Jews was minimal.

The reservations of biblical commentators about mediaeval Jewish writings were not shared by those whose interests revolved around the mystical tradition. For John Dee, and those of a like mind, the Kabbalah had an enduring fascination. To their way of thinking, the solution of many theological and intellectual problems lay in the application of arcane ideas which had their origin in the Oral Law delivered to Moses on Sinai. Dee's vast library testifies to his passionate concern with this mystical lore of the Jews. In common with Pico and Reuchlin he appropriated the Jewish Kabbalah for his own religious purposes.

The final section of our study covered the opportunities afforded for the development of Hebraic studies among English Christians. This led to an examination of the teaching facilities provided by universities, schools and private households, and of the availability of suitable books. When Pico, Reuchlin and Münster began learning Hebrew they had Jewish teachers to help them. But the first English students were not so fortunate, for the names of Jews, other than converts, connected with intellectual circles in England appear only at the beginning of the seventeenth century. Although the first recognised teacher was Robert Wakefield, the credit for introducing Hebraic studies into a college curriculum goes to John Fisher; others built on the foundations laid by him between 1509 and 1530 at Cambridge. By the mid-1540s the appointment of Regius professors had put Hebrew teaching on a sound financial basis and had secured a place for the language in the official university course. Nevertheless, English teachers of Hebrew were not plentiful. There was thus ample opportunity for continental scholars to find employment as instructors. During the second half of the century, a line of distinguished foreigners played a major part in maintaining a high standard of Hebrew teaching at both Oxford and Cambridge. In this way a practice introduced by Cranmer, who was personally responsible for inviting many eminent foreign scholars to settle in or simply to visit England, was perpetuated. Their reception was made possible by the generosity of various colleges. When life became difficult for English Protestants in their native land, the trend was reversed. The consequences of prolonged residence on the Continent by these religious refugees cannot be overestimated in the history of English education, as the extensive correspondence relating to this period shows. Those who left England to escape persecution were received with open arms and derived much profit from close contact with some of the finest Hebraists living. Another crucial factor was the development of collegiate instruction. As their wealth increased through endowments and benefactions, individual colleges were able to provide the institutional framework necessary for the expansion of the new learning by appointing lecturers. Provision was made for Hebrew teaching at those foundations which concentrated on the Classics and the scholarly study of the Bible. St John's, Cambridge, is the most notable example.

As a rule English students were introduced to Hebrew at the university, but by 1600 a handful of schools were providing their senior pupils with the necessary groundwork. More would have done so, and thereby kept to their foundation deed, if teachers had been readily available. Private households too made their contribution to

the dissemination of Semitic studies. Since the scholarly remains of the
Tudor gentry are not abundant, any definite appraisal of the place of
Hebrew in their educational pattern is virtually impossible. But the
very fact that Francis Willoughby, Jane Grey, James Whitelocke,
Lady Falkland and other prominent lay people studied the language
indicates that the Hebrew Bible was not regarded solely as the
province of scholarly theologians.

The study of the Hebraic tradition, like every other branch of
Renaissance and Reformation learning, benefited greatly from the
invention of printing. Thanks to the great continental scholar-
publishers, men who were devoted to the learned languages and to an
enlightened study of the Scriptures, sources hitherto unavailable to
Christians found their way into English libraries. Inventories and
library catalogues demonstrate that by the end of the sixteenth century
there was, in addition to Hebrew Bibles and rabbinic commentaries, a
surprising range of manuals and dictionaries on the market. Since the
Targum, the Talmud and the major mediaeval rabbinic works were, in
their original languages, beyond the grasp of the majority of English
Hebraists, the Latin translations provided by Pagninus, Münster,
Fagius and others assumed considerable importance. Both Catholics
and Protestants participated in this drive to provide aids to the study of
Hebrew, but taking the century as a whole, Protestant publications
outnumber those of Catholics.

By the end of the Tudor period the foundations had been laid in
English intellectual circles for sound Hebrew scholarship. Even
allowing for the early biographers' capacity for flattery and
posthumous exaggeration, England could boast of a small but
impressive group of gifted linguists who had a wide knowledge of
Hebrew literature. It is as well to remember that when James I decided
in 1604 to have yet another version of the Bible in the vernacular, he
had no difficulty in finding twenty-five qualified translators who could
be trusted to render the Old Testament into the king's English and at
the same time to respect the *hebraica veritas*. It will be readily
admitted that none of them equalled in eminence the great continental
Hebraists such as Reuchlin and Pagninus, or devoted themselves to the
intensive study of the language as Münster did. But these Elizabethan
scholars certainly prepared the way for the weighty contributions of
later generations of English students to Semitic scholarship. They
imparted their enthusiasm for the Hebraic tradition to those who came
after them. The seed which they planted fell on good ground, and in

the following century bore much fruit.

Notes

1 *The University of Cambridge*, vol. II, p. 418.
2 *A History of the University of Oxford*, vol. II, p. 147.
3 *A Book of Essays*, p. 3. Cf. K. Charlton, *Education in Renaissance England*, London 1965, p. 160.
4 *A True Chronologie*, p. 202.
5 See above p. 32.

Appendix I

A partial list of those who held the Hebrew lectureship at St John's College, Cambridge from 1534 to 1605. The names are taken from the MS. lists of college rentals compiled by F. P. White.

1534–35	John Redman
1544–45	Robert Horne
1546–48	William Barker
1548	James Pilkington
1555–58	Christopher Brown
1558–59	Thomas Willan
1559–61	Thomas Wilson
1561–64	Richard Longworth
1564–66	Richard Curtes
1566–69	William Fulke
1569–72	Anthony Chevallier
1572–73	John Knewstubb
1573–75	Walter Barker
1575–80	Andrew Downes
1580–85	Dyas
1585–87	Richard Clayton
1587–90	?
1590–93	William Billingsley
1593–95	Thomas Playfere
1595–99	Arthur Johnson
1599–1605	Robert Spalding

Appendix II

A list of Hebrew and Aramaic books extracted from the catalogue of John Dee's private library. The catalogue was compiled by Dee himself and completed on 6 September 1583. The entries are copied verbatim from the copy of the catalogue which is in the British Library (MS. Harleian 1879). The books are numbered for easy reference.

Hebraïci. Chald. compacti.

1 Concordantiae hebraïcae Rabbi Mardochai Nathan. translatae per Anton. Reuchlin. H. Petri. Basil 1556.
2 R. David Kimchi liber radicum, sive thesaurus linguae sanctae vel dictionarium hebraïcum. Ven. Daniel Bomb.
3 Joh. Reuchlin Lexicon hebraïcum et in hebraeorum grammatican commentaria. Basil 1537.
4 Eliae Levitae Methurgeman, Sive Lexicon Chaldaïcum. Isnae 1541.
5 Psalterium hebraïcum, graecum, Arabicum et Chaldaïcum, cum tribus latinis interpretationibus et glossis per Augustinum Justinianum Genuensem. Genue 1516.
6 David Kiberi Tabulae decem gramm. heb. Basil 1546.
7 R. David Kimchi in psalmos, hebraïcè. Isnae.
8 Joh. Bolezaei Tabulae sive compendium ling. sanctae. Paris 1566.
9 Biblia hebraïca. Ven. Daniel Bomberg.
10 Pentateuchus Mosis cum quinque Magnis canticis, videl. Cantica Canticorum; Ruth; Threni; Ecclesiastes & Esther. hebraïcè cum latina versione & annotationibus ex rabbinorum, Augustini Justiniani. Ven. 1551.
11 Sanctis Pagnini Thesaurus linguae sanctae. contractior. Rob. Stephanus 1548.
12 Eiusdem Pagnini hebraïcarum institutionum seu gramm. libri quattuor. Rob. Stephanus 1549.
13 Eliae Levitae Grammatica hebraïca. Isnae.
14 Joh. Cellarii Gnostopolitae isagogicon in hebraeas literas. Haganoae Anshelm. 1518.
15 Joh. Merceri Grammatica chaldaïca. Item de abbreviaturis hebraeorum libellus. Paris Wilhel. Morel 1560.
16 Joh. Cheradami Rudimenta Grammaticae hebraïcae. Paris.
17 Gilberti Genebrardi Isagoge ad legenda rabinorum commentaria.
18 Eliae Levitae Thesbites, Seu lexicon Hebraïcum cum versione latina

Pauli Fagii. Isnae.
19 Sententiae Morales Ben Syrae hebraïcè cum versione Pauli Fagii. Item Tobias hebraïcè cum latina vers. Isnae 1542.
20 Sepher Aemanah. id est liber fidei, hebraïcè cum latina versione Pauli Fagii. Isnae 1540
21 Pauli Fagii exegesis dictionum in quatuor capita Geneseos. Isnae 1542.
22 Joh. Vallensis de prosodia hebraeorum libri quatuor. Paris 1545.
23 Genesis Mosis hebraïcè. Paris Wechel 1536.
24 Agathii Guidacerii in Cantica Canticorum Salomonis, expositio. Paris 1531.
25 Sebastiani Munsteri Grammatica chaldaica. Froben 1527.
26 Seb. Munsteri dictionarium chaldaicum. Froben 1527.
27 R. Abraham Hispani ben R. Haya Sephaera mundi ad annotationibus Munsteri. Basil 1546.
28 Elementa linguae Syriacae. Vicennes 1555.
29 R. Simeonis Logica hebraïca cum Munsteri versione latine. Froben 1527.
30 Evangelium Matthaei heb. latinum. Item Epistola ad Hebraeos per Munsterum. Basil HP [Henricus Petri] 1557.
31 Martin Martinez Grammatica hebraïca. Paris 1548.
32 Precationes Biblicae heb. graecae et latinae. Paris 1554.
33 Eliae Levitae anomala hebraïca latine per Seb. Munsterum. Basil HP 1536.
34 Agathii Guidacerii Grammatica hebraïca. Paris 1537.
35 Psalterium David cum radicibus in margine hebraïcè per Antonio Margarita genere Israelitum. Lipsiae 1533.
36 Eliae Levitae Composita verborum et nominum hebraïcorum latinè per Munsterum. Froben 1525.
37 Augustinus Sebastianus Nouzenus de prima sermonis hebraïci lectione. Marpurg 1532.
38 Item Nicolai Clenardi Grammatica heb. Col. 1561.
39 Munsteri dictionarium hebraïcum. Froben 1548.
40 R. David Kimchi liber Michlol gramm. ling. sanctae. Daniel Bombergus Venice 1534.
41 Praecepta Judaïca 613 affirmativa cum rabbinorum expositione per Seb. Munsterum. HP Basil 1533.
42 Wigandi Happelii Grammatica heb. Basil 1561.
43 Eliae Levitae Grammatica heb. a Seb. Munstero versa & scholiis illust. & Froben 1543.
44 Matthaei Aurogalli libellus de locis, populisque hebraeorum. Witeb. 1536.
45 Proverbia Salomonis heb latina cum annotationibus Seb. Munsteri. Froben. Basle.
46 Jonas propheta cum versione latina et exercitatione grammaticali Wigandi Happellii. Basileae 1561.
47 Joh. Isaaci defensio veritatis hebraicae sacrarum scripturarum adversus Wilhelmi Lindani libros tres de optimo scripturas interpretandi ratione. Colon. 1559.

48 Canticum Canticorum et Ecclesiastes Chaldaica paraphrasi cum versione latina Erasmi Oswaldi Schreckenfuchsii HP Bas. 1553.
49 Sanctis Pagnini Epitome Thesauri ling. sanctae. Plantin 1570.
50 Joh. Avenarii Grammatica hebraïca. Witeb. 1562.
51 Joh. Avenarii Grammatica hebraïca. Witeb. 1570.
52 Godescalci praetorii Grammatica hebraïca. Oporin. Basil 1558.
53 Eliae Levitae Grammatica hebraïca ex versione latina Munsteri cum aliis Munsteri. Froben 1537.
54 Eliae Levitae Capitula Cantica, specierum, proprietatum et officiorum in quibus scilicet agitur de literis, punctis et quibusdam accentibus hebraïcis cum versione lat Munsteri. Froben 1527.
55 Eliae Levitae accentuum hebraicorum liber. Eiusdem Sepher masoreth hammasoreth per Munsterum. Basle 1539.
56 Rabbi David Kimchi libri Michlol, grammatices linguae sanctae, pars prima cum versione lat ad verbum Agathii Guidacerii. Parisiis in collegio Italorum 1546.
57 Messias Christianorum et Judaeorum hebraïcè et lat per Munsterum. HP Basil 1539.
58 Michael Neandri Grammatica hebraïca. Oporin 1563.
59 Psalmi David hebraïcè. Froben 1538.

The following titles are listed in the general catalogue:

60 Concordantiae Bibliorum. R. Stephanus.
61 Joh. Forsteri Lexicon Hebraicum. Froben 1564.
62 Proverbia; Joel; Micheas; Zacharias; heb. chald. graec. latine et germanice per Joh. Draconitem Witeb. 1564.

Appendix III

Appended below is a list of Hebrew and Aramaic books owned by dons and booksellers in sixteenth-century Oxford and Cambridge. Except in the case of John Dorne, the titles come from the inventories made after the death of each individual. The date is that of probate. The approximate number of books in each person's study or bookshop is also recorded. Abbreviations have been expanded and some titles clarified.

Oxford

The following lists are compiled from the transcripts made by Walter Mitchell of the Bodleian Library from the registers of the Chancellor's Court. The inventory of Dorne's books has been published by F. Madan, *The Day Book of John Dorne*, Collectanea, Oxford 1920. The biographical details are taken from J. Foster, *Alumni Oxonienses*, Oxford 1891.

1520
John DORNE, Bookseller   Total books: 1851
   Alphabetum hebraicum

1530
William WOODROFE, After clandestine flight   Total books: 39
   Primarium hebraicum
   Alphabetum hebraicum

1543
Master BYSLEY, ?   Total books: 127
   Münster: Grammatica hebraica
   Grammatica hebraica chaldeaque
   Vetus Testamentum hebraice
   Genesis hebraice

1552
James BICTON, Fellow of Christ Church, B.A. 1545   Total books: 4
   Tabula hebraica

1566
Richard CLYFF, Chaplain of Christ Church, B.A. 1555   Total books: 256
   Alphabetum hebraicum
   Dictionarium hebraicum
   Dictionarium chaldaicum
   Biblia hebraica

Genesis hebraice
Psalterium hebraicum
Proverbia hebraice
Interpretatio nominum hebraicorum

1568
Thomas DAYE, Fellow of All Souls, B.C.L. 1521   Total books: 168
    Biblia cum annotationibus hebraicis

1570
Robert HERT, ?   Total books: 164
    Joel et Malachias hebraice

1571
Robert HOOPER, Master of Balliol, B.A. 1558   Total books: 77
    Grammatica hebraica

1575
Nicholas LUMBARD, Fellow of Magdalen, B.A. 1567–68   Total books: 150
    Avenarius: Grammatica hebraica
    Isaacus: Grammatica hebraica
    Quinquarboreus: Grammatica hebraica
    Biblia hebraica Stephani

1576
Philip JOHNSON, Principal of St Edmund Hall, B.A. 1566   Total books: 330
    Campensis: Grammatica hebraica
    Münster: Grammatica hebraica
    Pagninus: Epitome lexicon hebraicum
    Biblia hebraica [7 vols]
    Münster: Annotaciones hebraice latine
John TATAM, Rector of Lincoln, B.A. 1563   Total books: 219
    Clenardus: Grammatica hebraica
    Pagninus: Epitome lexicon hebraicum

1577
Thomas STANDLEY, At Brasenose, B.A. 1574–75   Total books: 41
    Schyndlerus: Grammatica hebraica

1578
Nicholas CLIFTON, Bookseller,   Total books: 316
    Godescalcus: Grammatica hebraica
    Grammatica hebraica
    Reuchlin: De rudimentis linguae hebraeae
    Lexicon hebraicum
John HORNSLEY, Fellow of Magdalen, B.A. 1573   Total books: 88
    Avenarius: Grammatica hebraica
    Campensis: Grammatica hebraica
Thomas POPE, Student of Gloucester Hall, B.A. 1572   Total books: 39
    Genesis hebraice

Psalmi hebraice

1584

Thomas MORREY, Student of Christ Church, B.A. 1571–72   Total books: 186
   Grammatica hebraica
   5 Hebrew books
Anthony TYE, Fellow of Oriel, B.A. 1570–71   Total books: 108
   Campensis: Grammatica hebraica
   Münster: Grammatica hebraica
   Thesaurus Stephani
   Genesis hebraice
   Psalmi hebraice

1587

Edward HIGGINS, Fellow of Brasenose, B.A. 1575   Total books: 338
   Bertramus: Grammatica hebraica
   Clavius: Elementa linguae hebraeae
   Junius: Grammatica hebraica [2 copies]
   Tremellius et Isaacus: Grammatica hebraica
   Phrases hebraicae
   Pagninus: Thesaurus
   Biblia hebraica [7 vols]

1588

Thomas NEWBIE, Fellow of Lincoln, B.A. 1582–83   Total books: 43
   Clenardus: Grammatica hebraica
   Martinius: Grammatica hebraica
   Lexicon hebraicum
   Hosea in Hebrew
   Part of a Hebrew Bible

1597

R. PAINE, ?   Total books: 31
   Hebrew Grammar
   Hebrew Lexicon
   Hebrew Psalter

1599

William MITCHELL, Fellow of Queen's, B.A. 1584–85   Total books: 264
   Martinius: Grammatica hebraica
   Udall: Grammatica hebraica
   Vigandus: Grammatica hebraica
   Pagninus: Thesaurus
   Genesis hebraice

1603

George BARTON, Fellow of Brasenose, B.A. 1588   Total books: 12
   Two of my best Hebrew Grammars to Mr. Johnes. I give to my
   chamberfellow Mr. Taylor my Hebrew notes.

Cambridge

For the biographical details of the scholars mentioned below I have relied on J. and J. A. Venn, *Alumni Cantabrigienses*. The titles of books are taken from various sources: W. M. Palmer, 'College dons, country clergy and university coachmen', *Proceedings of the Cambridge Antiquarian Society*, 1912, pp. 190 ff; G. J. Gray and W. M. Palmer, *Abstracts from the Wills and Testamentary Documents of Printers, Binders and Stationers of Cambridge from 1504 to 1699*, Bibliographical Society, London 1915; transcripts of inventories containing book lists exhibited for probate in the Vice-Chancellor's court, drawn up by Dr E. S. Leedham-Green of Cambridge University Library.

1521
Bryan ROWE, Vice-Provost of King's, B.A. 1507   Total books: 101
    Alphabetum hebraicum
    Grammatica hebraica

1539
Edward MOORE, Fellow of St Catharine's, B.A. 1528–29   Total books: 111
    Bibliander: Grammatica hebraica
    Reuchlin: De accentibus et orthographia linguae hebraicae
    Münster: Dictionarium hebraicum
    Psalterium hebraicum cum radicibus
    Proverbia Salomonis cum libro compositione
    Ecclesiastes Münsteri
    Praecepta Mosaica Münster interprete
    De articulis fidei Iudaeorum

1540
Richard BULLAR, Fellow of Christ's, B.A. 1536–37   Total books: 73
    Proverbia Salomonis hebraica

?1543
? MALTBY, Christ's   Total books: 89
    Münster: Grammatica hebraica
    Dictionarium hebraicum

1545
Miles EGLESFIELD, Fellow of Christ's, B.A. 1537–38   Total books: 103
    Genesis hebraice
Benedict KYTBALDE, Fellow of Caius, B.A. 1540–41   Total books: 56
    Clenardus: Grammatica hebraica
Nicholas PILGRIM, Bookseller   Total books: 143
    Clenardus: Tabulae hebraicae [3 copies]
    Clenardus: Grammatica hebraica [2 copies]
    Fagius: Dictionarium hebraicum
    Levita: Thesbites hebraice
    Biblia hebraica et latina Münsteri

Psalterium hebraicum Campensis
Psalterium hebraicum cum commentario
Psalterium hebraicum grece et latine
Esaias hebraice et latine
Cantica Canticorum hebraice [Levita]
Evangelium Matthei hebraice [Münster]
Josephus hebraice et latine
John THOMAS, Lic. Chir. 1513   Total books: 60
  Bibliander: Grammatica hebraica
Edward WYGAN, Fellow of King's B.A. 1508–09   Total books: 186
  Capito: Grammatica hebraica

1546
Oliver AINSWORTH, Fellow of Jesus, B.A. 1529–30   Total books: 202
  Münster: Grammatica hebraica
  Grammatica hebraica
  Dictionarium hebraicum
  Reuchlin: Dictionarium hebraicum
  Genesis hebraice
  Psalterium hebraicum
  Interpretationes nominum hebraicorum
William BUCKMASTER, Fellow of King's Hall, B.A. 1513–14   Total books: 99
  Münster: Institutio hebraica
Alice EDWARDS, Widow of John Edwards, Fellow of Corpus, d. 1542   Total books: 21
  A Hebrew book
Thomas GREENWOOD, Fellow of Clare   Total books: 123
  Psalterium hebraicum
Roger SORESBYE, Fellow of Peterhouse, B.A. 1537–38   Total books: 198
  Grammatica hebraica
  Rudimenta hebraica [? Reuchlin]
  Dictionarium hebraicum
  Accentium hebraicorum
  Primus liber legis hebraici
  Annotationes in Proverbia hebraice

1547
Christopher LEVYNS, Scholar of Corpus, 1544   Total books: 24
  Cleonardus: Grammatica hebraica

1548
? NEVELL, Trinity Hall   Total books: 89
  Campensis: Grammatica hebraica
  Levita: Grammatica hebraica
  Reuchlin: Grammatica hebraica
  Clenardus: Grammatica hebraica
  Dictionarium hebraicum
  Biblia hebraica, greca et latina [4 vols.]

Psalterium hebraicum
Psalterium hebraicum et latinum
Psalterium quinque linguarum
Reuchlin: septem psalmos
5 libri hebraici

1549
Paul FAGIUS, Professor of Hebrew   Total books: 9
  Libri hebraici ligati et non ligati

1550
Edmund PIERPOINT, Master of Jesus, B.A. 1536–37   Total books: 83
  Grammatica hebraica
Godfrey GYLPYN, Fellow of Christ's, B.A. 1532–33   Total books: 121
  Reuchlin: De rudimentis hebraicis

1551
Richard GILDEN, Fellow of Jesus, B.A. 1548–49   Total books: 9
  Lexicon hebraicum
  Esaias hebraice, grece et latine
  Proverbia hebraice
  Job hebraice
Christopher WALKER, Fellow of Magdalen, B.A. 1547–48   Total books: 36
  Psalterium hebraicum

1556
William SEGRAVE, Corpus, Admitted 1552   Total books: 46
  Expositiones divi Jeronimi in hebraicas questiones
Nicholas SHAXTON, Fellow of Caius, B.A. 1506–07   Total books: 138
  Münster: Evangelium Matthei hebraice
  Psalterium quintuplex

1558
John ATKINSON, Fellow of Peterhouse, B.A. 1547–48   Total books: 129
  Grammatica hebraica [2 copies]
Christopher BROWN, Fellow of John's and Heb. Lect., B.A. 1535–36   Total books: 151
  Münster: Grammatica hebraica
  Martinius: Hebraicus liber unus [? Grammar]
  Lexicon hebraicum
  Thesaurus linguae hebraicae
  Dictionarium chaldaicum
  De accentibus hebraicis [? Reuchlin]
  Biblia hebraica cum commentario [2 vols.]
  Vetus Testamentum hebraice et latine
  Psalterium hebraicum
  Commentaria Rabbi hebraica
  Logica Rabbi hebraica
  Institutiones hebraicae [? Kimchi]

Kalendarium hebraicum Münster
Elia Hebreus [? Levita]
Several other Hebrew books of which the title could not be read
(Palmer, *op. cit.* p. 191)
William GOCKMAN, Fellow of St John's, B.A. 1539–40   Total books: 152
Grammatica hebraica
John SALT, Fellow of Pembroke, B.A. 1546–47   Total books: 71
Psalterium hebraicum
ANON 1, (this and the following three entries are possibly pre-
1558)   Total books: 101
Clenardus: Tabula hebraica
Bibliander: Grammatica hebraica
Münster: Grammatica hebraica
Münster: Dictionarium hebraicum
Levita: De punctis hebraicis
Fagius: De sententiis hebraicis
Institutiones hebraicae [? Kimchi]
Biblia hebraica
Genesis hebraice
Münster: Esaias hebraice, grece et latine
Psalterium hebraicum
Proverbia Salomonis hebraice
ANON 2   Total books: 83
Reuchlin: De rudimentis hebraicis
ANON 3   Total books: 60
Biblia hebraica
Psalterium hebraicum [2 copies]
Proverbia Salomonis hebraice
ANON 4   Total books: 89
Campensis: Grammatica hebraica
Clenardus: Grammatica hebraica
Levita: Grammatica hebraica
Reuchlin: Grammatica hebraica
Dictionarium hebraicum [2 copies]
Biblia hebraica, greca et latina
Psalterium hebraicum
Psalterium hebraicum et latinum
Liber hebraicus
4 libri hebraici

1559
John BATEMAN, Fellow of Caius, B.A. 1545–46   Total books: 425
Tabula in grammaticam hebraicam
Mercer: Tabula in grammaticam chaldaicam
Grammatica hebraica [5 copies]
Radices hebraicae [2 vols.]
Levita: hebraice
Lexicon chaldaicum

Dictionarium chaldaicum, grecum et latinum
Biblia hebraica
Quinque libri legis hebraice
Prophesia Ezechielis hebraice
Psalterium hebraicum
Precationes Biblia hebraica, greca et latina
Libri quattuor hebraicarum institutionum
Sententiae hebraeorum

Miles BUCKLEY, Fellow of St John's, B.A. 1551–52   Total books: 148
Grammatica hebraica
De accentibus hebreis
Levita: Thesbites hebraice
Vocabularium hebraicum chaldaicum
Institutiones hebraicae
Münster: In hebreicam [3 vols.]
Biblia hebraica cum commentario [2 vols.]
Biblia hebraica et latina
Psalterium hebraice, grece, arabice et chaldaeum
Quidam psalmi Davidis hebraice
Two other Hebrew books of the Bible
Sententiae morales hebraicae
Sententiae elegantiae hebraicae
13 small Hebrew books
Münster: Evangelium Matthei hebraice

Richard EDYLL, Fellow of Jesus, B.A. 1545–46   Total books: 44
Institutiones hebraicae
Dictionarium hebraicum
Quinque libri legis hebraice
Jeremias propheta hebraice

1560

Robert PEMBER, Fellow of Trinity, B.A. 1523–24   Total books: 160
Münster: Grammatica hebraica
Grammatica chaldaica
Dictionarium hebraicum
Dictionarium chaldaicum
Biblia hebraica
Prophetia Jeremie hebraice
Psalterium iuxta hebraicam veritatem [2 copies9
Septem psalmi penetentiales hebraice et latine [Reuchlin]
Proverbia Salomonis hebraice et latine
Ecclesiastes iuxta hebraicam veritatem
Liber hebraicus

George ALLSOPE/HAWSOPP, Fellow of Queens', B.A. 1550–51   Total books: 89
Capito: De hebraica [? Grammatica]
Pellican: hebraica [? Grammatica]
Reuchlin: De rudimentis hebraicis

1563
John LAKYN, Master of Jesus, B.A. 1552–53   Total books: 42
    Grammatica hebraica
    Kimchi: Institutiones hebraicae
    Vocabularium hebraicum
    Pars Biblia hebraica
    Psalterium hebraicum

1566
John DAKINS, Fellow of St John's, B.A. 1559–60   Total books: 46
    Münster: Grammatica hebraica
    Quinquarboreus: Grammatica hebraica

1567
Robert BEAUMONT, Master of Trinity, B.A. 1543–44   Total books: 118
    Biblia hebraica
Richard KYNGE, Fellow of Christ's, B.A. 1559–60   Total books: 65
    Dictionarium hebraicum
    Biblia hebraica

1568
John STOKES, Master of Queens', B.A. 1540–41   Total books: 94
    Münster: Dictionarium hebraicum

1569
William LYFFE, Fellow of Trinity, B.A. 1562–63   Total books: 122
    Isaacus: Grammatica hebraica
Martin PARKINSON, Fellow of Trinity, B.A. 1558–59   Total books: 151
    Grammatica chaldaica
    De lectione hebraica
    Münster: Dictionarium hebraicum
    Dictionarium chaldaicum

1571
Robert SMITH, Fellow of St John's, B.A. 1567–68   Total books: 57
    A Hebrew Grammar
    One half of a Hebrew Grammar
ANON 5, (Thomas F . . .)   Total books: 85
    Clenardus: Tabula hebraica

1573–4
ANON 6   Total books: 113
    Münster: Biblia hebraica et latina
    Genesis hebraice
    Proper mannes in Hebrew [? prophetae minores *or* interpretatio nominum
    hebraicorum]
ANON 7   Total books: 102
    Clenardus: Tabula hebraica
    Münster: Lexicon hebraicum
    Biblia hebraica Plantini
    Psalterium hebraicum

Pars Bibliae hebraicae manuscriptae

1576

Walter BARKER, Priest and pensioner of Jesus (? formerly Hebrew lecturer at John's)   Total books: 86
  Grammatica hebraica
  Martinius: Grammatica hebraica

Nicholas SHARPE, Fellow of Trinity, B.A. 1570–71   Total books: 113
  Avenarius: Grammatica hebraica
  Pagninus: Grammatica hebraica
  Isaacus: Grammatica hebraica
  Fabritius: Institutiones hebraicae
  Bertram: Liber hebraicus [? Grammar]
  Levita: De accentibus
  Biblia hebraica [2 copies]
  Paraphrasis Hosea prophetae hebraice
  Paraphrasis in Psalterium hebraicum
  Oratio R. Wakfeldi de laudibus et utilitate trium linguarum
  Liber hebraicus

1578

John DENYS, Bookseller   Total books: 523
  Chevalier: Grammatica hebraica
  Isaacus: Grammatica hebraica
  Martinius: Grammatica hebraica [3 copies]
  Biblia hebraica Plantini
  Biblia hebraica Plantini cum Novo Testamento greco

1579

William MYDSON, Fellow of Pembroke, B.A. 1575–76   Total books: 19
  Dictionarium hebraicum
  Genesis hebraice

Edmund ROBERTS, Fellow of St John's, B.A. 1572–73   Total books: 70
  Chevalier: Grammatica hebraica
  Clenardus: Grammatica hebraica
  Martinius: Grammatica hebraica
  Psalterium hebraicum

1581

Edward HAWFORD, Master of Christ's, B.A. 1542–43   Total books: 117
  Isaias hebraice

ANON 8   Total books: 118
  Isaias hebraicolatine

1583

Ambrose BARKER, Fellow of Christ's, B.A. 1571–72   Total books: 135
  Junius: Grammatica hebraica
  D. Kimchi: Hebraicae [? Institutiones]
  Pagninus: Lexicon hebraicum
  Münster: Dictionarium hebraicum

Biblia hebraica Plantini
Biblia hebraica
Biblia Complutensis
Psalterium hebraicum [3 copies]
Hester, Proverbia et Ecclesiastes hebraice
Robert WHITLIE, Chapel Clerk of Trinity   Total books: 51
Martinius: Grammatica hebraica

1586
Thomas BOUND, Fellow of Corpus, B.A. 1575–76   Total books: 48
Biblia hebraica

1588
ANON 9   Total books: 771
Bertram: Grammatica hebraica
Förster: Dictionarium hebraicum
Biblia hebraica [3 copies]
Prophetae Minores hebraice
Münster: Evangelium Mattei hebraicolatine
Talmud hebraice

1589
Andrew PERNE, Master of Peterhouse, B.A. 1537–38   Total books: 2540
Tabula hebraica
Clavis elementorum hebraicorum
Avenarius: Grammatica hebraica
Bayne: Grammatica hebraica
Clenardus: Grammatica hebraica
Shindlerus: Grammatica hebraica
Martinius: Grammatica hebraica
Fagius: Grammatica hebraica
Münster: Grammatica hebraica [2 copies]
Isaacus: Grammatica hebraica [2 copies]
Pagninus: Grammatica hebraica [2 copies]
Elenare: Grammatica hebraica
Haprorius: Grammatica hebraica
Junius: Grammatica hebraica
Münster: Grammatica chaldaica
Kimchi: Michlol
Avenarius: Lexicon hebraicum
Förster: Dictionarium hebraicum
Münster: Dictionarium hebraicum
Münster: Dictionarium trilingue
Pagninus: Dictionarium hebraicum
Pagninus: Thesaurus
Levita: Dictionarium hebraicum Thesbites
Levita: Lexicon chaldaicum
Dictionarium hebraicum unbound
Kimchi: Dictionarium hebraicum in comm.

Biblia hebraica cum commentariis hebraicis
Biblia hebraica Stephani [3 copies]
Biblia hebraica Hutteri
Biblia hebraica Arie Montani [8 vols.]
Biblia Münsteri duobus
Biblia hebraica Plantini
Idem cum apoc. greca
Biblia hebraica greca et latina Vatabli
Pentateuchum cum annotationibus hebraice
Jeremias et Ezekiel hebraice
Hosea hebraice cum commentariis
D. Kimchi in tres prophetas
Psalterium hebraicum
Psalmi hebraice
Proverbia hebraice
Commentarii in Psalmos hebraice [Kimchi]
Elias hebraice in Cantica
Leviticus hebraice [? Levita]
Selecte sententiae hebraice latine [Fagius]
Phrases linguae hebraicae [Stephanus]
Fagius super Thargum
Grammatica Quinquarborei [Targum on Lam., Ob., Jon.]
Josephus hebraice [Joseph ben Gorion]
Matheus hebraice [Münster: 2 copies]
Levita: Nomenclatura hebrea
Concordantiae hebraicae
Abraham TILLMAN, Fellow of Corpus, B.A. 1583–84   Total books: 79
    Biblia hebraica

1590
Reynold BRIDGES, Bookseller   Total books: 296
    Bertramus: Grammatica hebraica

1592
Michael BRISLEY, Fellow of Trinity Hall, Ll.B. 1588   Total books: 57
    Psalmi Davidis in Hebrew and Greek
John MOTE, ? (had many of Perne's books)   Total books: 500
    Psalterium hebraicum

1593
John COCK, Fellow of Emmanuel, B.A. 1579–80   Total books: 96
    Chevalier: Grammatica hebraica
    Martinius: Grammatica hebraica [2 copies]
    Levita: Grammatica hebraica
    Avenarius: Lexicon hebraicum
    Lexicon hebraicum
    Biblia hebraica [3 copies]
    Second part of the Hebrew Bible
    Proverbia Salomonis hebraice

Hebrew Concordance

1600
John SHAXTON, Fellow of Trinity, B.A. 1577–78   Total books: 97
  Bellarmine: Grammatica hebraica
  Martinius: Grammatica hebraica
  Pagninus: Lexicon hebraicum
  Biblia hebraica [2 copies]
  Biblia hebraice et latine

Select bibliography

Primary sources are cited in the notes, but are not listed in the bibliography.

Abrahams, I., 'Pico della Mirandola', *HUCA*, Jubilee vol. 1925.

Ackroyd, P. R. and Evans, C. F., *The Cambridge History of the Bible*, vol. I, Cambridge 1970.

Ages, A., 'Luther and the Rabbis', *JQR*, N.S., vol. LVIII, 1967–8.

Alexander, J. D., 'The Genevan Version of the Bible: its origin, translation and influence', unpublished D. Phil. thesis, University of Oxford 1957.

Allen, P. S. and H.M. (eds.), *Letters of Richard Fox 1486–1527*, Oxford 1929.

Anderson, C., *Annals of the English Bible*, London 1845.

Armstrong, E., *Robert Estienne: Royal Printer*, Cambridge 1954.

Attwater, A., *Pembroke College Cambridge: a Short History*, Cambridge 1936.

Baer, I., 'Rashi and the historical reality of his time', *Tarbiz*, vol. XX, 1949.

Bainton, R. H. and Lockwood, D. P., 'Classical and biblical scholarship in the age of the Renaissance and Reformation', *Church History*, vol X, No. 1, 1941.

Bainton, R. H. and Gritsch, E. W., *Bibliography of the Continental Reformation*, Archon Press, USA, 1972.

Baker, T., *History of the College of St John the Evangelist Cambridge*, ed. J. E. B. Mayor, Cambridge 1869.

Baldwin, T. W., *William Shakspere's Small Latine and Lesse Greeke*. Urbana 1944.

Barksdale, C., *A Remembrancer of Excellent Men*, London 1670.

Baron, S. W., *A Social and Religious History of the Jews*, vol. XIII, New York 1969.

——, 'John Calvin and the Jews', in *Harry Austryn Wolfson Jubilee Volume*, Jerusalem 1965.

Baroni, V., *La Contre-Réforme devant la Bible*, Lausanne 1943.

Barr, J., 'St. Jerome's appreciation of Hebrew', *BJRL*, vol. 49, No. 2, 1967.

Bataillon, M., *Erasme et l'Espagne*, Paris 1937.

Bauch, G., 'Die Einführung des Hebräischen in Wittenberg', *MGWJ*, Band 48, N.F. 12, 1904.

Bauckham, R. J., 'The career and thought of Doctor William Fulke (1537–1589)', unpublished Ph.D. thesis, University of Cambridge 1972.

——, *Tudor Apocalypse*, Appleford 1978.

Baumgartner, A. J., *Calvin hebraïsant et interprète de l'Ancien Testament*, Genève 1889.

——, *De l'Enseignement de l'hébreu chez les Protestants à partir de l'époque de la Réformation*, Lausanne 1889.

Becker, W., *Immanuel Tremellius: ein Proselyten-Leben in Zeitalter der Reformation*, 2nd ed., Leipzig 1891.

Bell, A. F. G., *Benito Arias Montano*, Hispanic Society of America 1922.

Bell, H. E., *An Introduction to the history and records of the Court of Wards and Liveries*, Cambridge 1953.

Blau, J. L., *The Christian Interpretation of the Cabala in the Renaissance*, New York 1944.

Bluhm, H., *Martin Luther: Creative Translator*, St Louis, Miss. 1965.

——, ' "Five Sundry Interpreters": the sources of the first printed English Bible', *Huntington Library Quarterly*, vol. XXXIX, 1975–6.

Boase, C. V. (ed.), *Register of the University of Oxford*, Oxford 1885.

Boehmer, H., *Road to Reformation*, Philadelphia, Pa. 1946.

Borgeaud, C., *Histoire de l'Université de Genève: l'Académie de Calvin 1559–1798*, Genève 1900.

Bornkamm, H., *Luther and the Old Testament*, Eng. trans. J. B. Mohr, Fortress Press 1966.

Bowman, J., 'A forgotten controversy', *Evangelical Quarterly*, vol. 20, 1948.

Box, G. H., 'Hebrew studies in the Reformation period and after: their place and influence', *The Legacy of Israel*, ed. C. Singer, Oxford 1928.

Brod, M., *Johannes Reuchlin und sein Kampf*, Stuttgart 1965.

Broderick, C., *Memorials of Merton College*, Oxford 1885.

Brosseder, J., *Luthers Stellung zu den Juden im Spiegel seiner Interpreten*, Munich 1972.

Breen, Q., *John Calvin: a study in French Humanism*, 2nd ed., Archon Books, Grand Rapids 1968.

Burmeister, K. H., *Sebastian Münster: eine Bibliographie mit 22 Abbildungen*, Wiesbaden 1964.

——, *Sebastian Münster: Versuch eines biographischen Gesamtbildes*, Basel und Stuttgart 1963.

Butterworth, C. C., *The Literary Lineage of the King James Bible, 1340–1611*, Philadelphia, Pa. 1941.

Callus, D. A., *Robert Grosseteste: Scholar and Bishop*, Oxford 1955.

Carlisle, N., *A Concise Description of the Endowed Grammar Schools of England and Wales*, London 1818.

Chadwick, O., 'The sixteenth century', in *The English Church and the Continent*, London 1959.

Chambers, R. W., *Thomas More*, London 1935.

Charlton, K., *Education in Renaissance England*, London 1965.

Chester, J. L., *John Rogers*, London 1861.

Chomsky, W. (ed.), *David Kimhi's Hebrew Grammar*, New York 1952.

Chrisman, M. V., *Strasbourg and the Reform*, New Haven, Conn. 1967.

Christ, K., *Die Bibliothek Reuchlins in Pforzheim*, Leipzig 1924.

Christen, E., *Zwingli avant la Réforme de Zurich*, Genève 1899.

Clair, C., *Christopher Plantin*, London 1960.

Clark, A., *Register of the University of Oxford*, Oxford 1887.

Clarke, J. W., *Endowments of the University of Cambridge*, Cambridge 1904.

Clarke, S., *The Lives of thirty-two English Divines*, London 1677.

Clebsch, W. A., *England's Earliest Protestants 1520–1535*, New Haven, Conn. 1964.

Cobban, A. B., *The King's Hall within the University of Cambridge in the Later Middle Ages*, Cambridge 1969.

Cohen, C., 'Martin Luther and his Jewish contemporaries', *Jewish Social Studies*, vol. 25, No. 3, 1963.

Collinson, P., *The Elizabethan Puritan Movement*, London 1967.

——, *Archbishop Grindal 1519–1583*, London 1979.

Cooper, C. H., *Athenae Cantabrigienses*, Cambridge 1858.

Courvoisier, J., 'Calvin et les Juifs', *Judaica*, vol. II, No. 3, 1946.

Costello, W. T., *The Scholastic Curriculum at Early Seventeenth-Century Cambridge*, Cambridge, Mass. 1958.

Cowley, A. E., 'Hebrew printing', *Bodleian Quarterly Record*, vol. I, No. 8, 1915.

Craig, H., 'The Geneva Bible as a political document', *Pacific Historical Review*, vol. VII, 1938.

Cross, C., *The Puritan Earl: the Life of Henry Hastings, Third Earl of Huntingdon, 1536–1595*, London 1966.

——, 'Continental students and the Protestant Reformation in England in the sixteenth century', in *Reform and Reformation: England and the Continent c1500–c1750, Studies in Church History*, Subsidia 2, ed. D. Baker, Blackwell, Oxford 1979.

Curtis, M. H., *Oxford and Cambridge in Transition 1558–1642*, Oxford 1959.

——, 'Library catalogues in Tudor Oxford and Cambridge', *Studies in the Renaissance*, vol. V, 1958.

Daiches, D., *The King James Version of the English Bible*, Chicago, Ill. 1941.

Darlow, T. H. and Moule, H. F., *Historical Catalogue of the Printed Editions of Holy Scripture*, London 1911.

Deanesly, M., *The Lollard Bible*, reprinted Cambridge 1966.

de Lange, N., *Origen and the Jews*, Cambridge 1976.

de Lubac, H., *Exégèse Médiévale: les quatre sens de l'Ecriture*, Paris 1959–64.

de Molen, R. L., 'Richard Mulcaster and the profession of teaching in sixteenth-century England', *JHI*, vol. 35, No. 1, 1974.

de Sola Pool, D., 'The influence of some Jewish apostates on the Reformation', *JR*, vol. 2, 1911–12.

de Vocht, H., *History of the Foundation and the Rise of the Collegium Trilingue Lovaniense 1517–1550*, Louvain 1951.

——, *Jerome Busleyden, Founder of the Louvain Collegium Trilingue: his life and writings*, Turnhout 1950.

——, 'Thomas Harding', *EHR*, vol. 35, 1920.

Dickens, A. G., *Robert Holgate: Archbishop of York and President of King's Council in the North*, London 1955.

Doumergue, E., *Les Hommes et les Choses du temps de Calvin*, vol. 1, Lausanne 1889.

Duhamel, P. A., 'The Oxford lectures of John Colet', *JHI*, vol. 14, No. 4, 1953.

Einstein, L., *The Italian Renaissance in England*, New York 1902.

Eissfeldt, O., 'Mathaeus Aurogallus' Hebräische Grammatick 1523', *Wissenschaftliche Zeitschrift der Universität Halle–Wittenberg gesellschaftswissenschaftlichsprachwissen-schaftliche*, Reihe VII, 1957–8.

Emden, A. B., *A Biographical Register of the University of Oxford A.D. 1501 to 1540*, Oxford 1974.

Epstein, Levine and Roth, *Essays Presented to J. H. Hertz, Chief Rabbi*, London 1942.

Faerber, R., 'La Communauté anglaise à Strasbourg pendant le règne de Marie (1553–1558)', in *Strasbourg au coeur religieux du XVI siècle*, eds. G. Livet and F. Rapp, Strasbourg 1977.

Farner, O., 'Leo Jud, Zwinglis treuster Helfer', *Zwingliana*, vol. 10, No. 4, 1955.

Fife, R. H., *The Revolt of Martin Luther*, New York 1957.

Firth, K. R., *The Apocalyptic Tradition in Reformation Britain 1530–1645*, Oxford 1979.

Flahiff, G. B., 'Ralph Niger: an introduction to his life and works', *Mediaeval Studies*, vol. II, 1940.

Fletcher, J. M. (ed.), *Registrum Annalium Collegii Mertonensis 1567–1603*, Oxford Hist. Soc. N.S. vol. XXIV, Oxford 1976.

Foster, J., *Alumni Oxonienses*, Oxford 1891–2.

French, P. J., *John Dee: the World of an Elizabethan Magus*, London 1972.

Friedman, J., 'Sebastian Münster, the Jewish mission, and Protestant antisemitism', *Archiv für Reformationsgeschichte*, vol. 70, 1979.

——, 'Sixteenth-century Christian-Hebraica: scripture and the Renaissance myth of the past', *Sixteenth Century Journal*, vol. XI, No. 4, 1980.

Galliner, H., 'Agathias Guidacerius 1477?–1540: an early Hebrew grammarian in Rome and Paris', *Historia Judaica*, vol. II, No. 1, 1940.

Ganoczy, A., *La Bibliothèque de l'Académie de Calvin: le catalogue de 1572 et ses enseignements*, Geneva 1969.

Garrett, C. H., *The Marian Exiles*, Cambridge 1938.

Gauthier, J. D., 'Sanctes Pagninus O.P.', *CBQ*, vol. 7, No. 2, 1945.

Geddes, A., *A Prospectus of a New Translation of the Holy Bible*, Glasgow 1786.

Geiger, L., *Johann Reuchlin: sein Leben und seine Werke*, Leipzig 1871 (reprinted 1964).

——, *Das Studium der hebräischen Sprache in Deutschland vom Ende des XV bis zur mitte des XVI Jahrhunderts*, Breslau 1870.

Godfrey, W. R., 'John Colet of Cambridge', *Archiv für Reformationsgeschichte*, vol. 65, 1974.

Godwin, T., *A Catalogue of the Bishops of England*, London 1615.

Greenslade, S. L. (ed.), *The Work of William Tindale*, London 1938.

——, *The Cambridge History of the Bible*, vol. 3, Cambridge 1963.

Gundersheimer, W. L., *French Humanism 1470–1600*, London 1969.

——, 'Erasmus, humanism and the Christian Cabala', *JWCI*, vol. XXVI, 1963.

Guppy, H., *A Brief Sketch of the History of the Transmission of the Bible*, Manchester 1936.

Hailperin, H., *Rashi and the Christian Scholars*, Pittsburgh, Pa. 1963.

——, 'The Hebrew heritage of Mediaeval Christian biblical scholarship', *Historia Judaica*, vol. V, 1943.

Hall, B., *The Great Polyglot Bibles*, San Francisco, Cal. 1966.

——, *The Genevan Version of the English Bible*, London 1957.

——, *John Calvin: Humanist and Theologian*, London 1956.

——, 'The Reformation city', *BJRL*, vol. 54, No. 1, 1971.

——, 'The Trilingual College of San Ildefonso and the making of the Complutensian Polygot Bible', in *The Church and Academic Learning: Studies in Church History*, vol. 5, ed. G. J. Cuming, Leiden 1969.

Hamilton, A., *The Angel of Syon*, London 1905.

Hammond, G., 'William Tyndale's Pentateuch: its relation to Luther's German Bible and the Hebrew original', *Renaissance Quarterly*, vol. 33, No. 3, 1980.

Harbison, E. H., *The Christian Scholar in the Age of the Reformation*, New York 1956.

Herminjard, J., *Correspondance des Réformateurs*, Paris 1866.

Hexter, J. H., 'The education of the aristocracy in the Renaissance', *Journal of Modern History*, vol. XXII, No. 1, 1950.

Heywood, J., *Collection of Statutes for the University and Colleges of Cambridge*, London 1840.

Hirsch, S. A., *A Book of Essays*, London 1905.

Hirschfeld, H., *A Literary History of Hebrew Grammarians and Lexicographers*, Oxford 1926.

Hobbs, G., 'Martin Bucer on Psalm 22: a study in the application of rabbinic exegesis by a Christian Hebraist', in *Histoire de l'exégèse au XVIe siècle*, eds. O. Fatio and P. Fraenkel, Geneva 1978.

Holborn, H., *Ulrich von Hutten and the German Reformation*, Eng. trans. by R. H. Bainton, New Haven, Conn. 1937.

Holmio, A. K. E., *The Lutheran Reformation and the Jews*, Hancock, 1949.

Hopf, C., *Martin Bucer and the English Reformation*, Oxford 1946.

Horden, J. (ed.), *Icones 1580*, London 1971.

Hunter, A. M., 'The education of Calvin', *Evangelical Quarterly*, vol. 9, 1937.

——, 'The erudition of John Calvin', *Evangelical Quarterly*, vol. 18, 1946.

Hyma, A., 'The origins of English humanism', *Huntington Library Quarterly*, vol. IV, No. 1, 1940.

Ikin, R. G., *Notes on the history of Ely Cathedral Grammar School*, Cambridge 1931.

Jarrot, C. A. L., 'Erasmus' biblical humanism', *Studies in the Renaissance*, vol. 17, 1970.

Jayne, S., *John Colet and Marsilio Ficino*, Oxford 1963.

Jedin, H., *A History of the Council of Trent*, Eng. trans. E. Graf, London 1957–61.

Jewels, E. N., *A History of Archbishop Holgate's Grammar School, York 1546–1946*, York 1963.

Jones, J. G., 'The Wynn family and estate of Gwydir: their origins, growth and development up to 1674', unpublished Ph.D. thesis, University of

Wales 1974.

Josten, C. H., 'A translation of John Dee's "Monas Hieroglyphica" (Antwerp 1564), with an introduction and annotations', *Ambix*, vol. XII, 1964.

Karpman, D., 'William Tyndale's response to the Hebraic tradition', *Studies in the Renaissance*, vol. 14, 1967.

Kearney, H., *Scholars and Gentlemen: Universities and Society in pre-industrial Britain*, London 1970.

Kedar-Kopfstein, B., 'The Vulgate as a translation', unpublished Ph.D. thesis, Hebrew University, Jerusalem 1968.

Kisch, G., *Zasius und Reuchlin*, Constance 1961.

Kittelson, J. M., *Wolfgang Capito: from Humanist to Reformer*, Leiden 1975.

Knappen, M. M., *Tudor Puritanism*, Chicago 1939.

Koenig, W., 'Luther as a student of Hebrew', *Concordia Theological Monthly*, vol. 24, 1953.

Krebs, M. (ed.), *Johannes Reuchlin 1455–1522*, Pforzheim 1955.

Lambert, A., 'Arias Montano', *Dictionnaire d'Histoire et de Géographie Ecclésiastiques*, vol. IV, Paris 1930.

Lefranc, J., *La Jeunesse de Calvin*, Paris 1888.

——, *Histoire du Collège de France*, Paris 1893.

Lehmberg, S. E., *Sir Walter Mildmay and Tudor Government*, Austin, Tex. 1964.

Lenhardt, J. M., 'Protestant Latin Bibles of the Reformation from 1520–1570: a bibliographical account', *CBQ*, vol. 8, No. 4, 1946.

Lewis, J., *The Life and Death of Dr. John Fisher*, London 1885.

Locher, G. W., 'Calvin spricht zu den Juden', *Theologische Zeitschrift*, vol. 23, No. 2, 1967.

Loewe, R. 'The mediaeval history of the Latin Vulgate', *CHB*, vol. 2.

——, 'The mediaeval Christian Hebraists of England', *TJHSE*, vol. 17, 1951–2.

——, 'Jewish scholarship in England', in *Three Centuries of Anglo-Jewish History*, ed. V. D. Lipman, Cambridge 1961.

——, 'Alexander Neckam's knowledge of Hebrew', *Mediaeval and Renaissance Studies*, vol. IV, 1958.

——, 'Herbert of Bosham's commentary on Jerome's Hebrew Psalter: a preliminary investigation into its sources', *Biblica*, vol. 34, 1953.

——, 'Christian Hebraists (1100–1890)', *EJ*, vol. 8.

Logan, F. D., 'The origins of the so-called Regius Professorships: an aspect of the Renaissance in Oxford and Cambridge', in *Renaissance and Renewal in Christian History: Studies in Church History*, vol. 14, ed. D. Baker, Blackwell, Oxford 1977.

Lupton, J. H., *The Life of John Colet, D.D.*, 2nd ed., London 1909.

Lupton, L., *A History of the Geneva Bible*, vols. I–XII, London 1966–80.

McConica, J. K., *English Humanists and Reformation Politics*, Oxford 1961.

——, 'Humanism and Aristotle in Tudor Oxford', *EHR*, vol. 94, 1979.

McDonnell, M. F. J., *A History of St Paul's School*, London 1909.

Mcnally, R. E., 'The Council of Trent and vernacular Bibles', *Theological*

Studies, (New York), vol. XXVII, No. 2, 1966.

Macray, W. D., *A Register of the Members of St Mary Magdalen College, Oxford*, N.S. London 1897.

Maitland, S. R., *A List of some of the Early Printed Books in the Archiepiscopal Library at Lambeth*, London 1843.

Marc'Hadour, G., *The Bible in the Works of St Thomas More*, Holland 1971.

Marcus, J., *The Jew in the Mediaeval World*, New York 1960.

Martin, C., *Les Protestants anglais réfugiés à Genève au temps de Calvin*, Genève 1915.

Marx, A., 'Aldus and the first use of Hebrew type in Venice', *Papers of the Bibliographical Society of America*, vol. 13, 1919.

Masek, R., 'The humanistic interests of the early Tudor episcopate', *Church History*, vol. 39, No. 1, 1970.

Mayor, J. E. B., *Early Statutes of St John's College, Cambridge*, Cambridge 1859.

Mesnard, P., 'The pedagogy of Johann Sturm (1507–1589) and its evangelical inspiration', *Studies in the Renaissance*, vol. 13, 1966.

Miles, L., 'John Colet: an appreciation', *Moreana*, vol. 6, No. 23, 1969.

Monter, E. W., *Calvin's Geneva*, New York 1966.

Moore, G. F., 'Christian writers on Judaism', *HTR*, vol. XIV, No. 3, 1921.

Mozley, J. F., *William Tyndale*, London 1937.

——, *Coverdale and His Bibles*, London 1953.

——, 'Tyndale's knowledge of Hebrew', *JTS*, vol. XXXVI, 1935.

Mullinger, J. B., *The University of Cambridge from the Earliest Times to the Royal Injunctions of 1535*, Cambridge 1873.

——, *The University of Cambridge from the Royal Injunctions of 1535 to the Accession of Charles I*, Cambridge 1884.

Mumford, A. A., *Hugh Oldham 1452(?)–1519*, London 1936.

Nauert Jr., C. G., *Agrippa and the Crisis of Renaissance Thought*, Urbana, Ill. 1965.

Netanyahu, B., *Don Isaac Abravanel: Statesman and Philosopher*, 2nd. ed., Philadelphia, Pa. 1968.

Newman, J. H., *The Cistercian Saints of England*, London 1844.

Newman, L. I., *Jewish Influence on Christian Reform Movements*, New York 1925.

Nijenhuis, W., *Ecclesia Reformata: Studies on the Reformation*, Leiden 1972.

Nordman, A., 'Histoire des Juifs à Genève de 1281 à 1780', *Revue des Etudes Juives*, vol. 80, 1925.

Norton, F. J., 'The library of Bryan Rowe, Vice-Provost of King's College', *TCBS*, vol. II, 1954.

O'Malley, J. W., *Giles of Viterbo on Church and Reform*, Leiden 1968.

Omont, H., *Alphabets Grecs et Hébreux publiés à Paris au XVIe siècle*, Paris 1885.

Ottley, R. L., *Lancelot Andrewes*, 2nd ed. rev., London 1905.

Overfield, J. H., 'A new look at the Reuchlin affair', *Studies in Mediaeval and Renaissance History*, vol. VIII, ed. H. L. Adelson, Lincoln, Neb. 1971.

Pantin, W.A., 'The conception of the universities in England in the period of the Renaissance', in *Les Universités Européennes du XIVe au XVIIIe siècle: aspects et problèmes*, Geneva 1967.

Paquier, J., *Jérôme Aléandre*, Paris 1900.

Parks, G. B., *The English Traveller to Italy*, Rome 1954.

Peile, J., *Christ's College*, Cambridge 1900.

——, *A Biographical Register of Christ's College 1505–1905*, Cambridge 1910.

Pestalozzi, C., 'Leo Jud', in *Leben und ausgewählte Schriften der Väter und Begründer der reformierten Kirche*, vol. IX, ed. K. R. Hagenbach, Leipzig 1861.

Pocock, N., 'Some notices of the Genevan Bible', *The Bibliographer*, vol. III, 1882.

Pollard, A. W. (ed.), *Records of the English Bible*, London 1911.

Pope, H., *English Versions of the Bible*, revised ed. S. Bullough, St Louis, Miss. 1952.

Porter, H. C., *Reformation and Reaction in Tudor Cambridge*, Cambridge 1958.

——, *Puritanism in Tudor England*, London 1970.

Potter, G. R., *Zwingli*, Cambridge 1976.

Preus, J. S., *From Shadow to Promise: Old Testament Interpretation from Augustine to the Young Luther*, Cambridge, Mass. 1969.

Rashdall, H., *The Universities of Europe in the Middle Ages*, 2nd. ed. Powicke and Emden, Oxford 1936.

Raubenheimer, R., *Paul Fagius*, Grünstadt 1957.

Rekers, B., *Benito Arias Montano 1527–98*, London 1972.

Reu, J. M., *Luther's German Bible*, Columbus, Oh. 1934.

Reuss, E., 'Fragments littéraires et critiques relatifs à l'histoire de la Bible française', *Revue de Théologie*, IV. 3, Strasbourg 1865–66.

Rillet, J., *Zwingli: Third Man of the Reformation*, Eng. trans. H. Knight, London 1964.

Rosenfeld, A. (ed.), *The Authorized Selichot for the Whole Year*, London 1956.

Rosenthal, E. I. J., *Studia Semitica*, vol. I, Jewish Themes, Cambridge 1971.

——, (ed.), *Saadya Studies*, Manchester 1943.

Rosenthal, F., 'Robert Wakefield and the beginnings of biblical study in Tudor England', *Crozer Quarterly*, vol. 29, 1952.

——, 'The rise of Christian Hebraism in the sixteenth century', *Historia Judaica*, VII, No. 3, 1945.

Roth, C., 'Thomas Bodley – Hebraist', *Bodleian Library Record*, vol. VII, No. 5, 1966.

Routh, E. M. G., *Sir Thomas More and his Friends 1477–1535*, London 1934.

Schper, A., 'Christian Hebraists in sixteenth-century England', unpublished Ph.D. thesis, London 1944.

Schwarz, W., *Principles and Problems of Biblical Translation*, Cambridge 1955.

——, 'Studies in Luther's attitude towards humanism', *JTS*, N.S. vol. VI, Pt. 1, 1955.

Schwiebert, E. G., *Luther and his Times*, St Louis, Miss. 1950.

Scribner, R. W., 'Reformation, society and humanism in Erfurt, *c.* 1450–1530', unpublished Ph.D. thesis, University of London 1972.

Secret, F., *Les Kabbalistes Chrétiens de la Renaissance*, Paris 1964.

——, 'L'Ensis Pauli de Paulus de Heredia, *Sefarad*, vol. 26, 1966.

Seebohm, F., *The Oxford Reformers of 1498*, 3rd ed., London 1896.

Shulvass, M., *The Jews of the World of the Renaissance*, Leiden 1973.

Siirala, A., 'Luther and the Jews', *Lutheran World*, vol. 11, No. 3, 1964.

Simon, J., *Education and Society in Tudor England*, Cambridge 1966.

Simon, R., *Histoire Critique du Vieux Testament*, Rotterdam 1678. Eng. trans. A Person of Quality, London 1682.

Singer, S., 'Jews and coronations', *TJHSE*, vol. V, 1902–05.

Slater, J. R., *The Sources of Tyndale's Version of the Pentateuch*, Chicago, Ill. 1906.

Smalley, B., 'An early twelfth century commentator on the literal sense of Leviticus', *RTAM*, Tome 36, 1969.

——, *The Study of the Bible in the Middle Ages*, 2nd ed., Oxford 1952.

Smith, M. H., 'Some humanist libraries in early Tudor Cambridge', *Sixteenth Century Journal*, vol. V, No. 1, 1974.

Smith, P., 'Englishmen at Wittenberg in the sixteenth century', *EHR*, vol. 36, No. 134, 1921.

Southgate, W. M., 'The Marian Exiles and their influence on John Calvin', *History*, vol. XXVII, 1942.

Spitz, L. W., *The Religious Renaissance of the German Humanists*, Cambridge, Mass. 1963.

Stern, S., *Josel of Rosheim: Commander of Jewry in the Holy Roman Empire of the German Nation*, Eng. trans. G. Hirschler, Philadelphia, Pa. 1965.

Stocks, G. A., *The Records of Blackburn Grammar School*, Chetham Society vol. 66, 1909.

Stokes, F. G. (ed.), *Epistolae Obscurorum Virorum*, London 1909.

Stopes, C. C., *Shakespeare's Environment*, London 1914.

Strype, J., *The Life and Acts of Matthew Parker*, Oxford 1821.

Sturge, C., *Cuthbert Tunstal: Churchman, Scholar, Statesman, Administrator*, London 1938.

Sucher, C. B., *Luthers Stellung zu den Juden: eine Interpretation aus germanistischer Sicht*, Nieuwkoop 1977.

Surtz, E., *The Works and Days of John Fisher*, Cambridge, Mass. 1967.

Sutcliffe, E. F., 'Jerome', *CHB*, vol. 2.

——, 'The Venerable Bede's knowledge of Hebrew', *Biblica*, vol. 16, 1953.

——, 'The Council of Trent on the "Authentica" of the Vulgate', *JTS*, vol. 49, 1948.

Synan, E. A., *The Popes and the Jews in the Middle Ages*, New York 1965.

Talmage, F. E., *David Kimhi: the Man and the Commentaries*, Cambridge, Mass. 1975.

Thompson, K. M., *Ruthin School: the first Seven Centuries*, Denbigh 1974.

Thomson, S. H., *The Writings of Robert Grosseteste*, Cambridge 1940.

Tittler, R., 'Education and the gentleman in Tudor England: the case of Sir Nicholas Bacon', *History of Education*, vol. 5, No. 1, 1976.

Trend, J. B. and Loewe, H., *Isaac Abravanel*, Cambridge 1937.

Trinterud, L. J., 'A reappraisal of William Tyndale's debt to Martin Luther', *Church History*, vol. 31, No. 1, 1962.

Venn, J., *The Works of John Caius . . . with a Memoir of his Life*, Cambridge 1912.

——, *A Biographical History of Gonville and Caius College 1349–1901*, Cambridge 1901.

Venn, J. and J. A., *Alumni Cantabrigienses*, Cambridge 1922.

Vischer, W., 'Calvin, exégète de l'Ancien Testament', *La Revue Réformée*, vol. 18, 1967.

Voet, L., *The Golden Compasses*, Amsterdam 1969.

Walker, T. A., *A Biographical Register of Peterhouse Men*, Cambridge 1927.

Watson, F., 'Notes and materials on religious refugees in their relation to education in England before the revocation of the Edict of Nantes, 1685', *Proceedings of the Huguenot Society of London*, vol. IX, No. 3, 1911.

——, *The English Grammar Schools to 1660: their Curriculum and Practice*, Cambridge 1908.

——, *The Old Grammar Schools*, new impr. London 1968.

Wegg, J., *Richard Pace: a Tudor Diplomatist*, London 1932 (repr. 1971).

Weiss, R., 'England and the decree of the Council of Vienne on the teaching of Greek, Arabic, Hebrew and Syriac', *Bibliothèque d'Humanisme et Renaissance*, Tome XIV, 1952.

——, *Humanism in England during the Fifteenth Century*, 3rd ed., Oxford 1967.

Westcott, B. F., *A General View of the History of the English Bible*, 3rd ed., London 1905.

Wieder, N., *The Judean Scrolls and Karaism*, London 1962.

Williams, A. L., *Adversus Judaeos*, Cambridge 1935.

Williams, C. H., *William Tyndale*, London 1969.

Williams, G., *Bywyd ac Amserau'r Esgob Richard Davies*, Cardiff 1953.

Wilson, H. B., *The History of Merchant-Taylors' School*, London 1812.

Wirszubski, Ch., 'Giovanni Pico's companion to kabbalistic symbolism', in *Studies in Mysticism and Religion presented to G. Scholem*, Jerusalem 1967.

——, 'Giovanni Pico's Book of Job', *JWCI*, vol. XXXII, 1969.

Wolf, L., ' "Yosippon" in England', *TJHSE*, vol. VI, 1908–10.

——, 'Immanuel Tremellius', *Papers read at the Anglo-Jewish Historical Exhibition*, London 1887.

Wood, A., *Athenae Oxonienses*, 3rd ed. rev. P. Bliss, London 1813–20.

——, *The History and Antiquities of the University of Oxford*, Oxford 1786.

Wood, N., *The Reformation and English Education*, London 1931.

Yates, F. A., *Giordano Bruno and the Hermetic Tradition*, London 1964.

——, *Theatre of the World*, London 1969.

——, *The Occult Philosophy in the Elizabethan Age*, London 1979.

Zeeveld, W. G., *Foundations of Tudor Policy*, Cambridge, Mass. 1948.

Zika, C., 'Reuchlin's *De Verbo Mirifico* and the magic debate of the late fifteenth century', *JWCI*, vol. XXXIX, 1976.

——, 'Reuchlin and Erasmus: humanism and occult philosophy', *Journal of*

Religious History, vol. 9, 1977.
Zinberg, I., *A History of Jewish Literature*, vols. 1–12, New York 1972–77.

Index

The Appendices are not indexed.

Biblical references

Persons and subjects